Shojo Beat

Rasetsu

Vol. 5

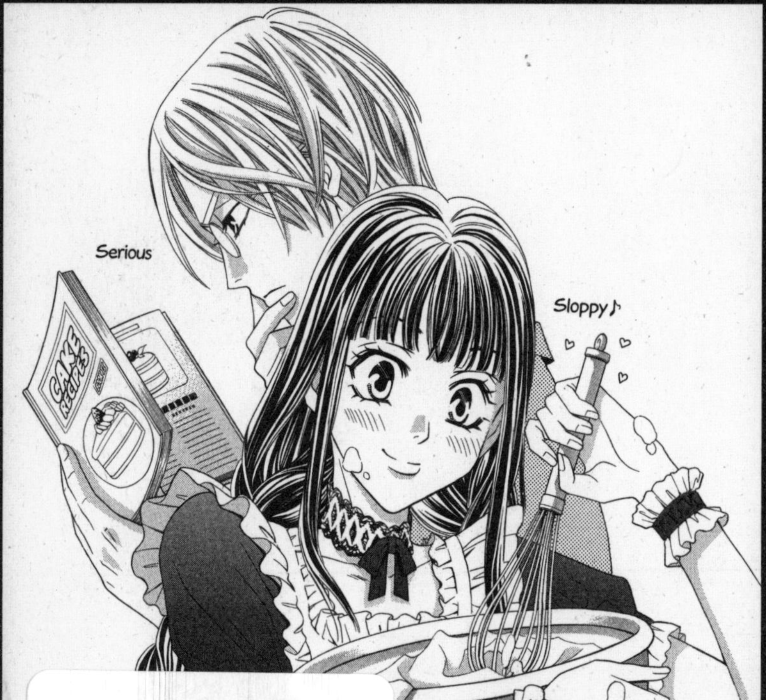
Serious
CAKE RECIPES
Sloppy♪

…Art by

Chika Shiomi

Characters

Rasetsu Hyuga

A powerful 19-year-old exorcist, Rasetsu has a flowerlike mark on her chest—a memento left by a demon. Rasetsu eats lots of sweets to recharge her psychic powers. She's currently looking for a boyfriend.

Yako Hoshino

An ace psychic who controls water, Yako was headhunted by Rasetsu. He still has feelings for the spirit he was in love with in high school…

Hiichiro Amakawa

The chief of the agency where Rasetsu and Yako work. A very powerful psychic.

Kuryu Iwatsuki

A psychic who uses *kotodama* (spiritual power manifested through words). His power works on humans and animals alike.

Aoi Kugi

Does administrative work for the agency. Ever since Yako came to the office, however, he's been left with nothing to do.

Story

The Hiichiro Amakawa Agency deals with exorcisms, and Rasetsu, Kuryu and Yako are psychics who work there. Rasetsu is actually cursed by an evil spirit, and the only way for her to break the curse is to find true love before she turns 20! She starts to develop feelings for Yako, but he's too oblivious to notice. On Rasetsu's 19th birthday, the evil spirit shows up and takes over Aoi's body. He swears that he'll come back for Rasetsu next year. Rasetsu is crushed after seeing the spirit's strength. Then Kuryu kisses her and says that he loves her…!

Rasetsu

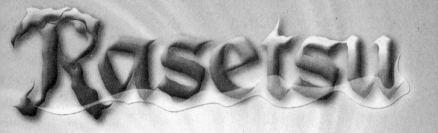

Volume 5

Contents

Rasetsu

Chapter 17

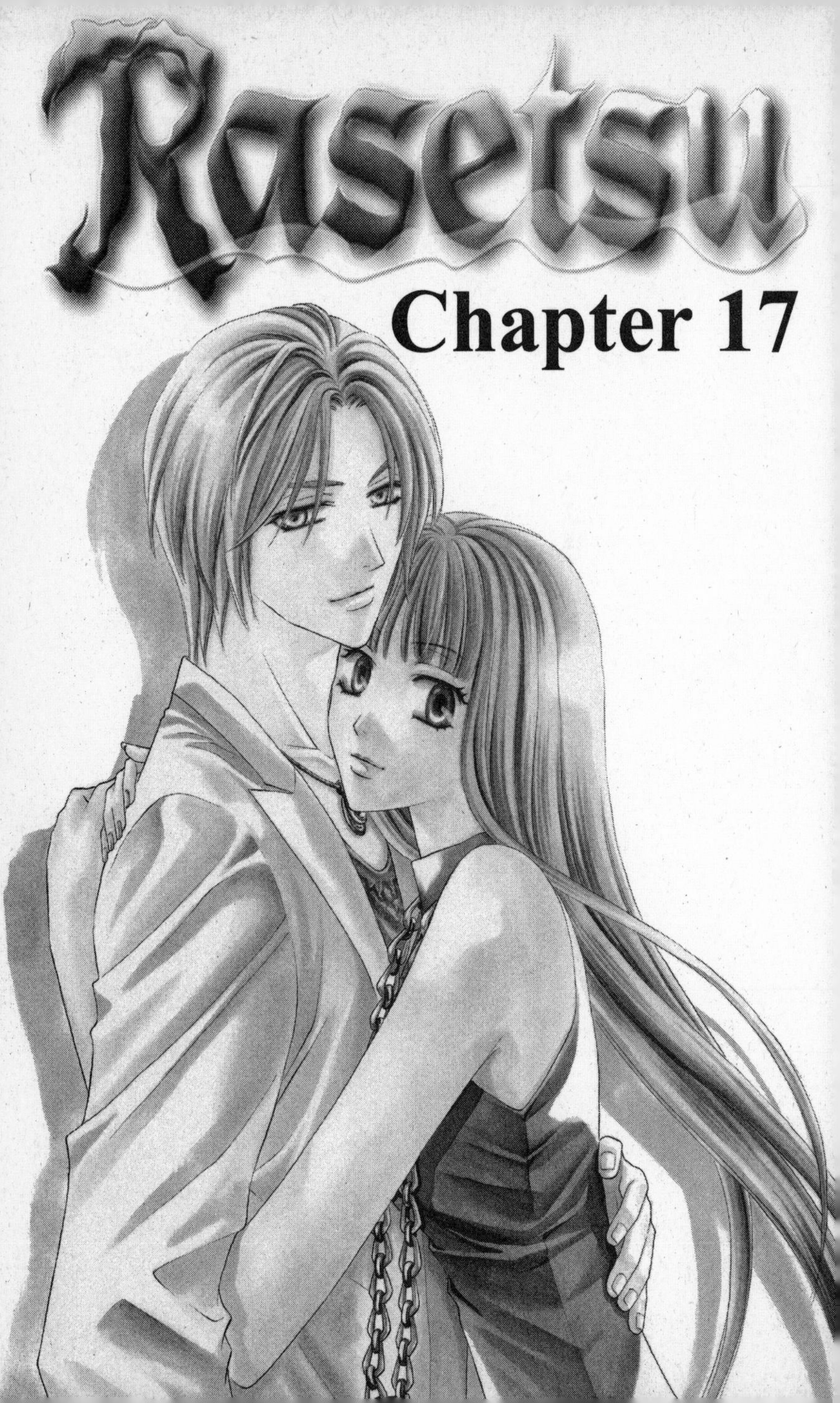

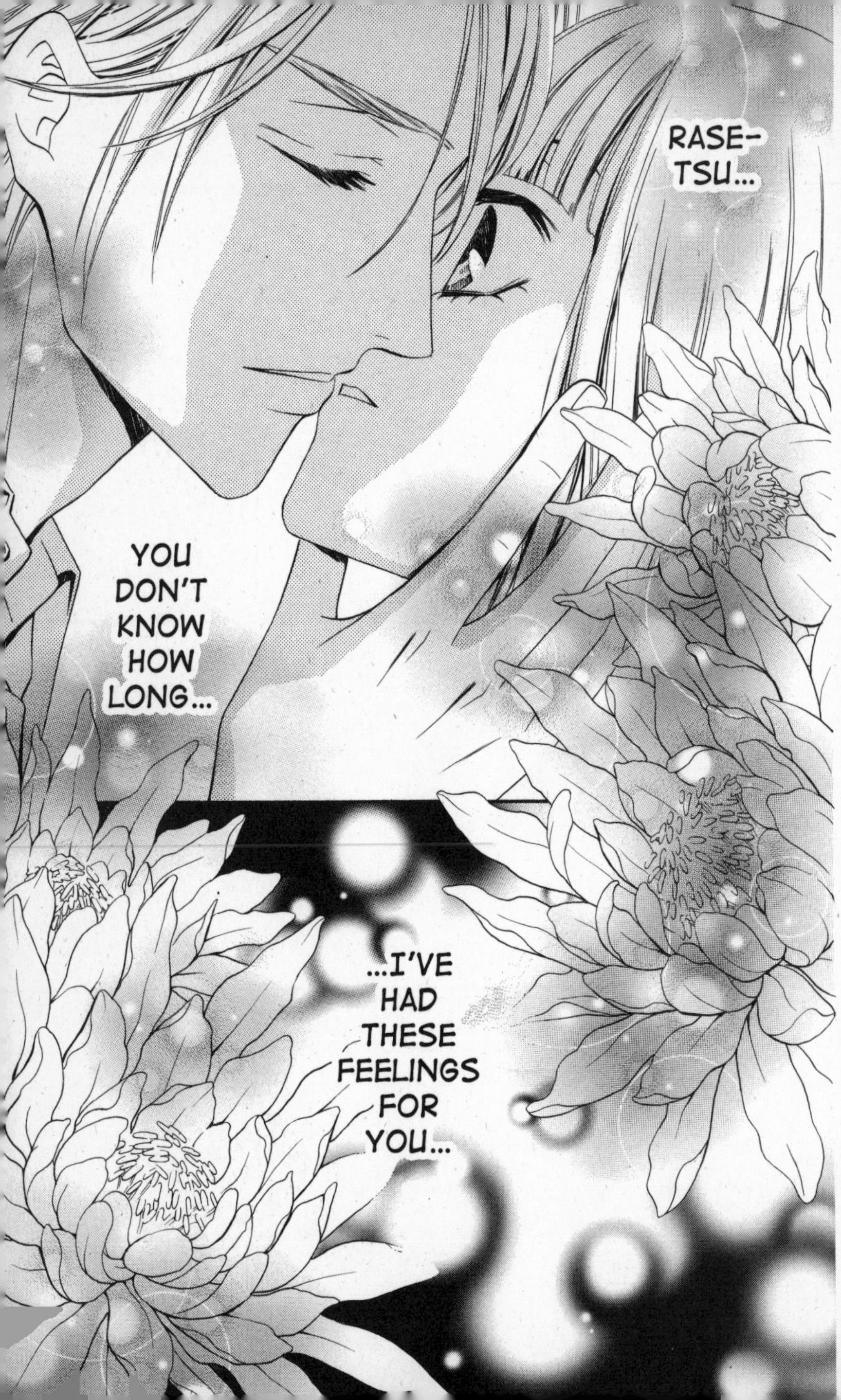
RASE-TSU...
YOU DON'T KNOW HOW LONG...
...I'VE HAD THESE FEELINGS FOR YOU...

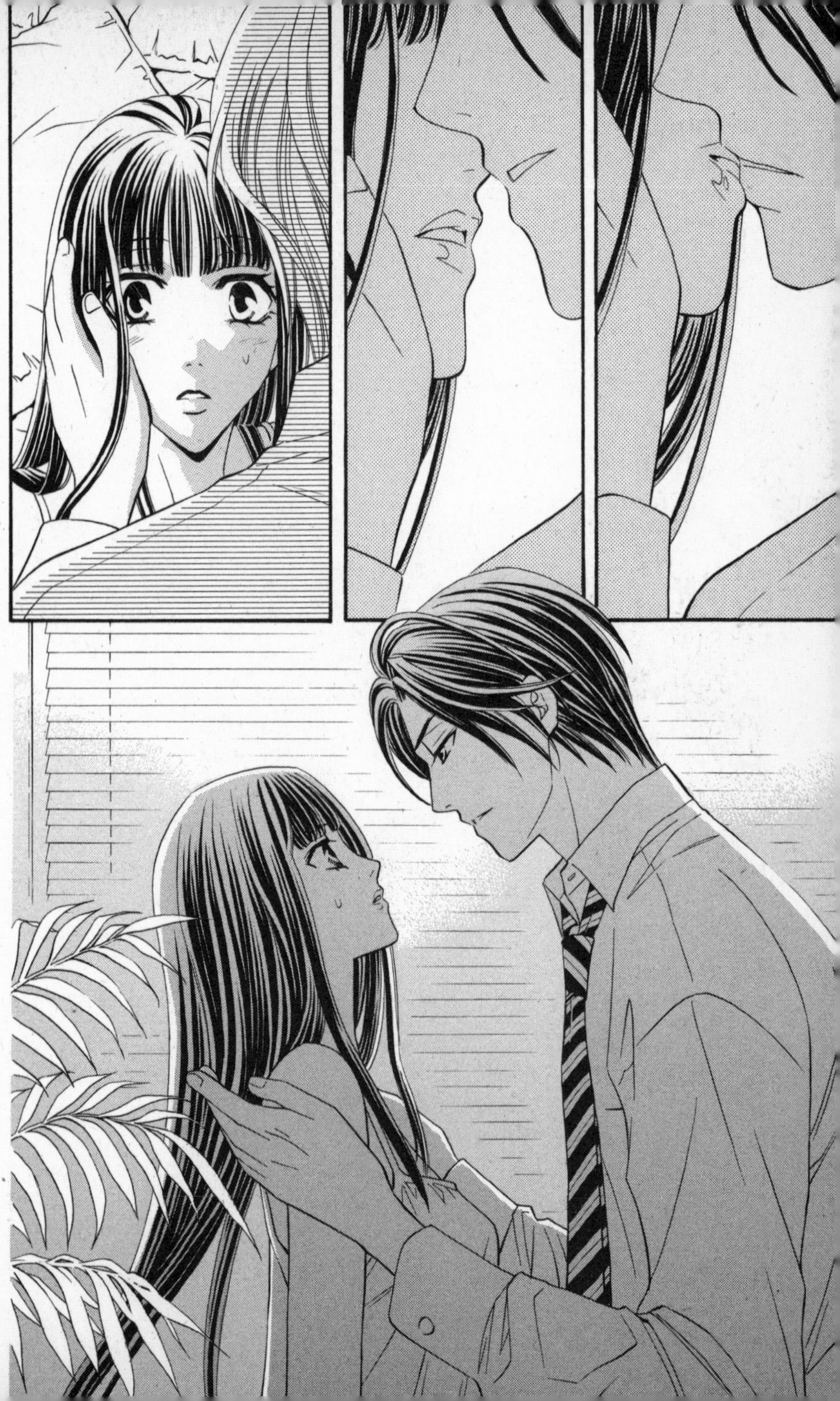

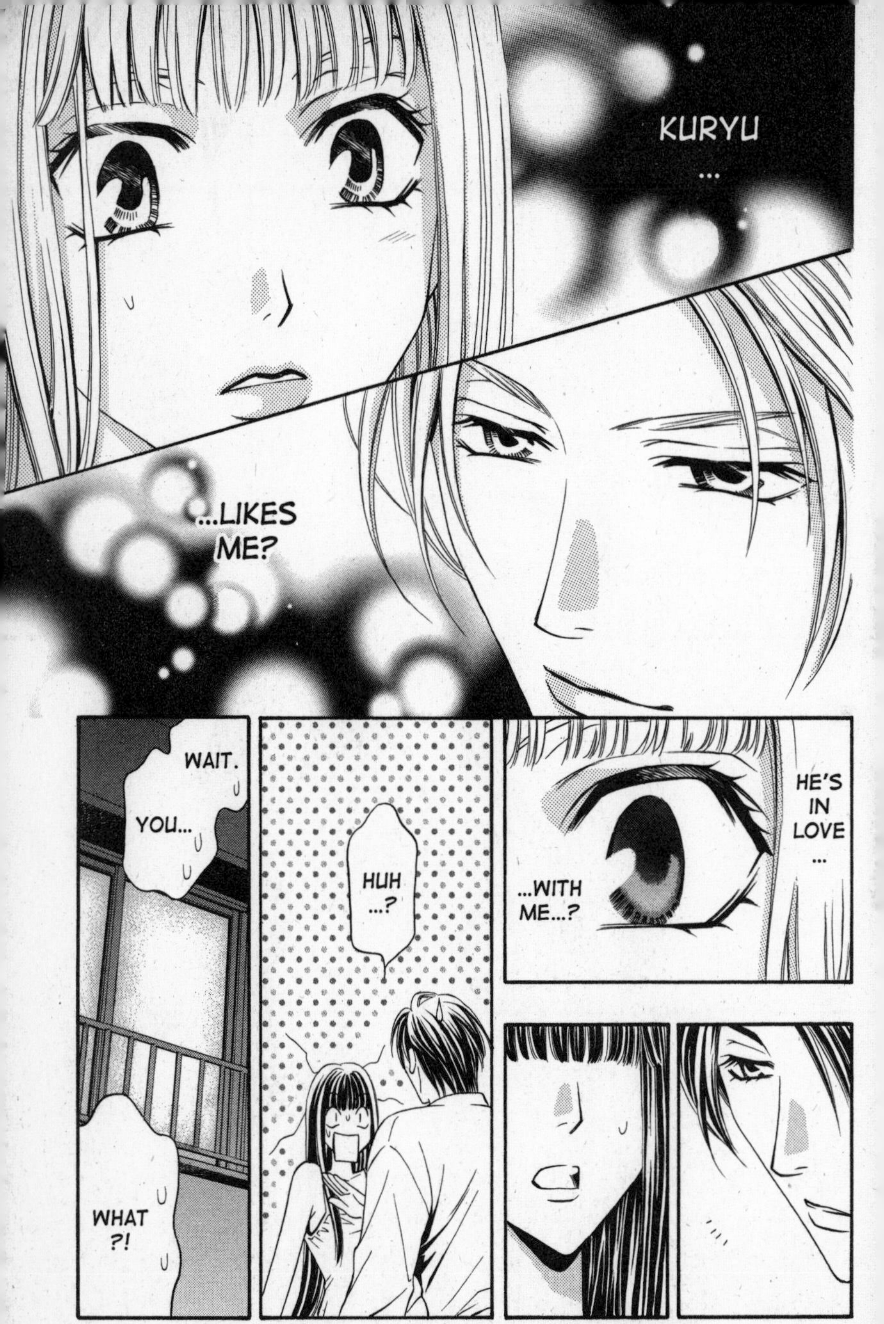
KURYU ...
...LIKES ME?
HE'S IN LOVE ...
...WITH ME...?
HUH ...?
WAIT.
YOU...
WHAT ?!

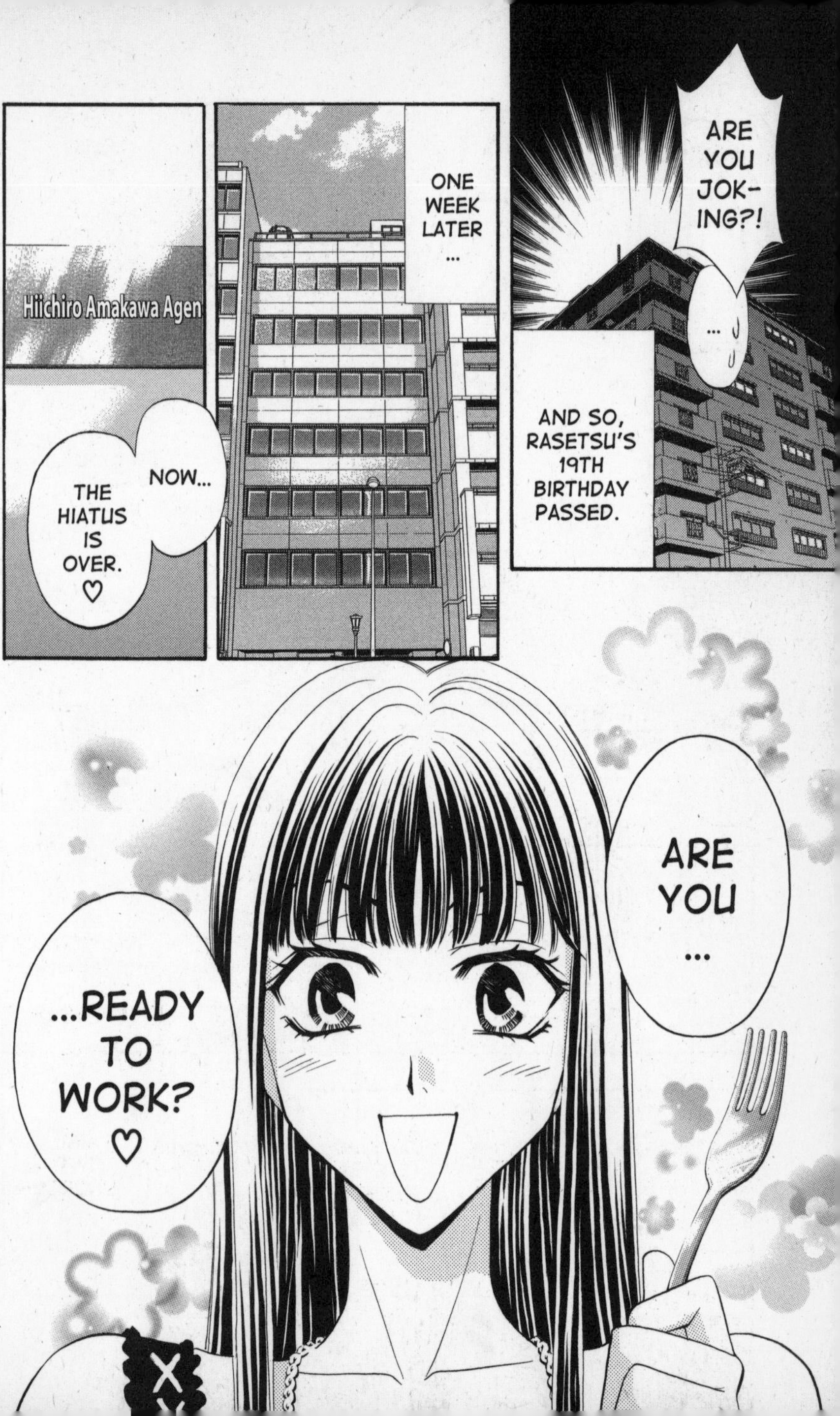
ARE YOU JOK-ING?!
... ;;
AND SO, RASETSU'S 19TH BIRTHDAY PASSED.
ONE WEEK LATER ...
Hiichiro Amakawa Agen
NOW...
THE HIATUS IS OVER. ♡
ARE YOU ...
...READY TO WORK? ♡

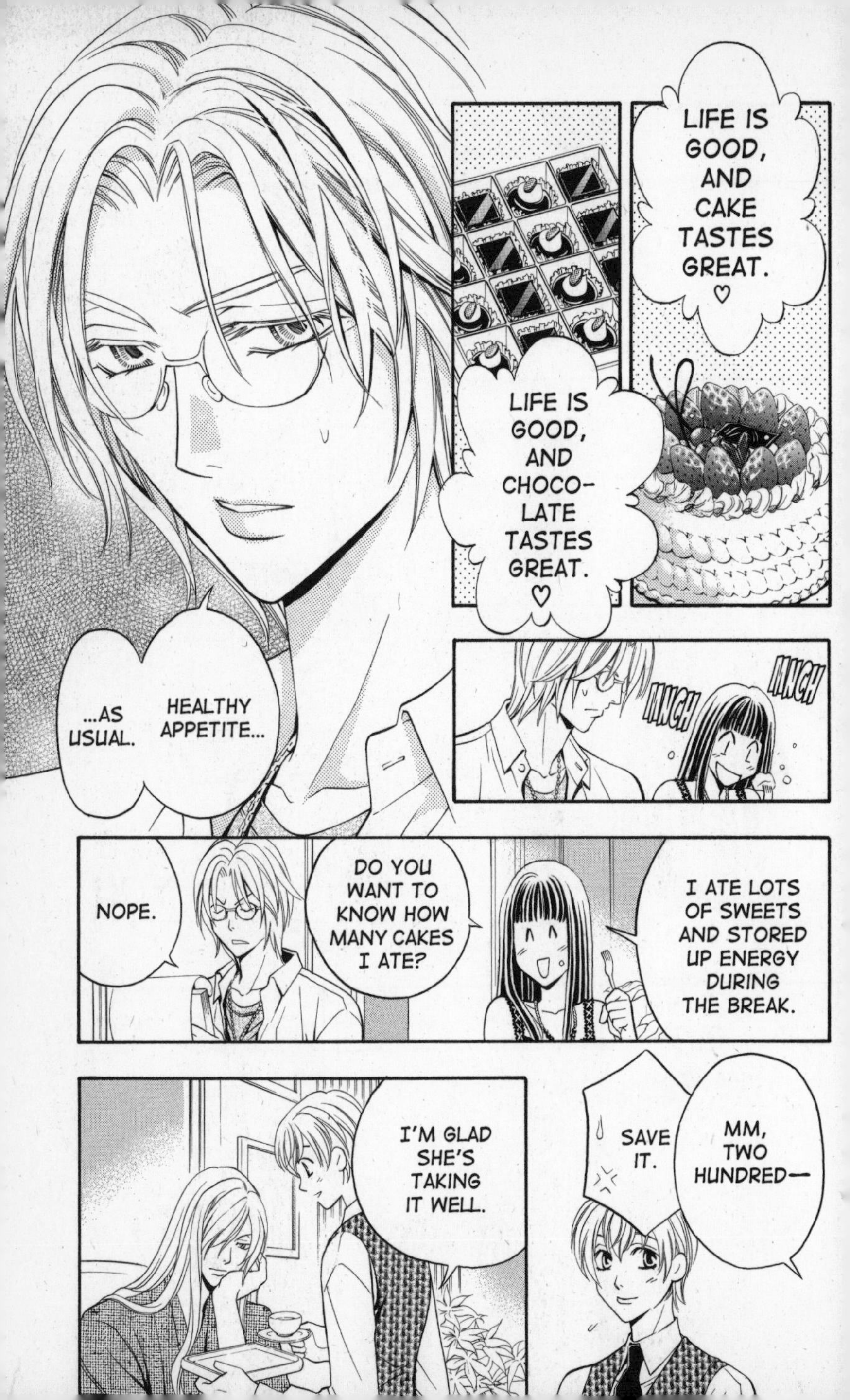
LIFE IS GOOD, AND CAKE TASTES GREAT. ♡
LIFE IS GOOD, AND CHOCOLATE TASTES GREAT. ♡
MUNCH
MUNCH
HEALTHY APPETITE...
...AS USUAL.
I ATE LOTS OF SWEETS AND STORED UP ENERGY DURING THE BREAK.
DO YOU WANT TO KNOW HOW MANY CAKES I ATE?
NOPE.
MM, TWO HUNDRED—
SAVE IT.
I'M GLAD SHE'S TAKING IT WELL.

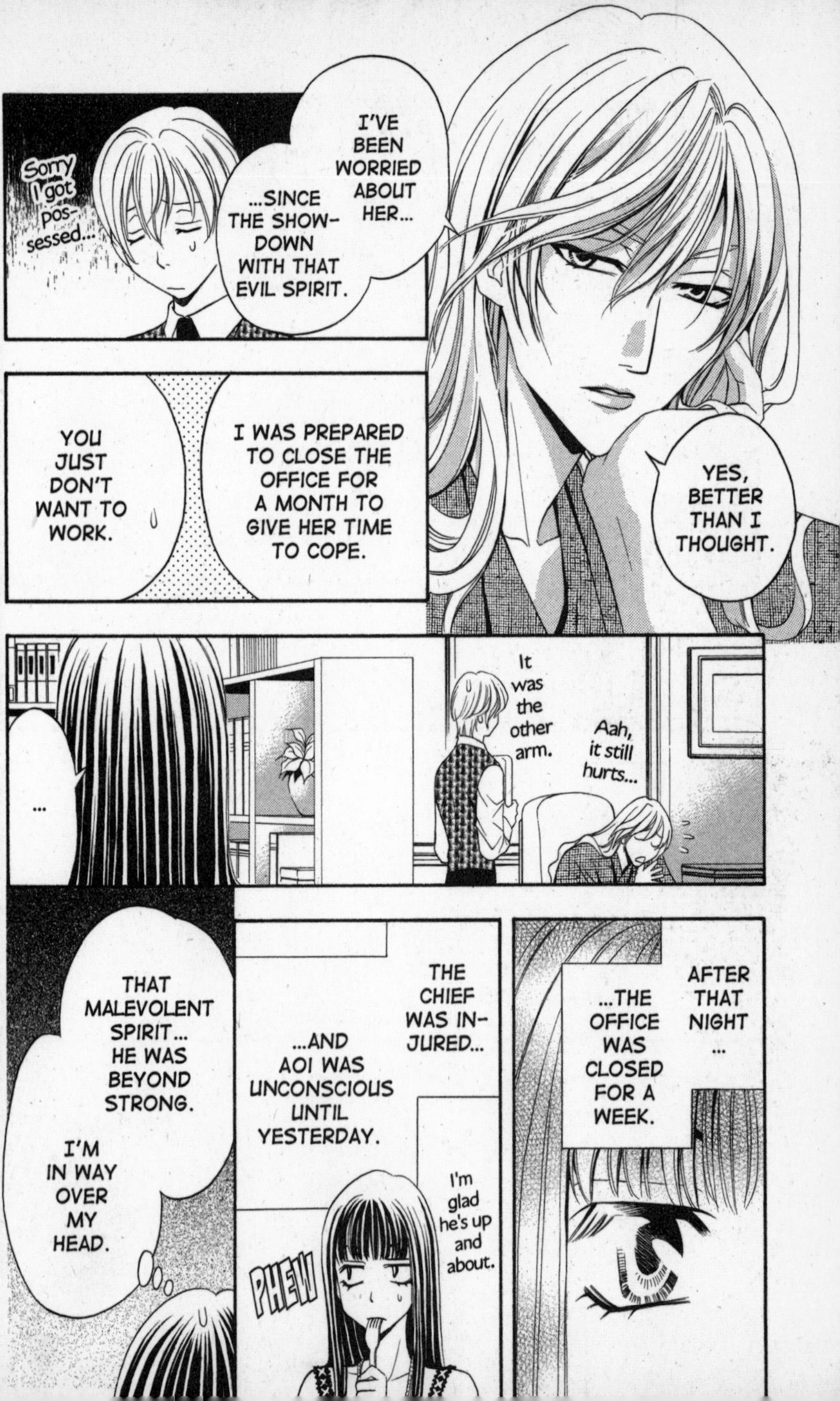
YES, BETTER THAN I THOUGHT.
I'VE BEEN WORRIED ABOUT HER...
...SINCE THE SHOWDOWN WITH THAT EVIL SPIRIT.
Sorry I got possessed...
I WAS PREPARED TO CLOSE THE OFFICE FOR A MONTH TO GIVE HER TIME TO COPE.
YOU JUST DON'T WANT TO WORK.
Aah, it still hurts...
It was the other arm.
...
AFTER THAT NIGHT...
...THE OFFICE WAS CLOSED FOR A WEEK.
THE CHIEF WAS INJURED...
...AND AOI WAS UNCONSCIOUS UNTIL YESTERDAY.
I'm glad he's up and about.
PHEW
THAT MALEVOLENT SPIRIT... HE WAS BEYOND STRONG.
I'M IN WAY OVER MY HEAD.

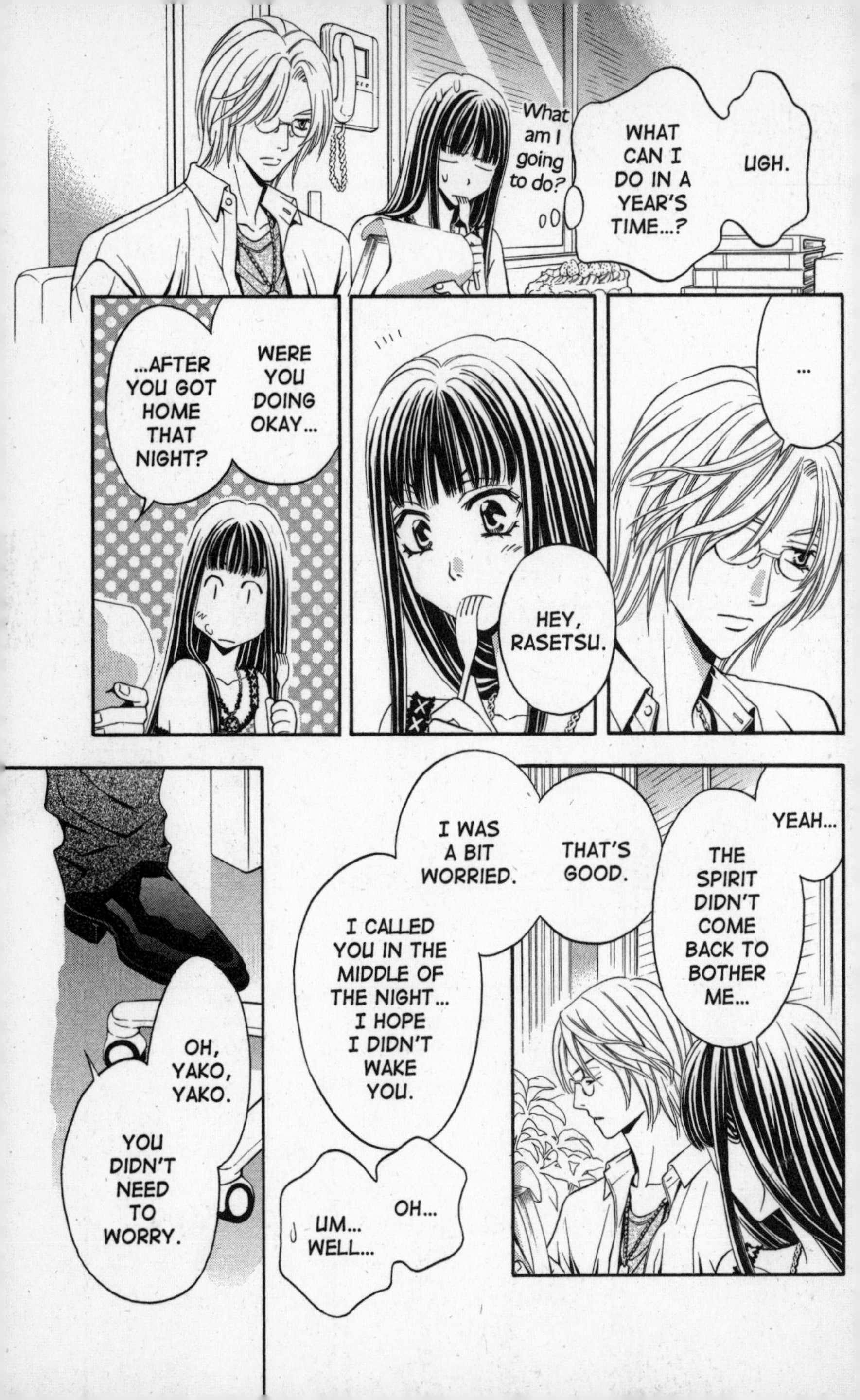
UGH.
WHAT CAN I DO IN A YEAR'S TIME...?
What am I going to do?
...
HEY, RASETSU.
WERE YOU DOING OKAY...
...AFTER YOU GOT HOME THAT NIGHT?
YEAH... THE SPIRIT DIDN'T COME BACK TO BOTHER ME...
THAT'S GOOD.
I WAS A BIT WORRIED.
I CALLED YOU IN THE MIDDLE OF THE NIGHT... I HOPE I DIDN'T WAKE YOU.
OH...
UM... WELL...
OH, YAKO, YAKO.
YOU DIDN'T NEED TO WORRY.

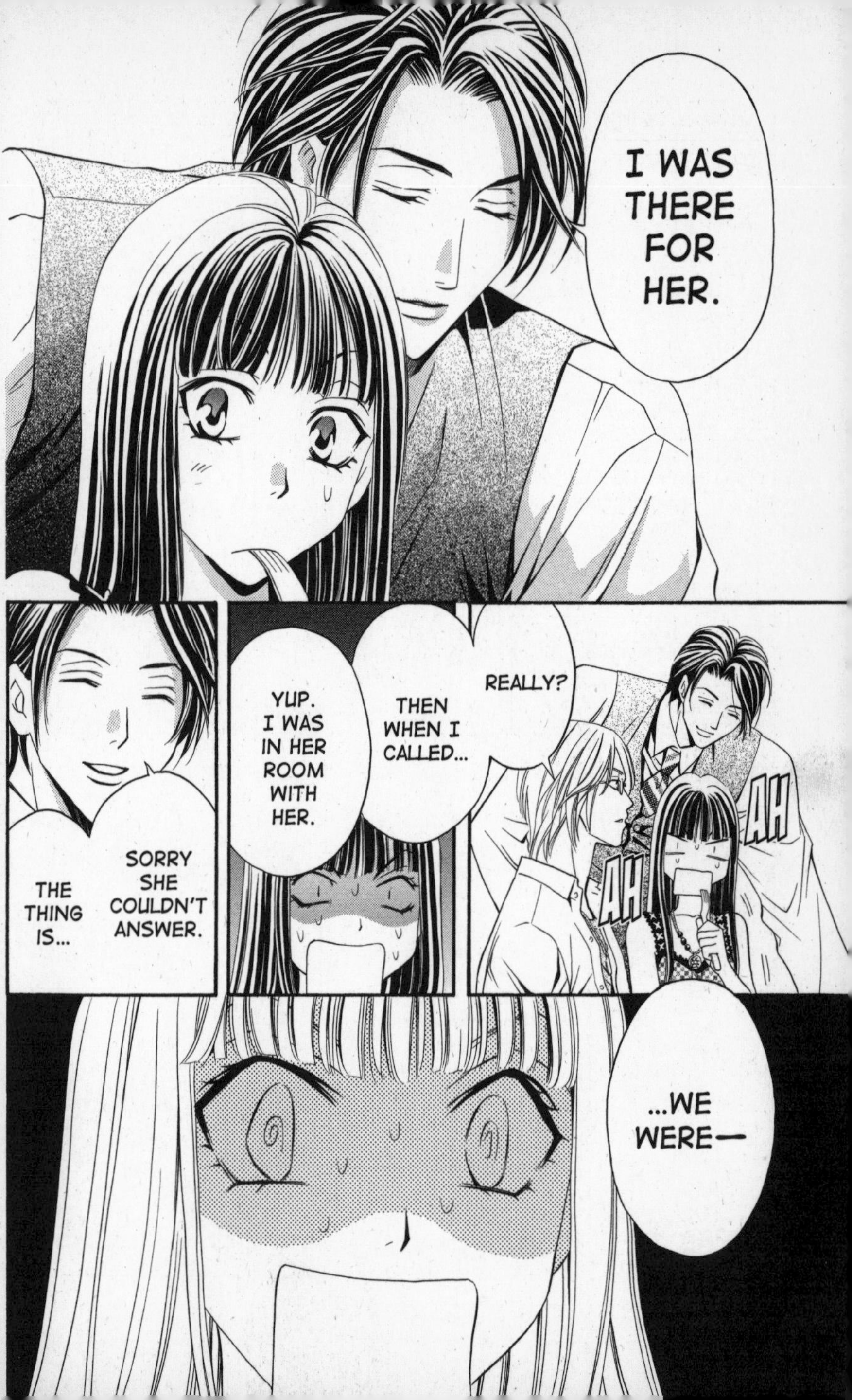
I WAS THERE FOR HER.
REALLY?
THEN WHEN I CALLED...
AH
AH
YUP. I WAS IN HER ROOM WITH HER.
SORRY SHE COULDN'T ANSWER.
THE THING IS...
...WE WERE—

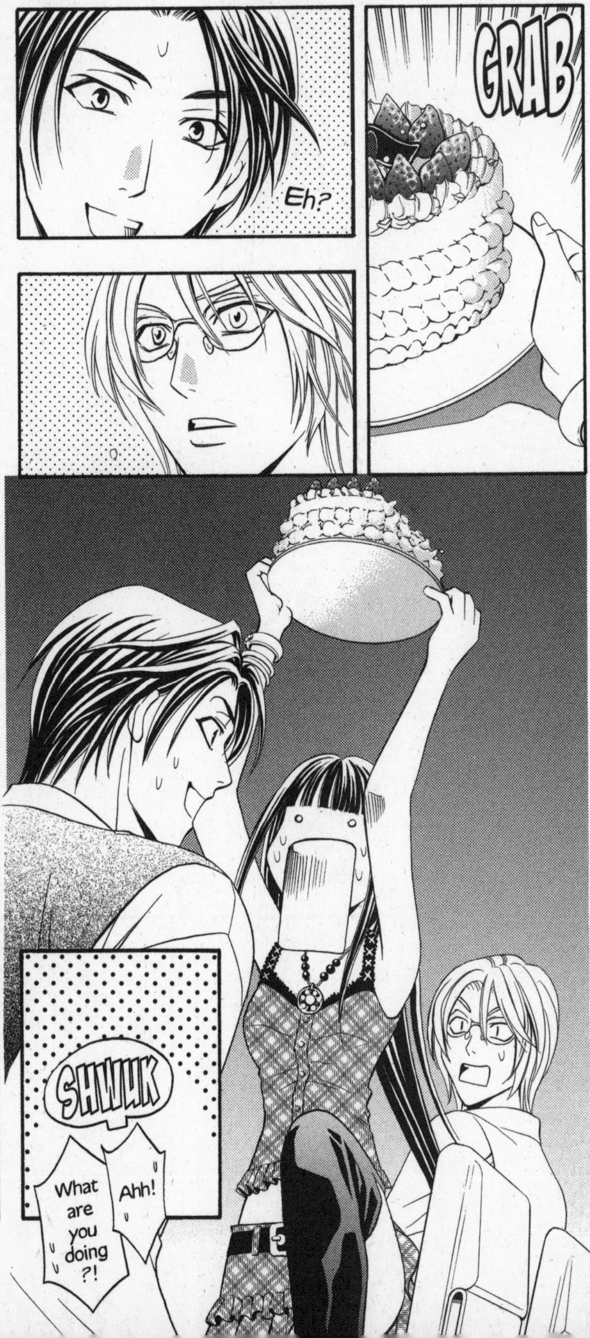
GRAB
Eh?
SHWUK
Ahh!
What are you doing?!

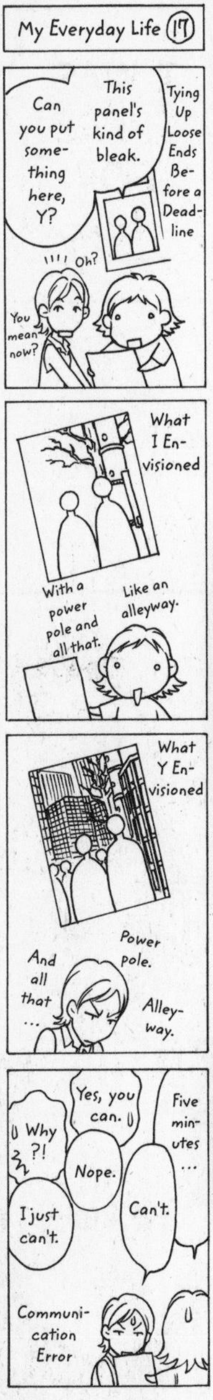
My Everyday Life 17
Tying Up Loose Ends Before a Deadline
This panel's kind of bleak.
Can you put some-thing here, Y?
Oh?
You mean now?
What I Envisioned
Like an alleyway.
With a power pole and all that.
What Y Envisioned
Power pole.
Alley-way.
And all that...
Five min-utes...
Yes, you can.
Why?!
Can't.
Nope.
I just can't.
Communi-cation Error

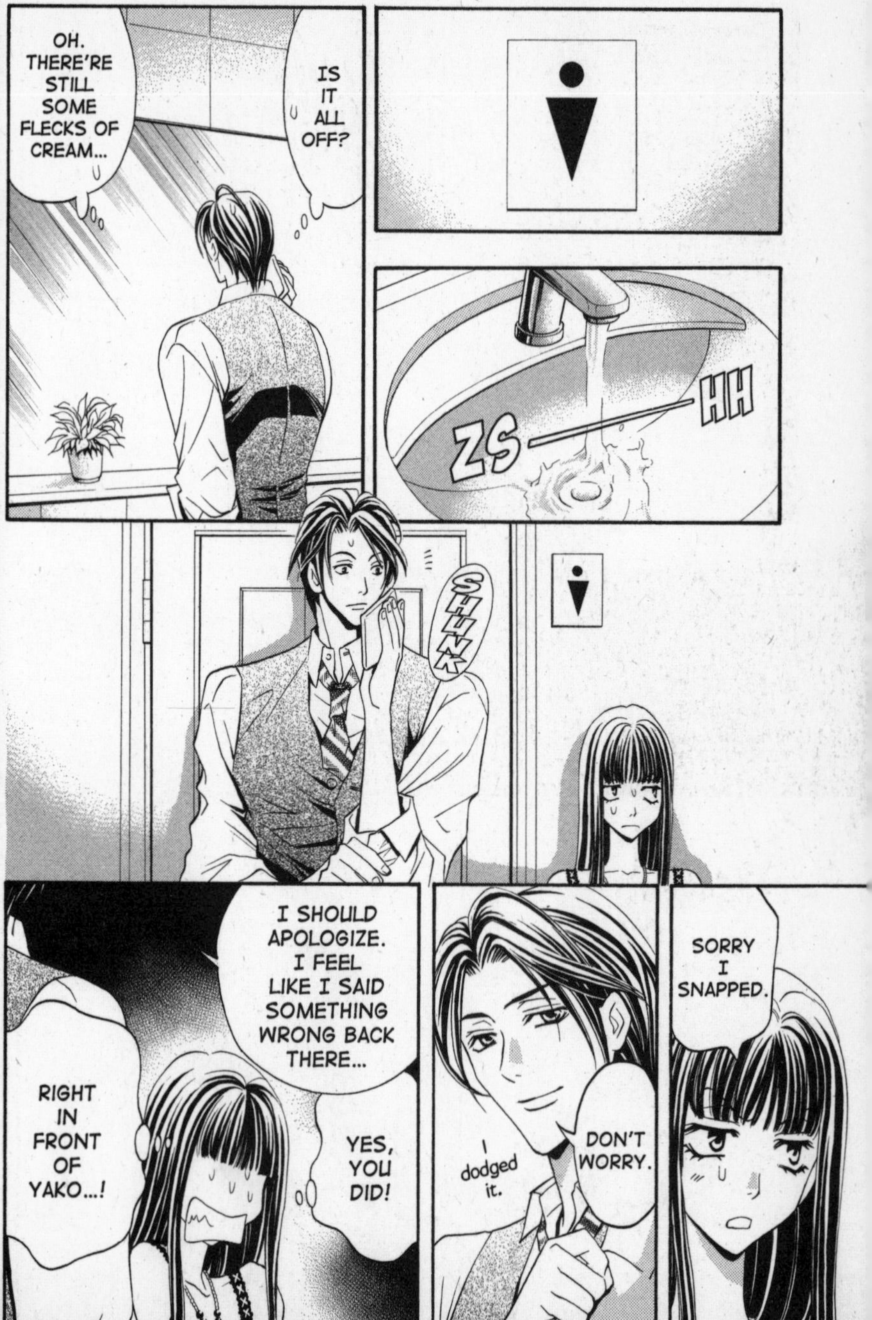
ZS—HH
IS IT ALL OFF?
OH. THERE'RE STILL SOME FLECKS OF CREAM...
SHUNK
SORRY I SNAPPED.
DON'T WORRY.
I dodged it.
I SHOULD APOLOGIZE. I FEEL LIKE I SAID SOMETHING WRONG BACK THERE...
YES, YOU DID!
RIGHT IN FRONT OF YAKO...!

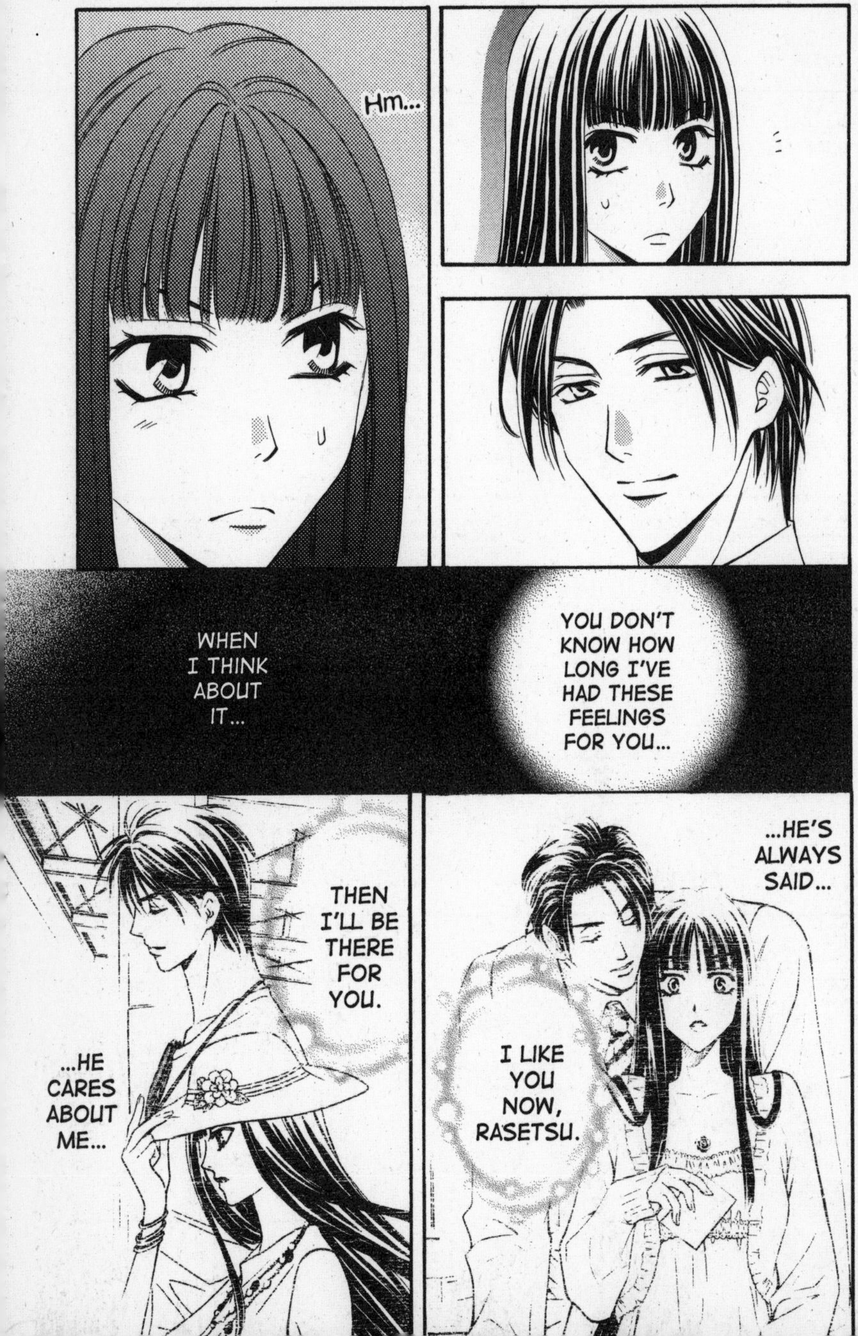
Hm...
YOU DON'T KNOW HOW LONG I'VE HAD THESE FEELINGS FOR YOU...
WHEN I THINK ABOUT IT...
...HE'S ALWAYS SAID...
I LIKE YOU NOW, RASETSU.
THEN I'LL BE THERE FOR YOU.
...HE CARES ABOUT ME...

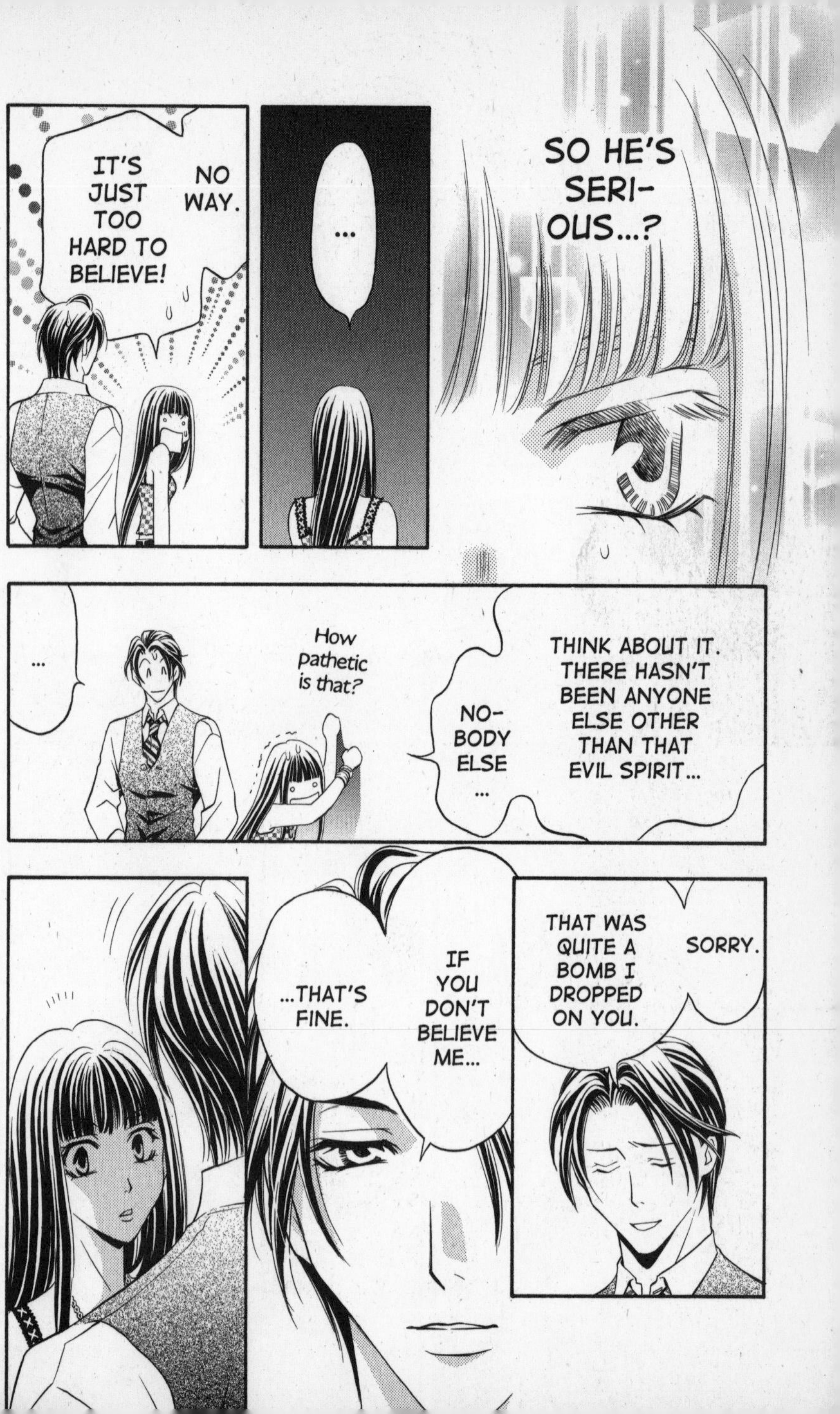
SO HE'S SERI-OUS...?
...
NO WAY.
IT'S JUST TOO HARD TO BELIEVE!
THINK ABOUT IT. THERE HASN'T BEEN ANYONE ELSE OTHER THAN THAT EVIL SPIRIT...
NO-BODY ELSE...
How pathetic is that?
...
SORRY.
THAT WAS QUITE A BOMB I DROPPED ON YOU.
IF YOU DON'T BELIEVE ME...
...THAT'S FINE.

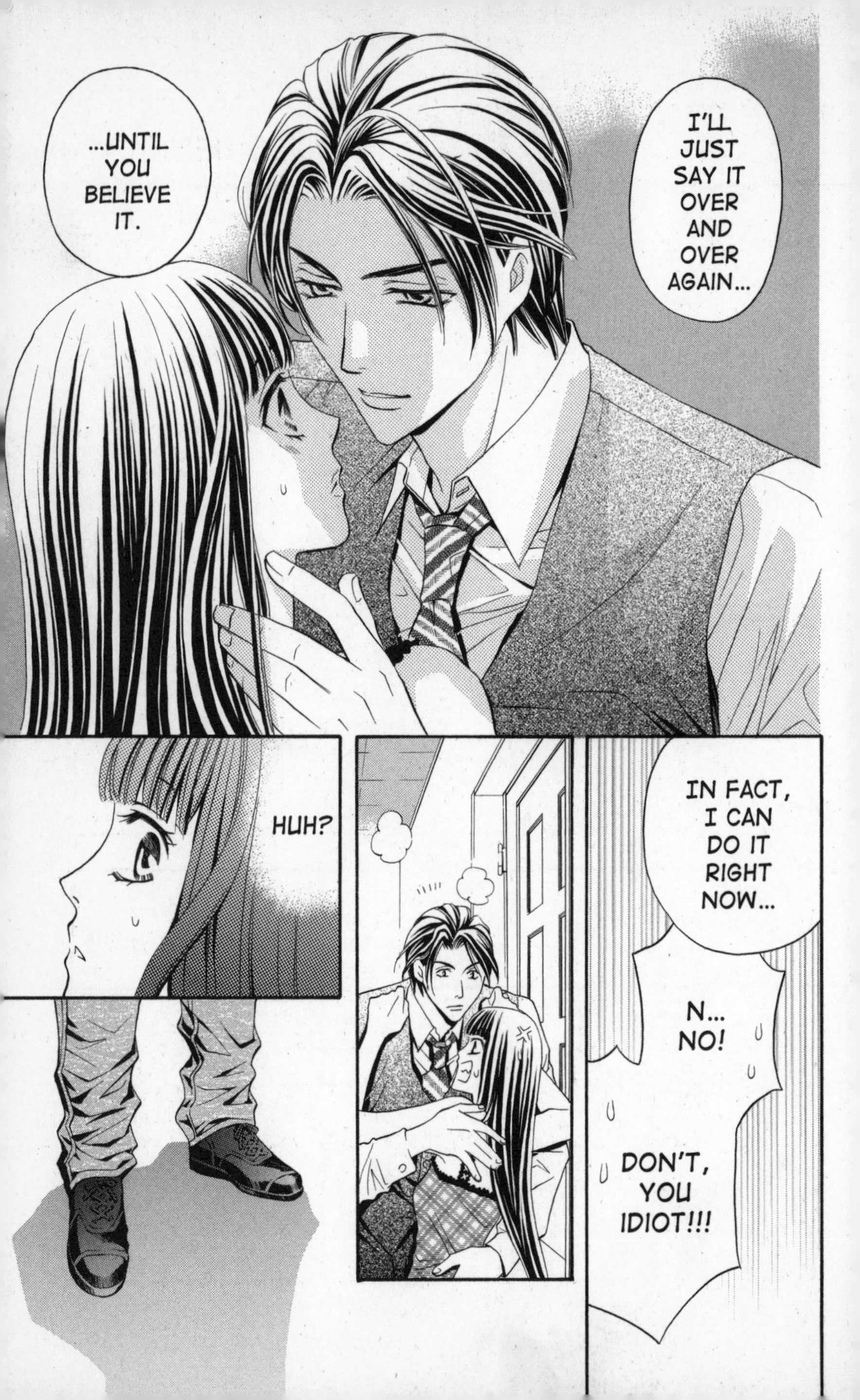
I'LL JUST SAY IT OVER AND OVER AGAIN...
...UNTIL YOU BELIEVE IT.
IN FACT, I CAN DO IT RIGHT NOW...
N... NO!
DON'T, YOU IDIOT!!!
HUH?

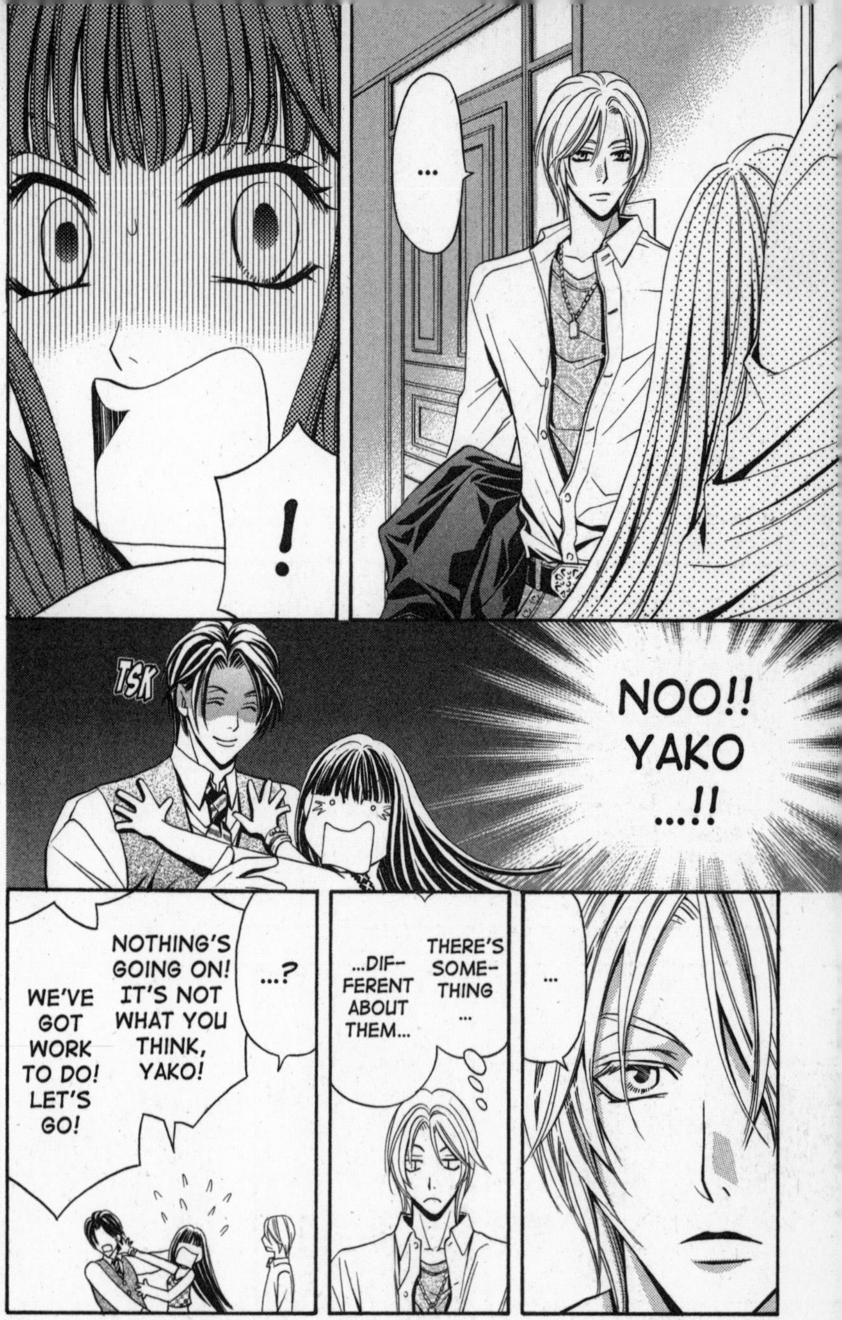
...
!
NOO!! YAKO ...!!
TSK
...
THERE'S SOME-THING ...
...DIF-FERENT ABOUT THEM...
...?
NOTHING'S GOING ON! IT'S NOT WHAT YOU THINK, YAKO!
WE'VE GOT WORK TO DO! LET'S GO!

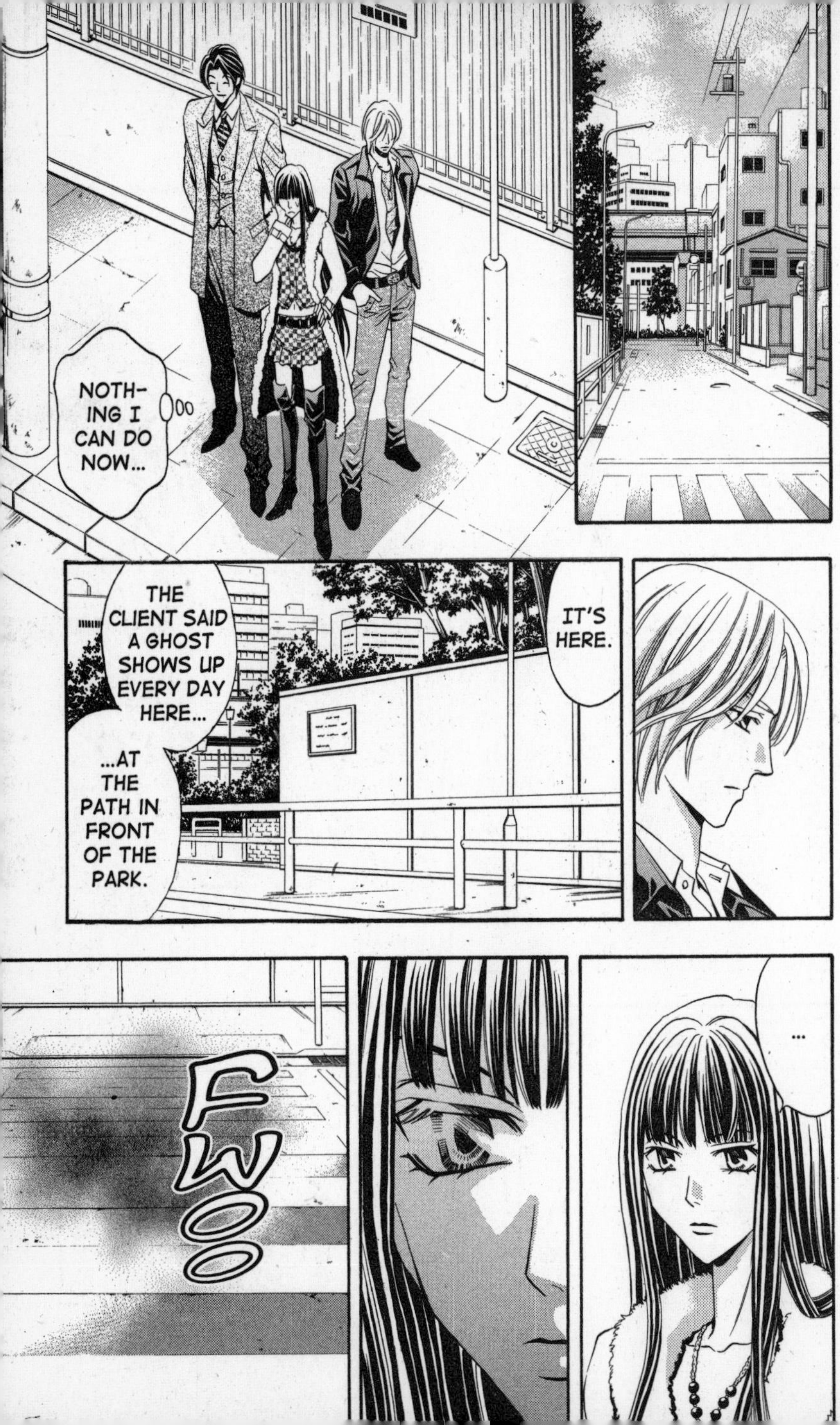
NOTHING I CAN DO NOW...
IT'S HERE.
THE CLIENT SAID A GHOST SHOWS UP EVERY DAY HERE...
...AT THE PATH IN FRONT OF THE PARK.
...
FWOO

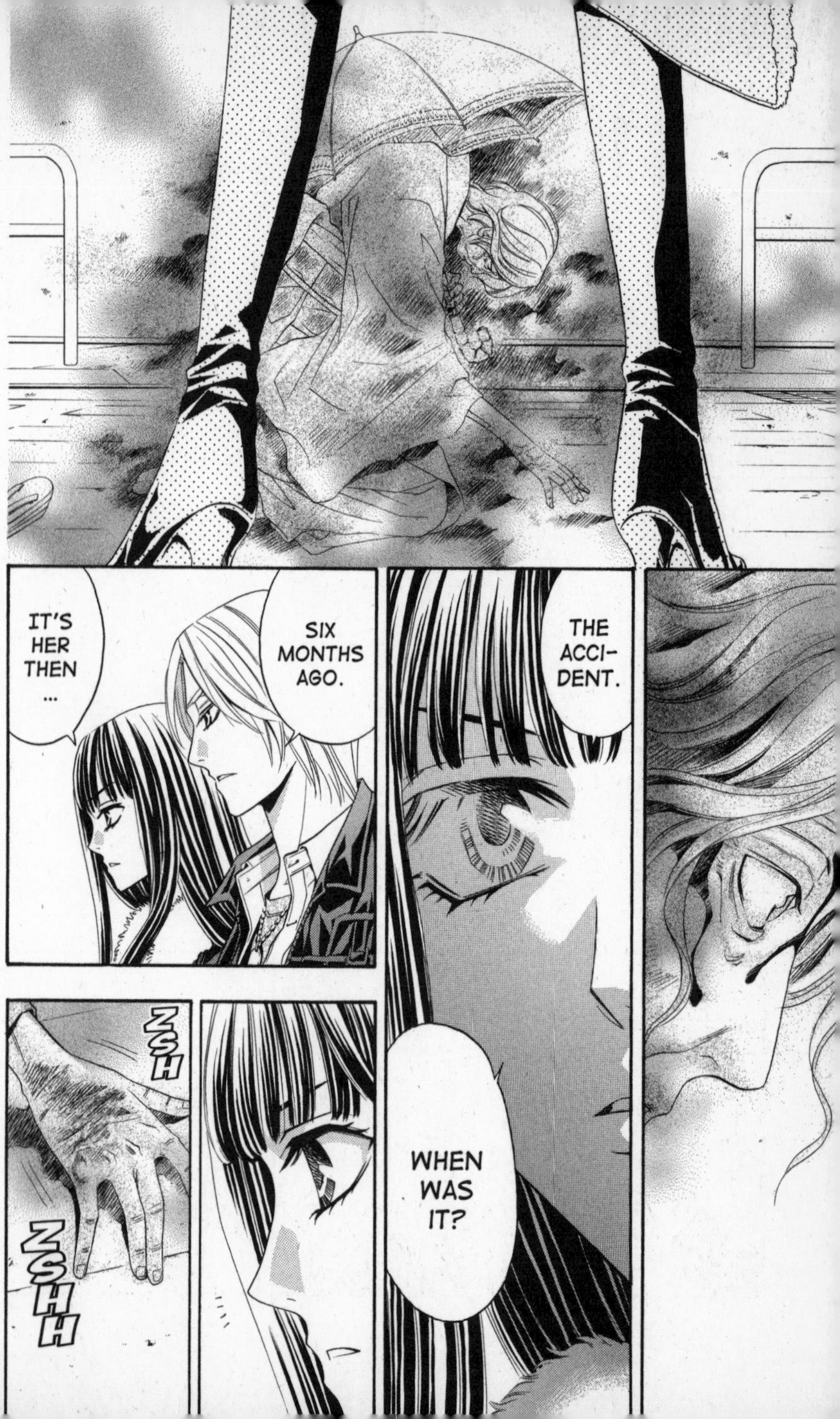
THE ACCI-DENT.
WHEN WAS IT?
SIX MONTHS AGO.
IT'S HER THEN ...
ZSH
ZSHHH

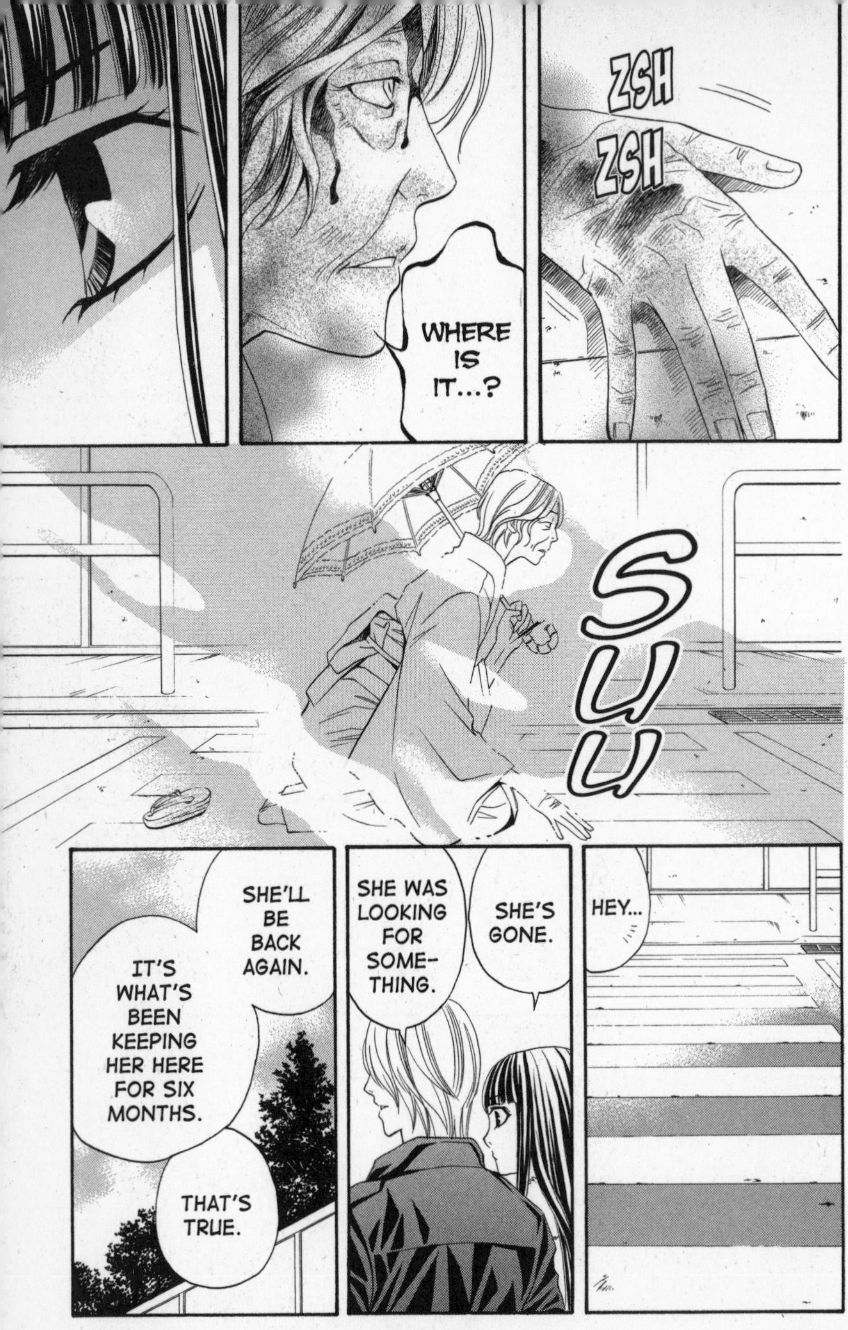
ZSH ZSH
WHERE IS IT...?
SUU
HEY...
SHE'S GONE.
SHE WAS LOOKING FOR SOME-THING.
SHE'LL BE BACK AGAIN.
IT'S WHAT'S BEEN KEEPING HER HERE FOR SIX MONTHS.
THAT'S TRUE.

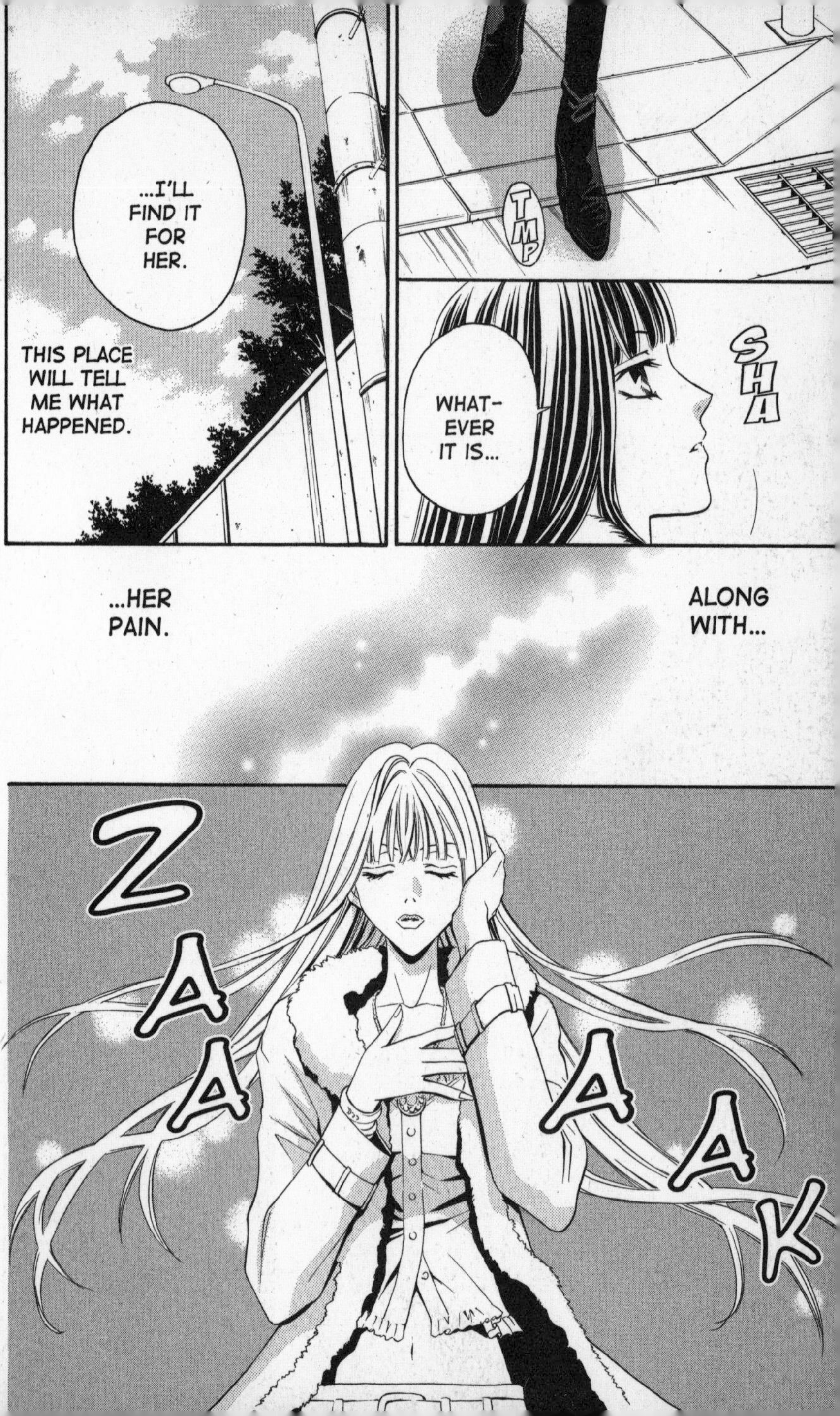
TMP
WHAT-EVER IT IS...
SHA
...I'LL FIND IT FOR HER.
THIS PLACE WILL TELL ME WHAT HAPPENED.
ALONG WITH...
...HER PAIN.
ZAAAAK

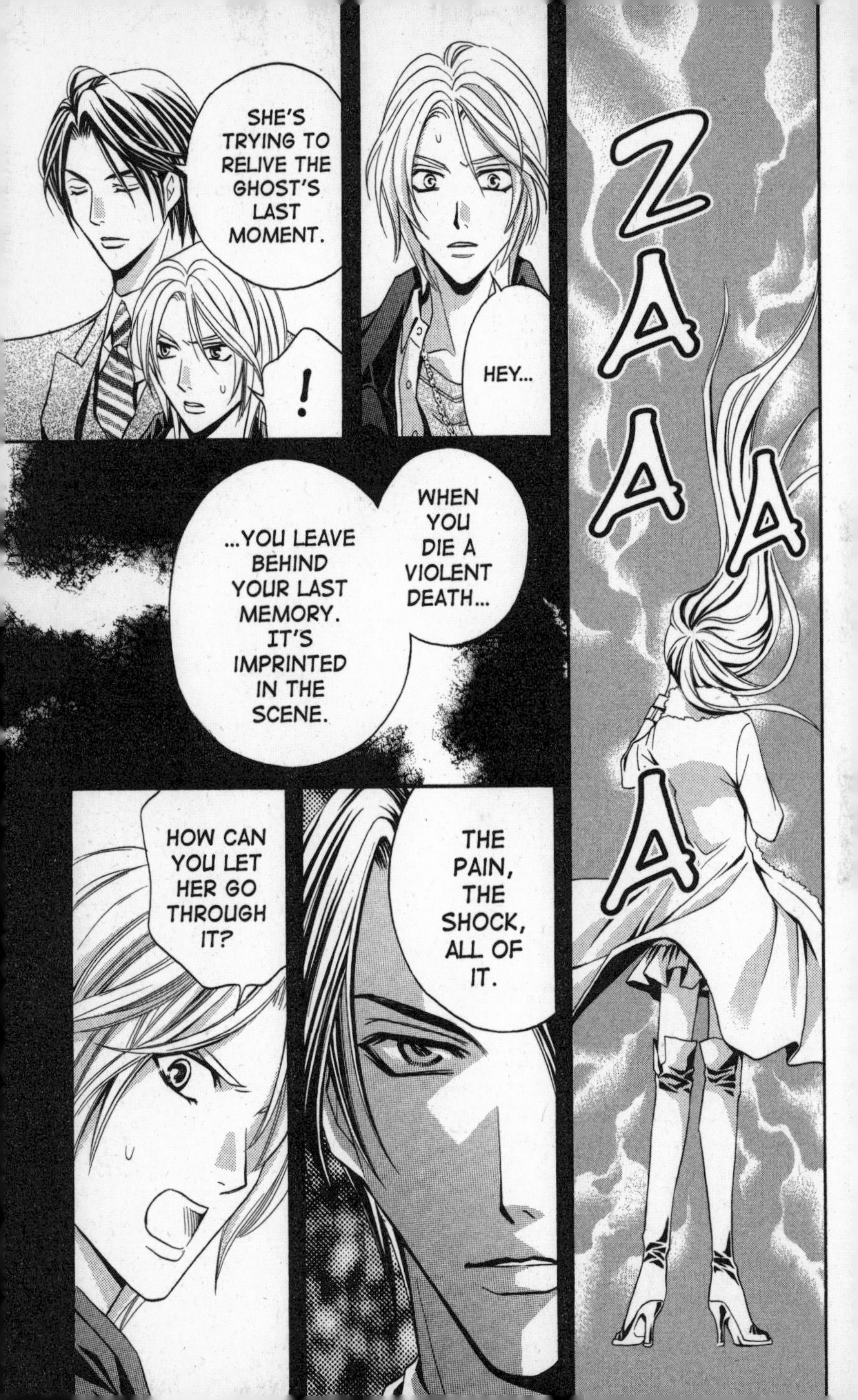
ZAAAA
HEY...
SHE'S TRYING TO RELIVE THE GHOST'S LAST MOMENT.
!
WHEN YOU DIE A VIOLENT DEATH...
...YOU LEAVE BEHIND YOUR LAST MEMORY. IT'S IMPRINTED IN THE SCENE.
THE PAIN, THE SHOCK, ALL OF IT.
HOW CAN YOU LET HER GO THROUGH IT?

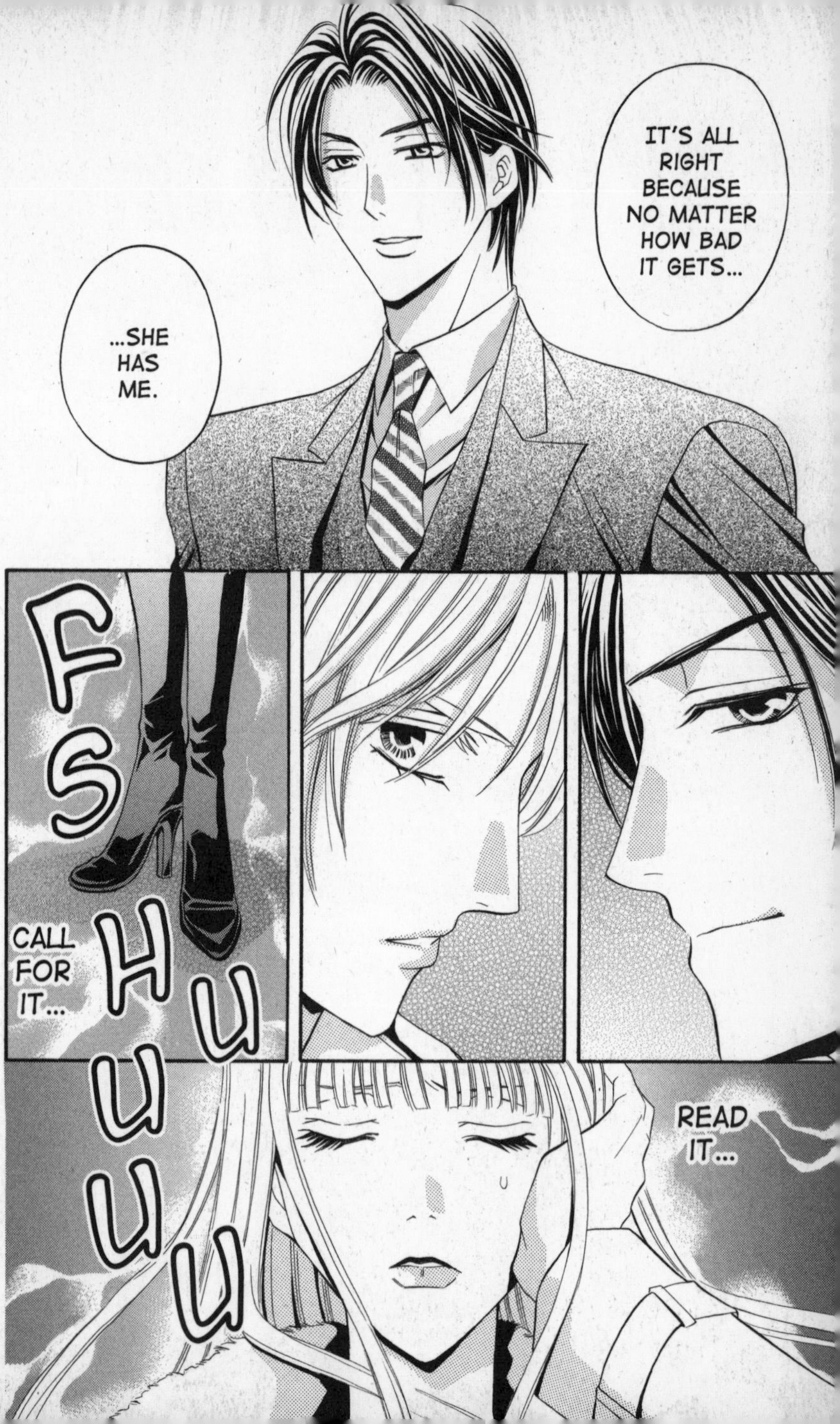
IT'S ALL RIGHT BECAUSE NO MATTER HOW BAD IT GETS...
...SHE HAS ME.
CALL FOR IT...
FSHUUUU
READ IT...

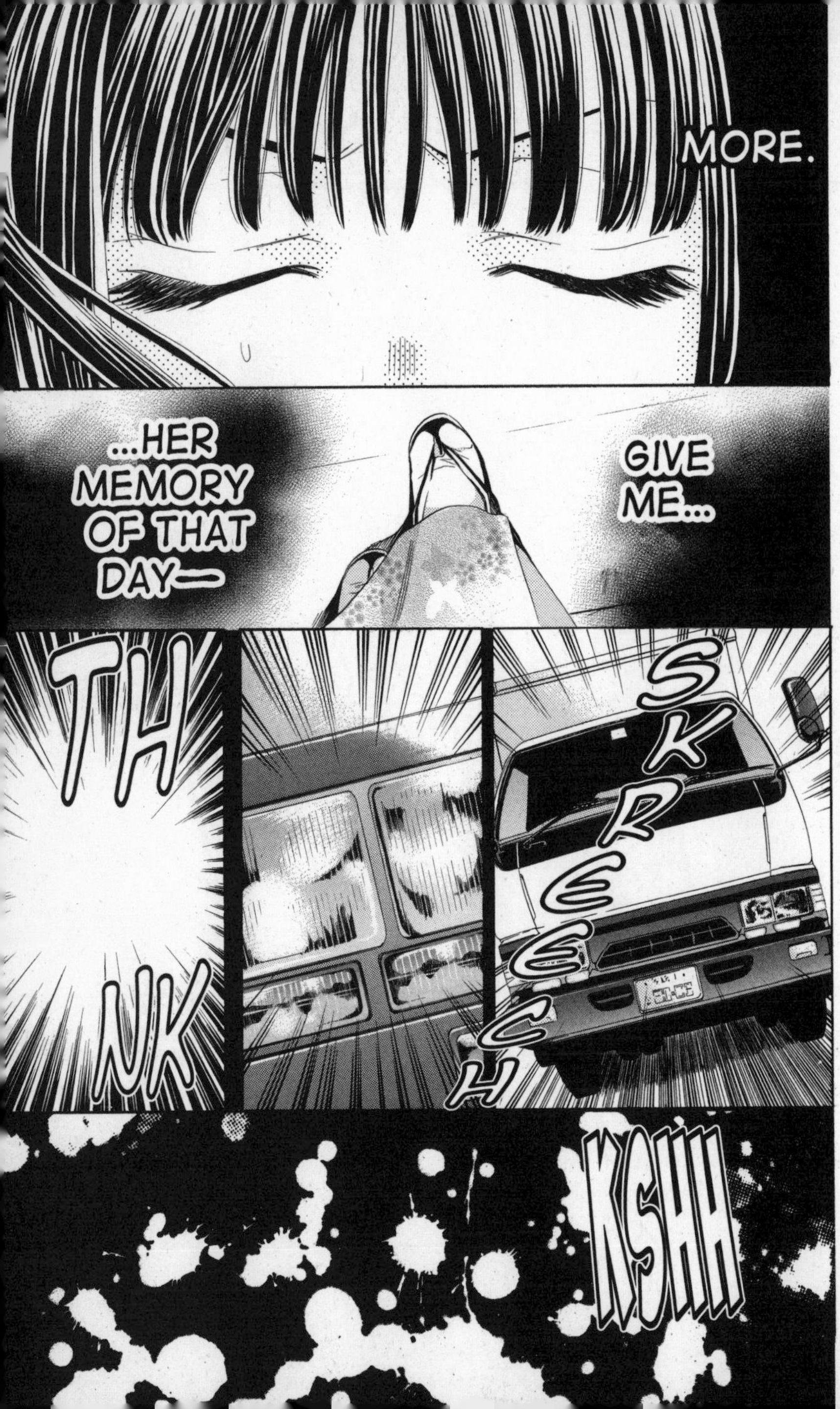
MORE.
GIVE ME...
...HER MEMORY OF THAT DAY—
SKREEEECH
THNK
KSHH

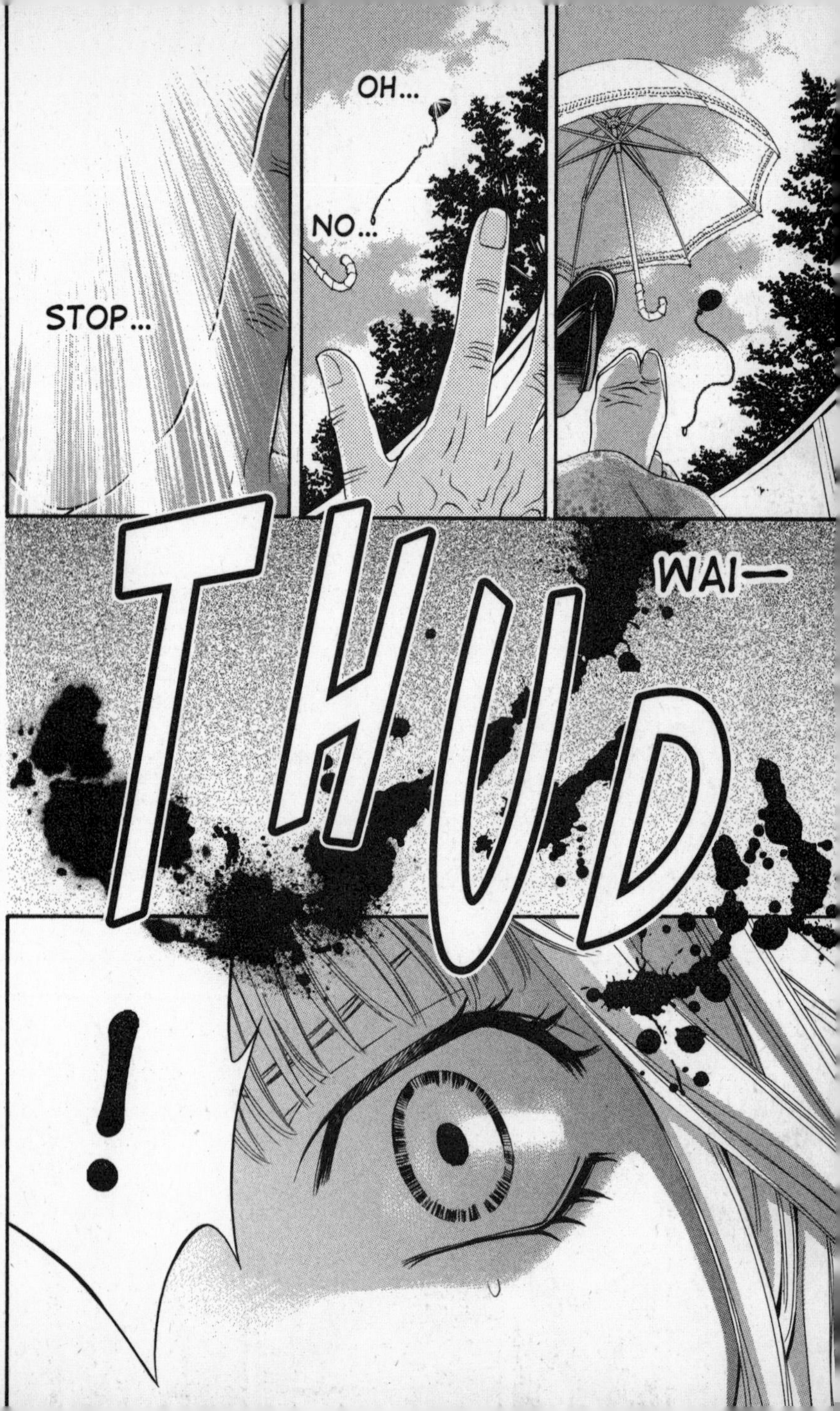
OH...
NO...
STOP...
WAI—
THUD
!

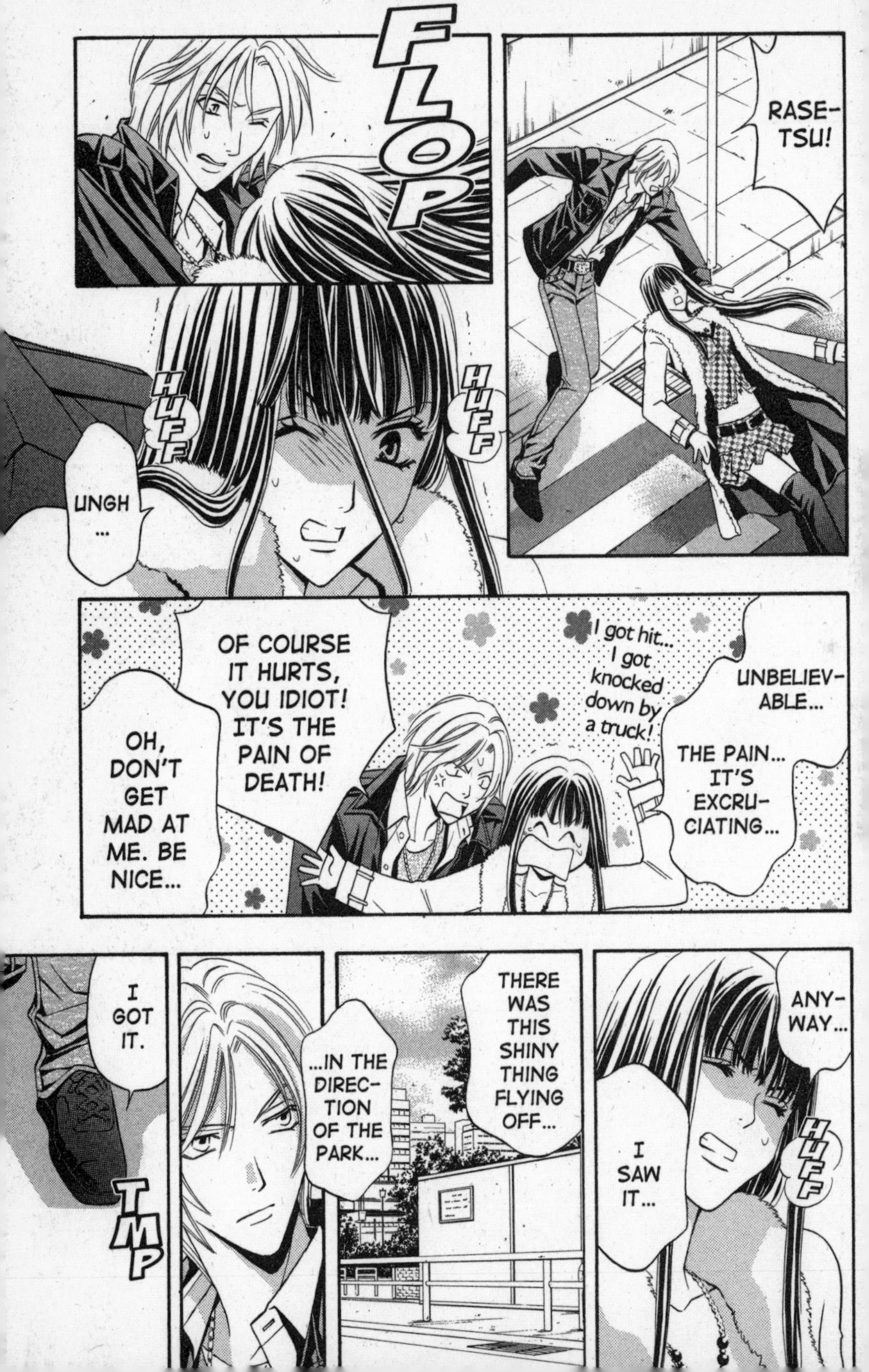
RASETSU!
FLOP
HUFF HUFF
UNGH...
UNBELIEVABLE...
THE PAIN... IT'S EXCRUCIATING...
I got hit... I got knocked down by a truck!
OF COURSE IT HURTS, YOU IDIOT! IT'S THE PAIN OF DEATH!
OH, DON'T GET MAD AT ME. BE NICE...
ANYWAY...
I SAW IT...
HUFF
THERE WAS THIS SHINY THING FLYING OFF...
...IN THE DIRECTION OF THE PARK...
I GOT IT.
TMP

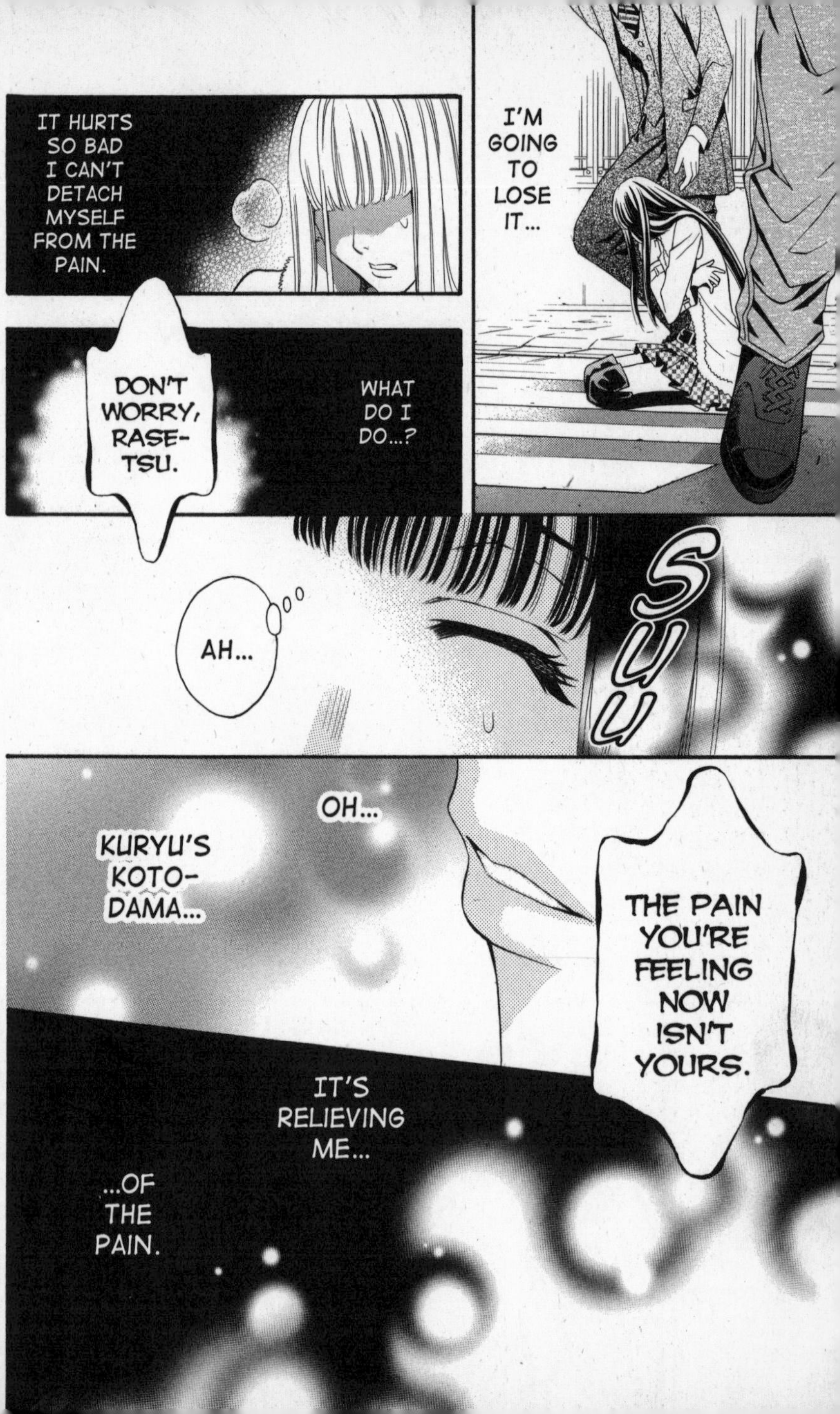
I'M GOING TO LOSE IT...
IT HURTS SO BAD I CAN'T DETACH MYSELF FROM THE PAIN.
WHAT DO I DO...?
DON'T WORRY, RASE-TSU.
SUU
AH...
THE PAIN YOU'RE FEELING NOW ISN'T YOURS.
OH...
KURYU'S KOTO-DAMA...
IT'S RELIEVING ME...
...OF THE PAIN.

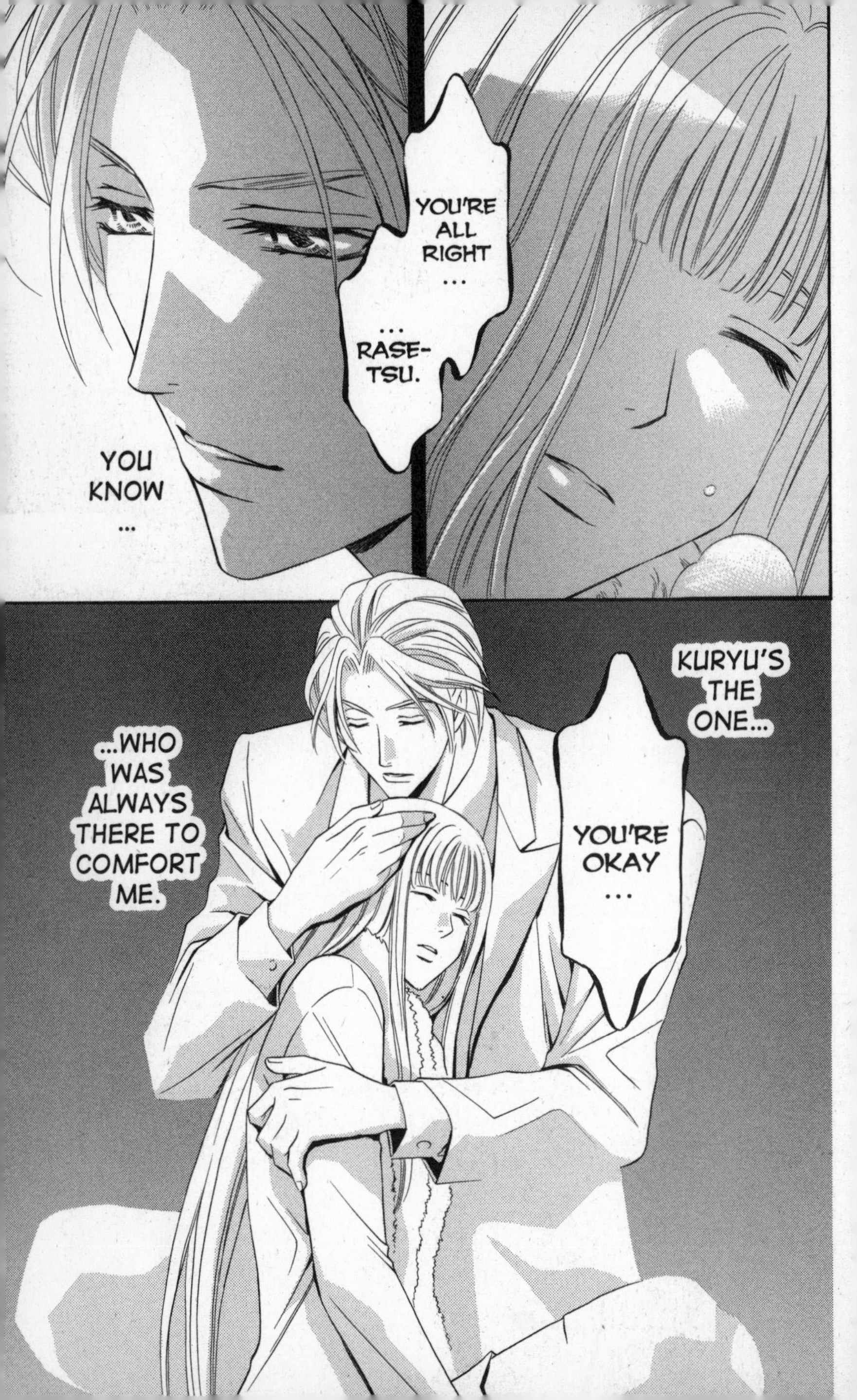
YOU'RE ALL RIGHT ... ... RASE-TSU.
YOU KNOW ...
KURYU'S THE ONE...
YOU'RE OKAY ...
...WHO WAS ALWAYS THERE TO COMFORT ME.

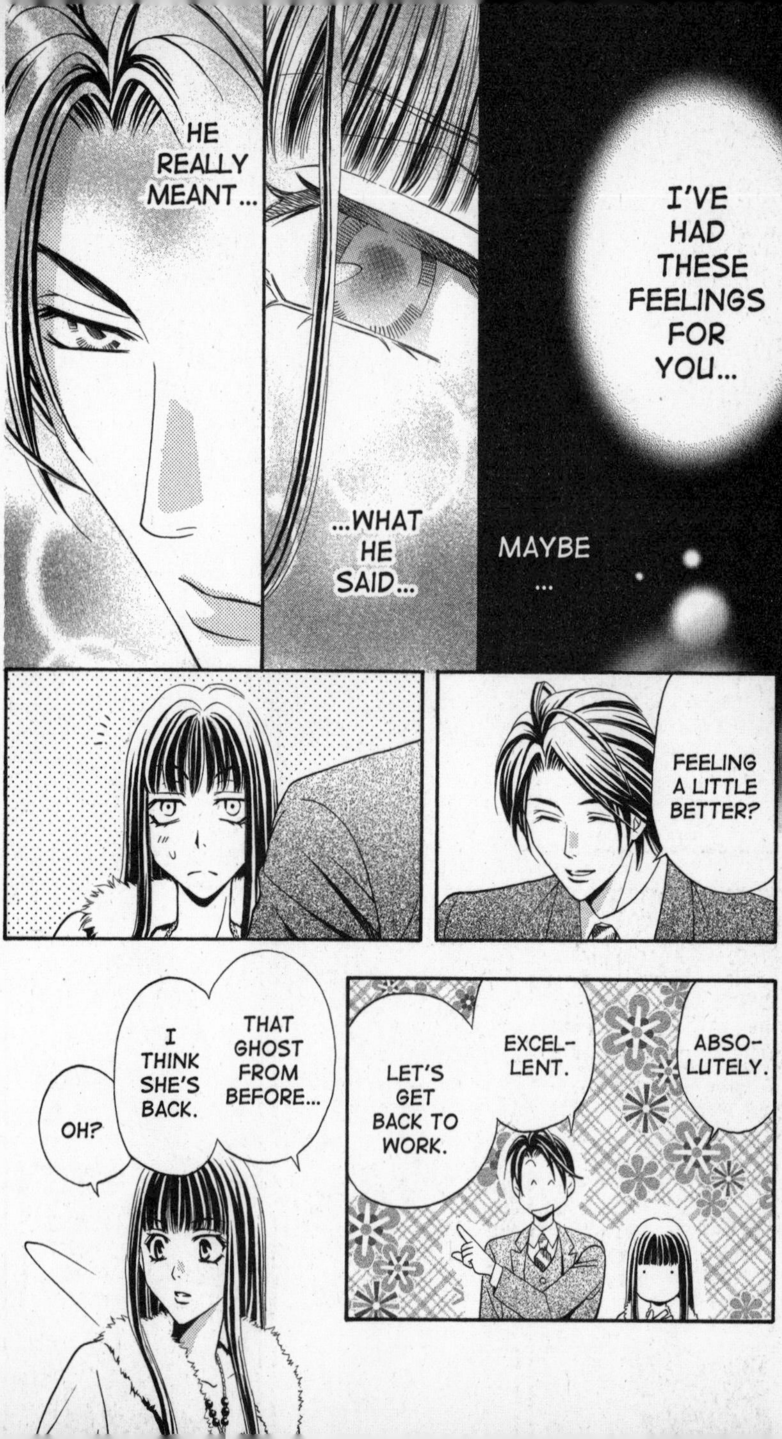
I'VE HAD THESE FEELINGS FOR YOU...
MAYBE ...
...WHAT HE SAID...
HE REALLY MEANT...
FEELING A LITTLE BETTER?
ABSO-LUTELY.
EXCEL-LENT.
LET'S GET BACK TO WORK.
THAT GHOST FROM BEFORE...
I THINK SHE'S BACK.
OH?

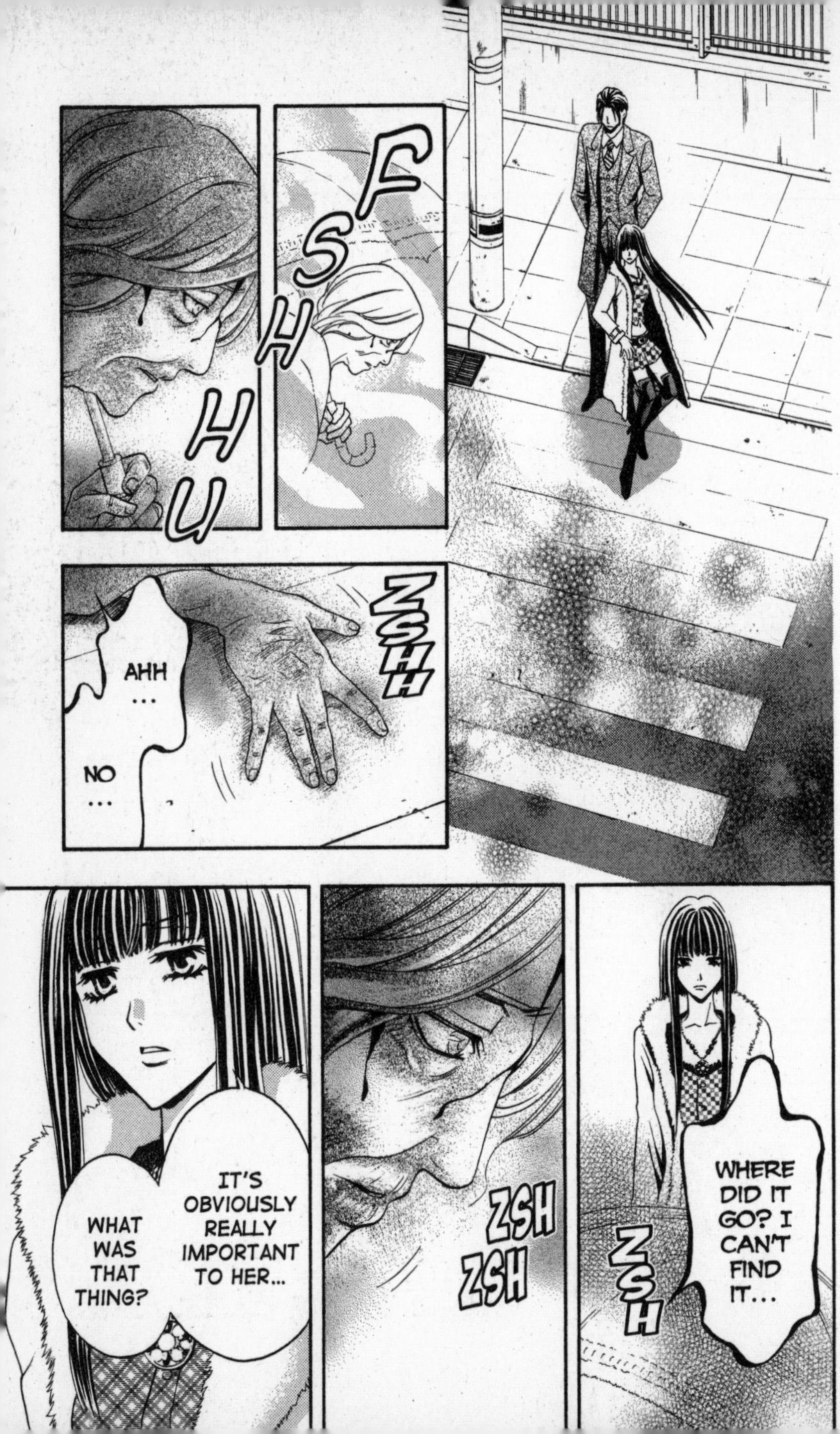
FSHHU
ZSHH
AHH ...
NO ...
WHERE DID IT GO? I CAN'T FIND IT...
ZSH
ZSH ZSH
IT'S OBVIOUSLY REALLY IMPORTANT TO HER...
WHAT WAS THAT THING?

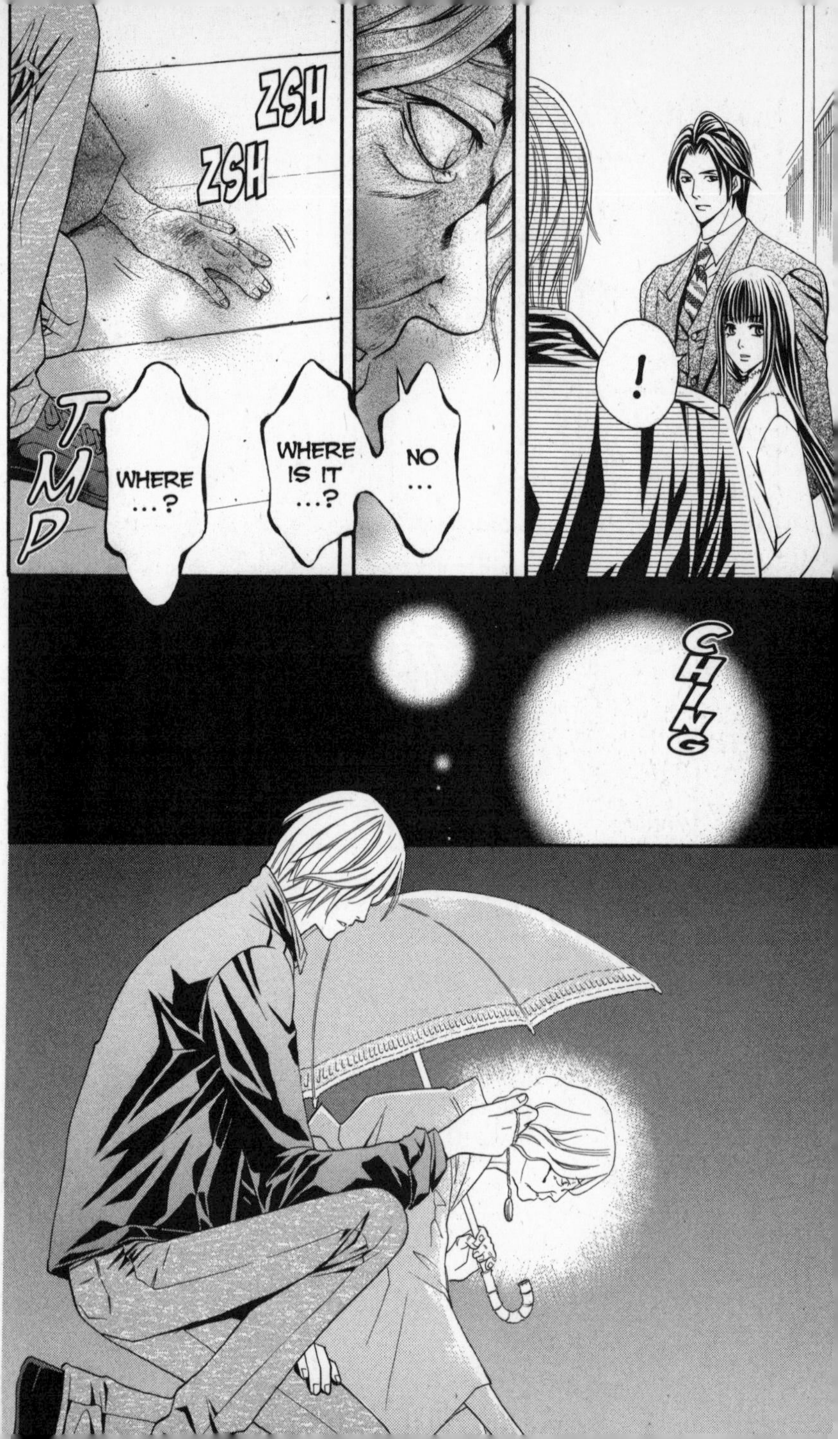
!
NO ...
WHERE IS IT ...?
ZSH
ZSH
WHERE ...?
TMD
CHING

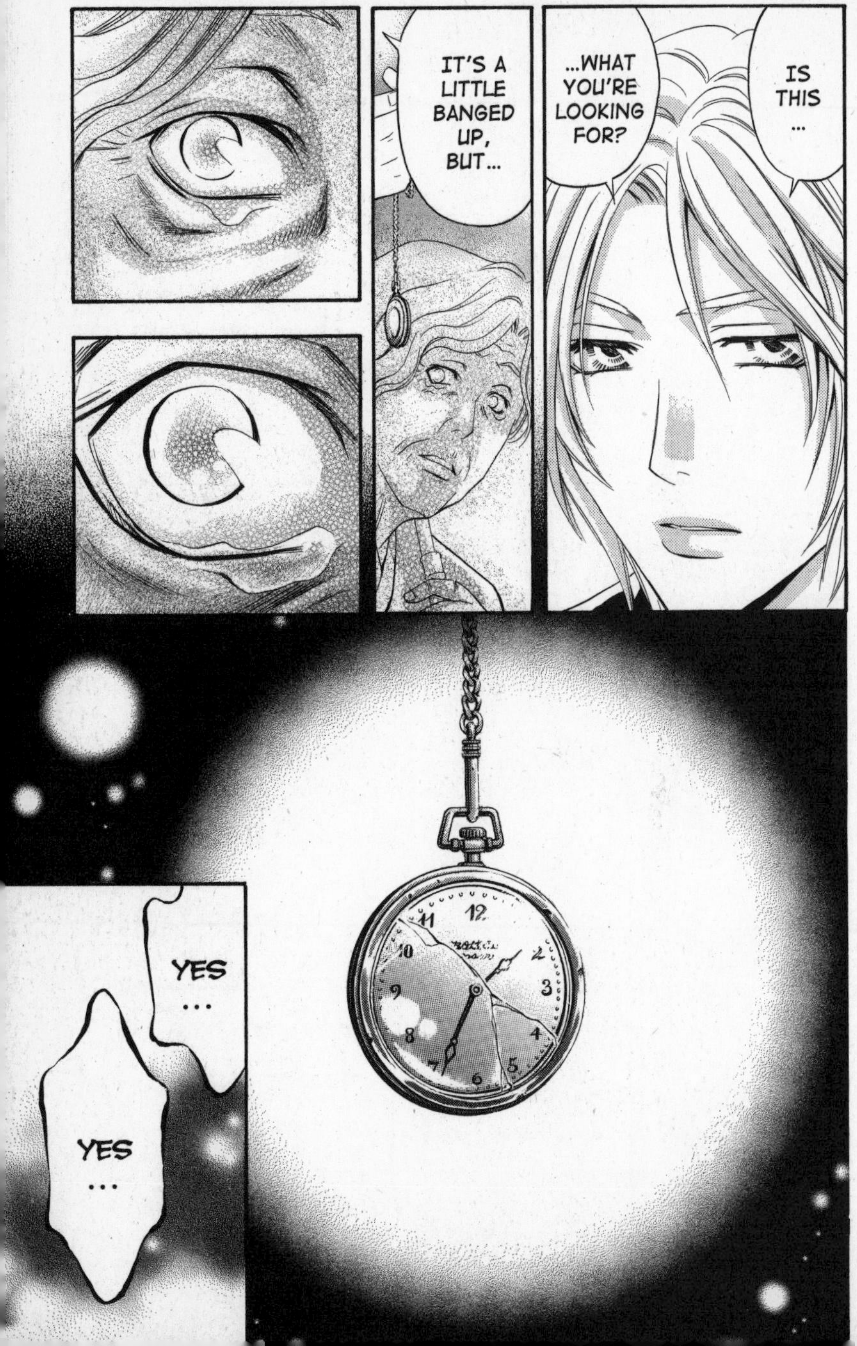
IS THIS ...
...WHAT YOU'RE LOOKING FOR?
IT'S A LITTLE BANGED UP, BUT...
YES ...
YES ...

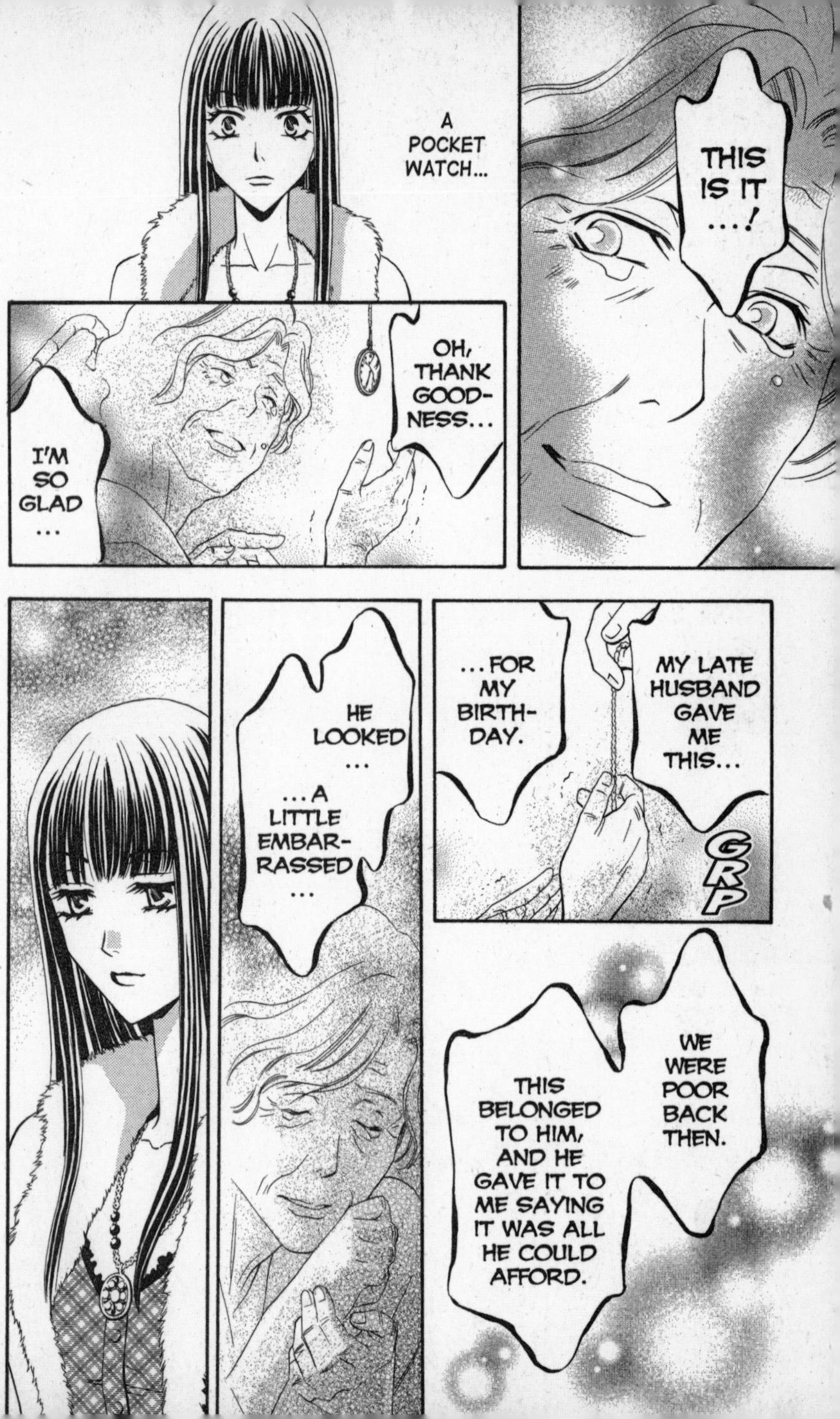
THIS IS IT ...!
A POCKET WATCH...
OH, THANK GOODNESS...
I'M SO GLAD ...
MY LATE HUSBAND GAVE ME THIS...
...FOR MY BIRTHDAY.
GRP
WE WERE POOR BACK THEN.
THIS BELONGED TO HIM, AND HE GAVE IT TO ME SAYING IT WAS ALL HE COULD AFFORD.
HE LOOKED ...
...A LITTLE EMBARRASSED ...

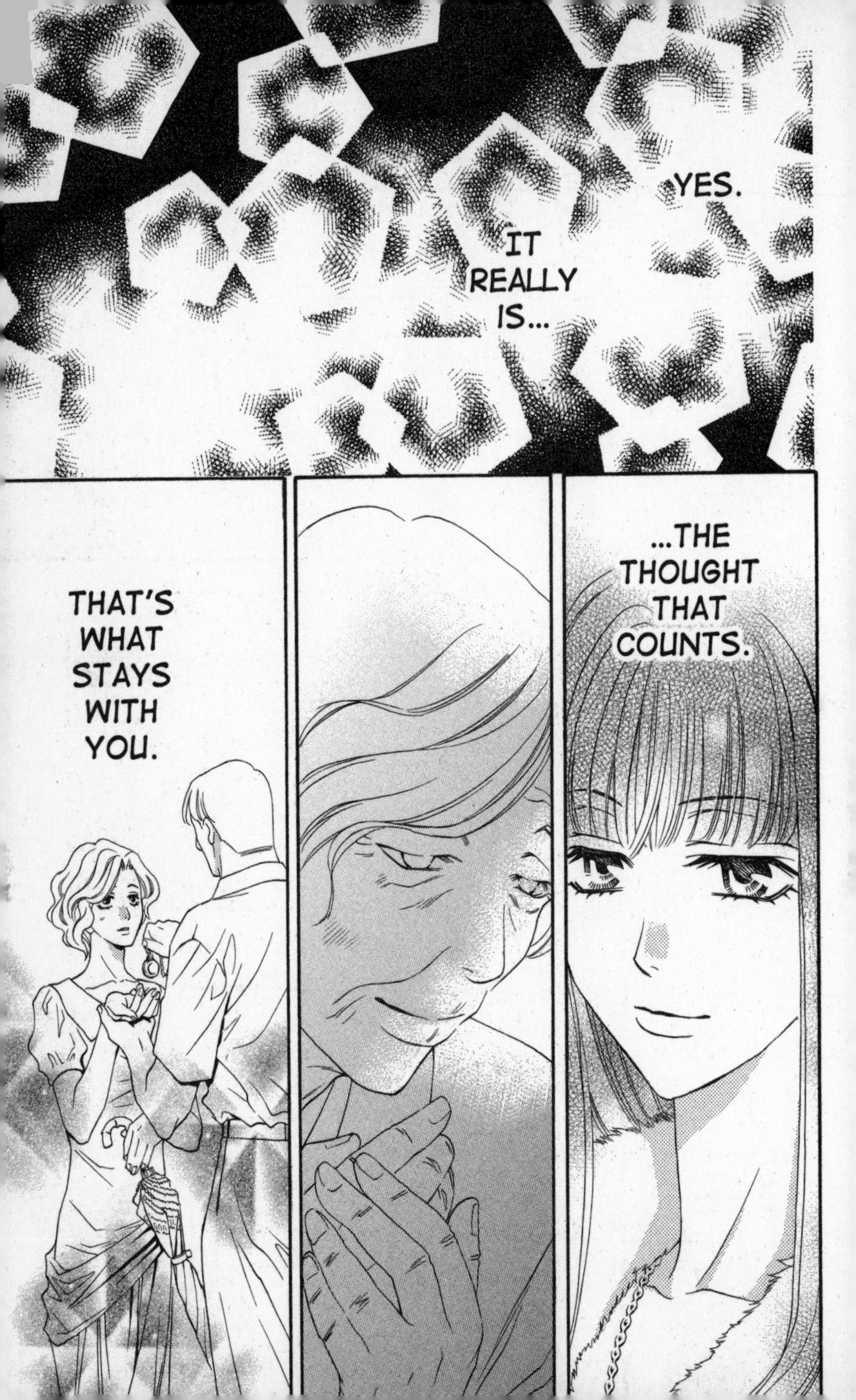
YES.
IT REALLY IS...
...THE THOUGHT THAT COUNTS.
THAT'S WHAT STAYS WITH YOU.

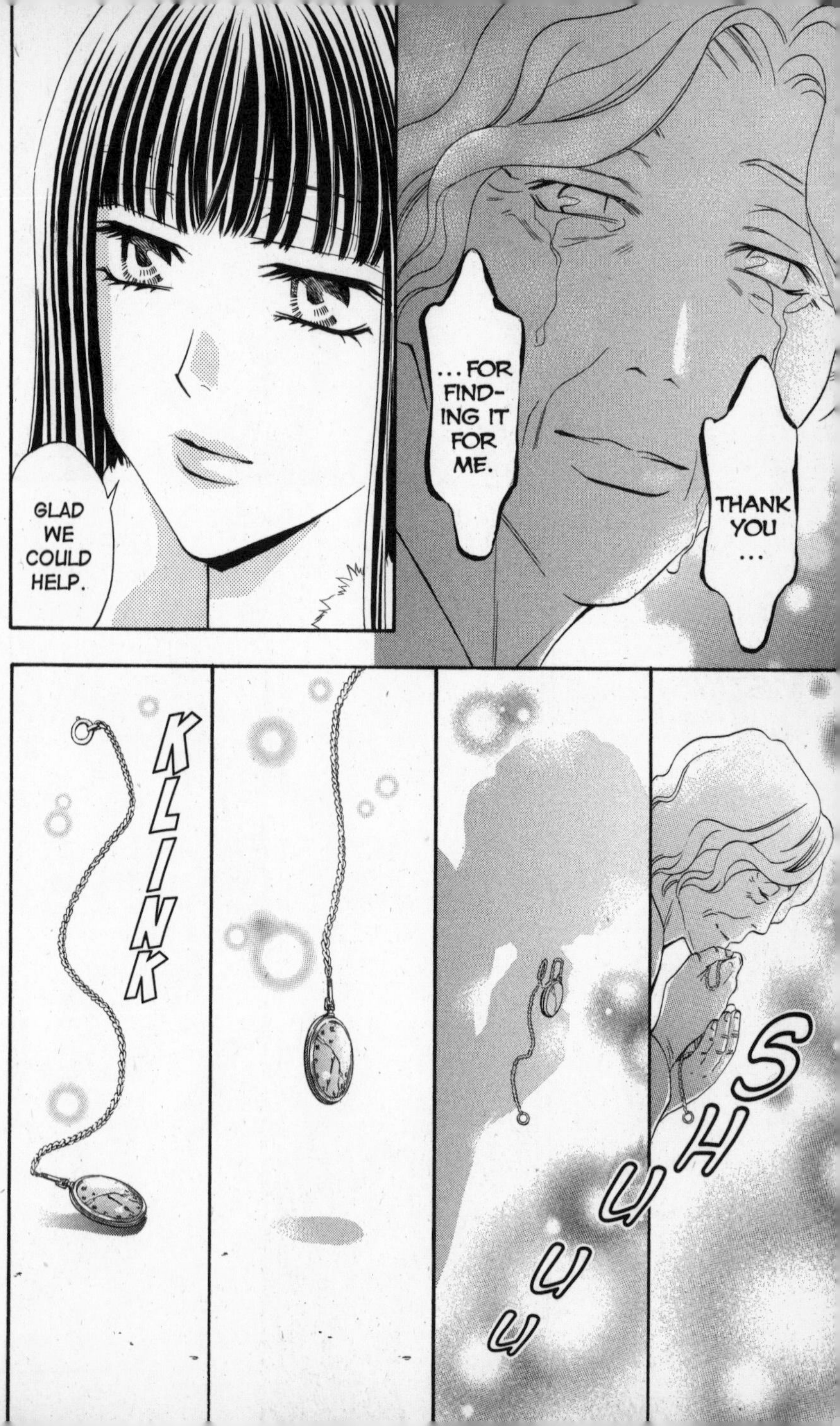
THANK YOU ...
...FOR FIND-ING IT FOR ME.
GLAD WE COULD HELP.
SHHUUUU
KLINK

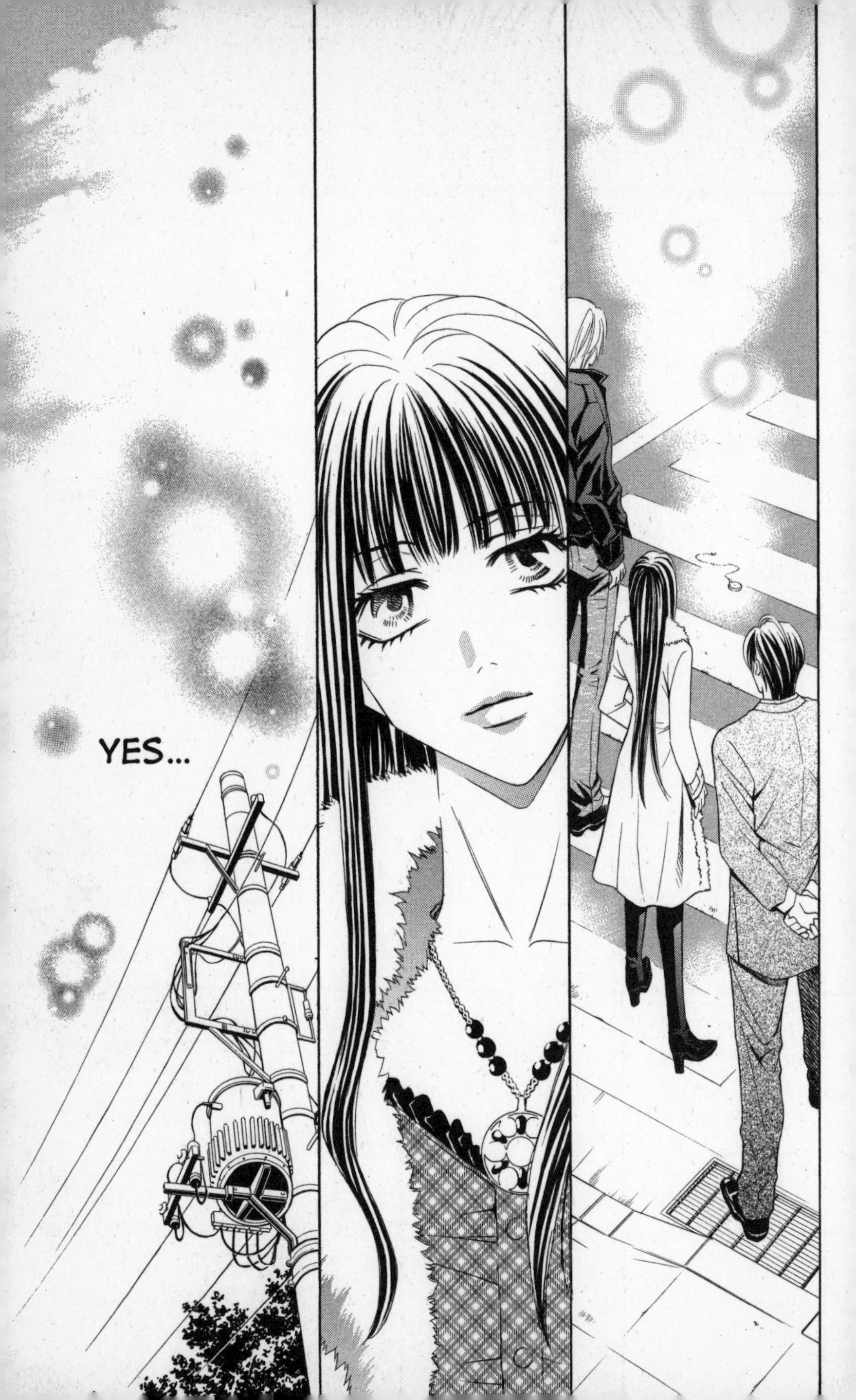
YES...

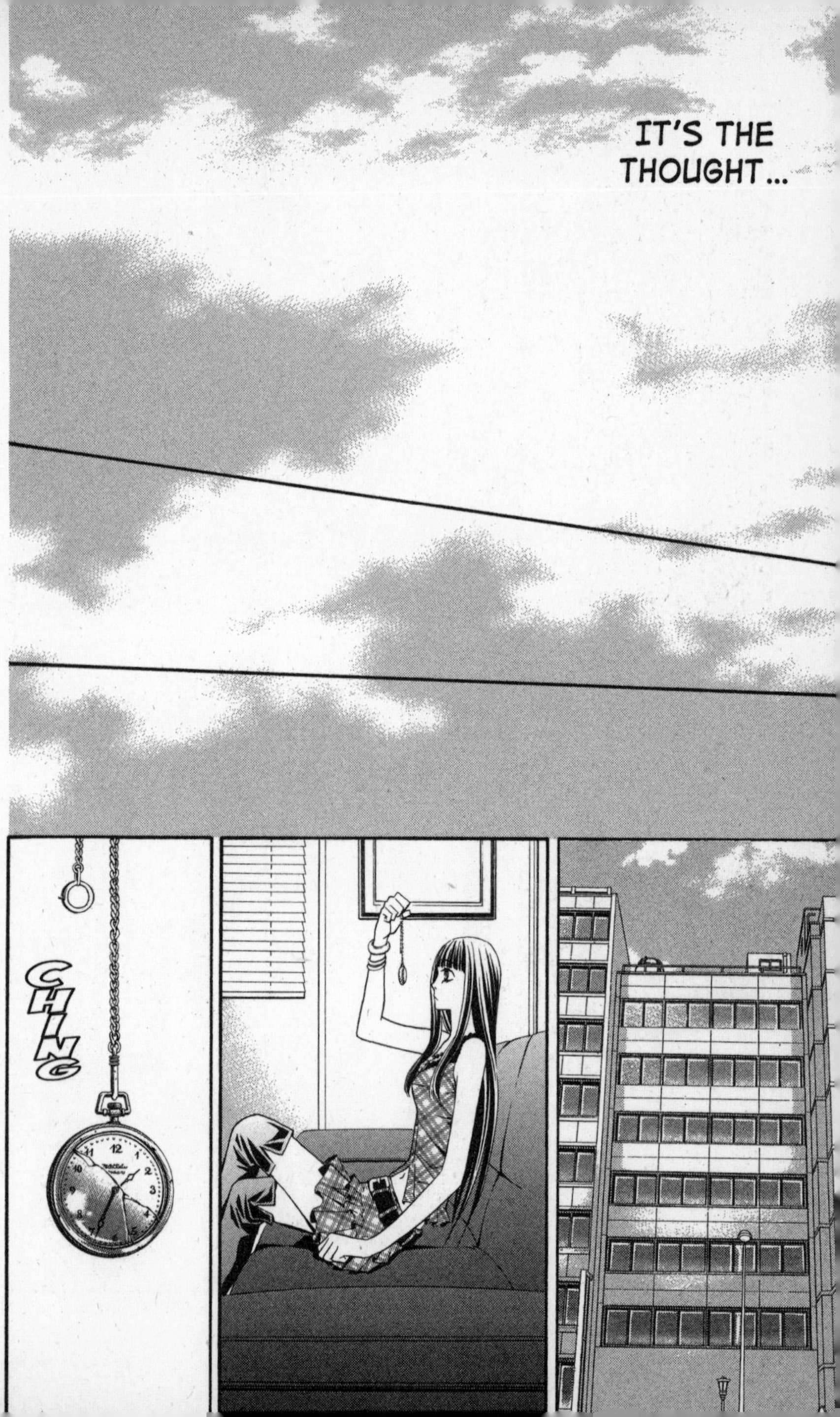
IT'S THE THOUGHT...
CHING

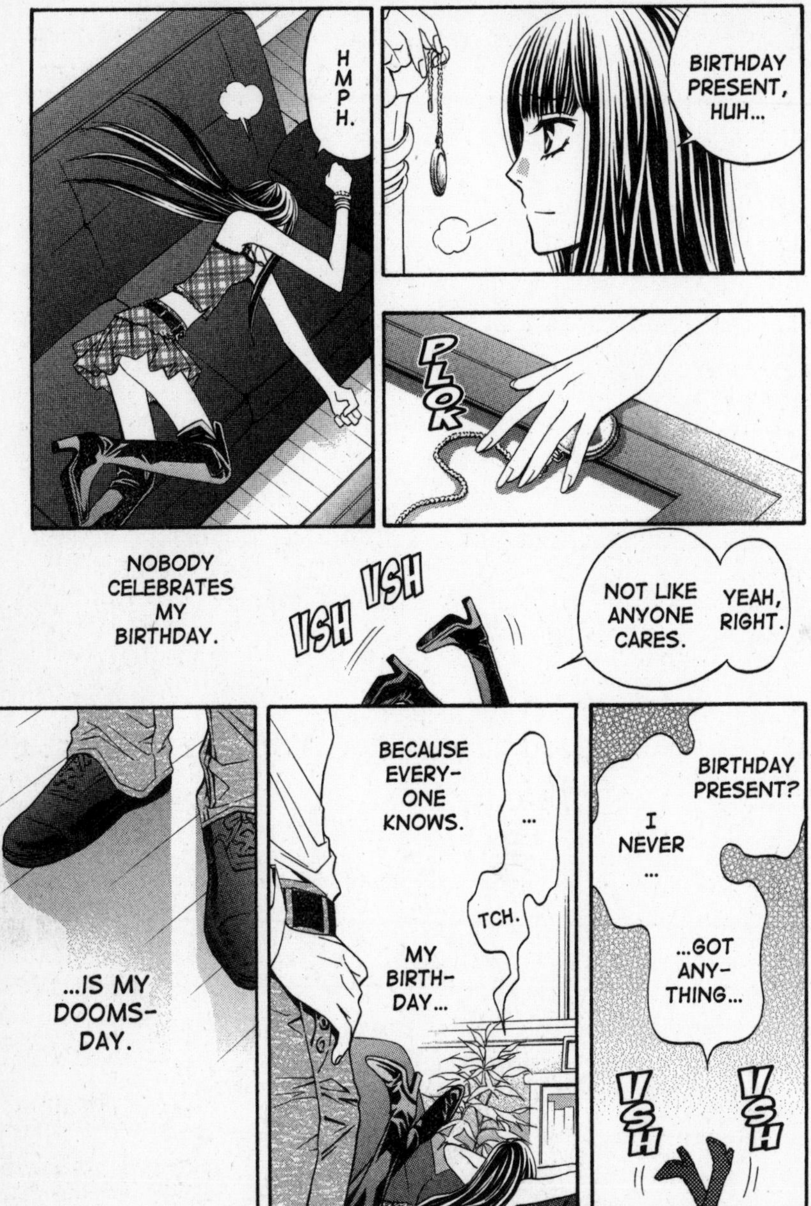
BIRTHDAY PRESENT, HUH...
PLOK
HMPH.
YEAH, RIGHT.
NOT LIKE ANYONE CARES.
VSH VSH
NOBODY CELEBRATES MY BIRTHDAY.
BIRTHDAY PRESENT?
I NEVER ...
...GOT ANY-THING...
VSH VSH
...
BECAUSE EVERY-ONE KNOWS.
TCH.
MY BIRTH-DAY...
...IS MY DOOMS-DAY.

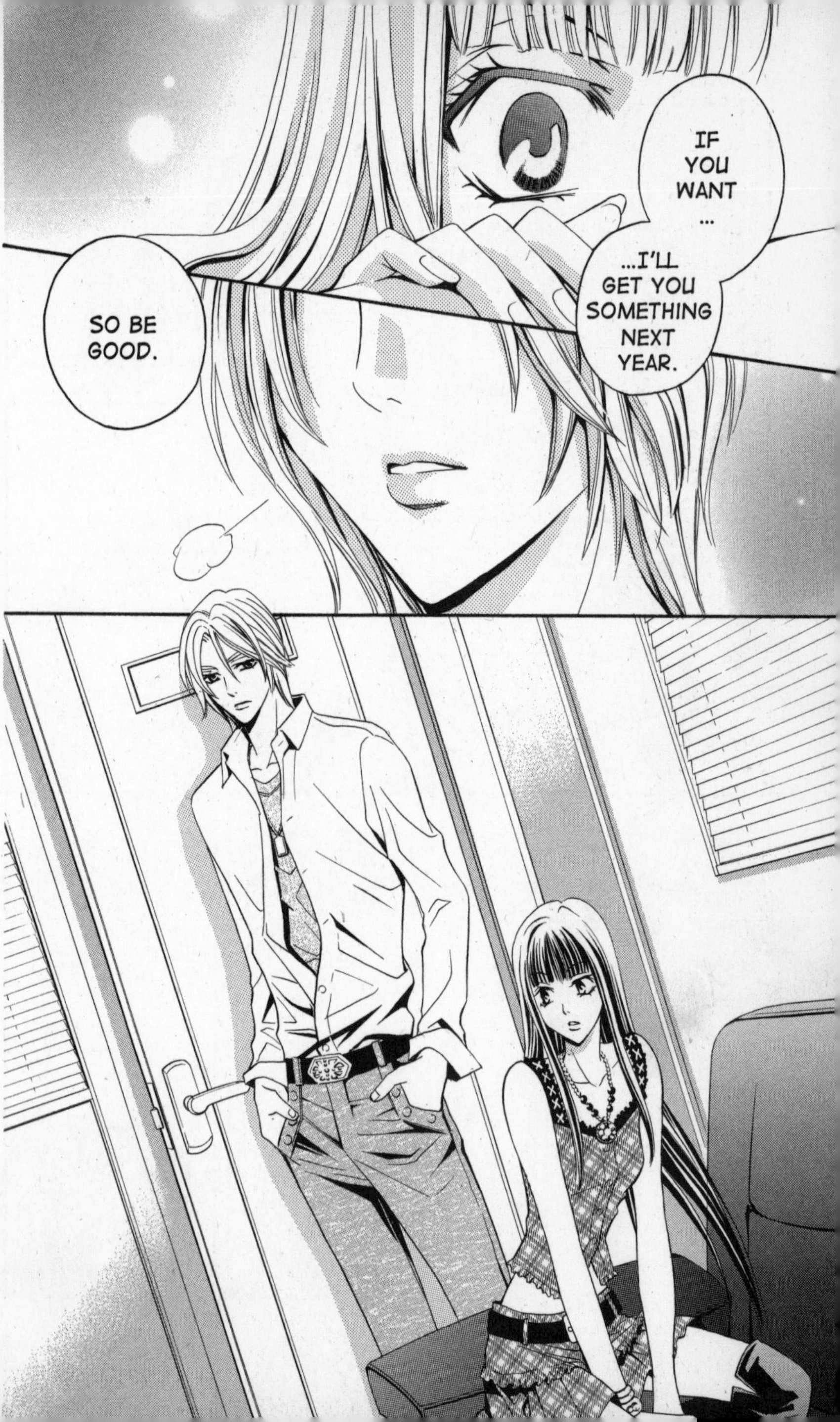
IF YOU WANT ...
...I'LL GET YOU SOMETHING NEXT YEAR.
SO BE GOOD.

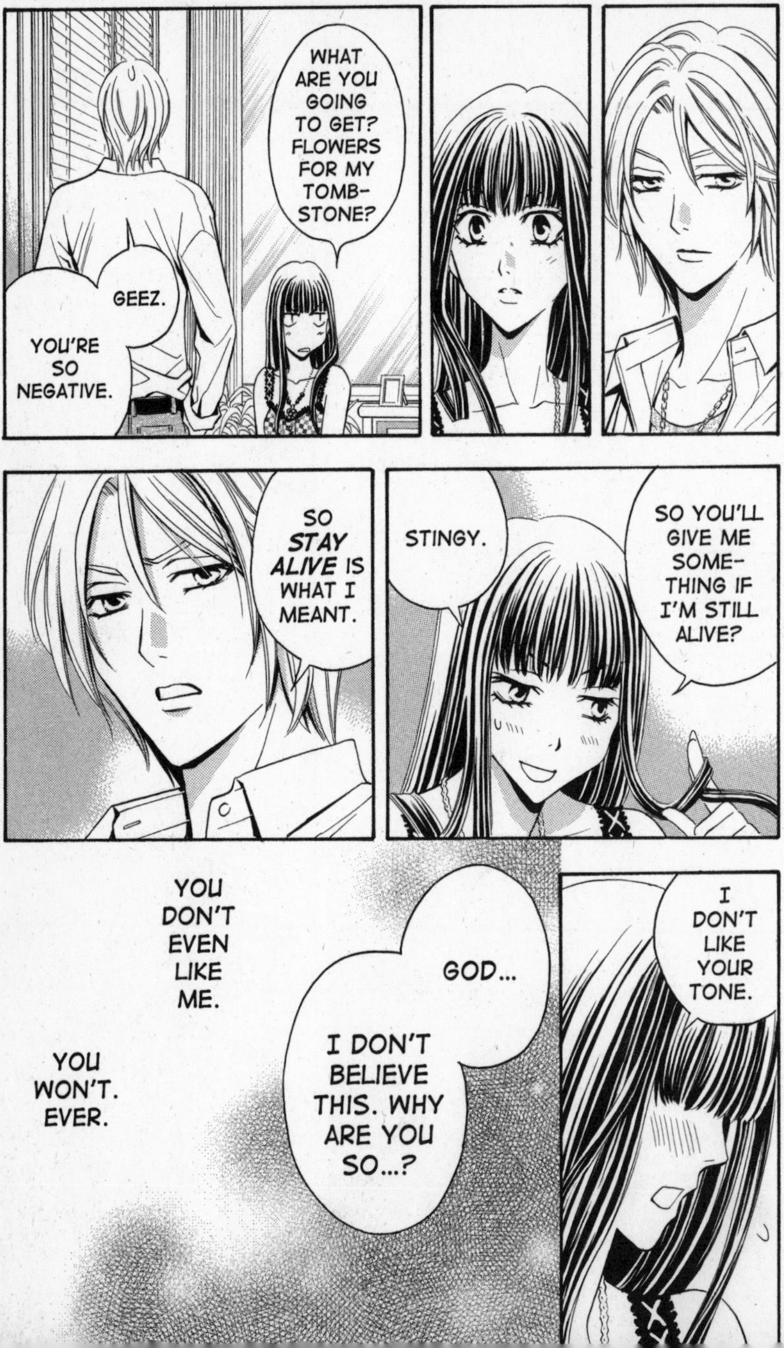
WHAT ARE YOU GOING TO GET? FLOWERS FOR MY TOMB-STONE?
GEEZ.
YOU'RE SO NEGATIVE.
SO YOU'LL GIVE ME SOME-THING IF I'M STILL ALIVE?
STINGY.
SO *STAY ALIVE* IS WHAT I MEANT.
I DON'T LIKE YOUR TONE.
GOD...
I DON'T BELIEVE THIS. WHY ARE YOU SO...?
YOU DON'T EVEN LIKE ME.
YOU WON'T. EVER.

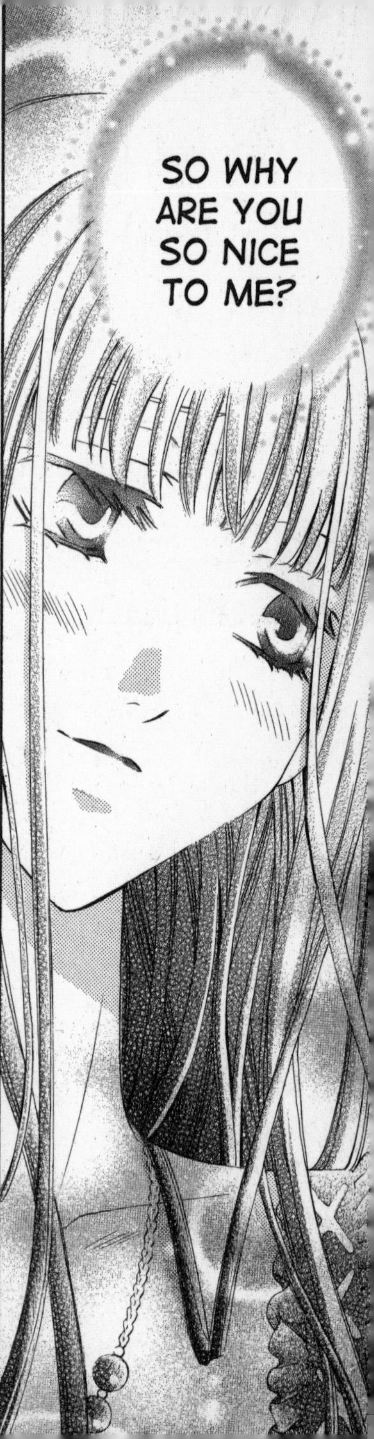
SO WHY ARE YOU SO NICE TO ME?

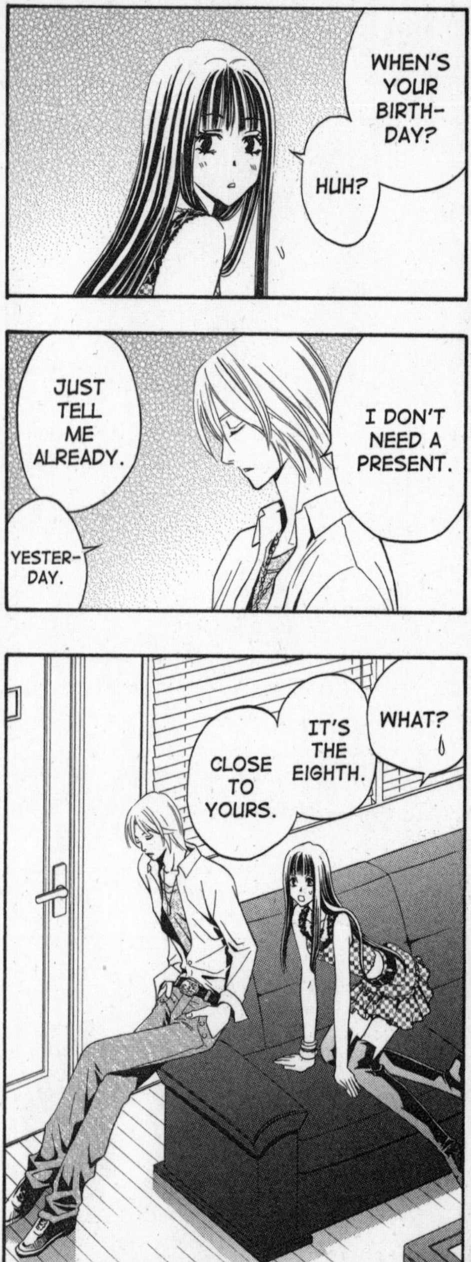
WHEN'S YOUR BIRTH-DAY?
HUH?
I DON'T NEED A PRESENT.
JUST TELL ME ALREADY.
YESTER-DAY.
WHAT?
IT'S THE EIGHTH.
CLOSE TO YOURS.

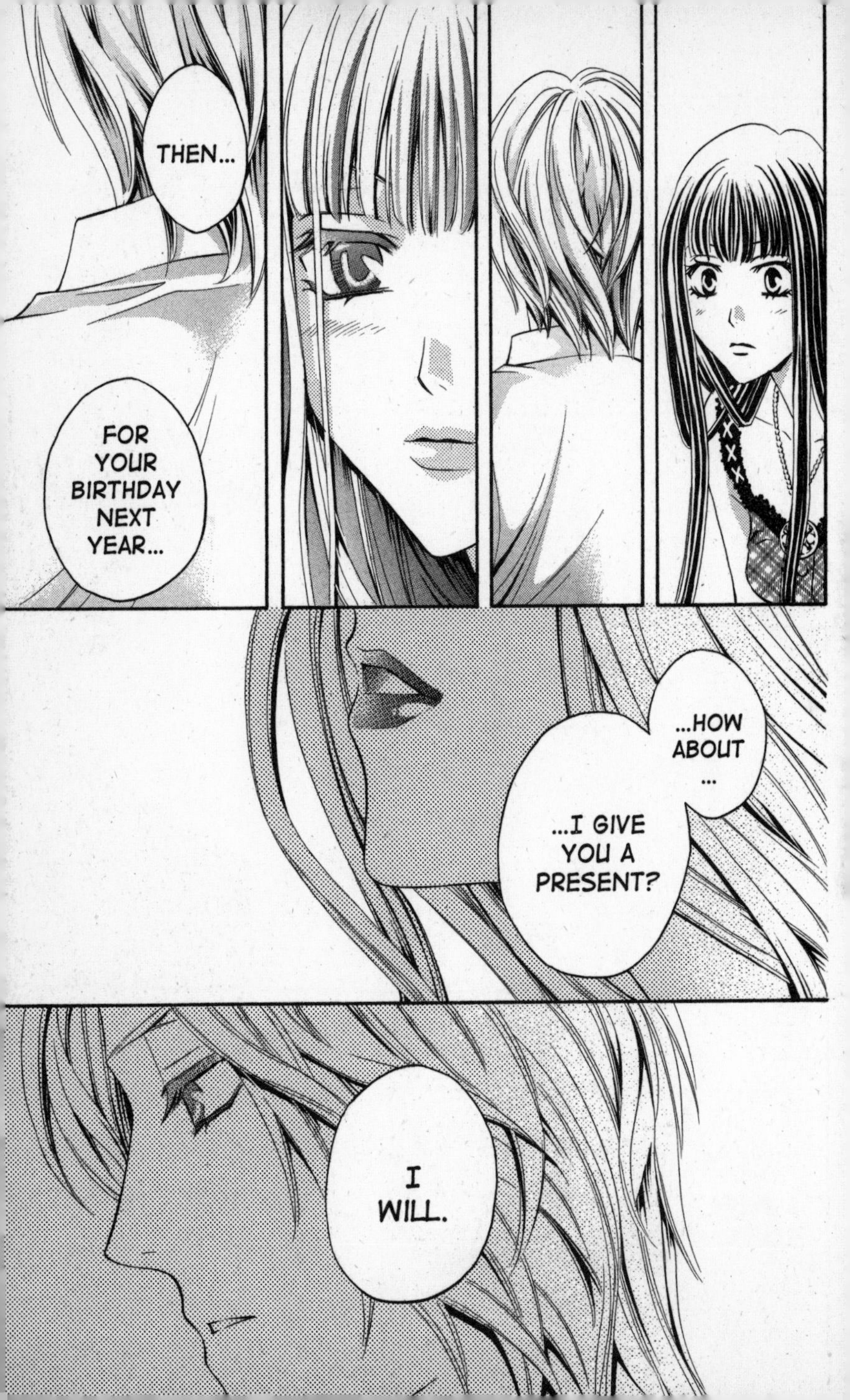
THEN...
FOR YOUR BIRTHDAY NEXT YEAR...
...HOW ABOUT ...
...I GIVE YOU A PRESENT?
I WILL.

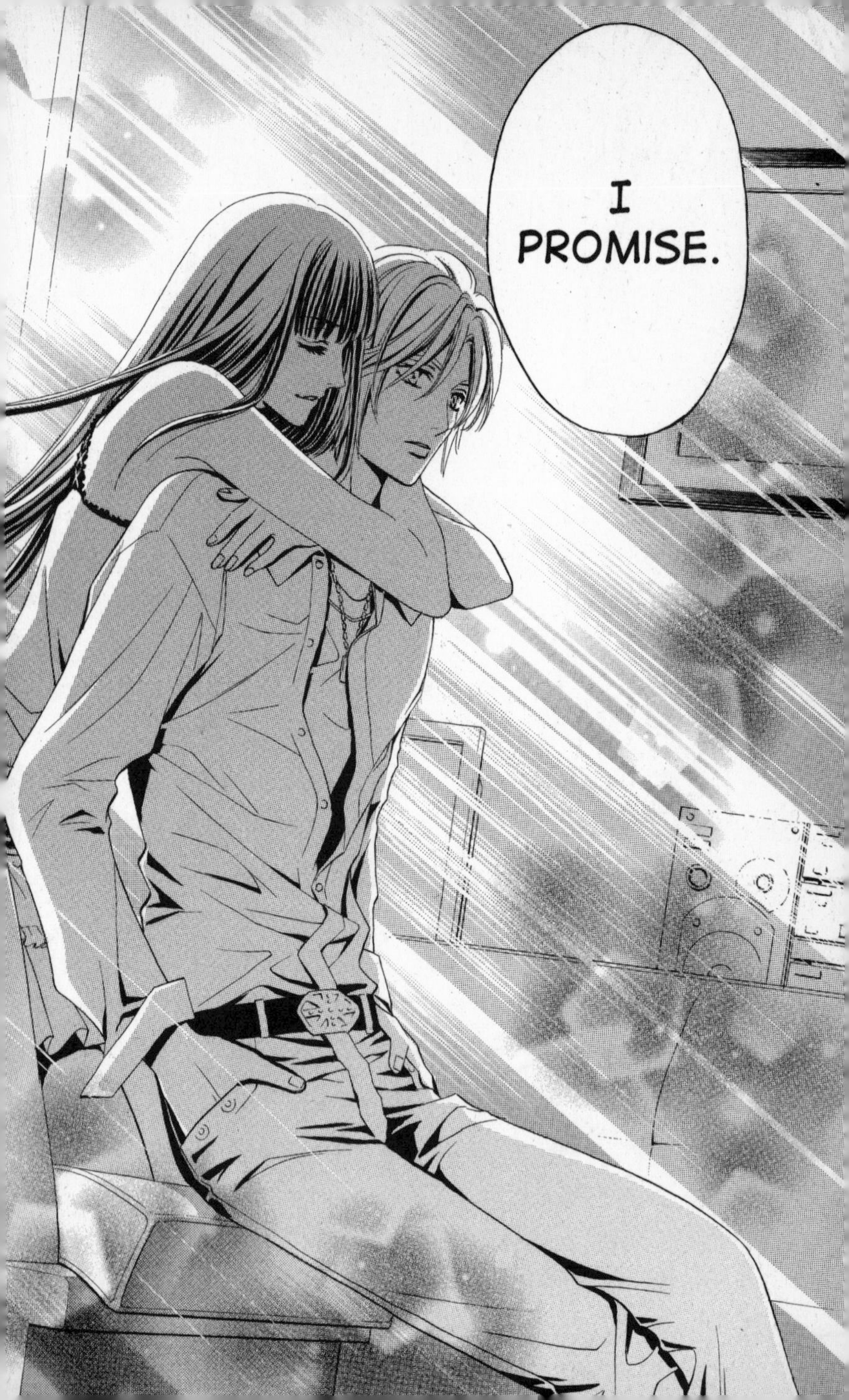
I PROMISE.

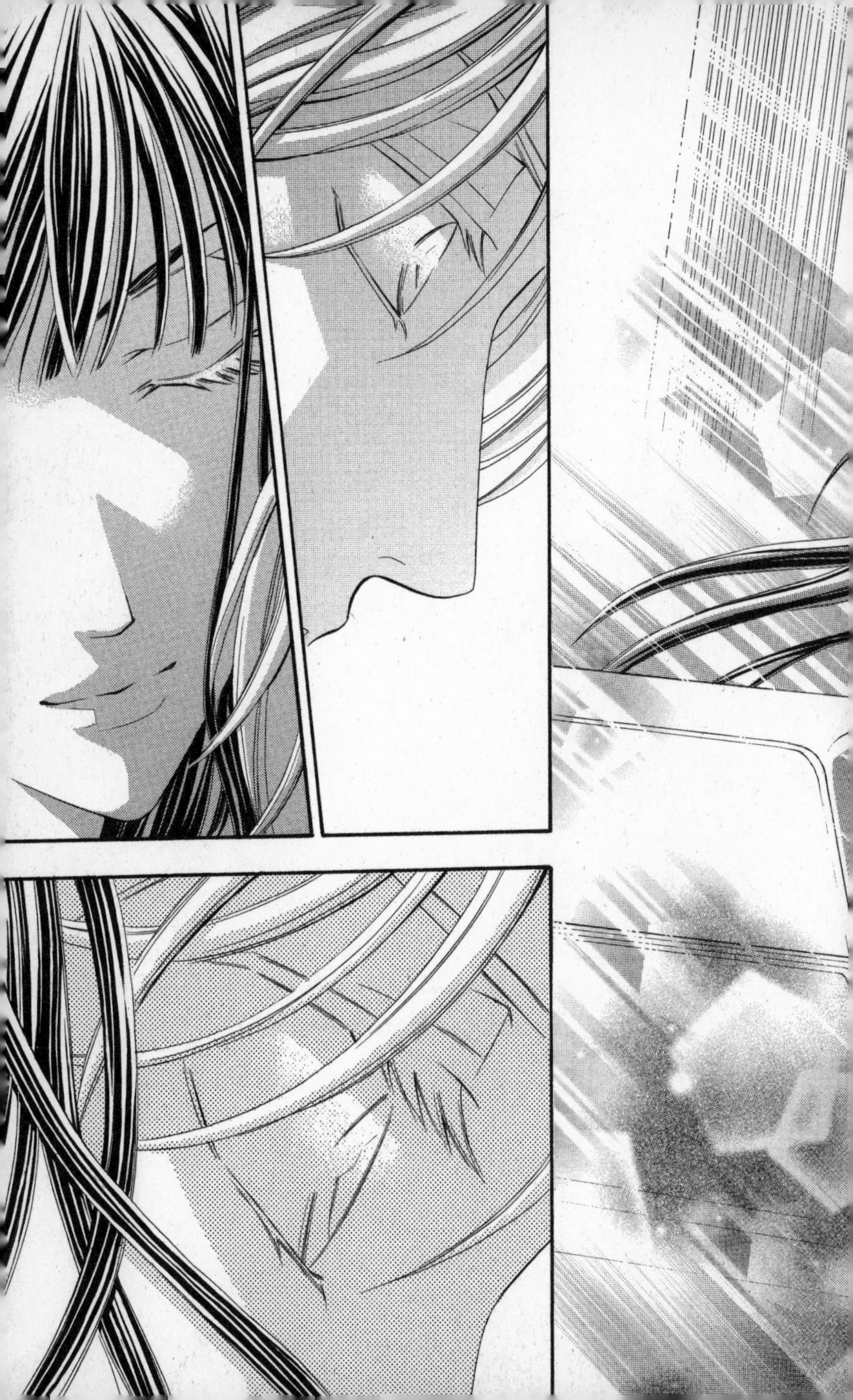

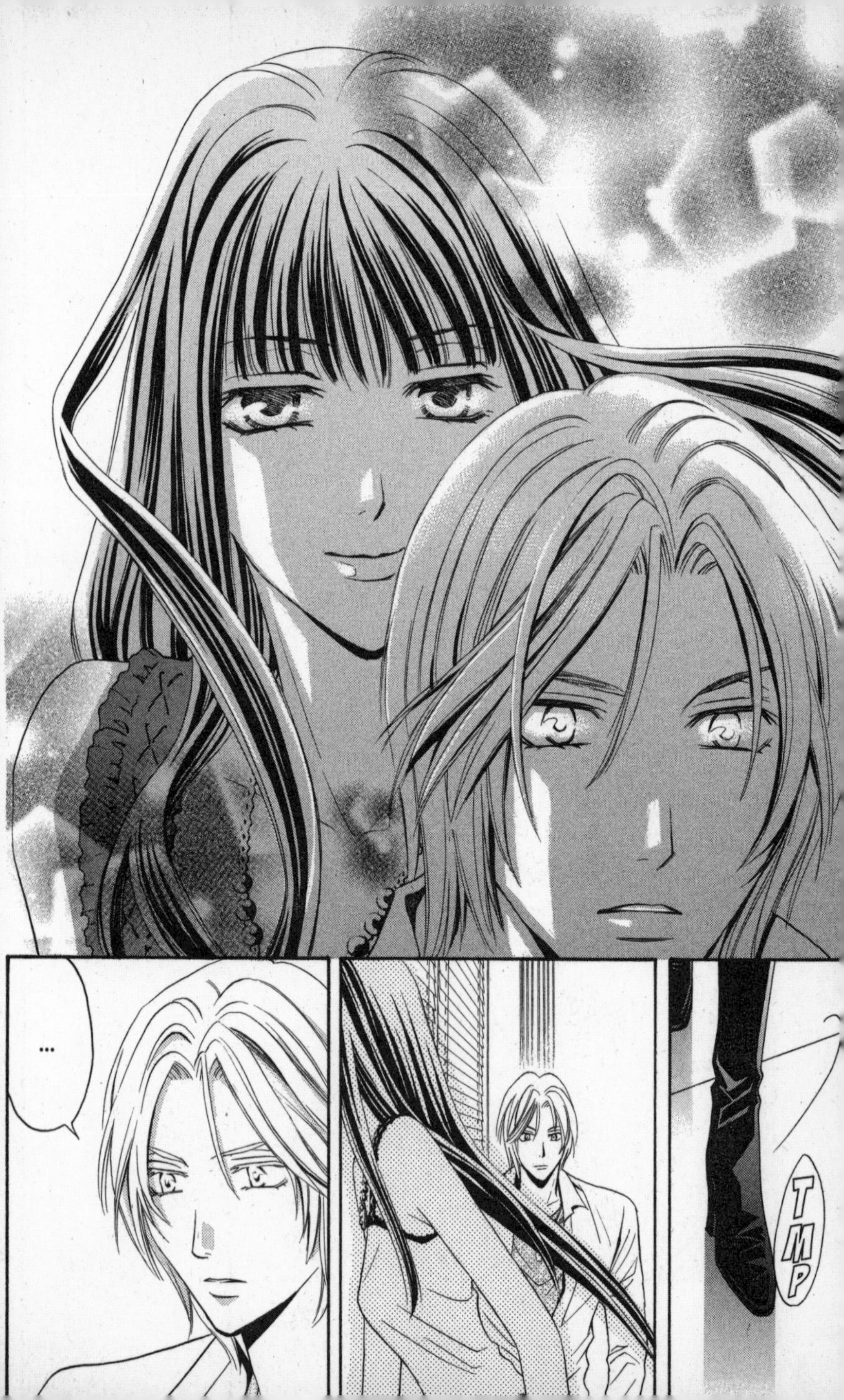
TMP
...

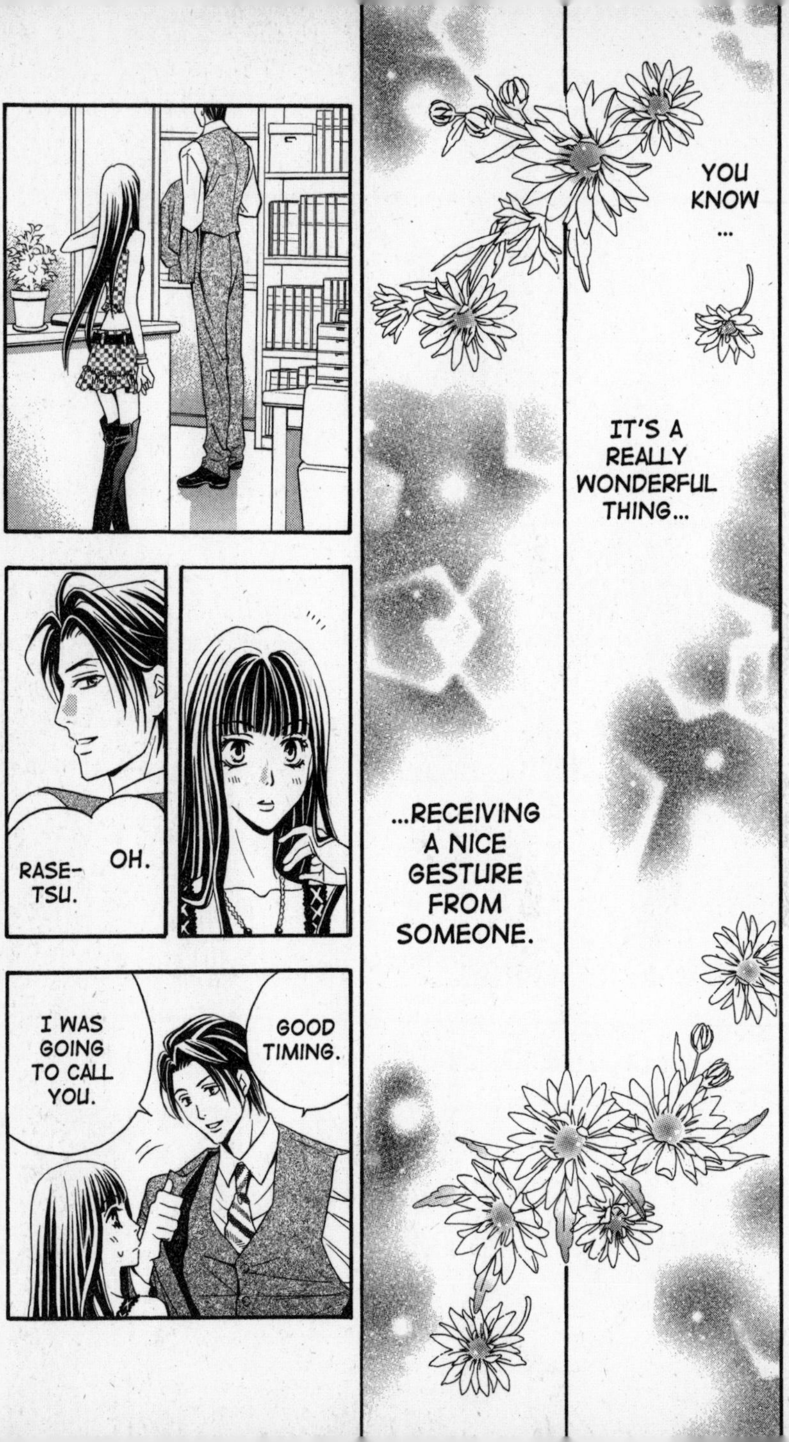
YOU KNOW ...
IT'S A REALLY WONDERFUL THING...
...RECEIVING A NICE GESTURE FROM SOMEONE.
OH.
RASE-TSU.
GOOD TIMING.
I WAS GOING TO CALL YOU.

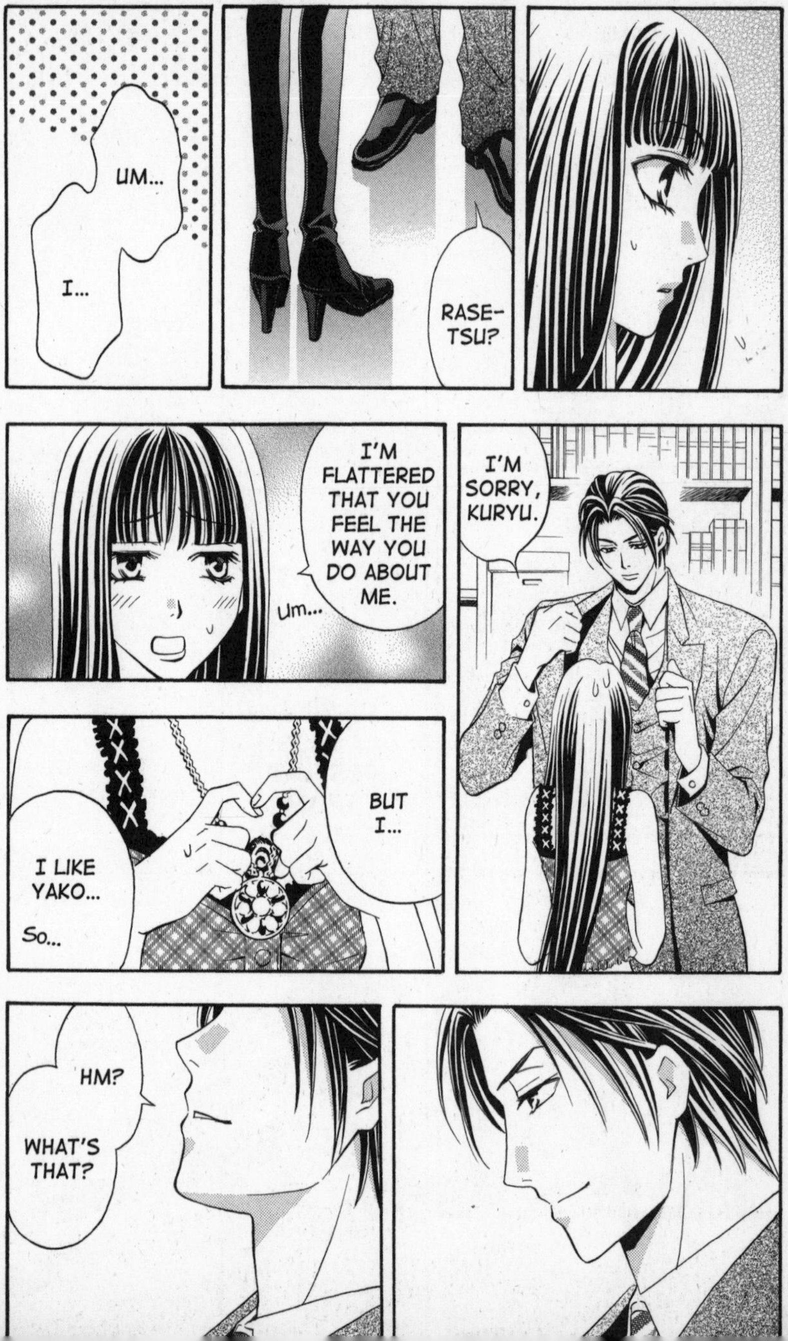
RASE-TSU?
UM...
I...
I'M SORRY, KURYU.
Um...
I'M FLATTERED THAT YOU FEEL THE WAY YOU DO ABOUT ME.
BUT I...
I LIKE YAKO...
So...
HM?
WHAT'S THAT?

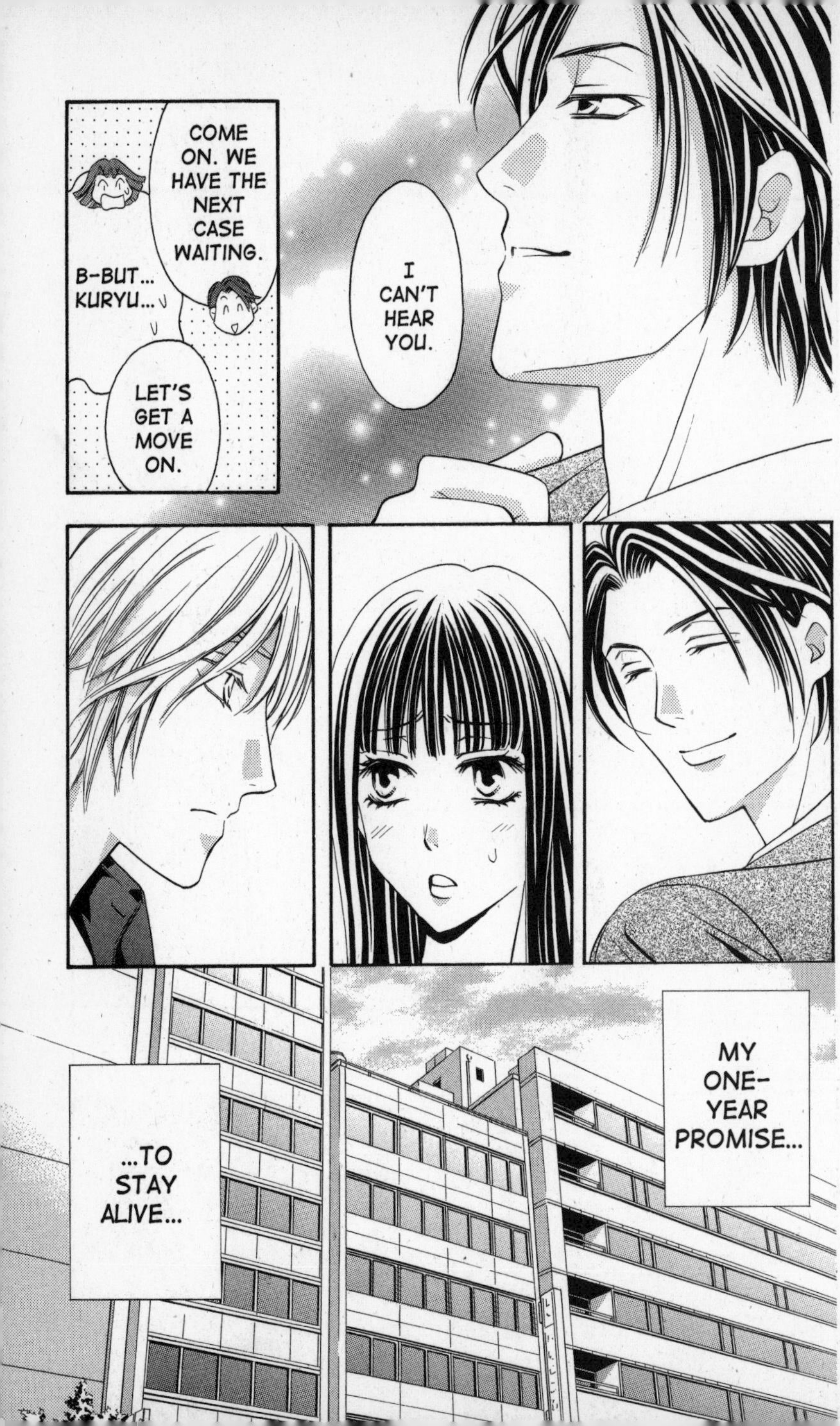
I CAN'T HEAR YOU.
COME ON. WE HAVE THE NEXT CASE WAITING.
B-BUT... KURYU...
LET'S GET A MOVE ON.
MY ONE-YEAR PROMISE...
...TO STAY ALIVE...

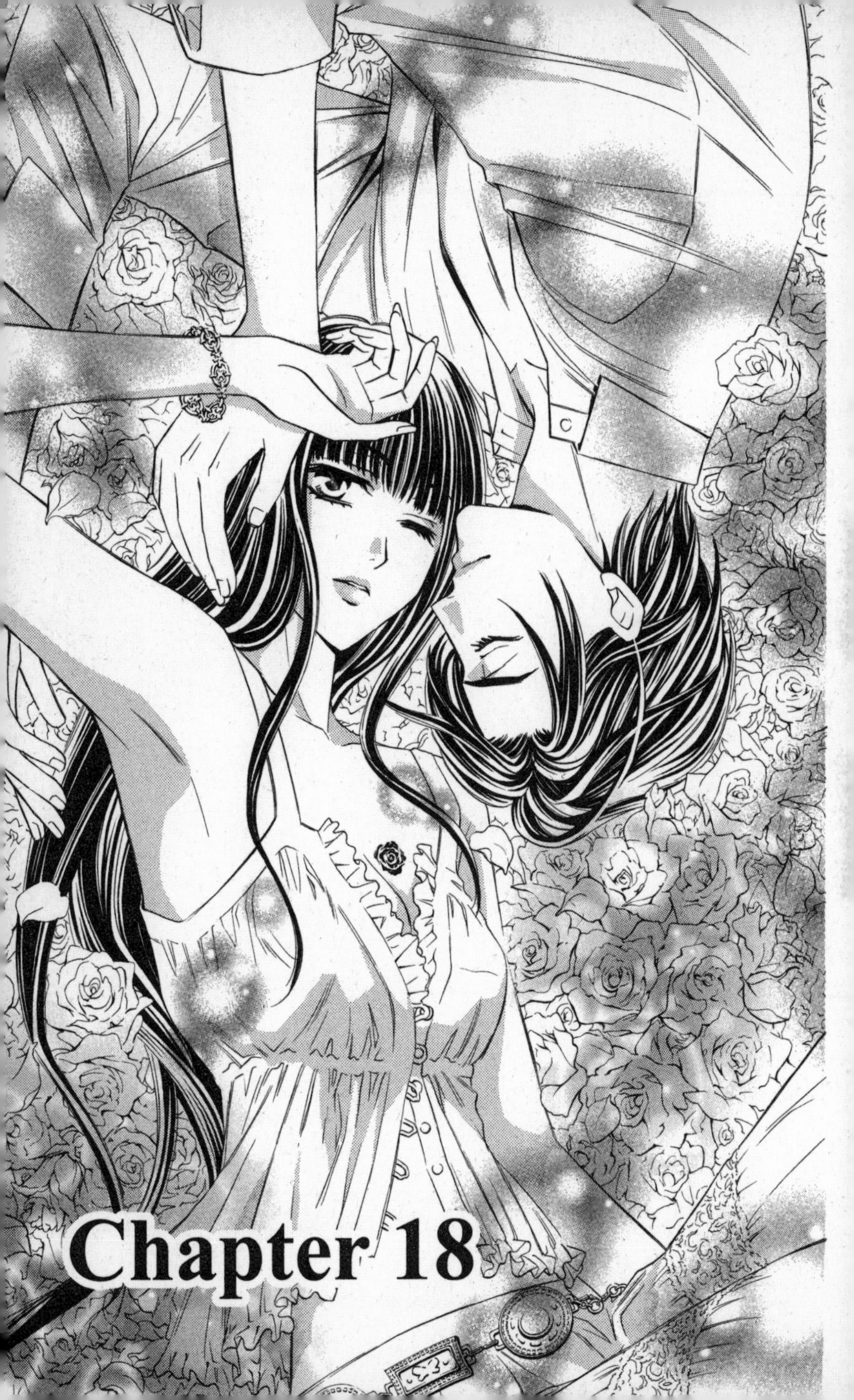
Chapter 18

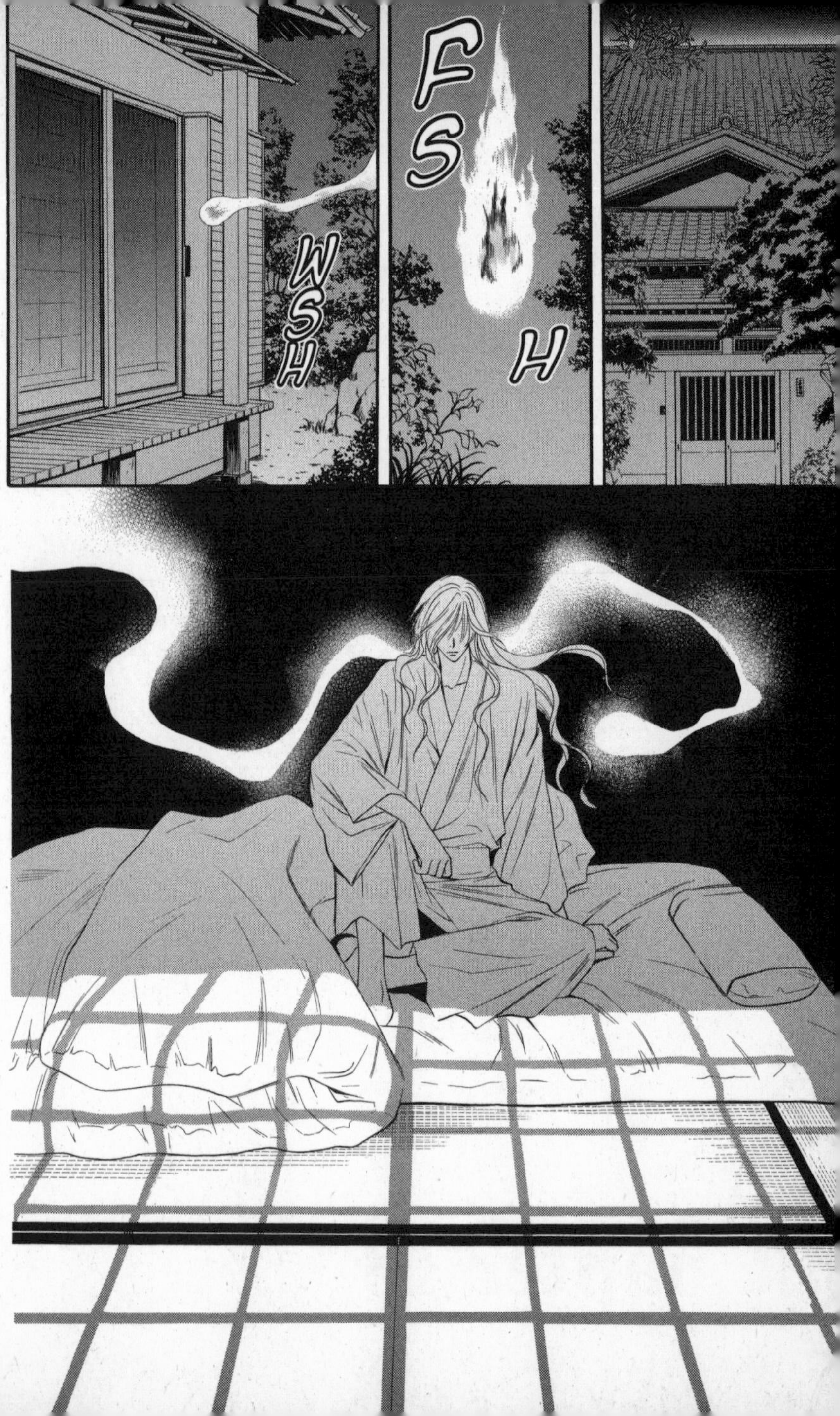
FSH
WSH

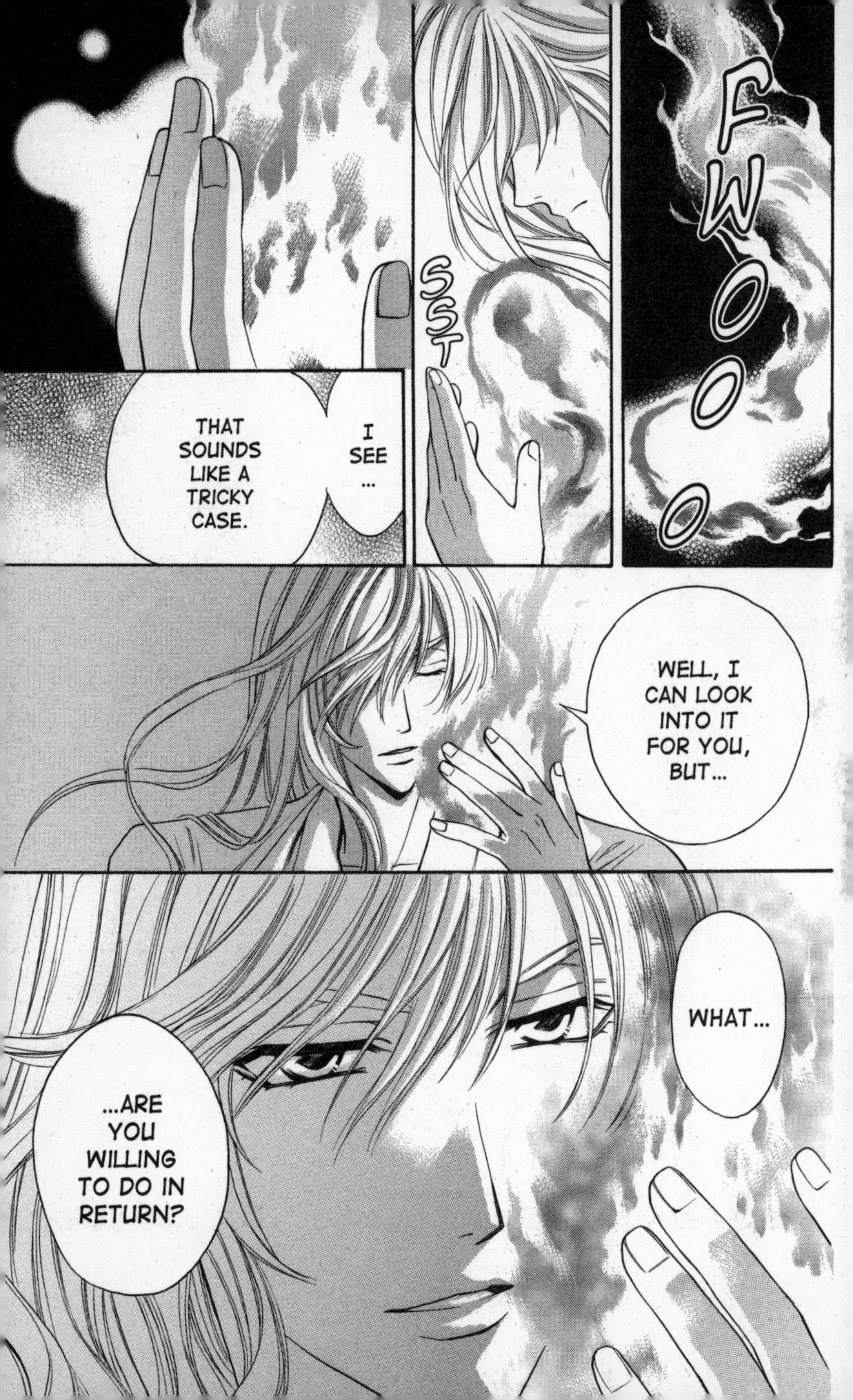
FWOOOO
SST
I SEE ...
THAT SOUNDS LIKE A TRICKY CASE.
WELL, I CAN LOOK INTO IT FOR YOU, BUT...
WHAT...
...ARE YOU WILLING TO DO IN RETURN?

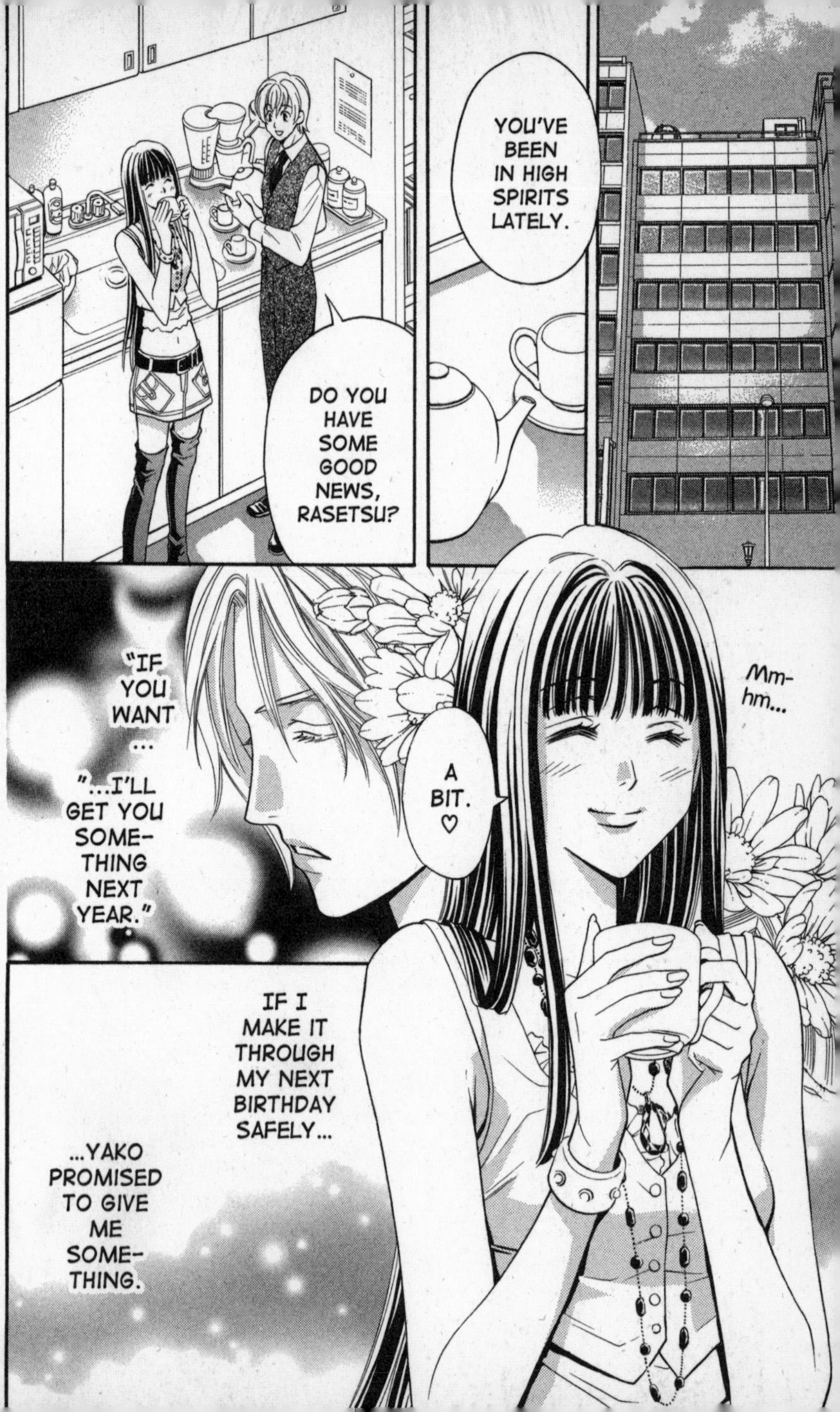
YOU'VE BEEN IN HIGH SPIRITS LATELY.
DO YOU HAVE SOME GOOD NEWS, RASETSU?
Mm-hm...
A BIT. ♡
"IF YOU WANT...
"...I'LL GET YOU SOMETHING NEXT YEAR."
IF I MAKE IT THROUGH MY NEXT BIRTHDAY SAFELY...
...YAKO PROMISED TO GIVE ME SOMETHING.

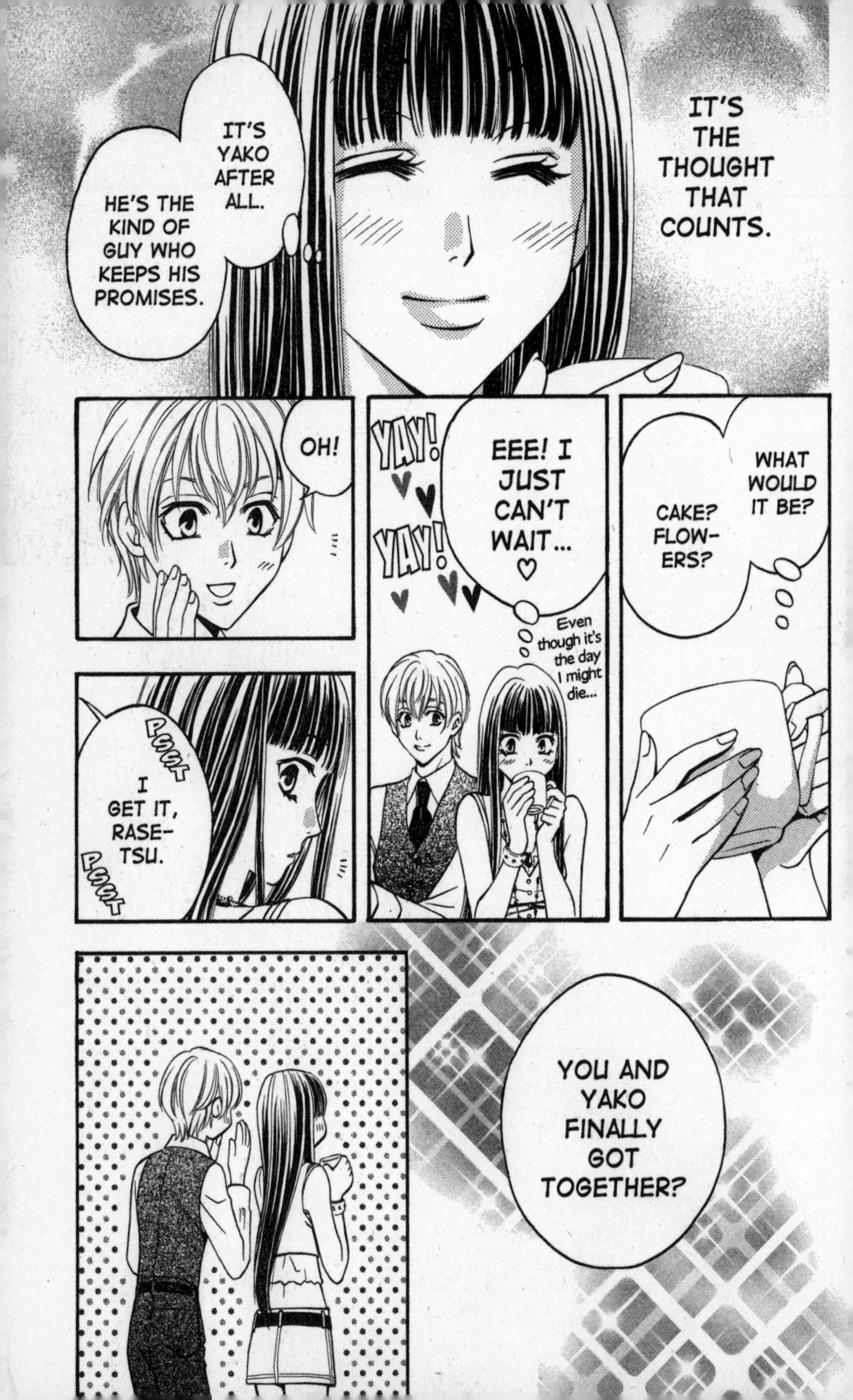
IT'S THE THOUGHT THAT COUNTS.
IT'S YAKO AFTER ALL.
HE'S THE KIND OF GUY WHO KEEPS HIS PROMISES.
WHAT WOULD IT BE?
CAKE? FLOWERS?
EEE! I JUST CAN'T WAIT... ♥
YAY! YAY!
Even though it's the day I might die...
OH!
PSST
I GET IT, RASETSU.
PSST
YOU AND YAKO FINALLY GOT TOGETHER?

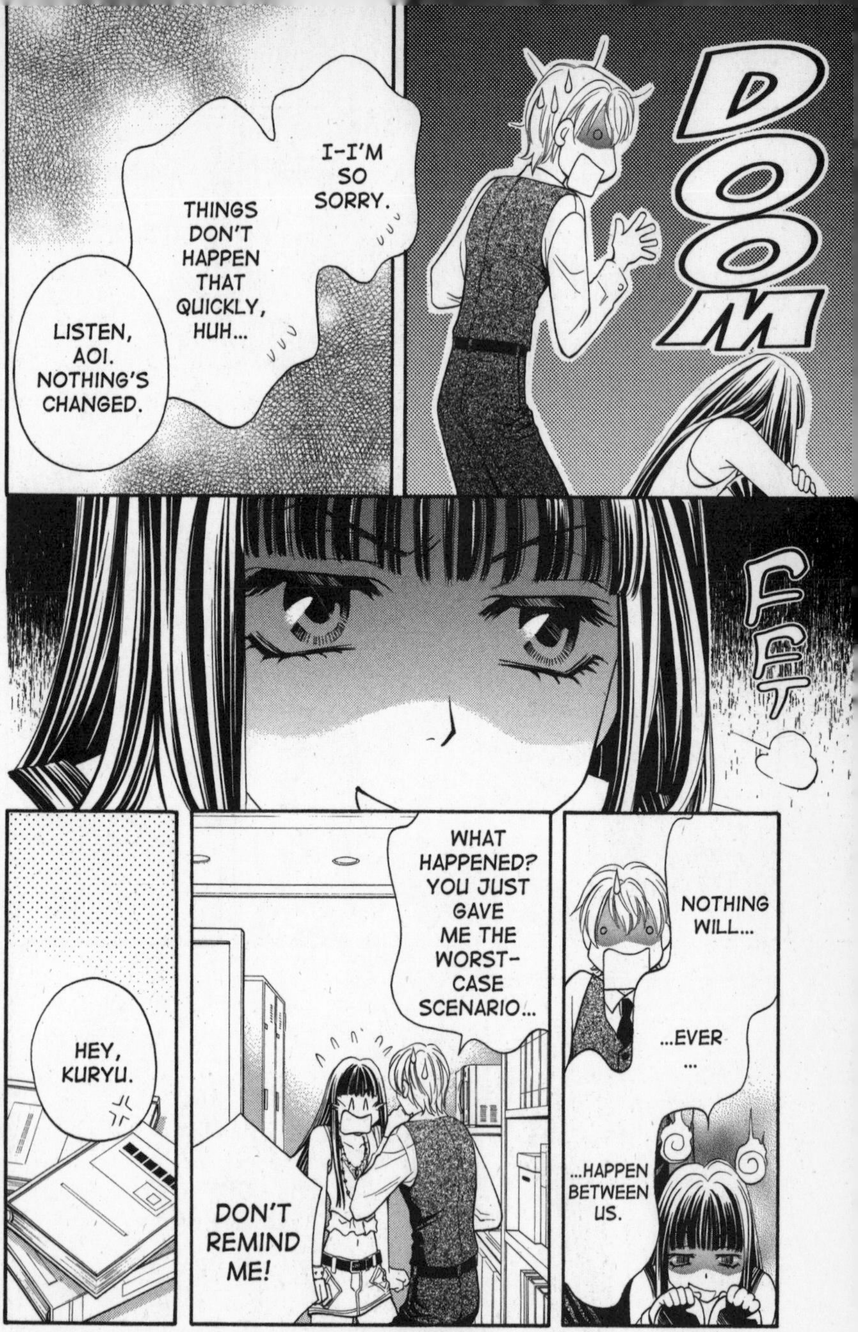
DOOM
I-I'M SO SORRY.
THINGS DON'T HAPPEN THAT QUICKLY, HUH...
LISTEN, AOI. NOTHING'S CHANGED.
FFFT
NOTHING WILL...
...EVER ...
...HAPPEN BETWEEN US.
WHAT HAPPENED? YOU JUST GAVE ME THE WORST-CASE SCENARIO...
DON'T REMIND ME!
HEY, KURYU.

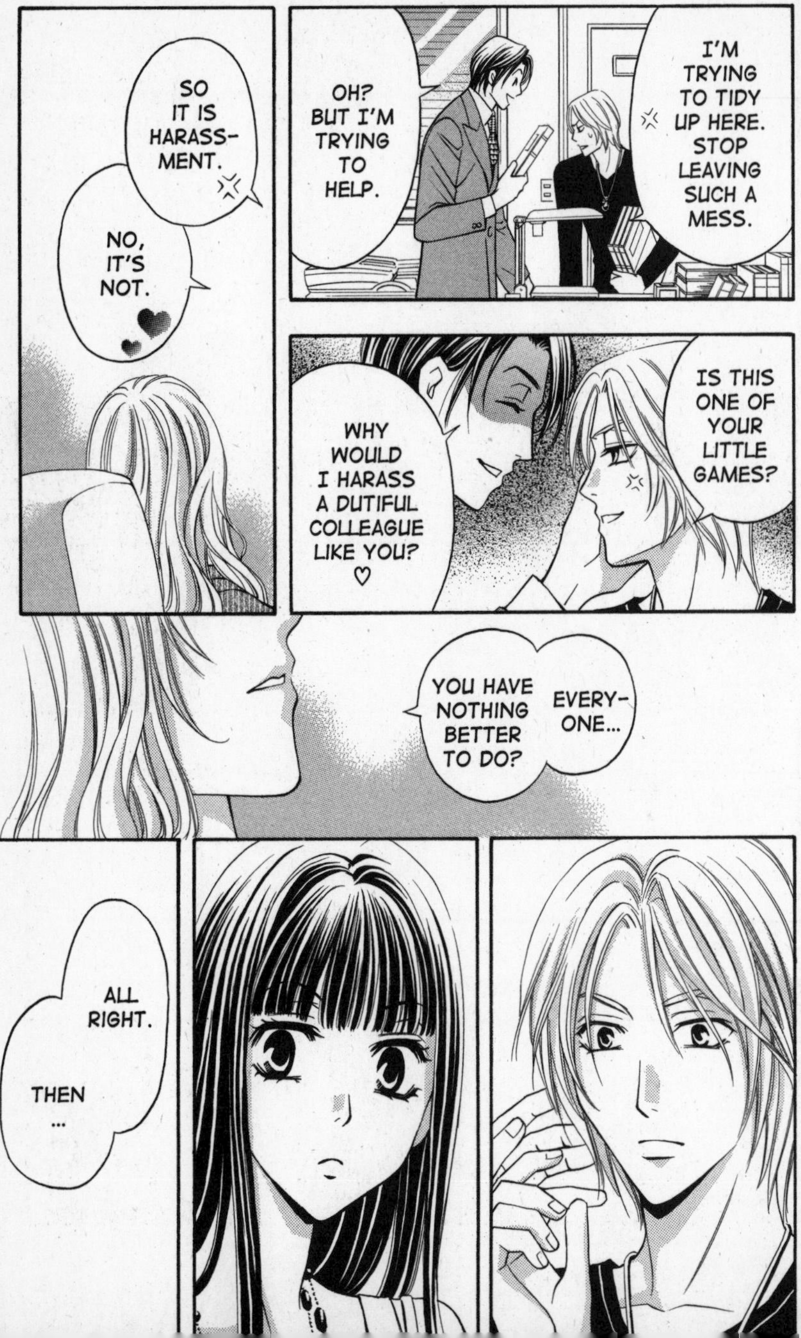
I'M TRYING TO TIDY UP HERE. STOP LEAVING SUCH A MESS.
OH? BUT I'M TRYING TO HELP.
IS THIS ONE OF YOUR LITTLE GAMES?
WHY WOULD I HARASS A DUTIFUL COLLEAGUE LIKE YOU? ♡
SO IT IS HARASSMENT.
NO, IT'S NOT.
EVERY-ONE...
YOU HAVE NOTHING BETTER TO DO?
ALL RIGHT.
THEN...

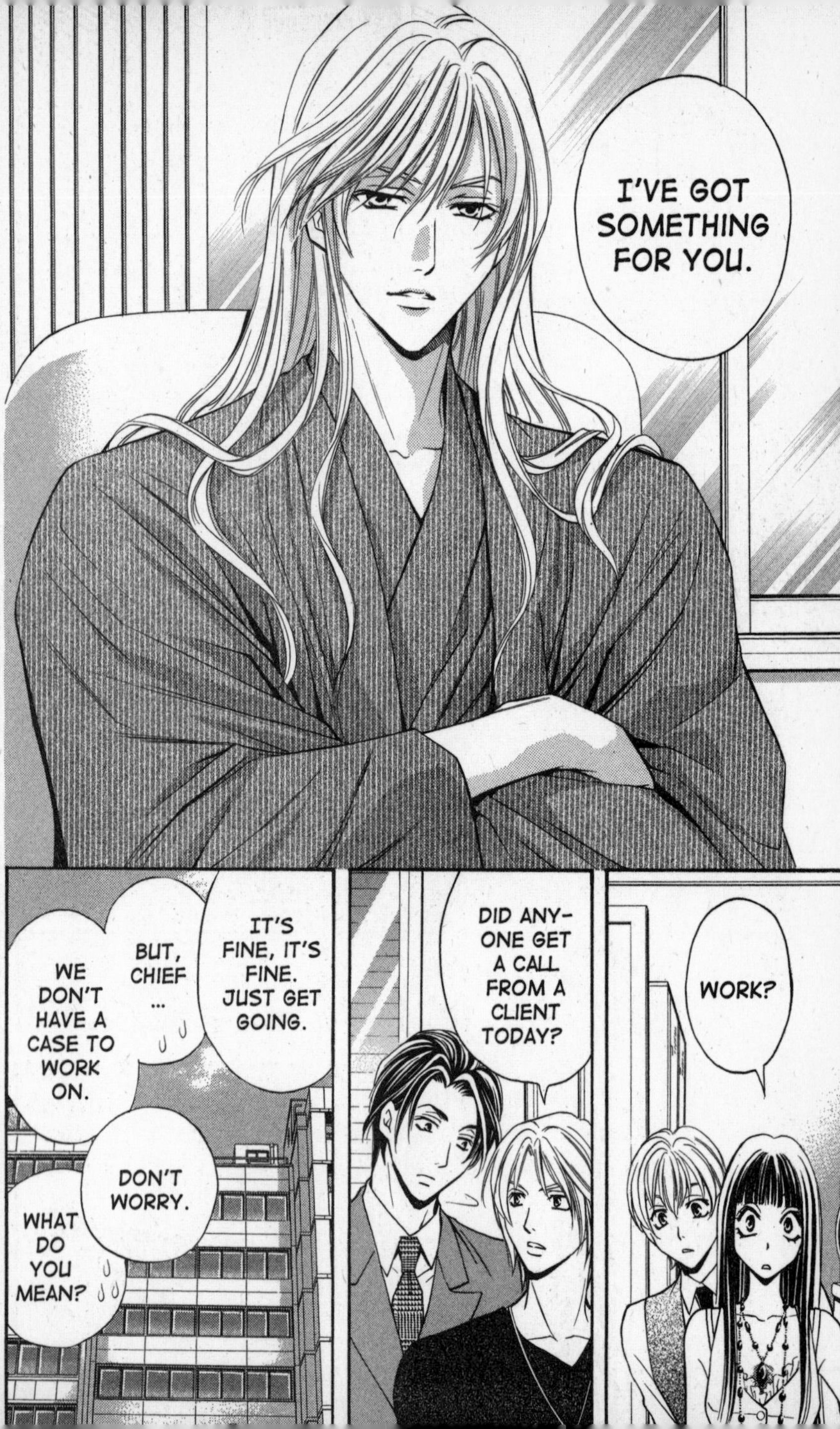
I'VE GOT SOMETHING FOR YOU.
WORK?
DID ANY-ONE GET A CALL FROM A CLIENT TODAY?
IT'S FINE, IT'S FINE. JUST GET GOING.
BUT, CHIEF ...
WE DON'T HAVE A CASE TO WORK ON.
DON'T WORRY.
WHAT DO YOU MEAN?

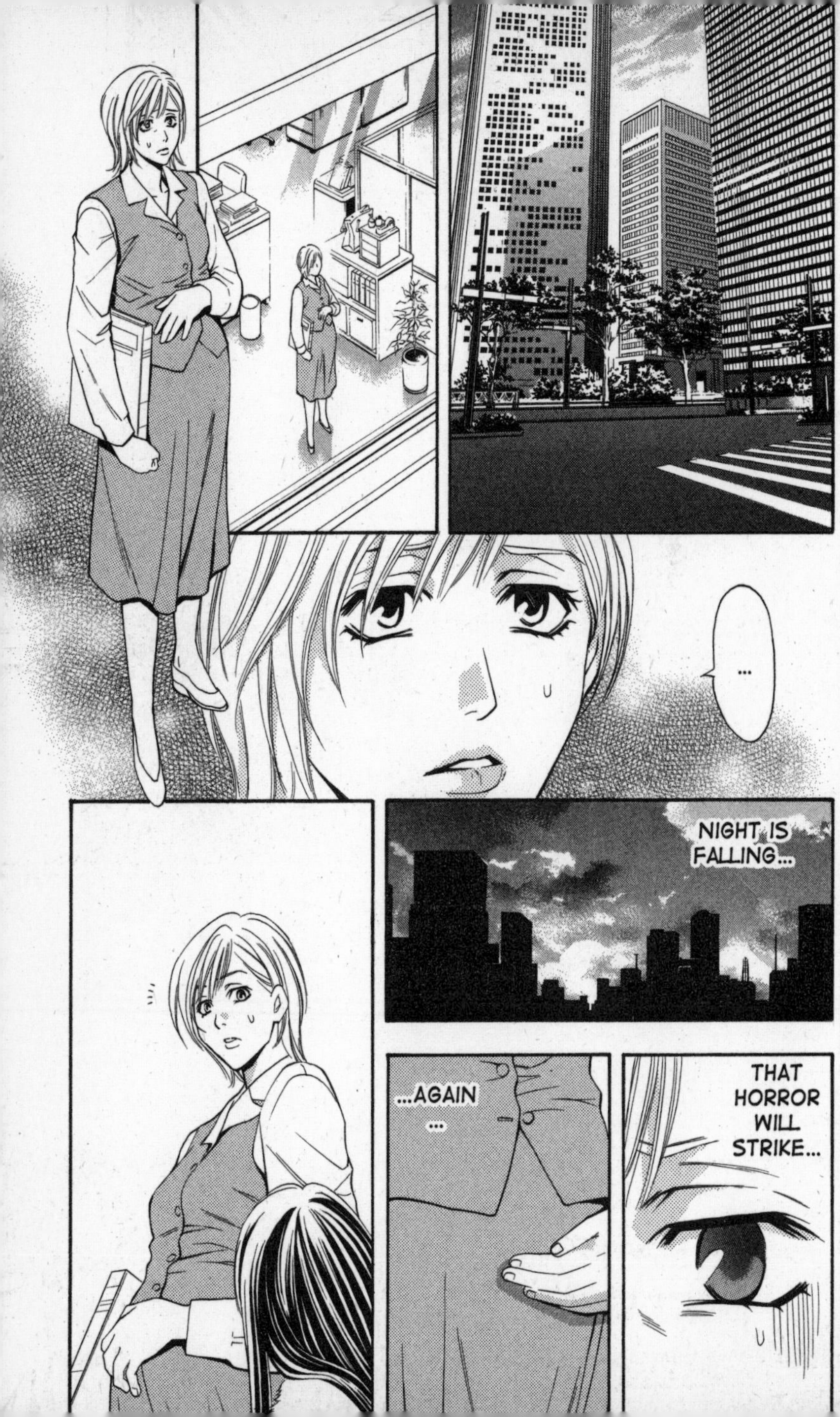
...
NIGHT IS FALLING...
THAT HORROR WILL STRIKE...
...AGAIN ...

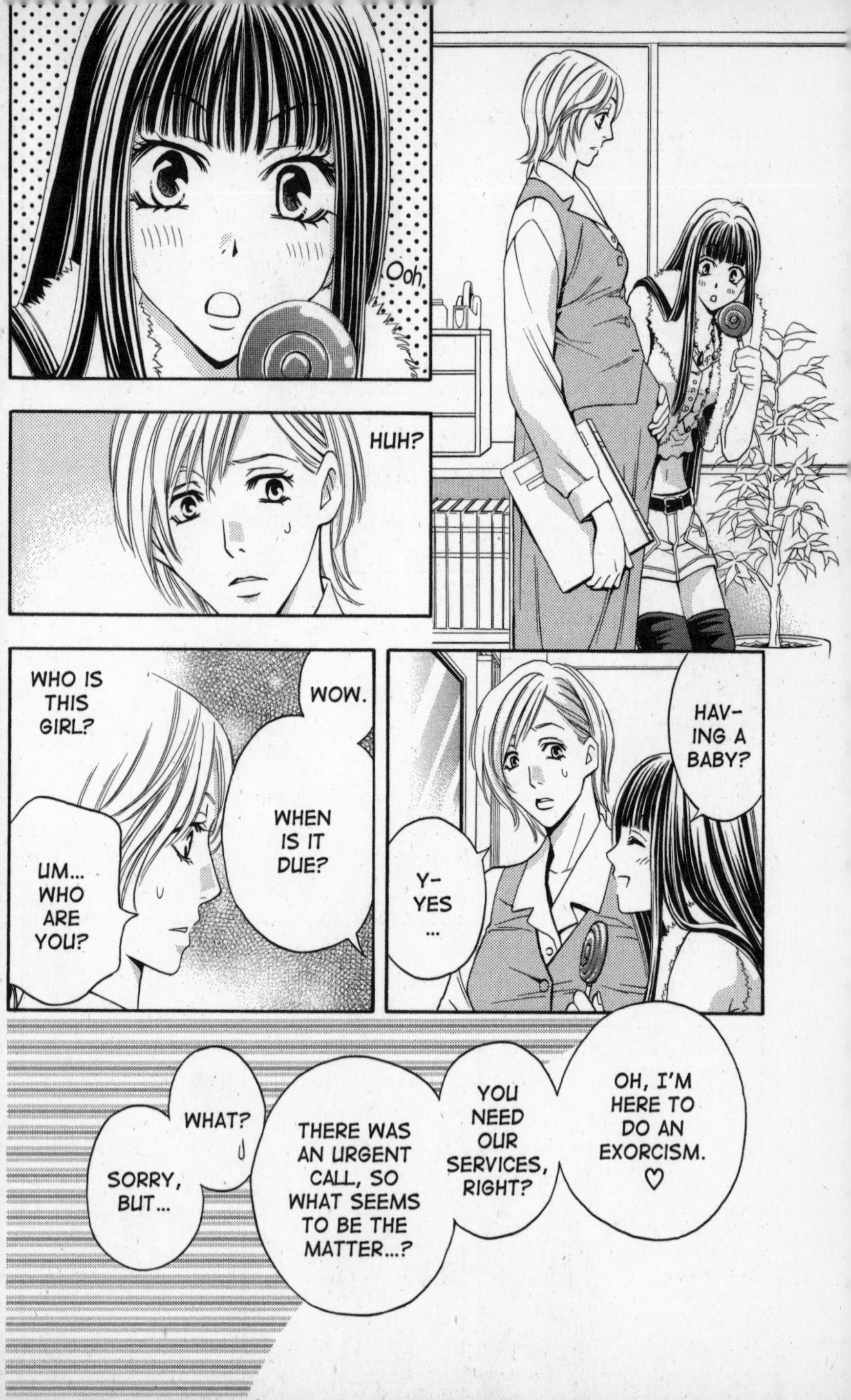
Ooh.
HUH?
HAV-ING A BABY?
Y-YES...
WOW.
WHEN IS IT DUE?
WHO IS THIS GIRL?
UM... WHO ARE YOU?
OH, I'M HERE TO DO AN EXORCISM. ♡
YOU NEED OUR SERVICES, RIGHT?
THERE WAS AN URGENT CALL, SO WHAT SEEMS TO BE THE MATTER...?
WHAT?
SORRY, BUT...

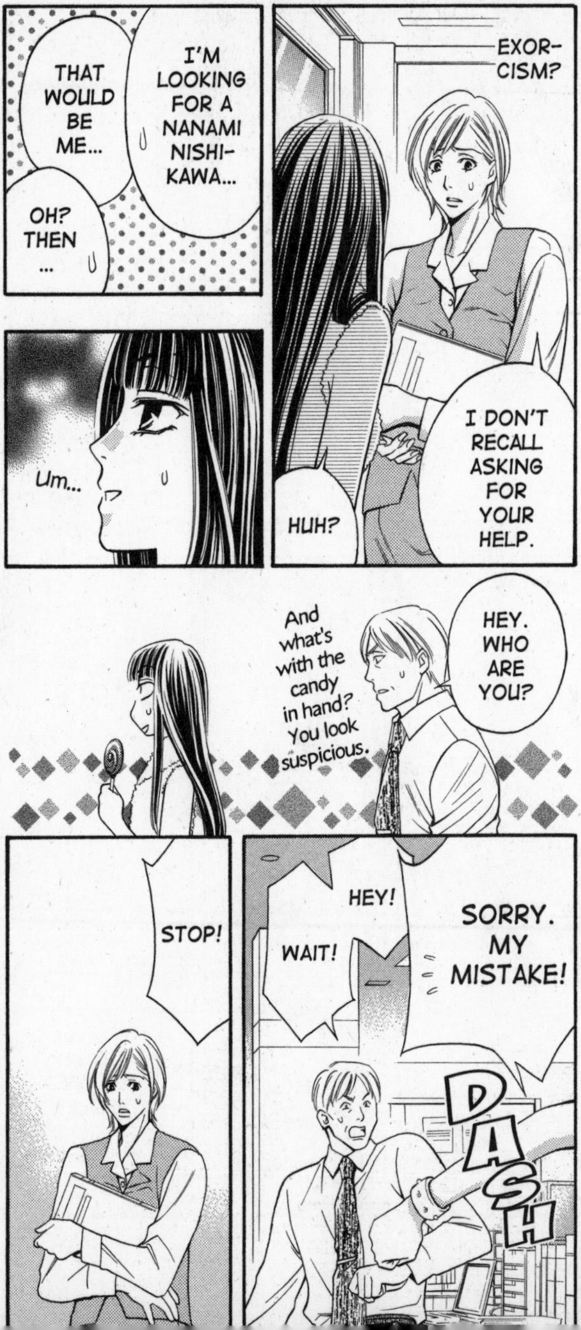
EXOR-CISM?
I DON'T RECALL ASKING FOR YOUR HELP.
HUH?
I'M LOOKING FOR A NANAMI NISHIKAWA...
THAT WOULD BE ME...
OH? THEN ...
Um...
HEY. WHO ARE YOU?
And what's with the candy in hand? You look suspicious.
SORRY. MY MISTAKE!
HEY!
WAIT!
DASH
STOP!

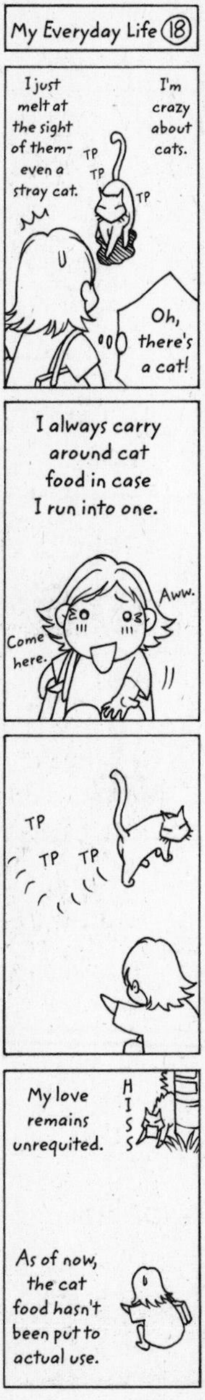
My Everyday Life ⑱
I'm crazy about cats.
I just melt at the sight of them—even a stray cat.
TP
TP
TP
Oh, there's a cat!
I always carry around cat food in case I run into one.
Aww.
Come here.
TP
TP
TP
My love remains unrequited.
HISS
As of now, the cat food hasn't been put to actual use.

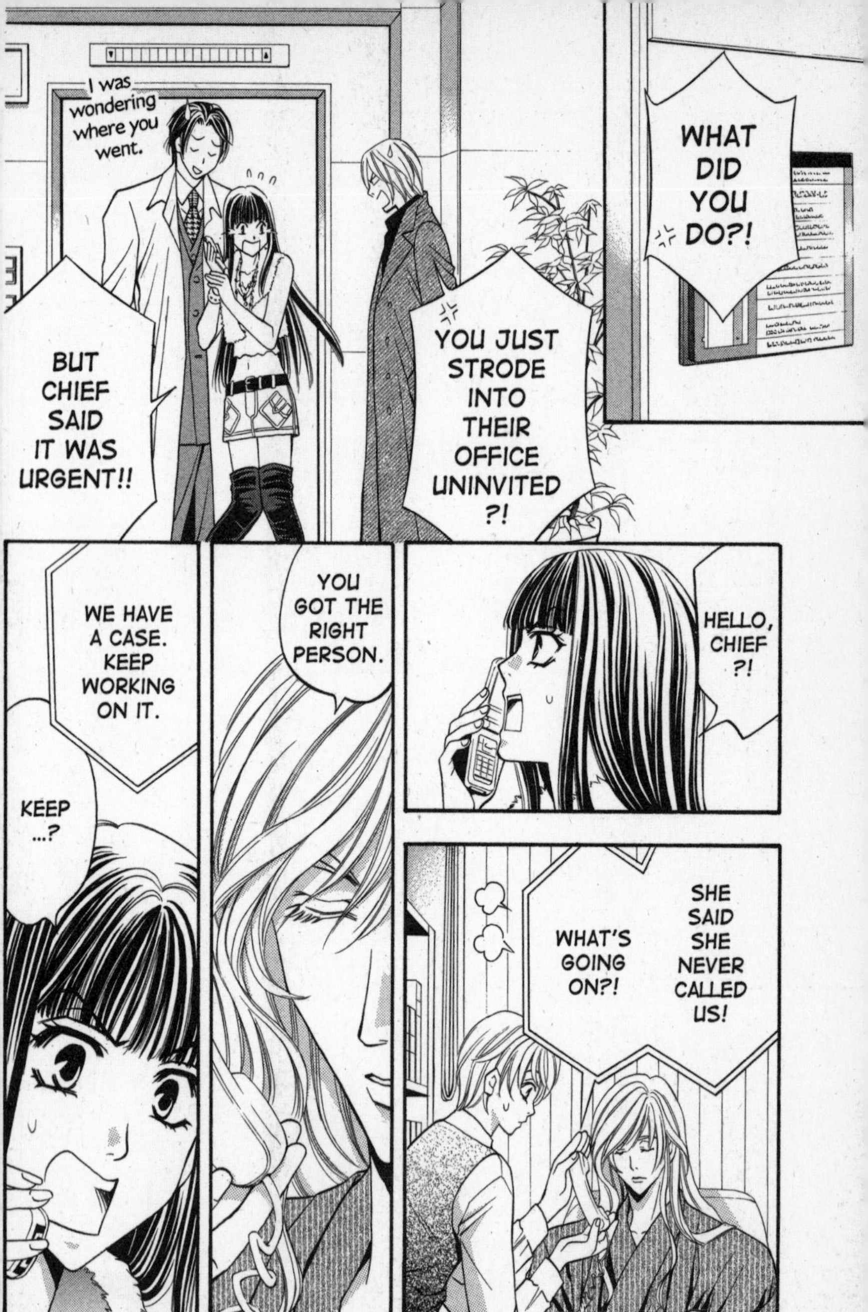
WHAT DID YOU DO?!
YOU JUST STRODE INTO THEIR OFFICE UNINVITED?!
BUT CHIEF SAID IT WAS URGENT!!
I was wondering where you went.
HELLO, CHIEF?!
SHE SAID SHE NEVER CALLED US!
WHAT'S GOING ON?!
YOU GOT THE RIGHT PERSON.
WE HAVE A CASE. KEEP WORKING ON IT.
KEEP ...?

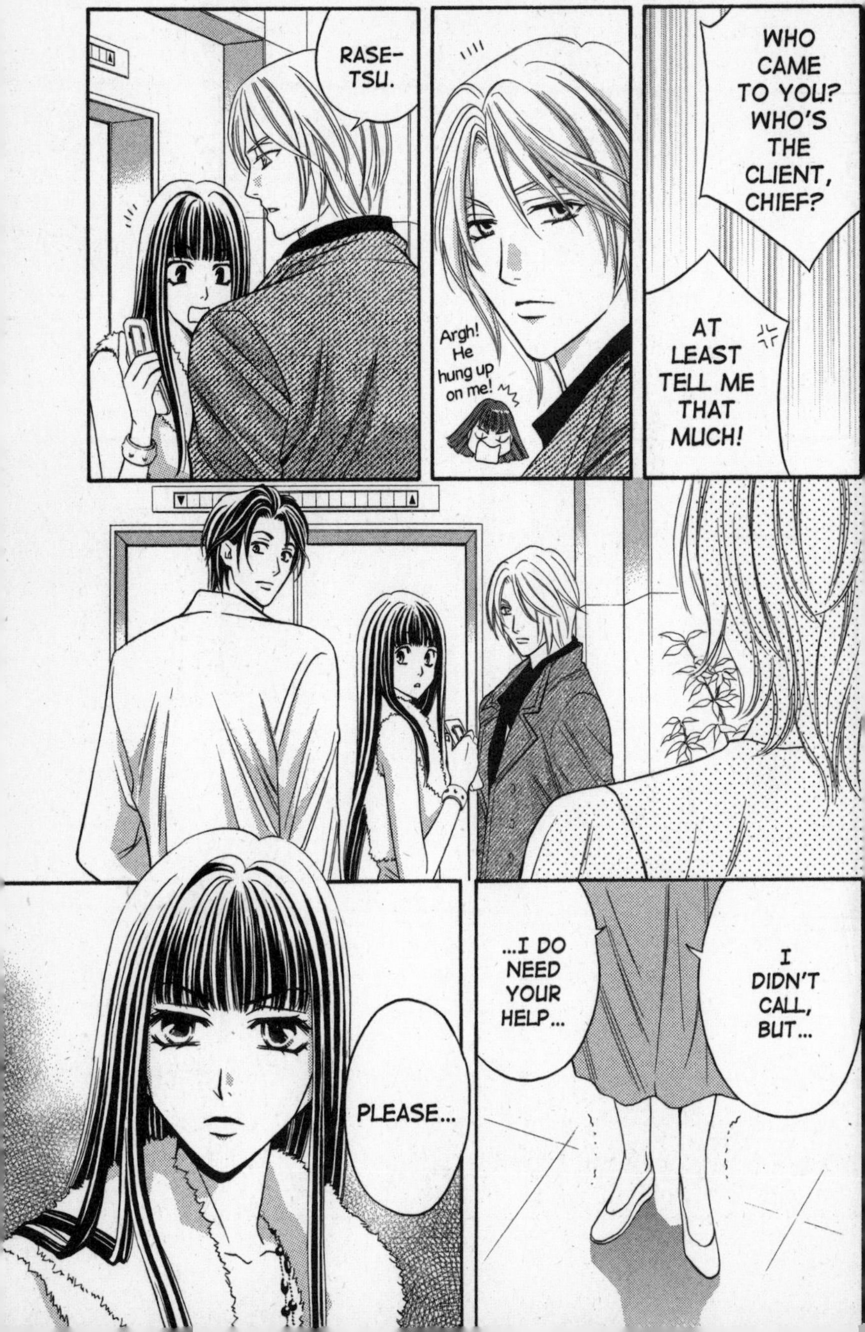
WHO CAME TO YOU? WHO'S THE CLIENT, CHIEF?
AT LEAST TELL ME THAT MUCH!
Argh! He hung up on me!
RASE-TSU.
I DIDN'T CALL, BUT...
...I DO NEED YOUR HELP...
PLEASE...

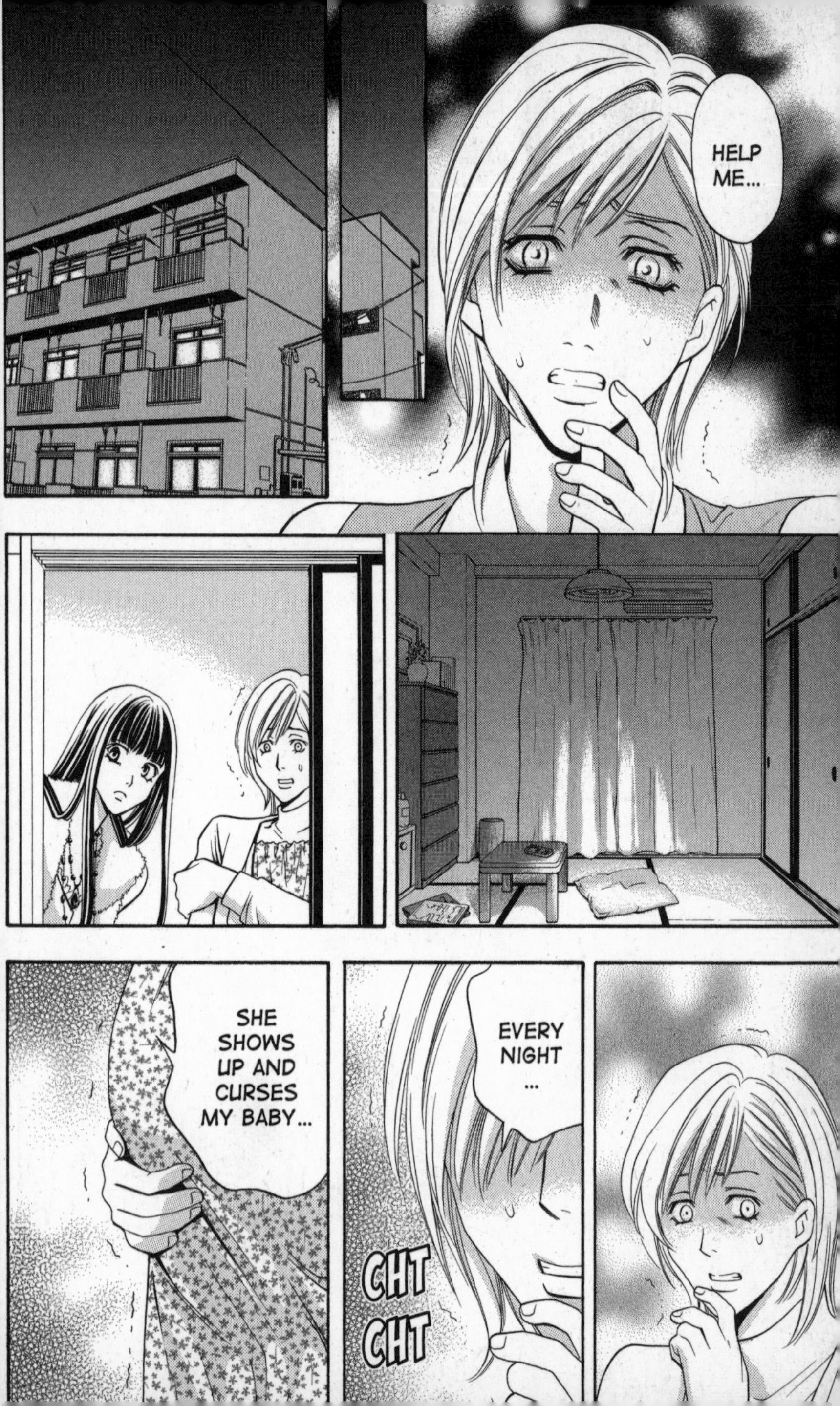
HELP ME...
EVERY NIGHT ...
SHE SHOWS UP AND CURSES MY BABY...
CHT CHT

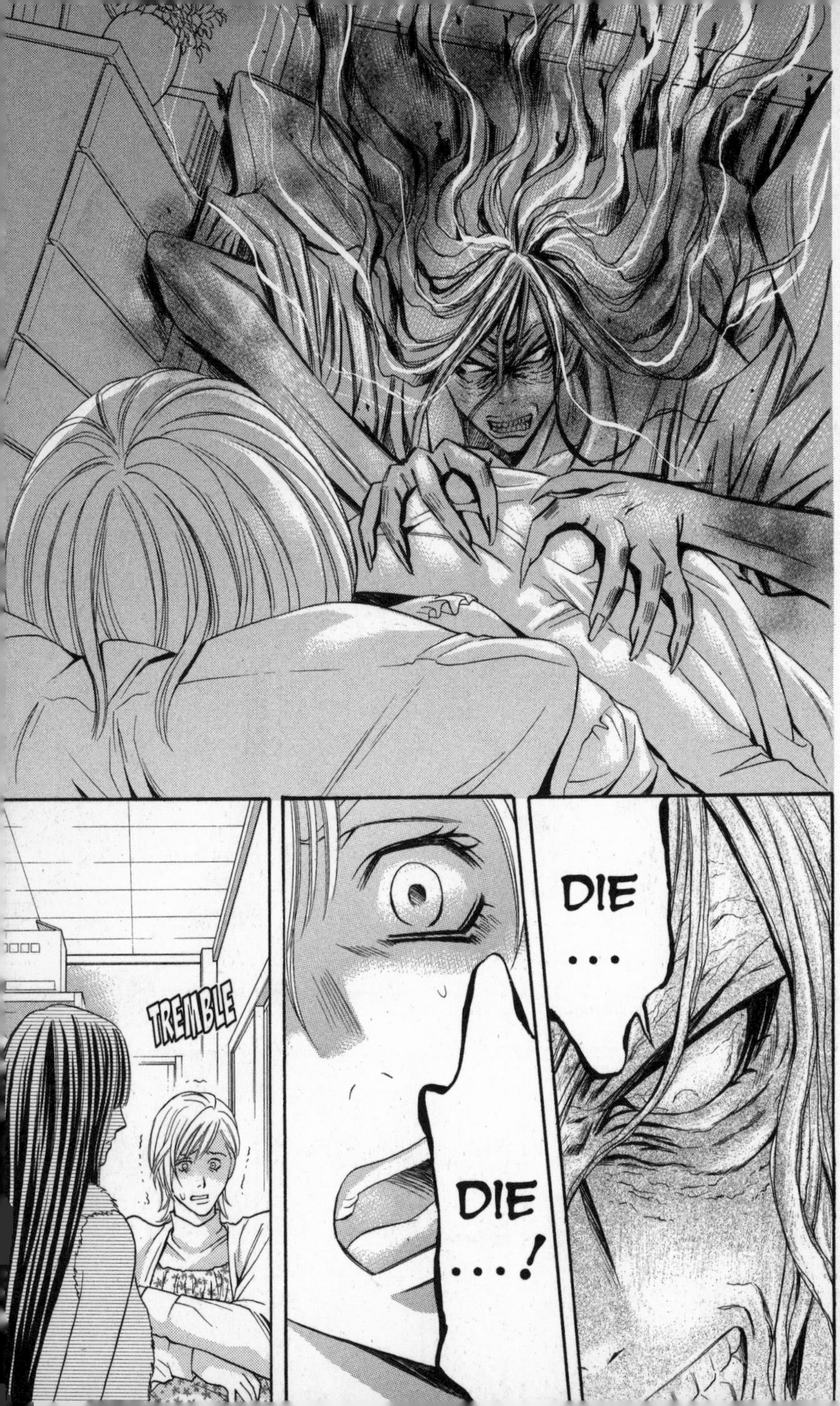
DIE ...
DIE ...!
TREMBLE

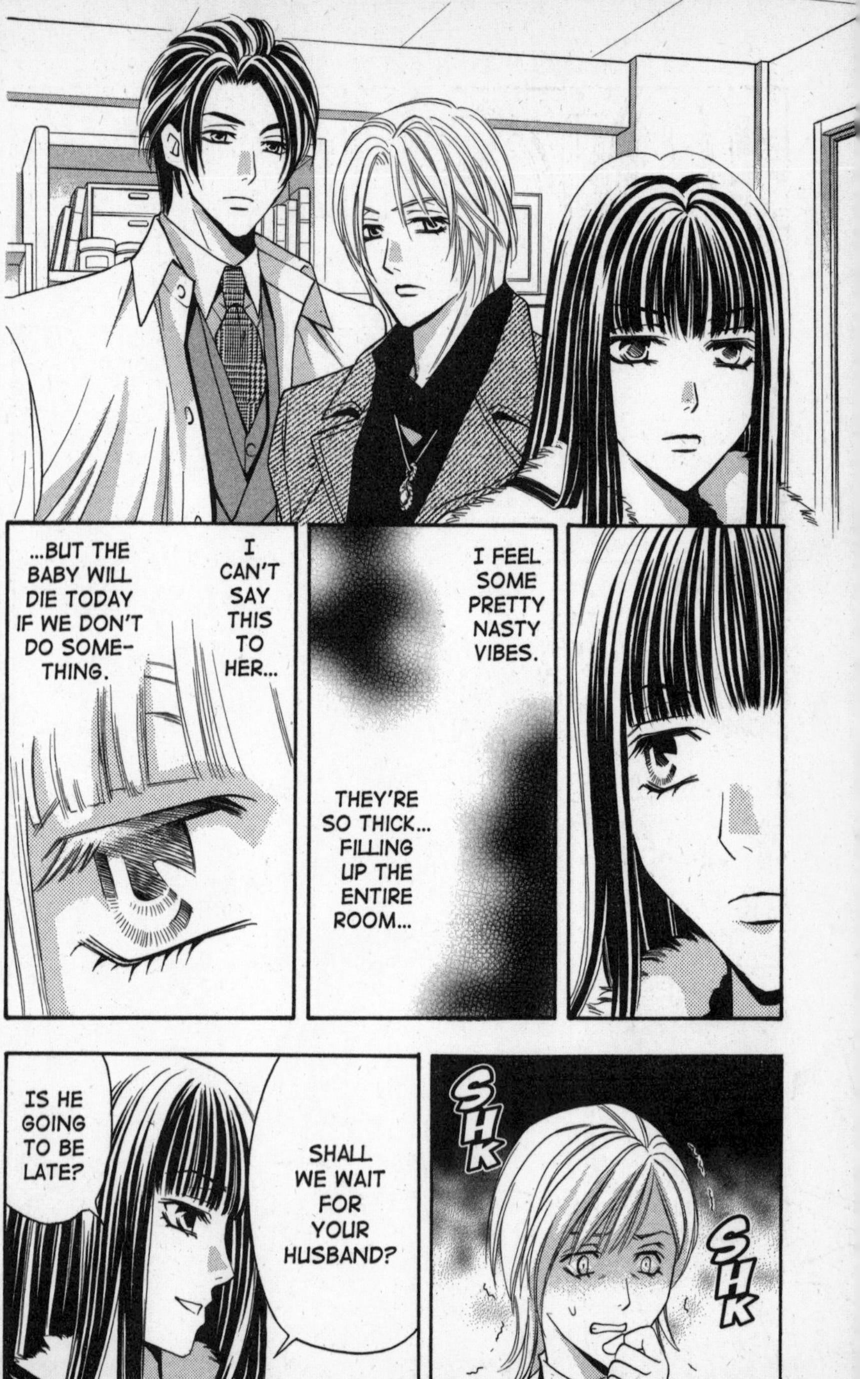
I FEEL SOME PRETTY NASTY VIBES.
THEY'RE SO THICK... FILLING UP THE ENTIRE ROOM...
I CAN'T SAY THIS TO HER...
...BUT THE BABY WILL DIE TODAY IF WE DON'T DO SOME-THING.
SHK
SHK
SHALL WE WAIT FOR YOUR HUSBAND?
IS HE GOING TO BE LATE?

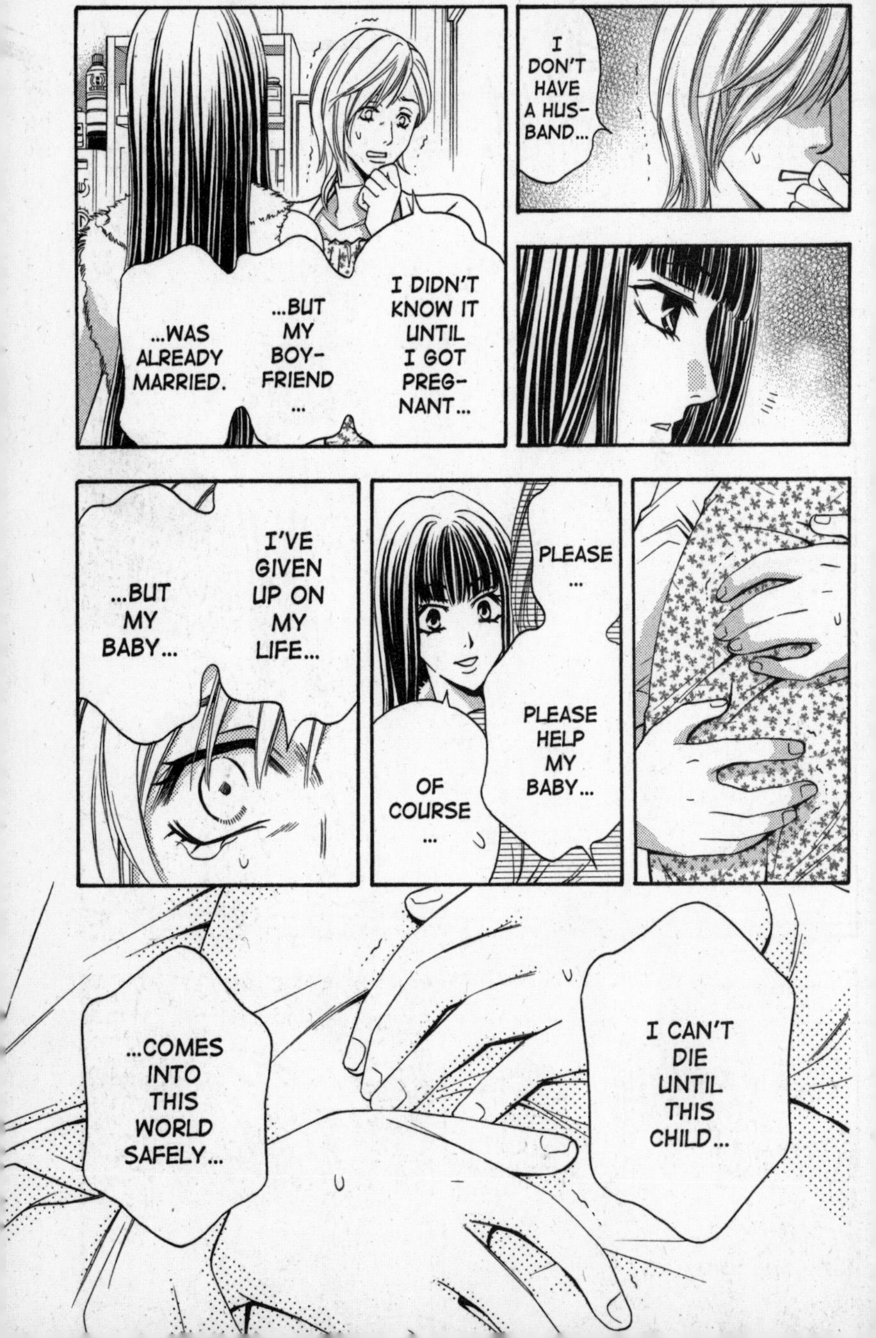
I DON'T HAVE A HUS-BAND...
I DIDN'T KNOW IT UNTIL I GOT PREG-NANT...
...BUT MY BOY-FRIEND ...
...WAS ALREADY MARRIED.
PLEASE ...
PLEASE HELP MY BABY...
OF COURSE ...
I'VE GIVEN UP ON MY LIFE...
...BUT MY BABY...
I CAN'T DIE UNTIL THIS CHILD...
...COMES INTO THIS WORLD SAFELY...

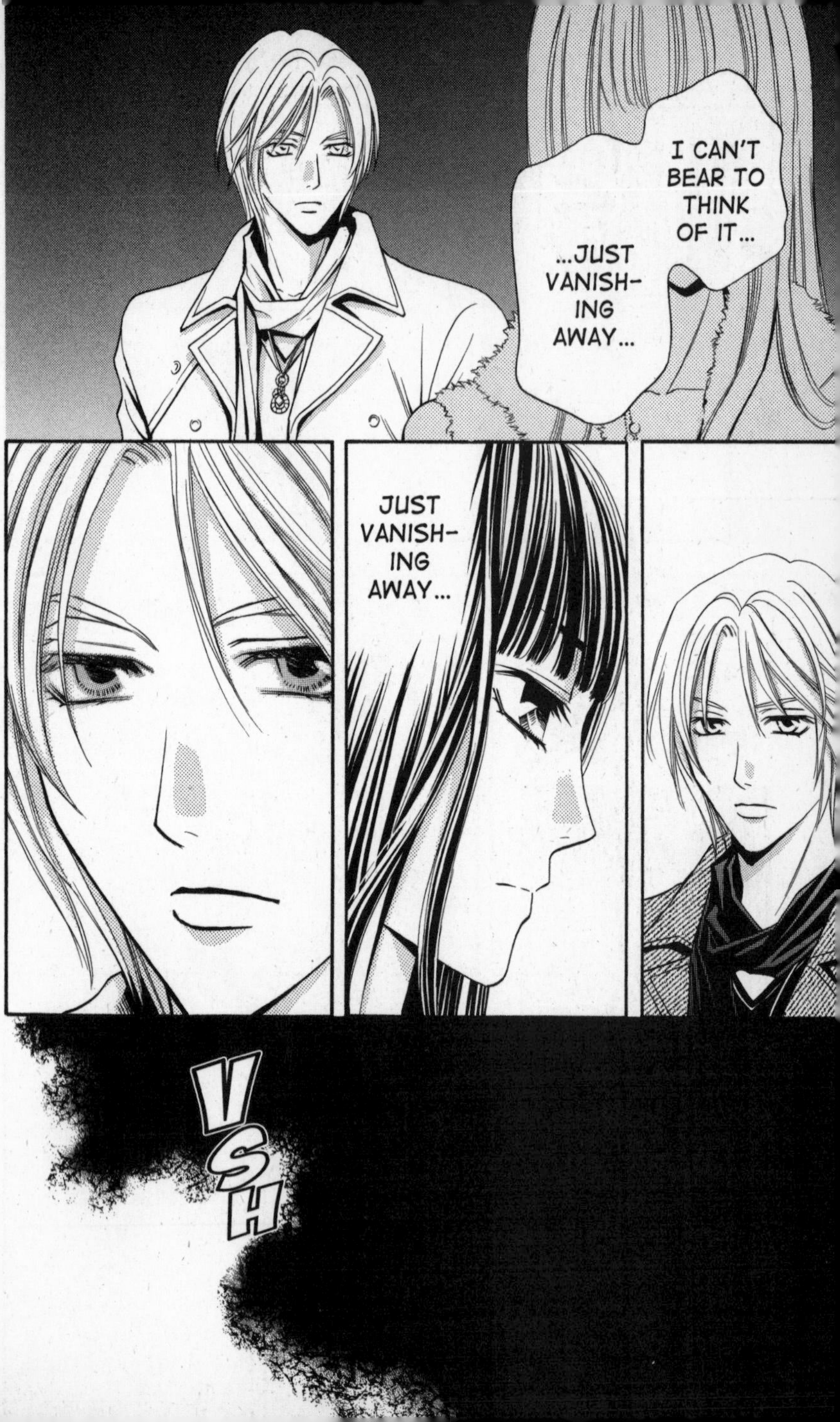
I CAN'T BEAR TO THINK OF IT...
...JUST VANISH-ING AWAY...
JUST VANISH-ING AWAY...
VSH

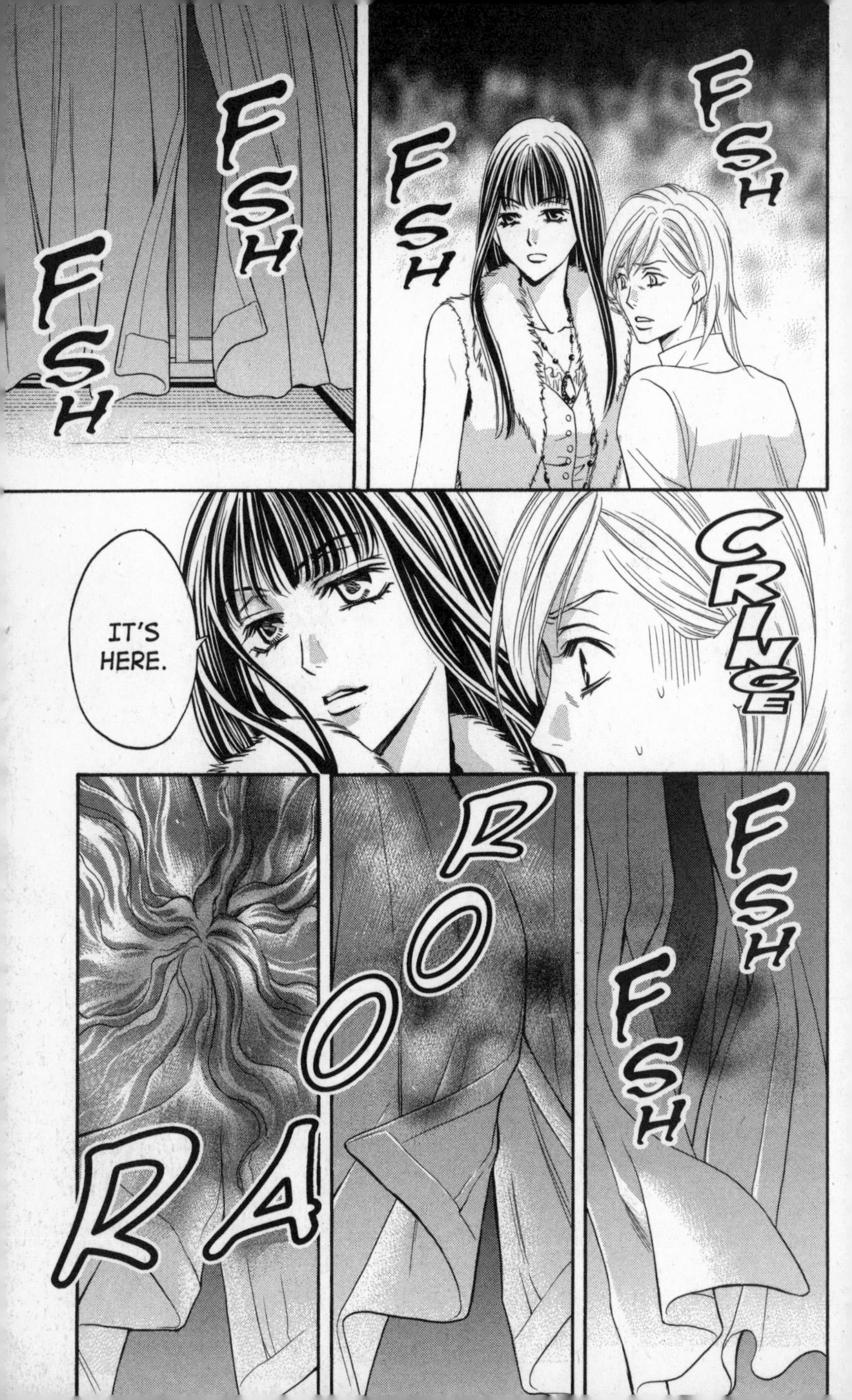
FSH
FSH
FSH
FSH
CRINGE
IT'S HERE.
FSH
FSH
ROO
RA

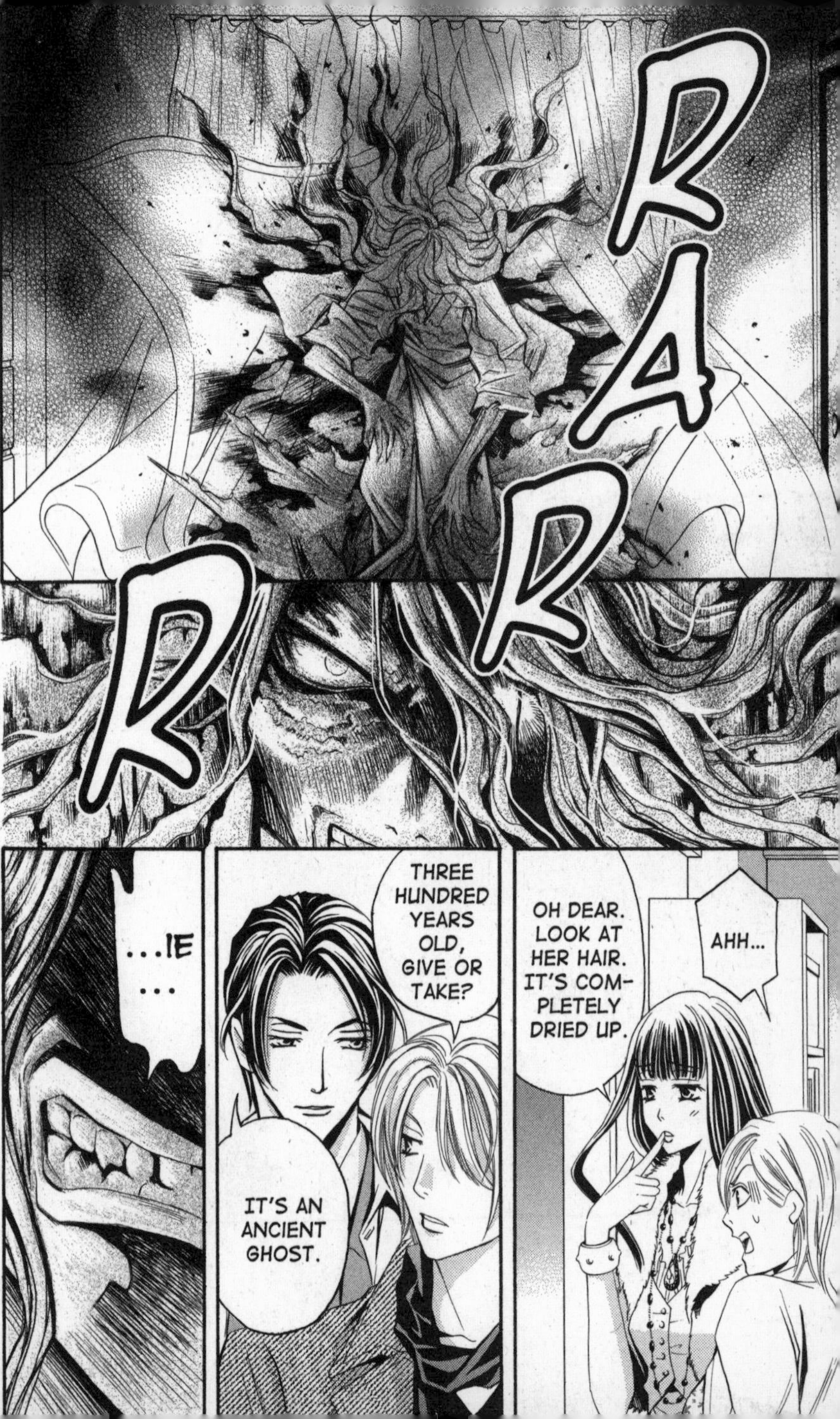
RARR
AHH...
OH DEAR. LOOK AT HER HAIR. IT'S COM-PLETELY DRIED UP.
THREE HUNDRED YEARS OLD, GIVE OR TAKE?
IT'S AN ANCIENT GHOST.
...IE ...

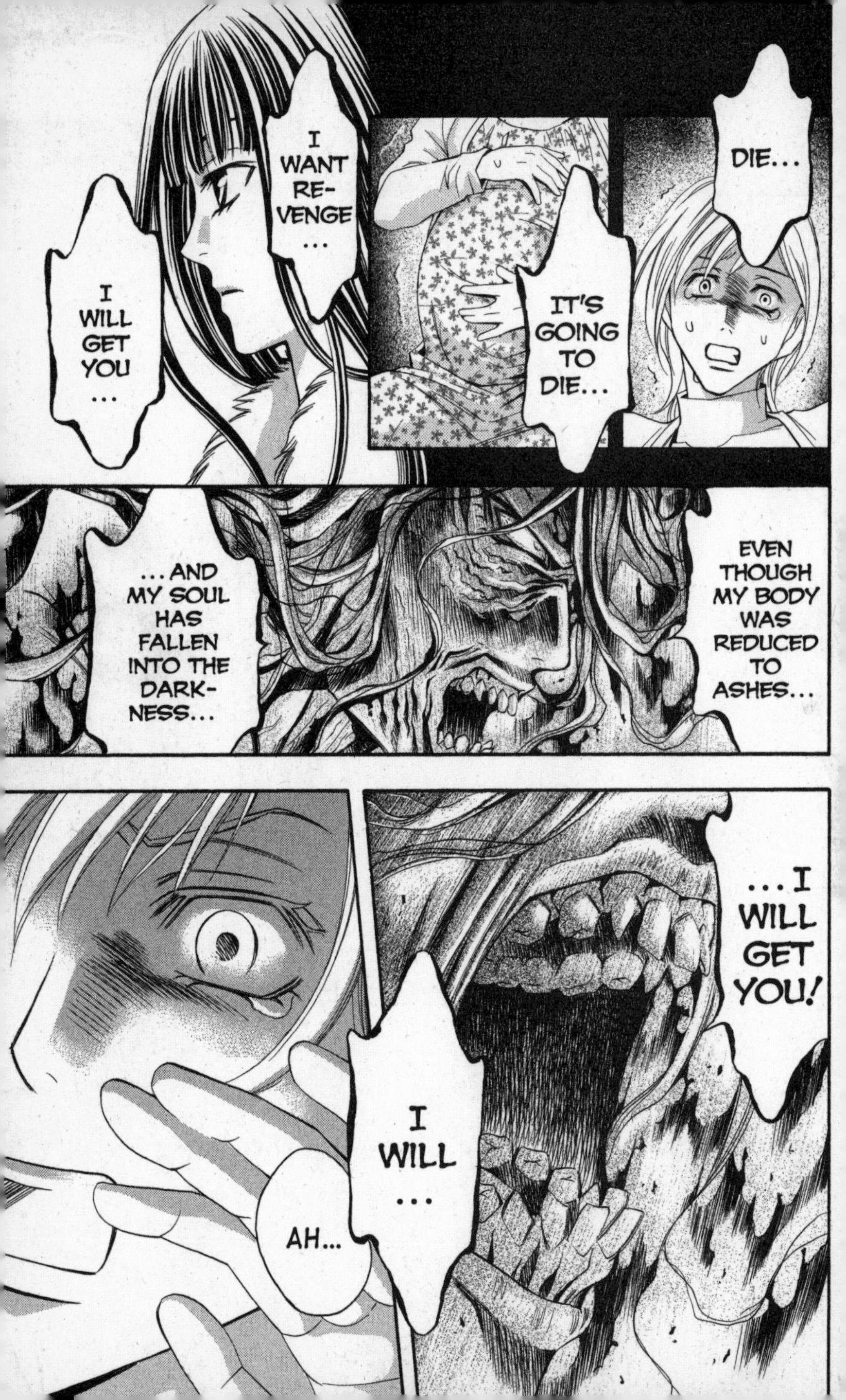
DIE...
IT'S GOING TO DIE...
I WANT RE-VENGE...
I WILL GET YOU...
EVEN THOUGH MY BODY WAS REDUCED TO ASHES...
...AND MY SOUL HAS FALLEN INTO THE DARK-NESS...
...I WILL GET YOU!
I WILL...
AH...

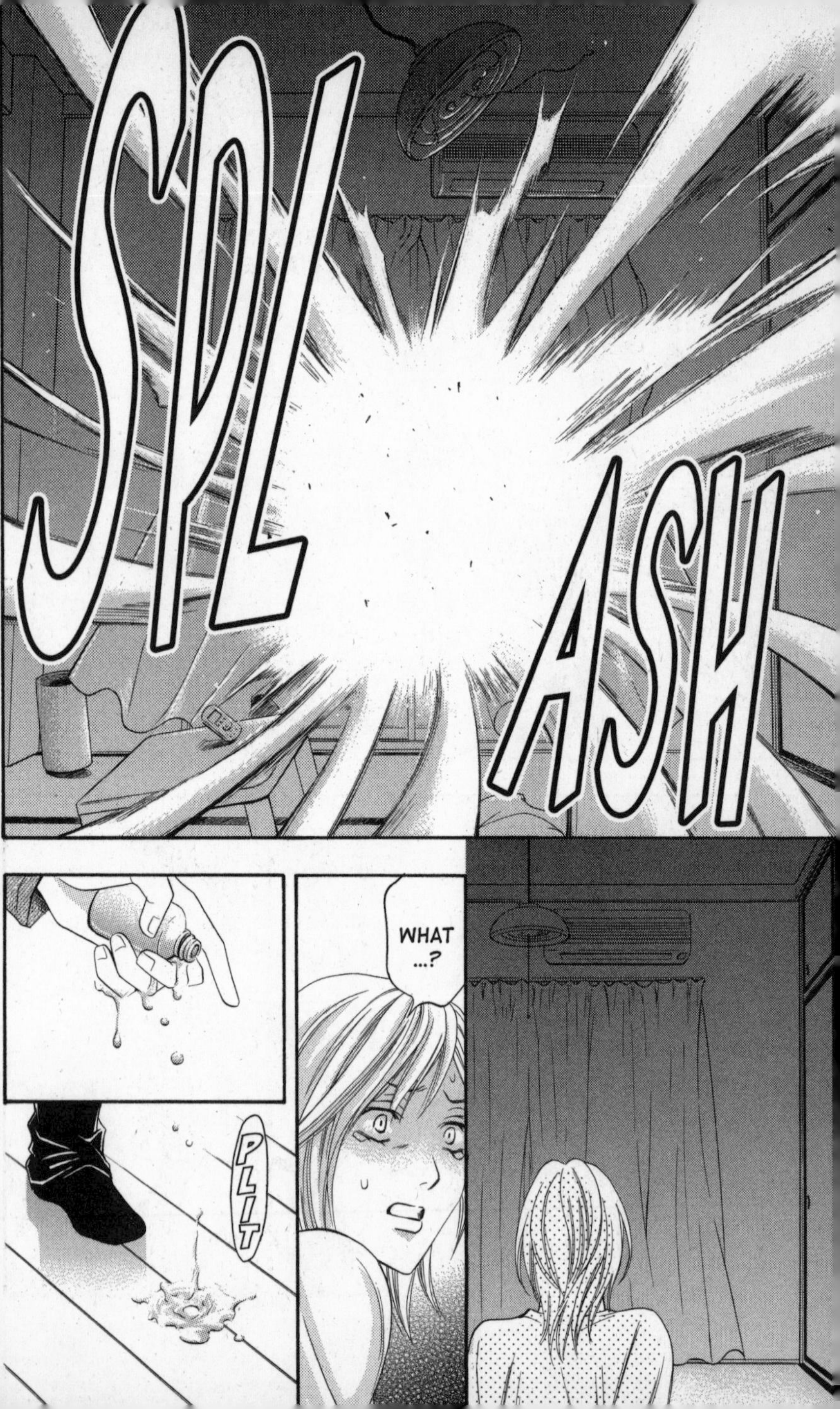
SPLASH
WHAT ...?
PLIT

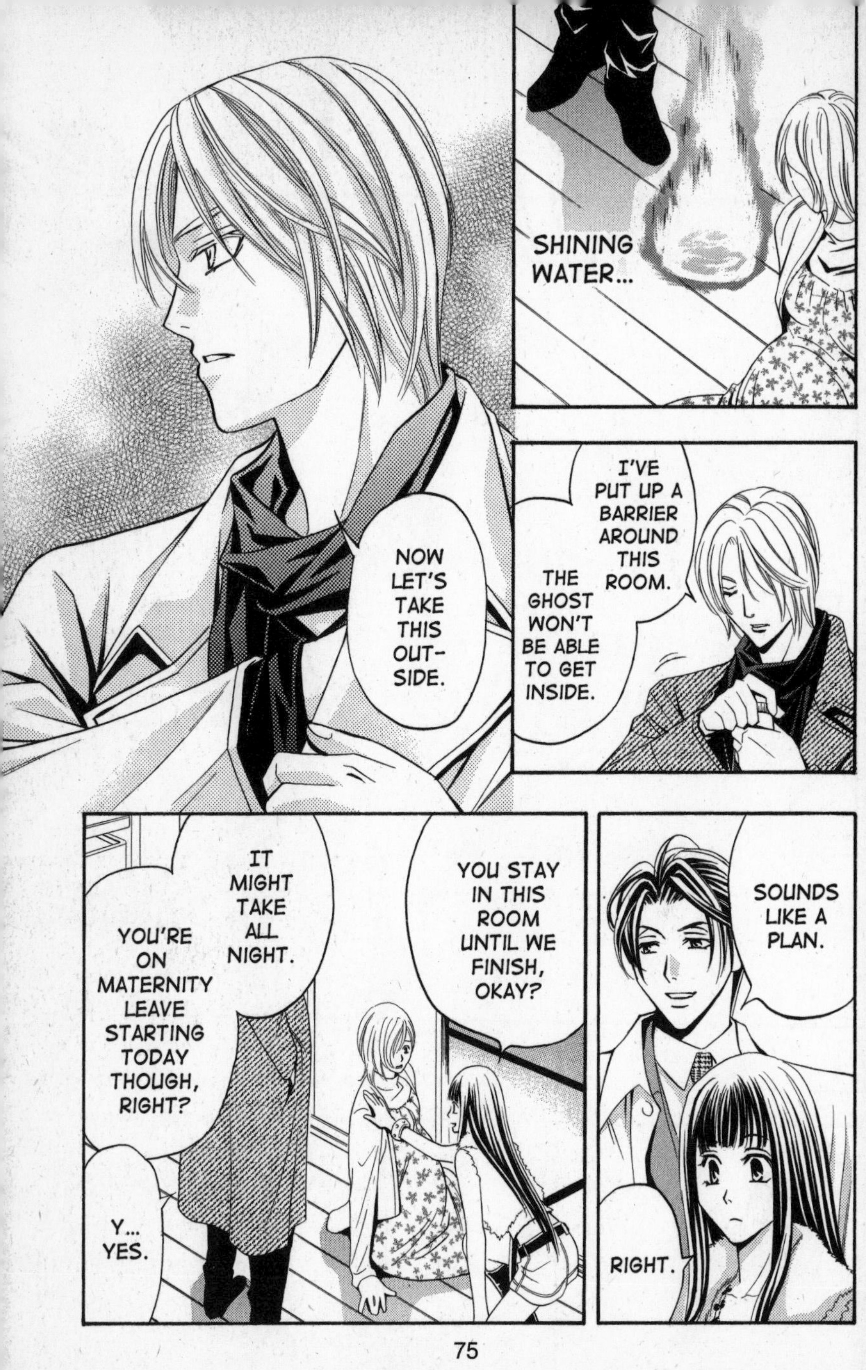
SHINING WATER...
I'VE PUT UP A BARRIER AROUND THIS ROOM.
THE GHOST WON'T BE ABLE TO GET INSIDE.
NOW LET'S TAKE THIS OUT-SIDE.
SOUNDS LIKE A PLAN.
RIGHT.
YOU STAY IN THIS ROOM UNTIL WE FINISH, OKAY?
IT MIGHT TAKE ALL NIGHT.
YOU'RE ON MATERNITY LEAVE STARTING TODAY THOUGH, RIGHT?
Y... YES.

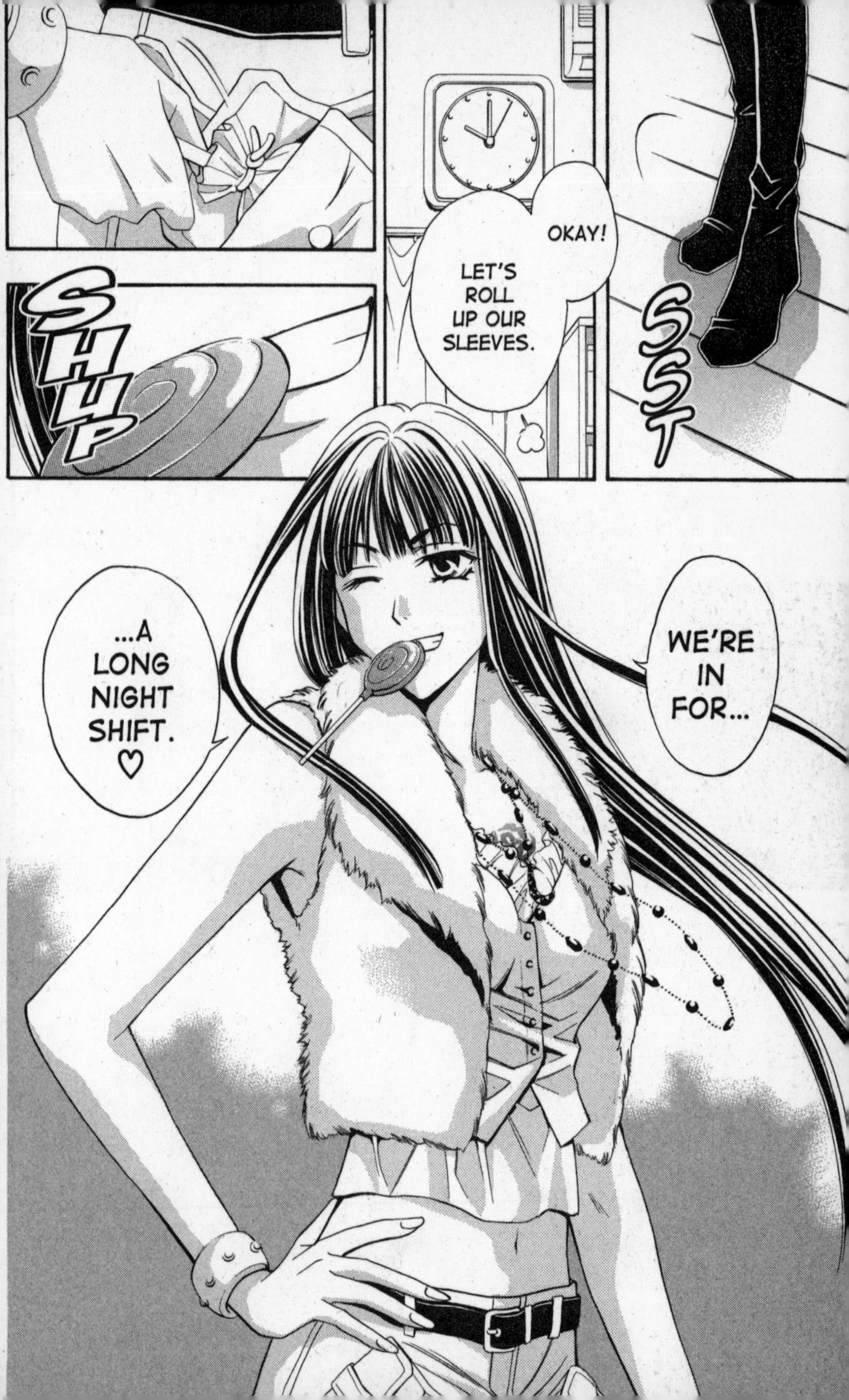
SST
OKAY!
LET'S ROLL UP OUR SLEEVES.
SHUP
WE'RE IN FOR...
...A LONG NIGHT SHIFT. ♡

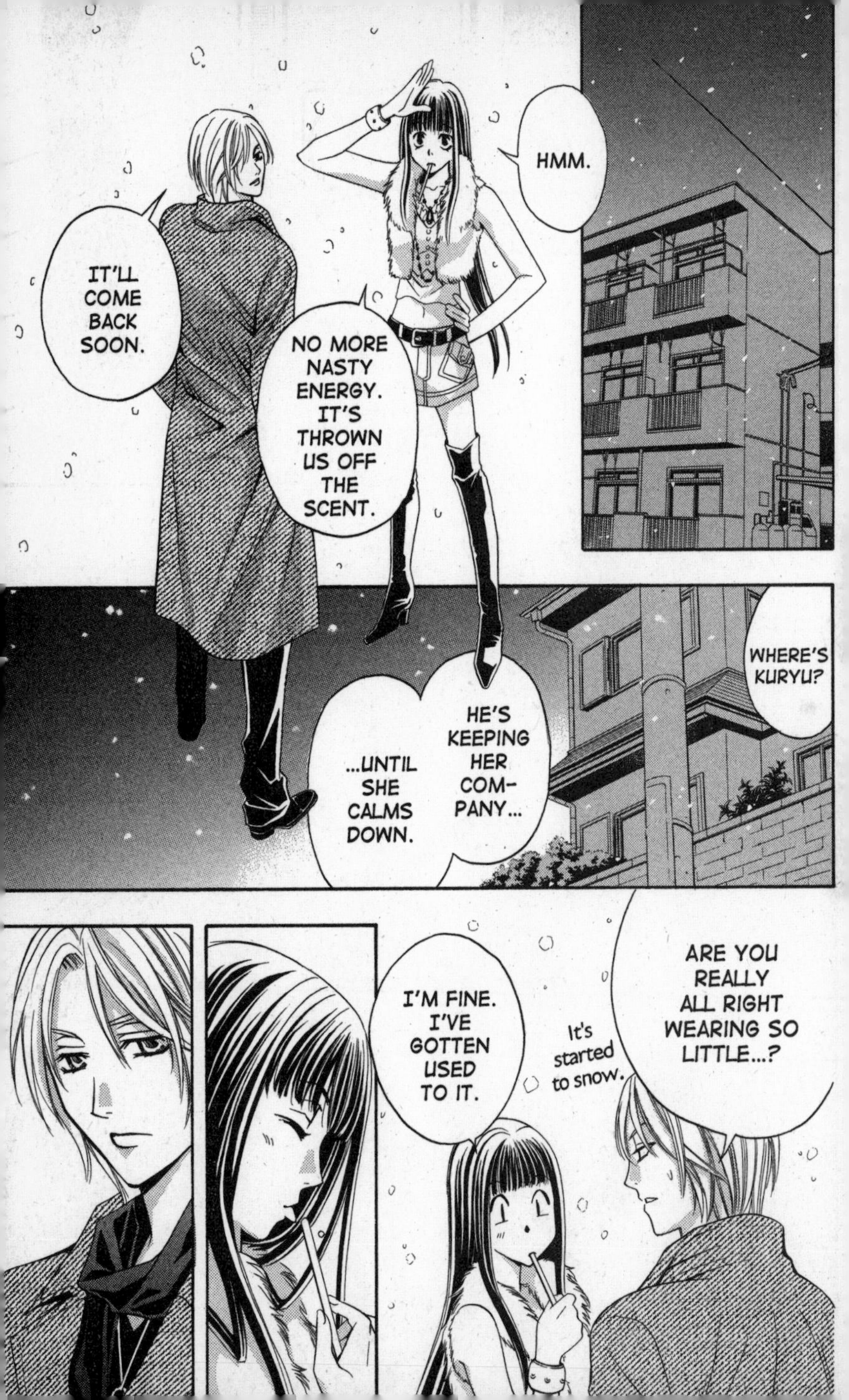
HMM.
NO MORE NASTY ENERGY. IT'S THROWN US OFF THE SCENT.
IT'LL COME BACK SOON.
WHERE'S KURYU?
HE'S KEEPING HER COMPANY...
...UNTIL SHE CALMS DOWN.
ARE YOU REALLY ALL RIGHT WEARING SO LITTLE...?
It's started to snow.
I'M FINE. I'VE GOTTEN USED TO IT.

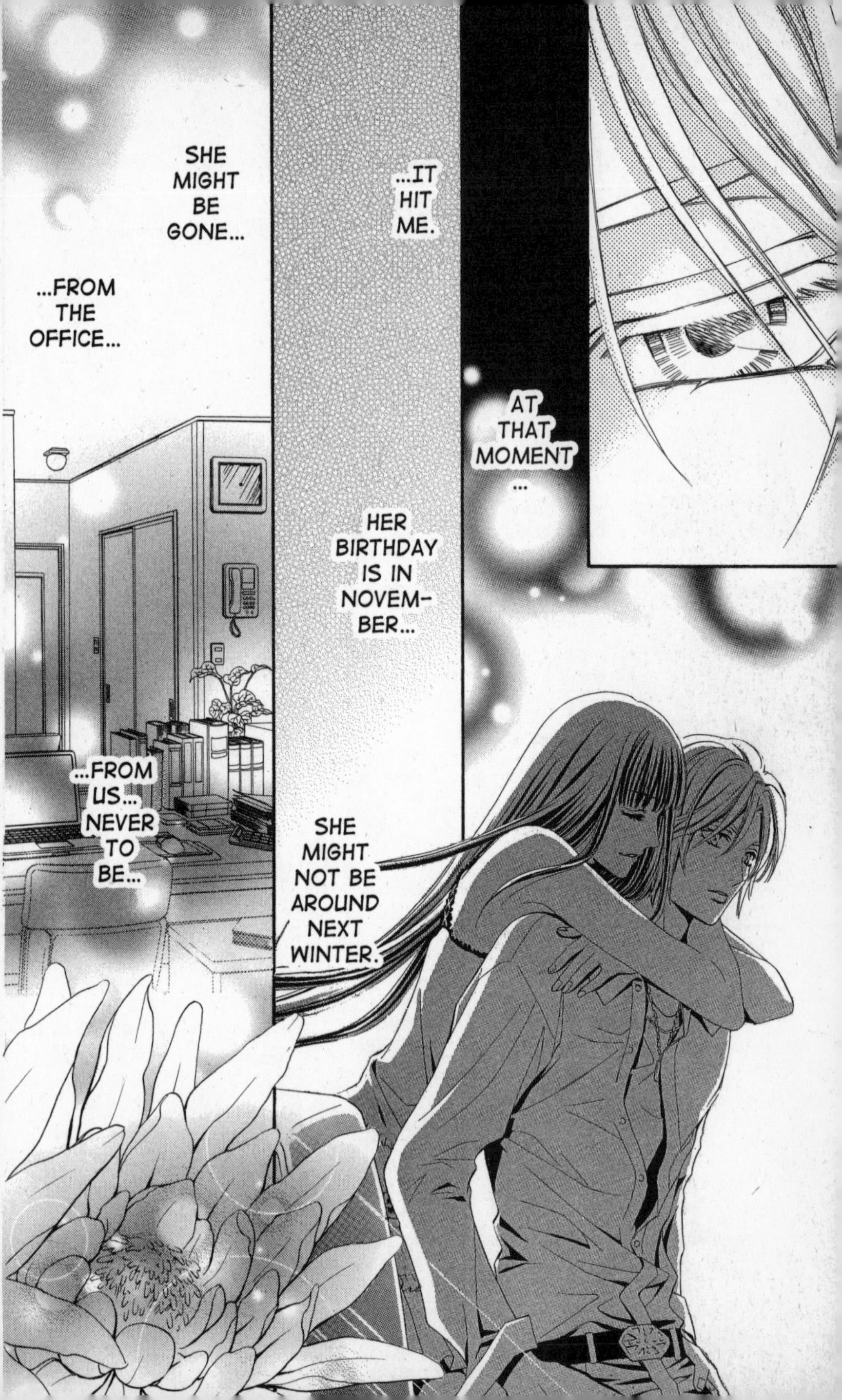
AT THAT MOMENT ...
...IT HIT ME.
HER BIRTHDAY IS IN NOVEMBER...
SHE MIGHT NOT BE AROUND NEXT WINTER.
SHE MIGHT BE GONE...
...FROM THE OFFICE...
...FROM US... NEVER TO BE...

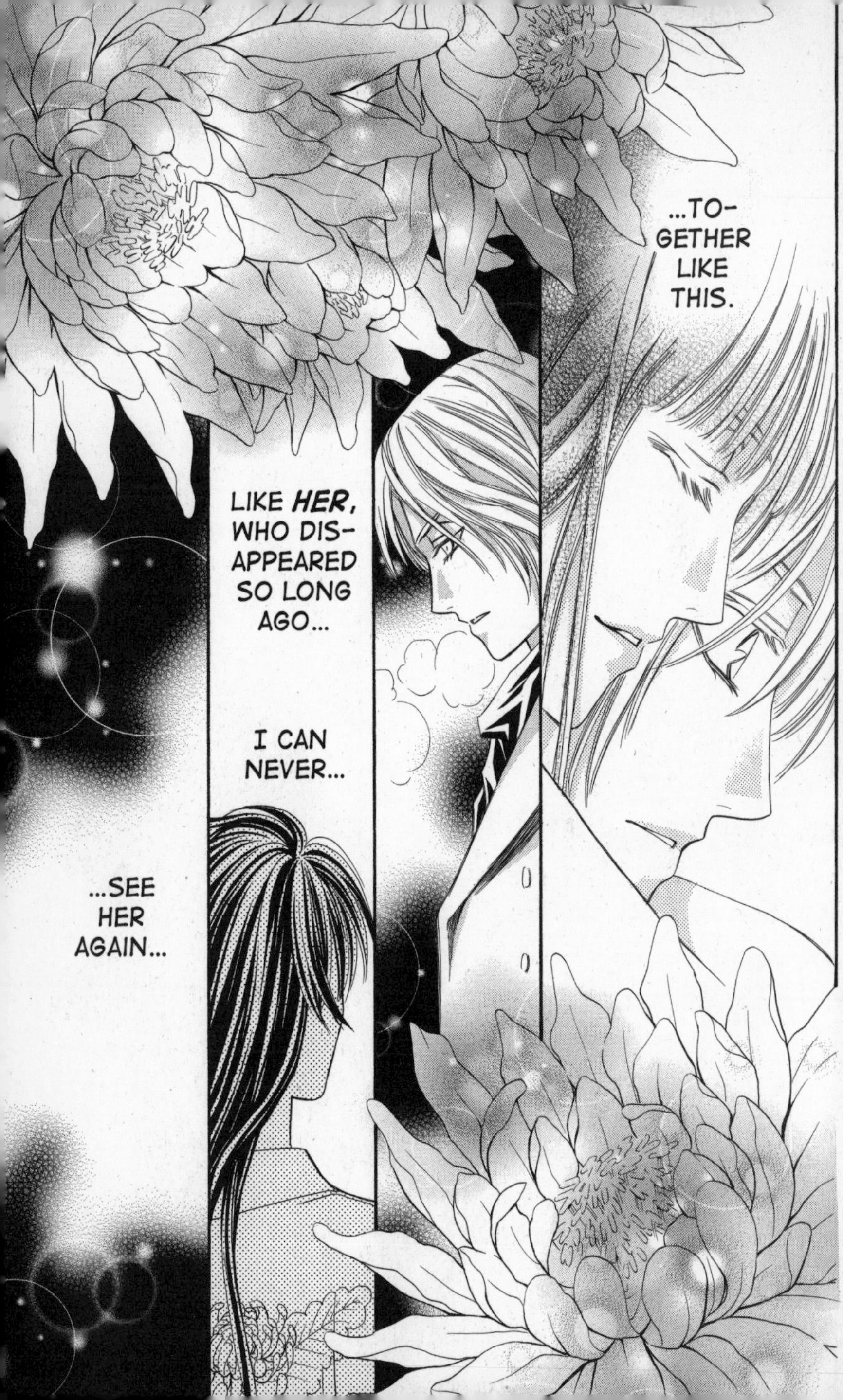
...TO-GETHER LIKE THIS.
LIKE *HER*, WHO DIS-APPEARED SO LONG AGO...
I CAN NEVER...
...SEE HER AGAIN...

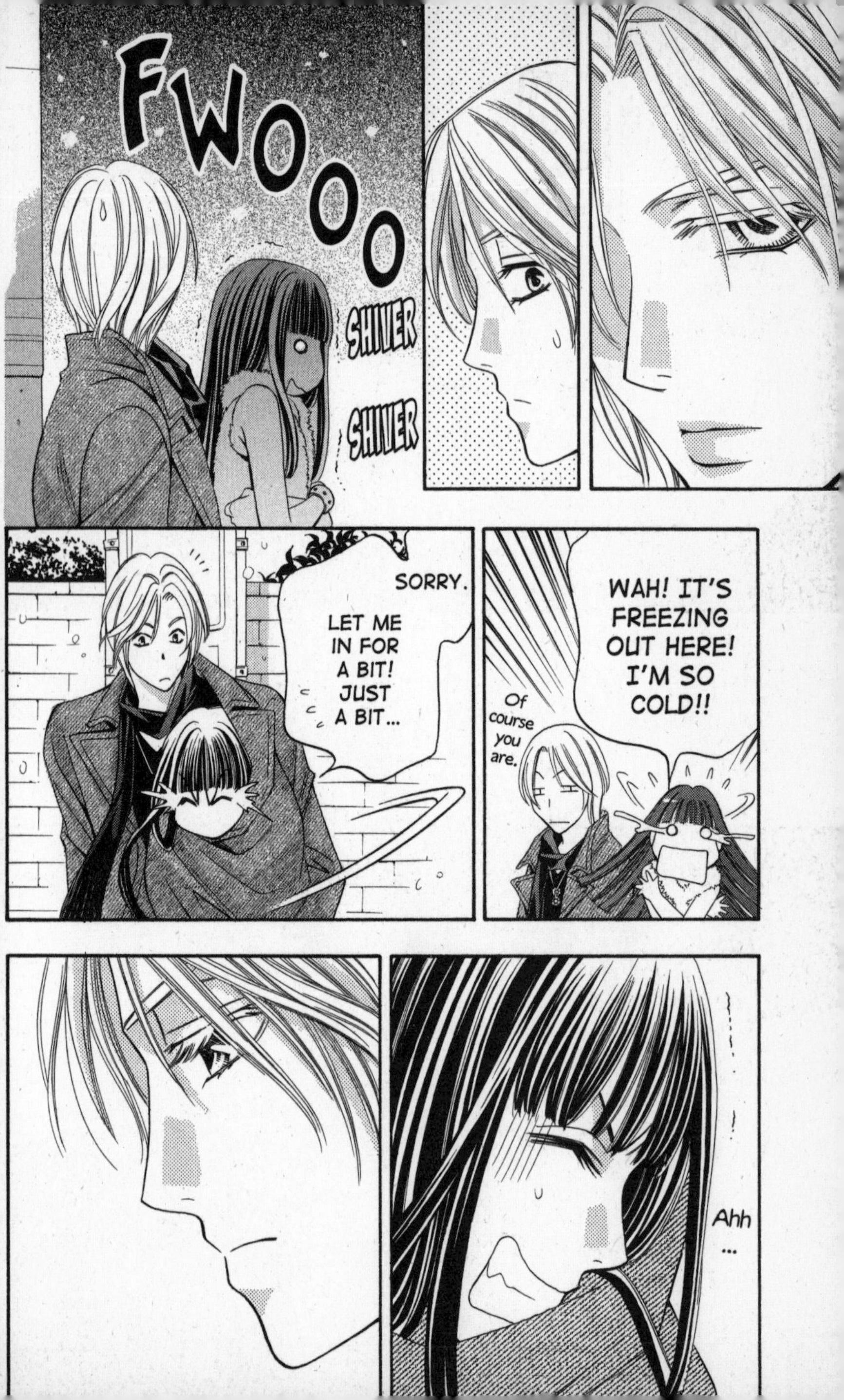
FWOOO
SHIVER
SHIVER
WAH! IT'S FREEZING OUT HERE! I'M SO COLD!!
Of course you are.
SORRY.
LET ME IN FOR A BIT! JUST A BIT...
Ahh ...

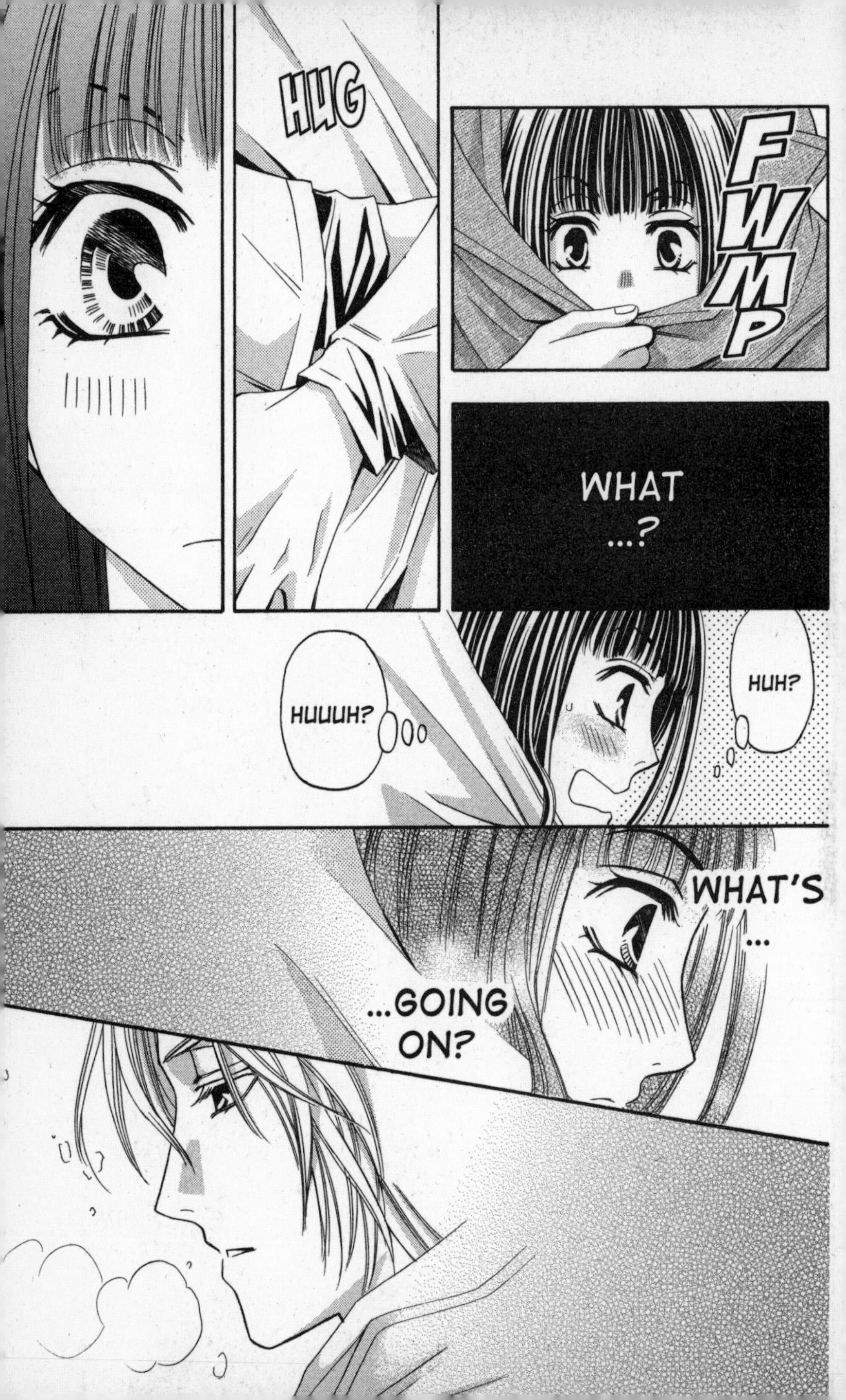
FWMP
WHAT ...?
HUG
HUH?
HUUUH?
WHAT'S ...
...GOING ON?

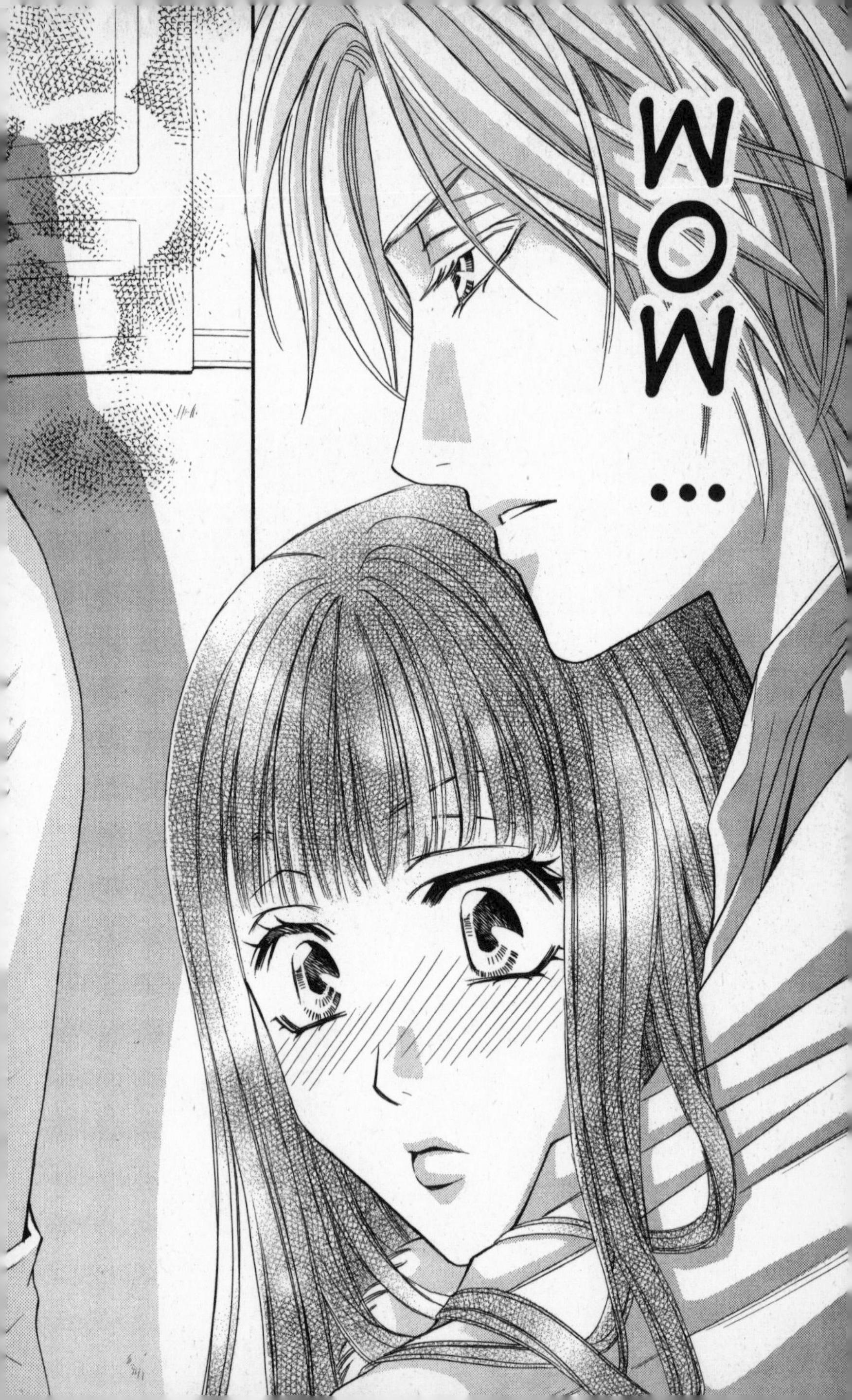
WOW...

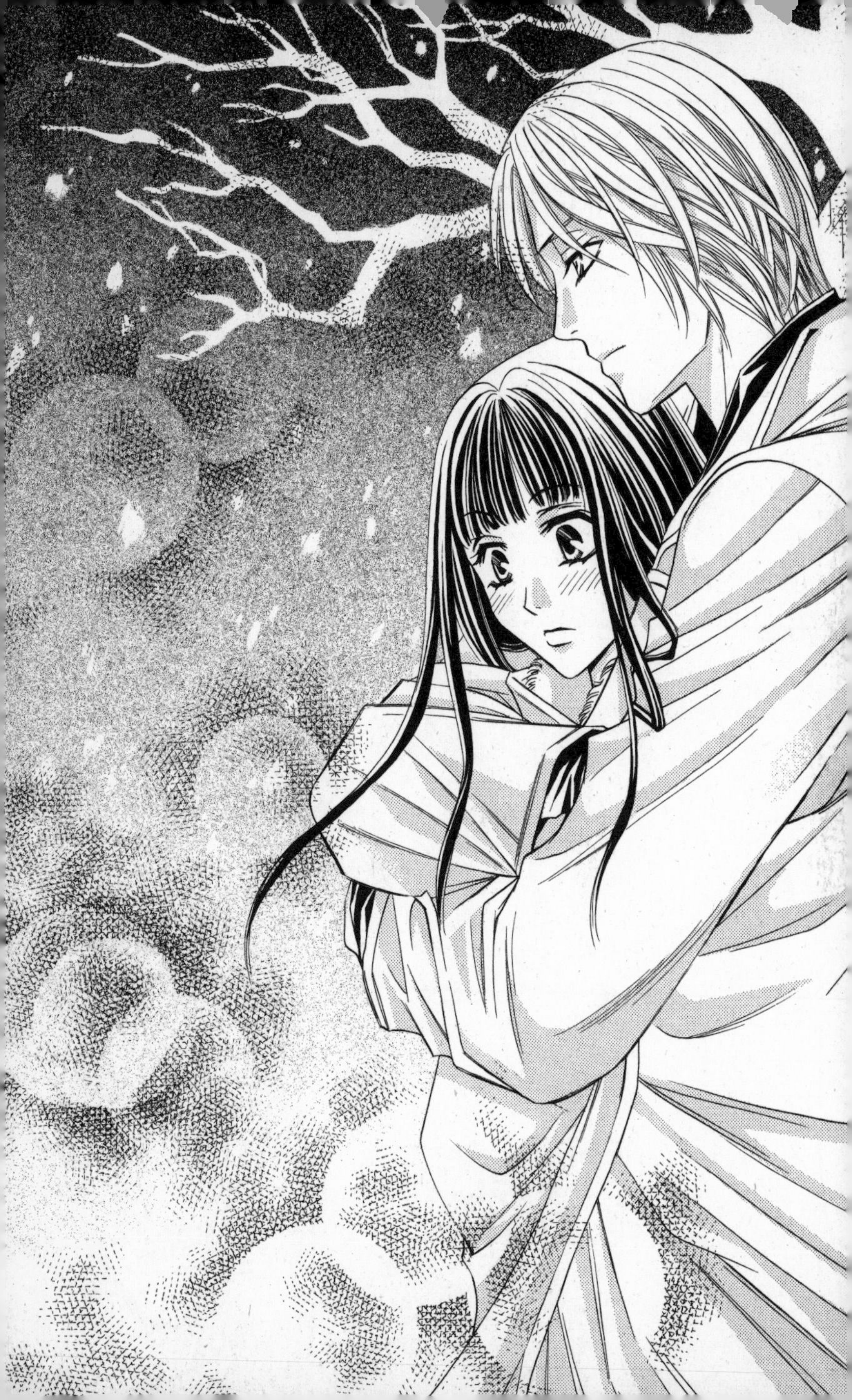

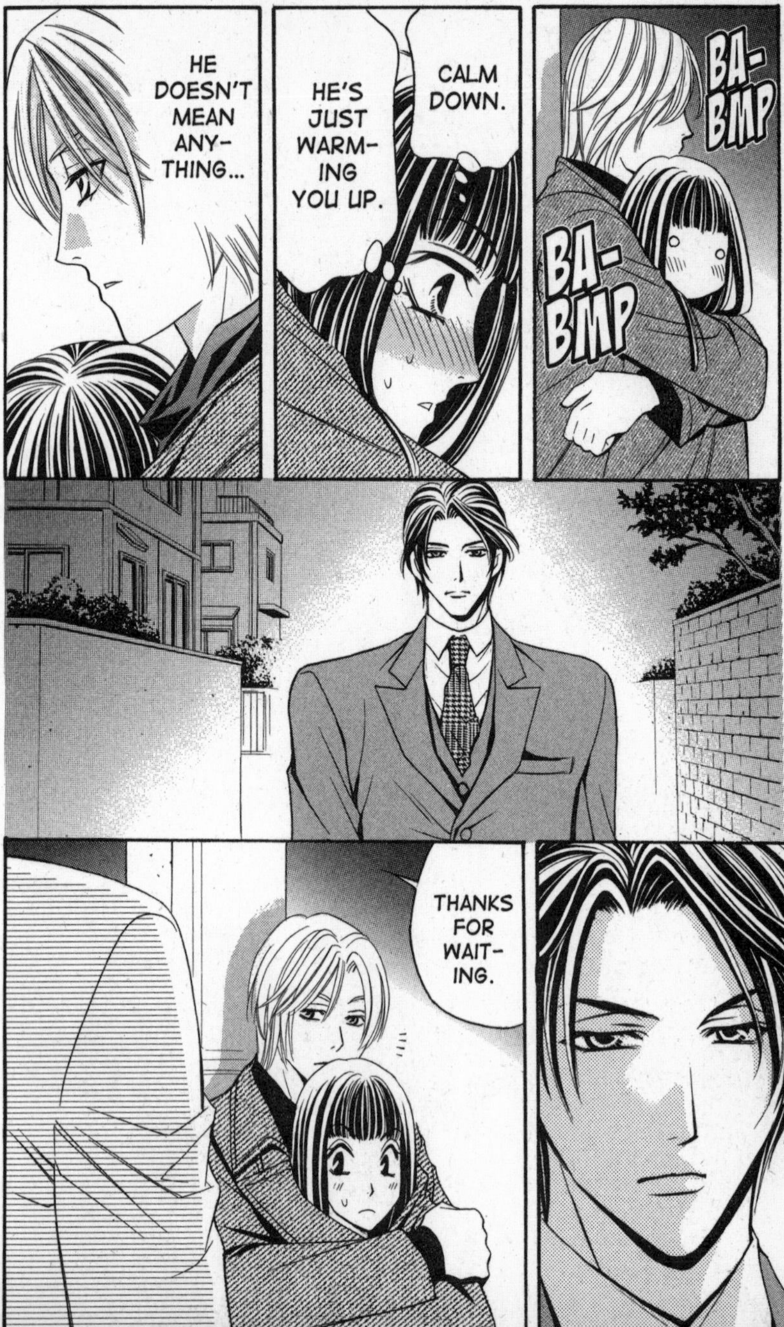
BA-BMP
BA-BMP
CALM DOWN.
HE'S JUST WARMING YOU UP.
HE DOESN'T MEAN ANY-THING...
THANKS FOR WAIT-ING.

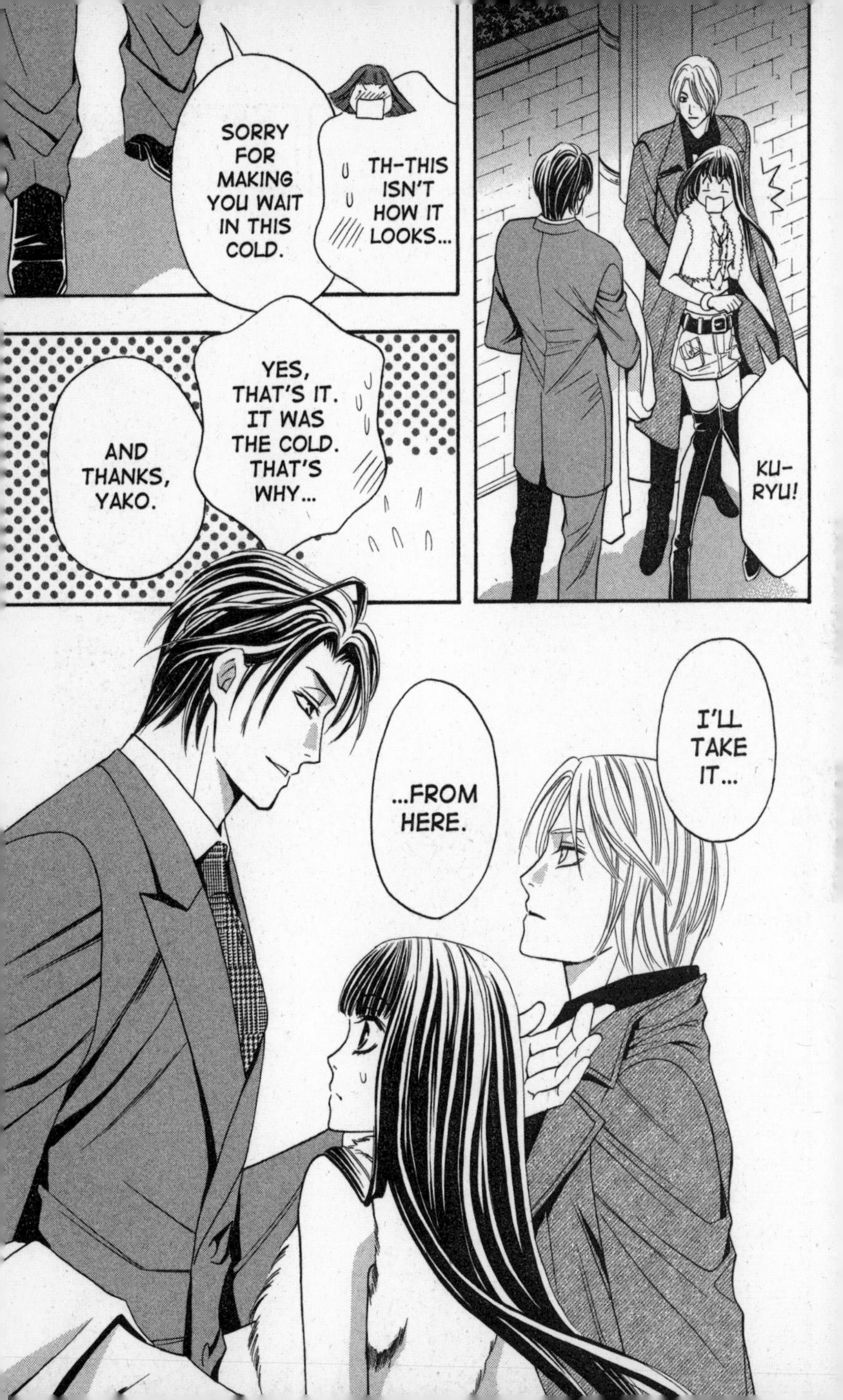
KU-RYU!
TH-THIS ISN'T HOW IT LOOKS...
SORRY FOR MAKING YOU WAIT IN THIS COLD.
YES, THAT'S IT. IT WAS THE COLD. THAT'S WHY...
AND THANKS, YAKO.
I'LL TAKE IT...
...FROM HERE.

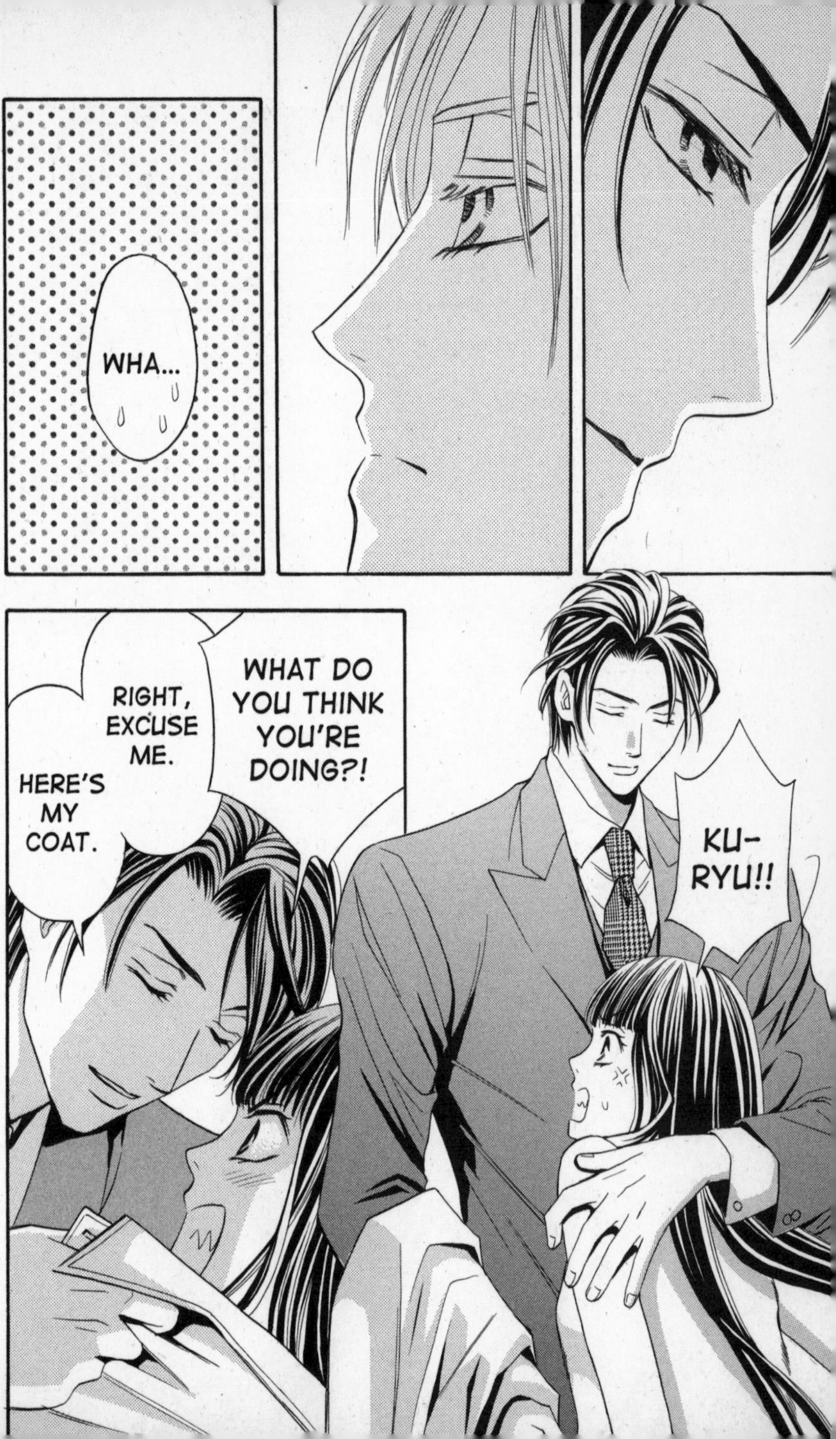
WHA...
WHAT DO YOU THINK YOU'RE DOING?!
RIGHT, EXCUSE ME.
HERE'S MY COAT.
KU-RYU!!

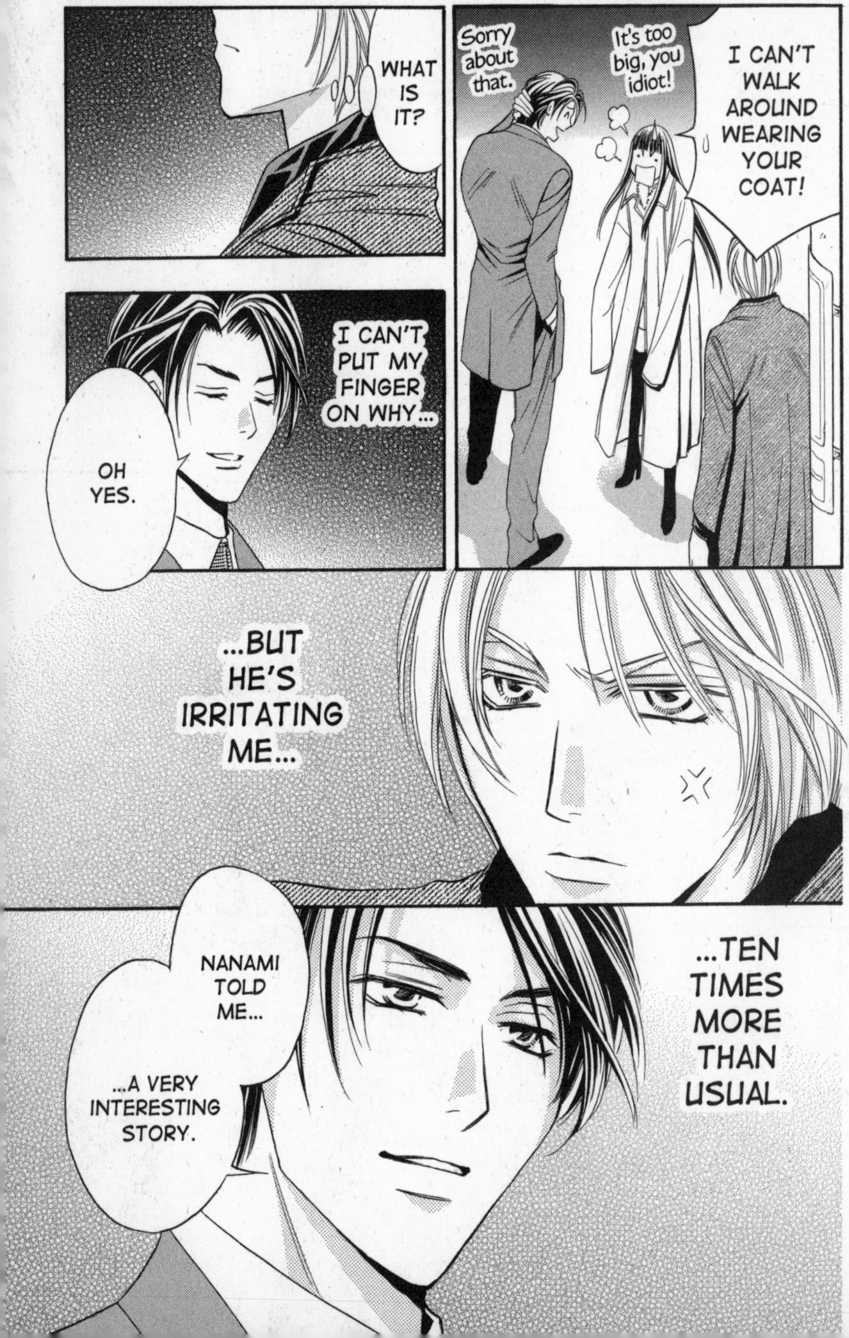
I CAN'T WALK AROUND WEARING YOUR COAT!
It's too big, you idiot!
Sorry about that.
WHAT IS IT?
I CAN'T PUT MY FINGER ON WHY...
OH YES.
...BUT HE'S IRRITATING ME...
...TEN TIMES MORE THAN USUAL.
NANAMI TOLD ME...
...A VERY INTERESTING STORY.

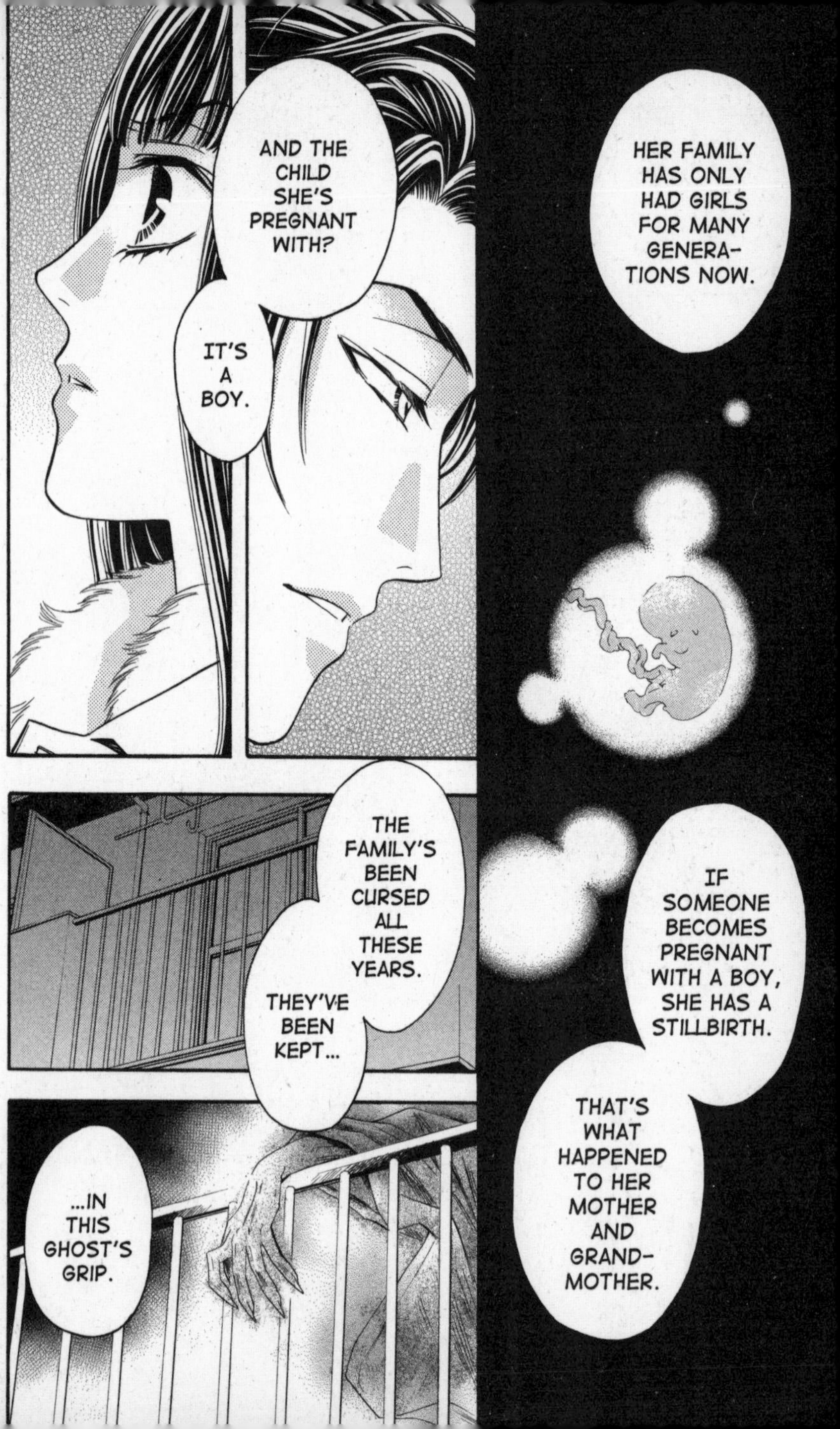
HER FAMILY HAS ONLY HAD GIRLS FOR MANY GENERA-TIONS NOW.
IF SOMEONE BECOMES PREGNANT WITH A BOY, SHE HAS A STILLBIRTH.
THAT'S WHAT HAPPENED TO HER MOTHER AND GRAND-MOTHER.
AND THE CHILD SHE'S PREGNANT WITH?
IT'S A BOY.
THE FAMILY'S BEEN CURSED ALL THESE YEARS.
THEY'VE BEEN KEPT...
...IN THIS GHOST'S GRIP.

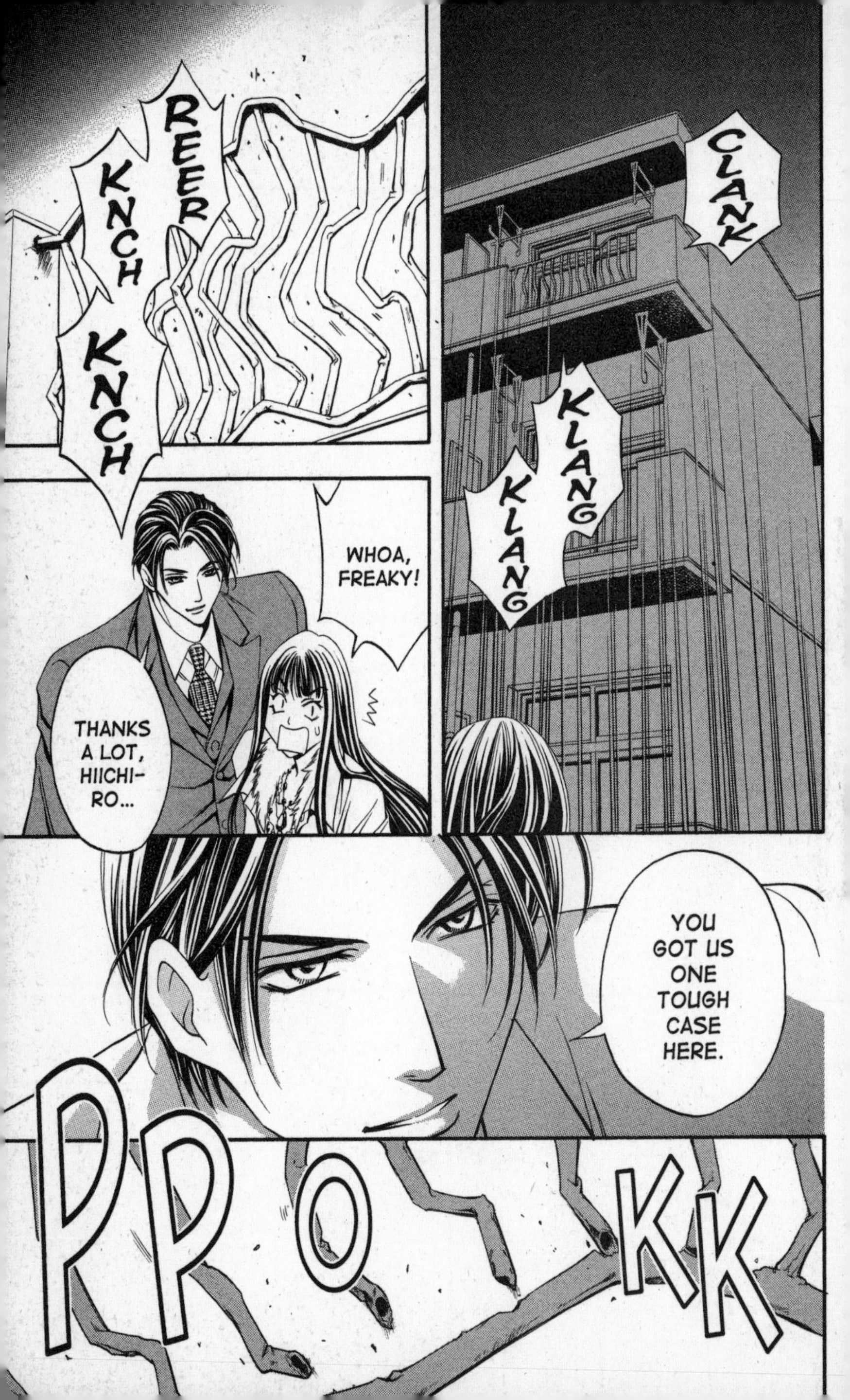
CLANK
KLANG KLANG
REEER
KNCH
KNCH KNCH
WHOA, FREAKY!
THANKS A LOT, HIICHIRO...
YOU GOT US ONE TOUGH CASE HERE.
PPOKK

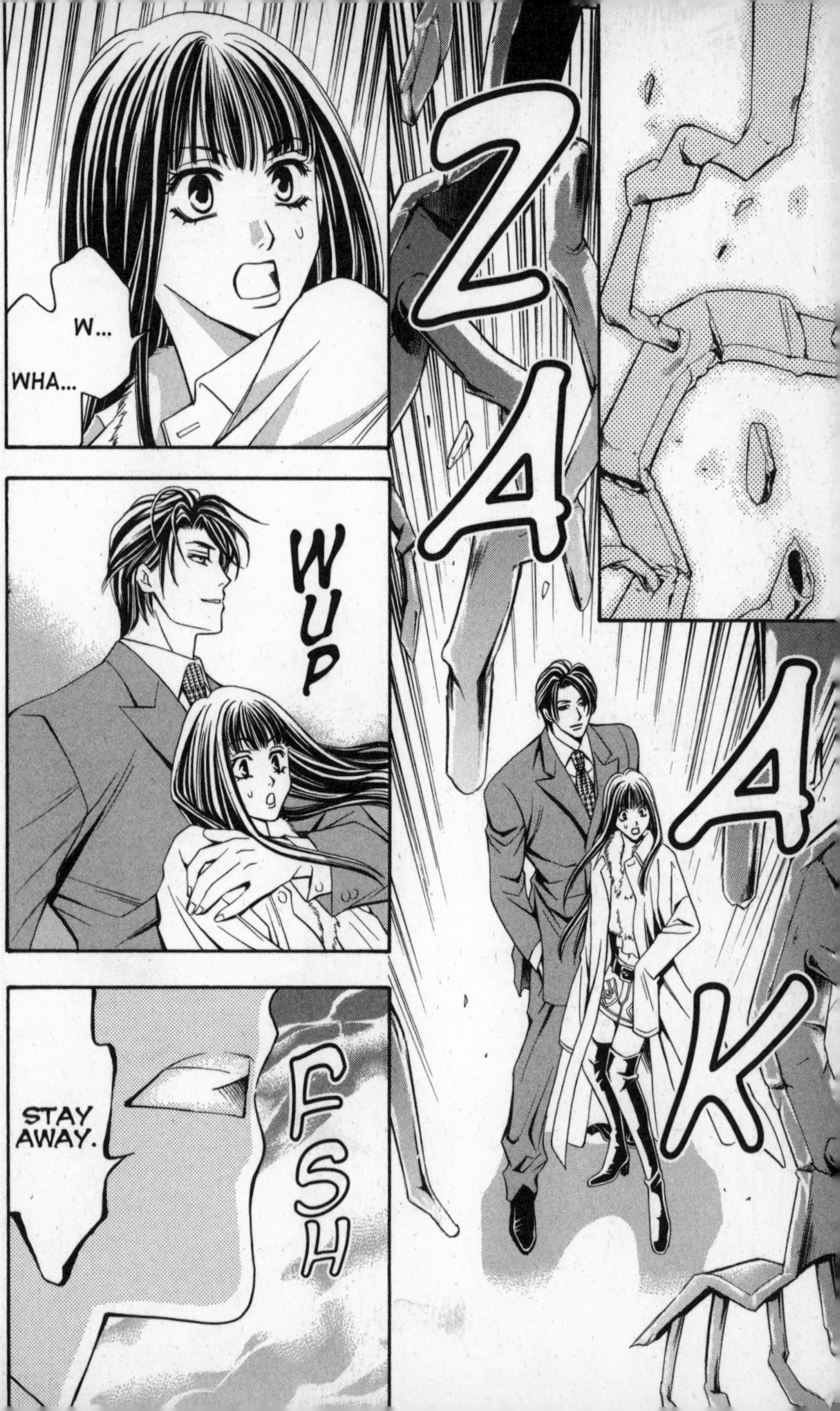
ZAAK
W...
WHA...
WUP
FSH
STAY AWAY.

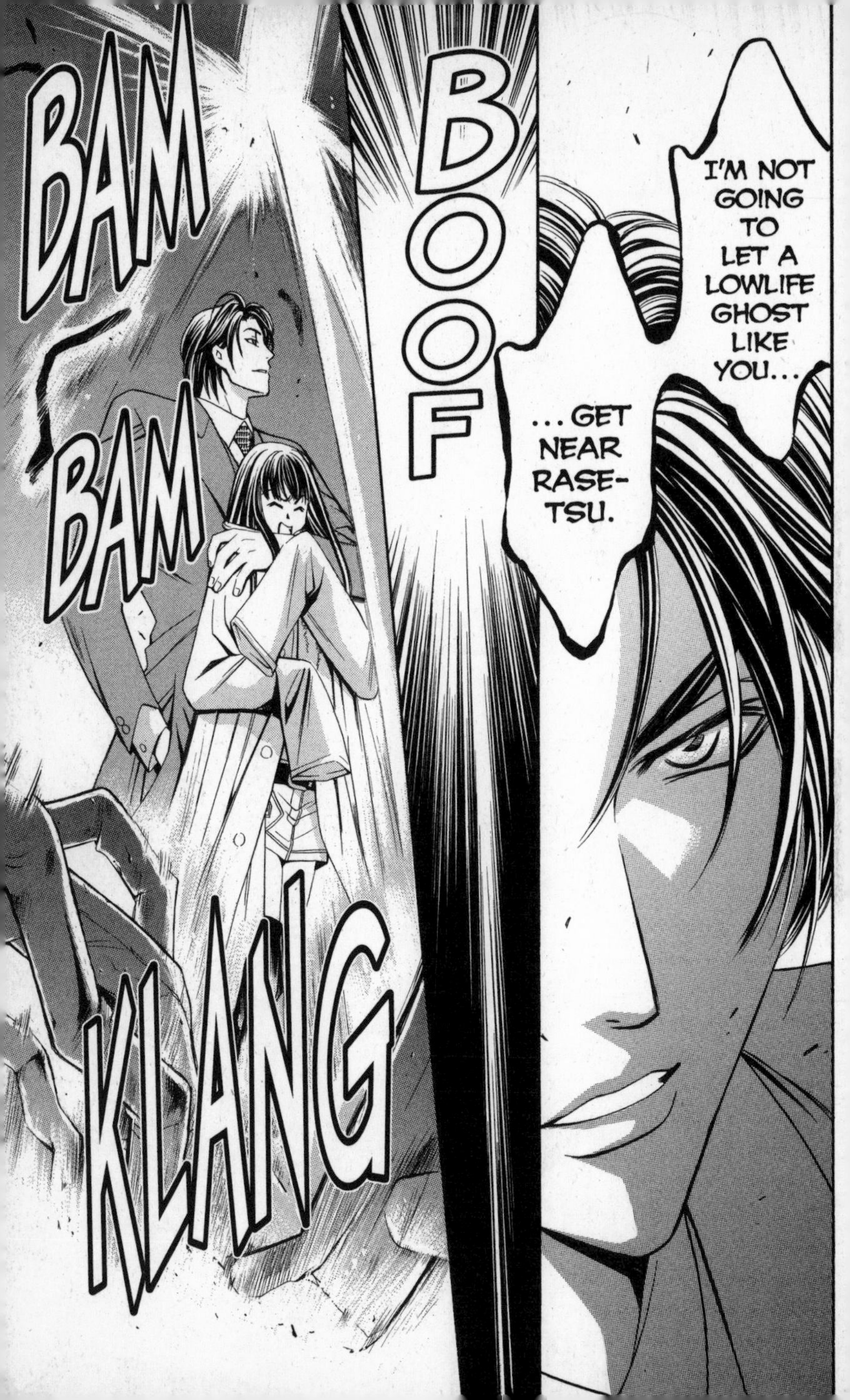
I'M NOT GOING TO LET A LOWLIFE GHOST LIKE YOU...
...GET NEAR RASE-TSU.
BOOOF
BAM
BAM
KLANG

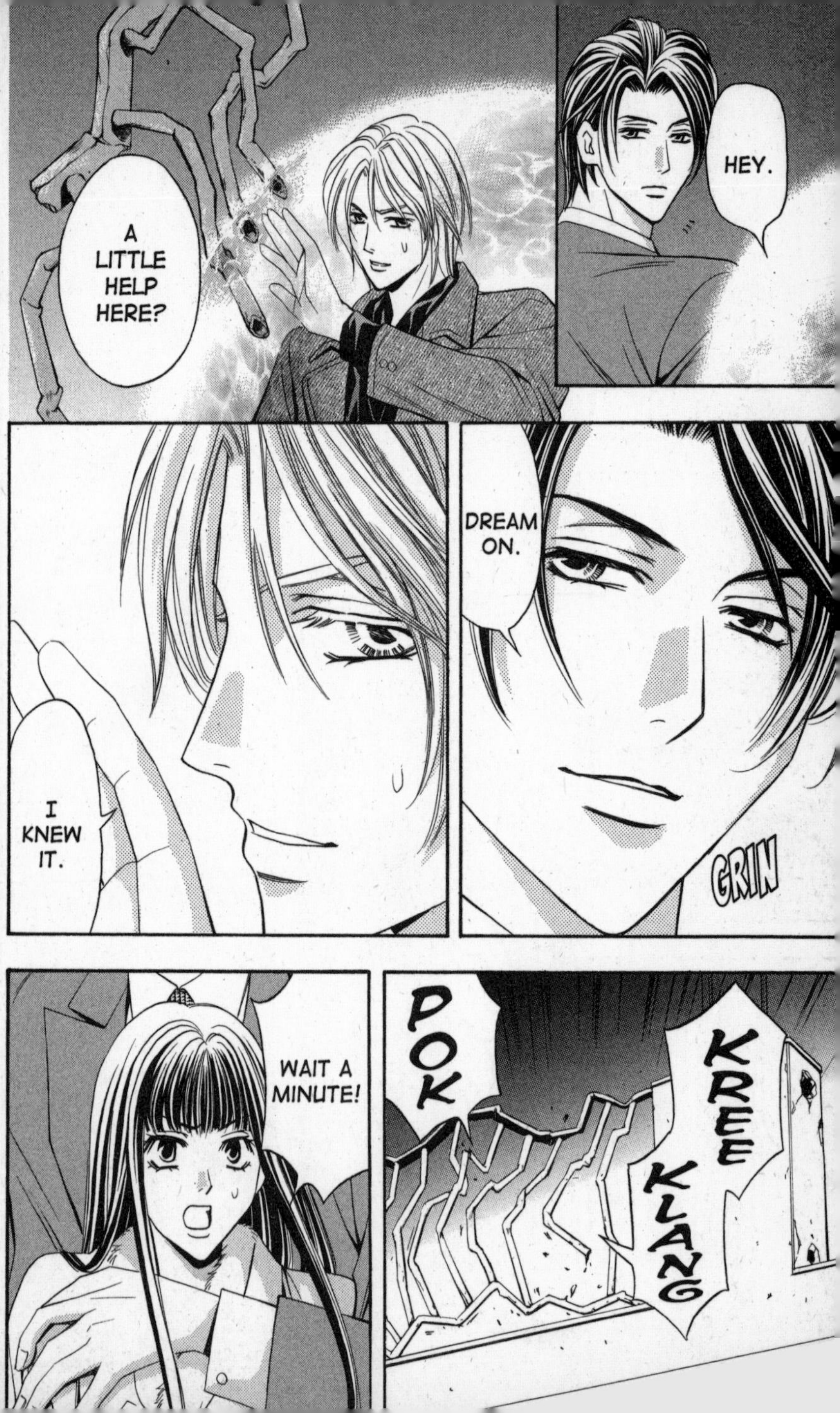
HEY.
A LITTLE HELP HERE?
DREAM ON.
GRIN
I KNEW IT.
POK
KREE KLANG
WAIT A MINUTE!

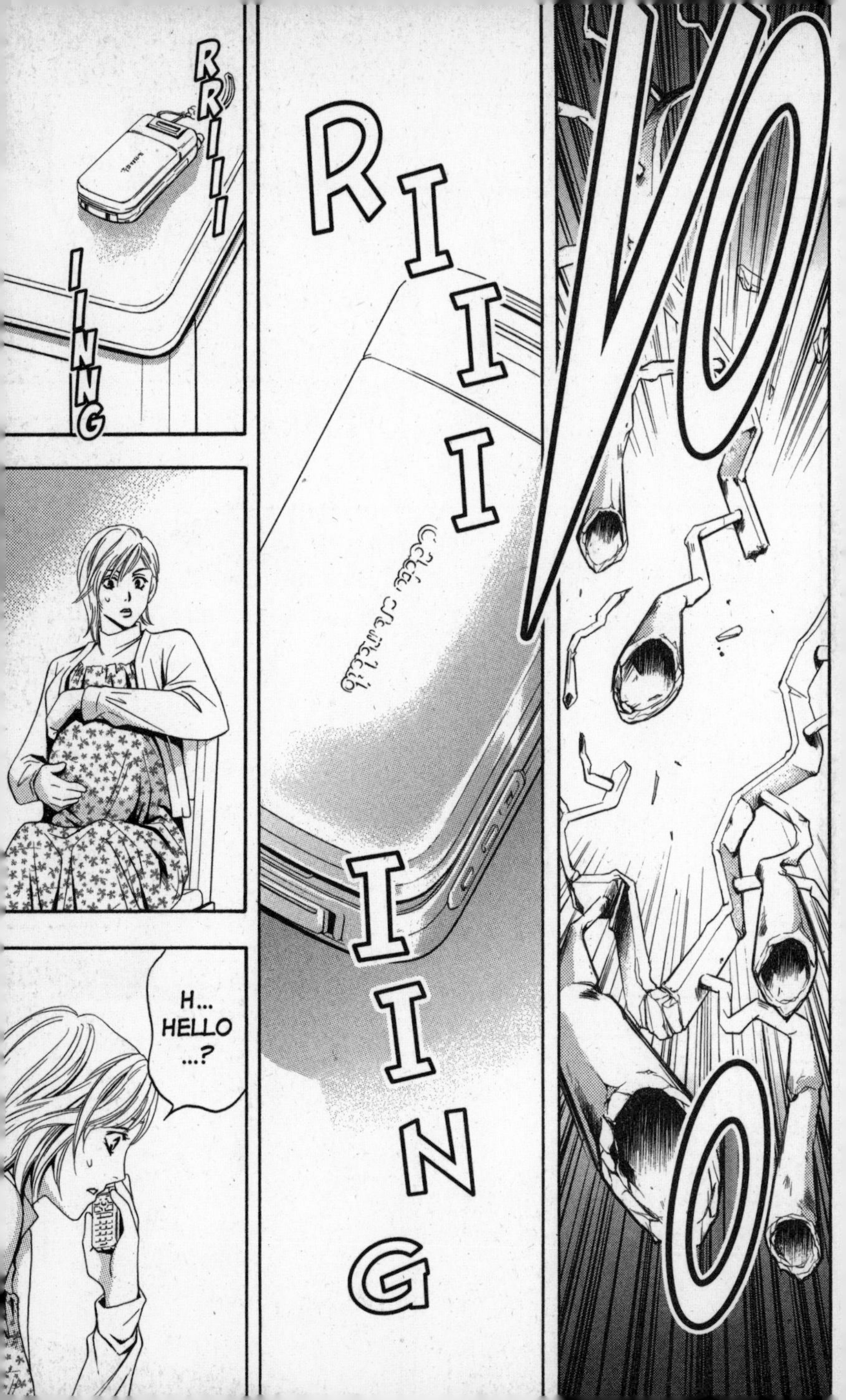
RIIIIING
RRIIIIINNG
H... HELLO ...?

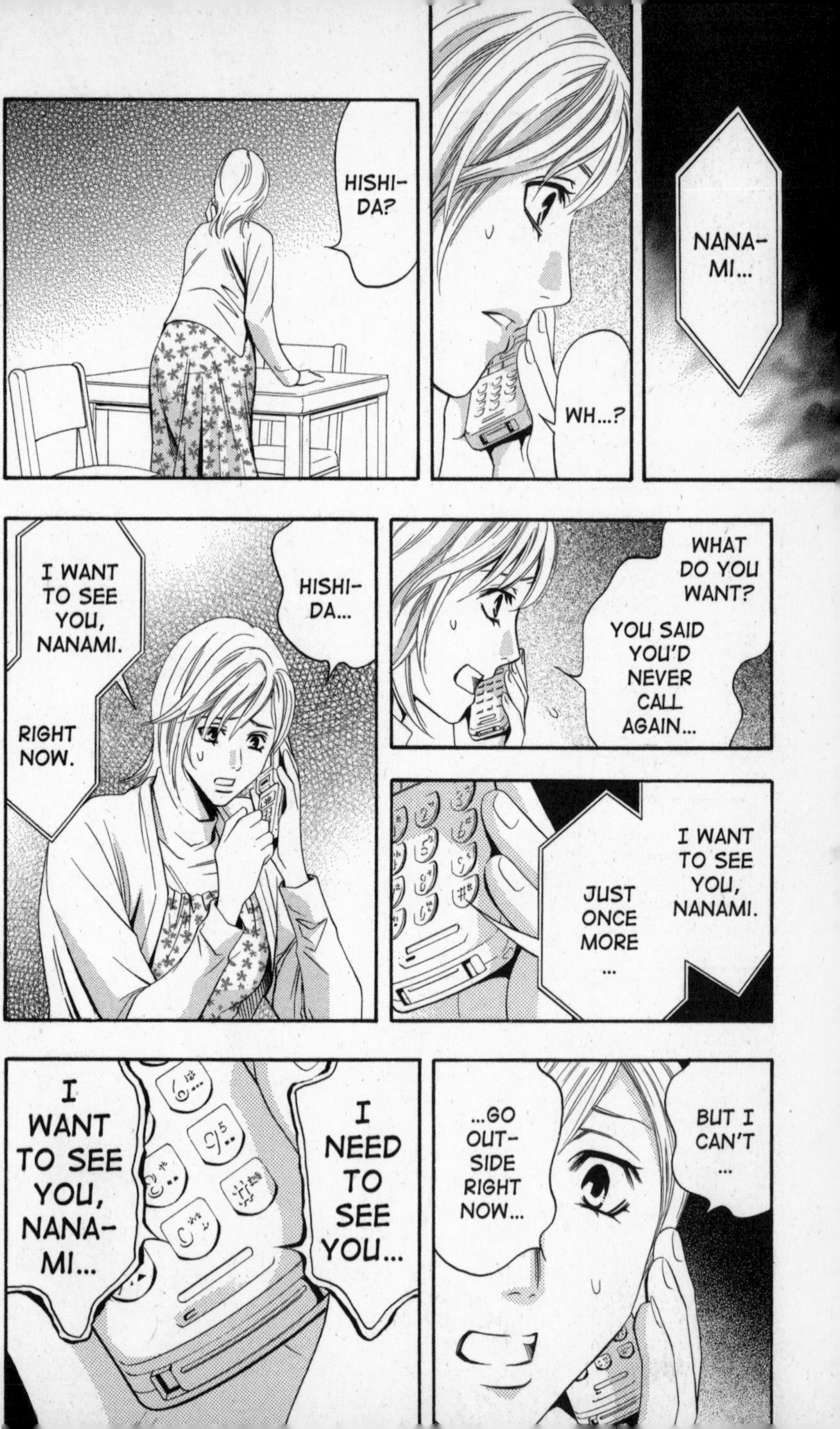
NANA-MI...
WH...?
HISHI-DA?
WHAT DO YOU WANT?
YOU SAID YOU'D NEVER CALL AGAIN...
I WANT TO SEE YOU, NANAMI.
JUST ONCE MORE ...
HISHI-DA...
I WANT TO SEE YOU, NANAMI.
RIGHT NOW.
BUT I CAN'T ...
...GO OUT-SIDE RIGHT NOW...
I NEED TO SEE YOU...
I WANT TO SEE YOU, NANA-MI...

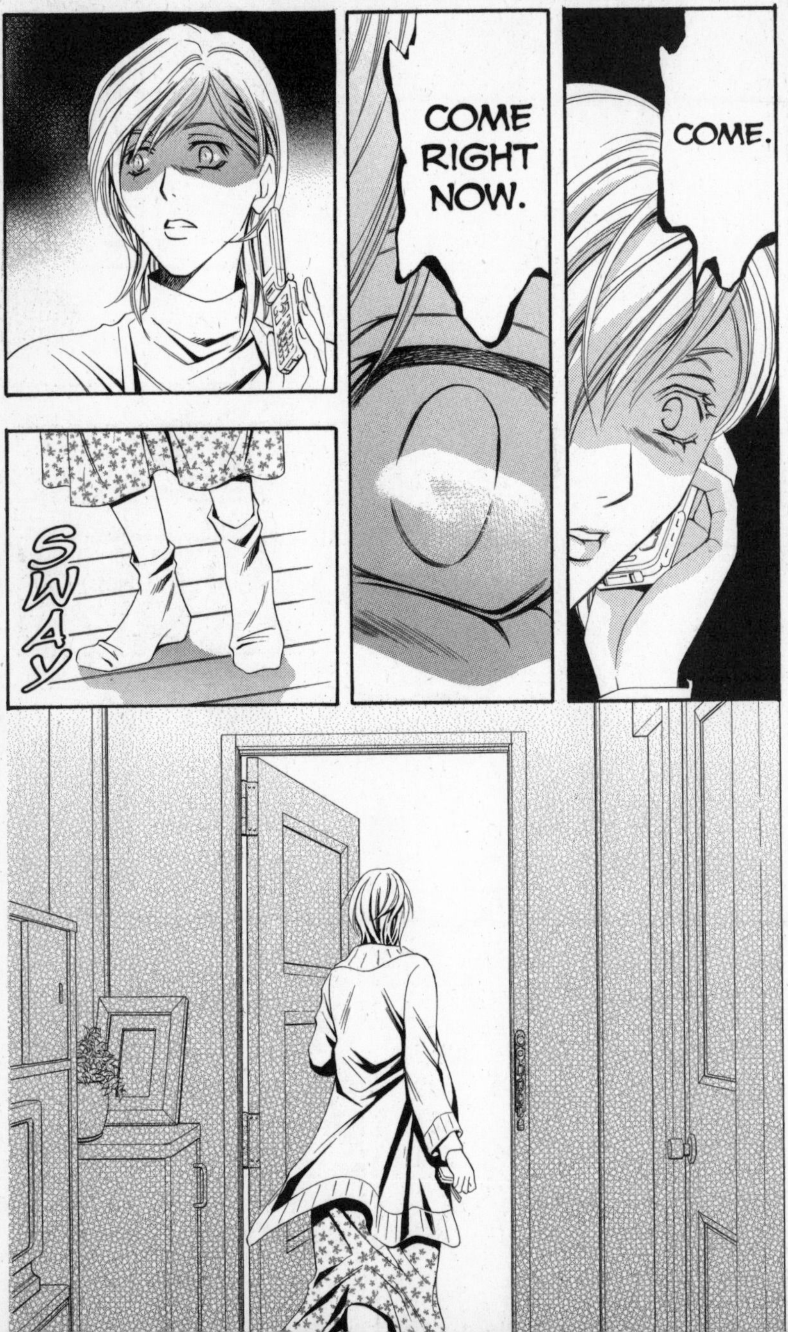
COME.
COME RIGHT NOW.
SWAY

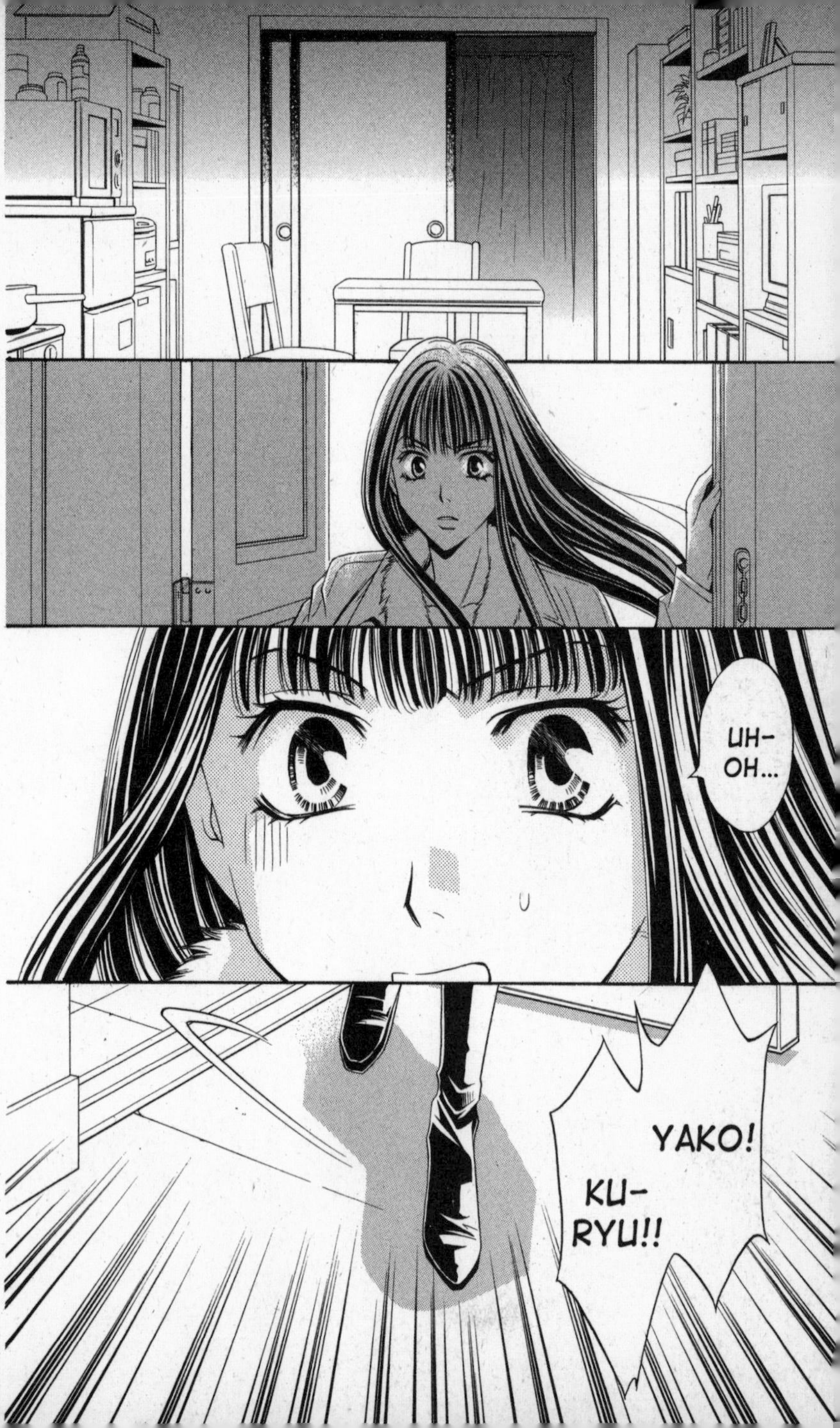
UH-OH...
YAKO! KU-RYU!!

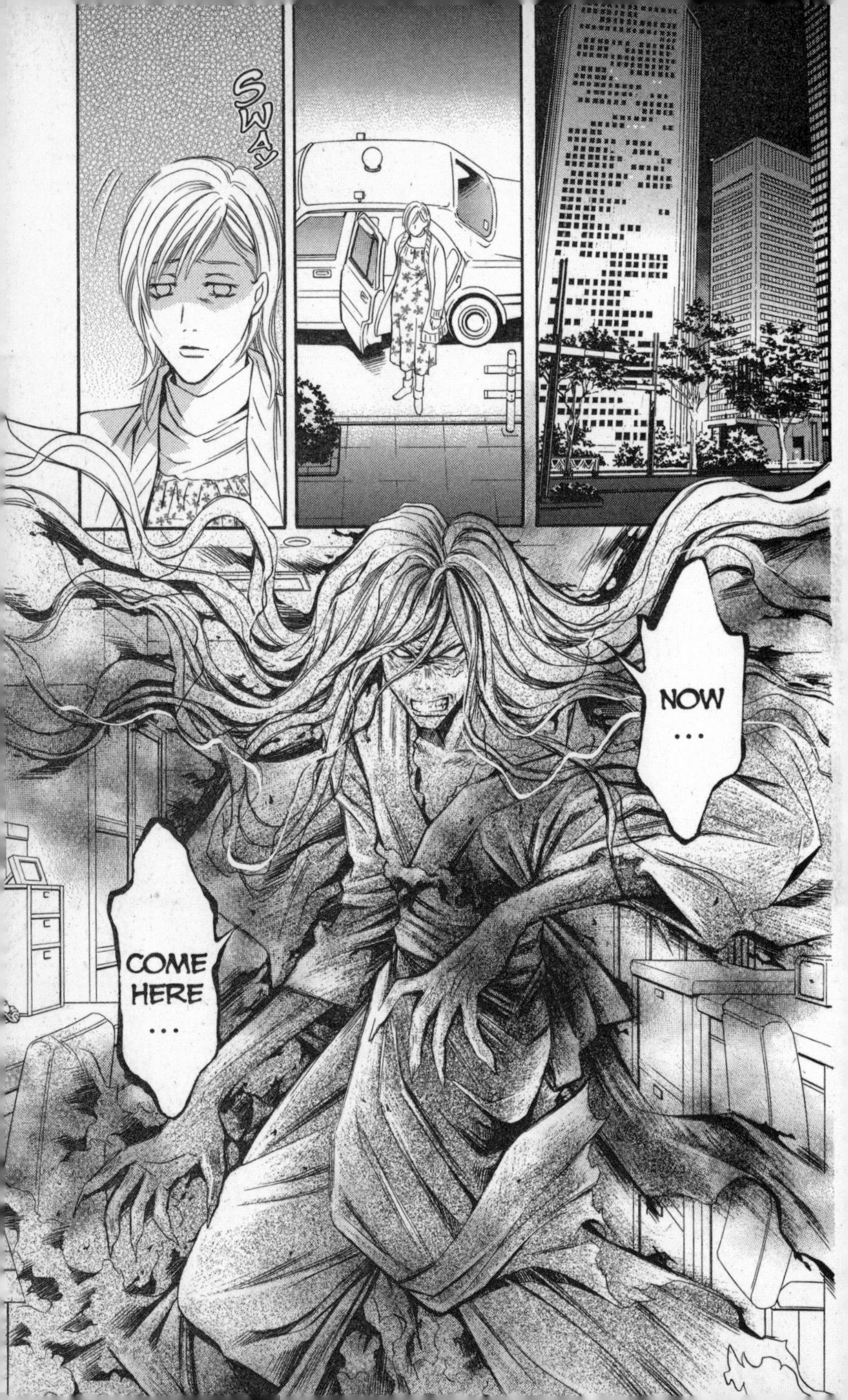
SWAY
NOW ...
COME HERE ...

BONUS MANGA
(AOI ROOTS FOR RASETSU)

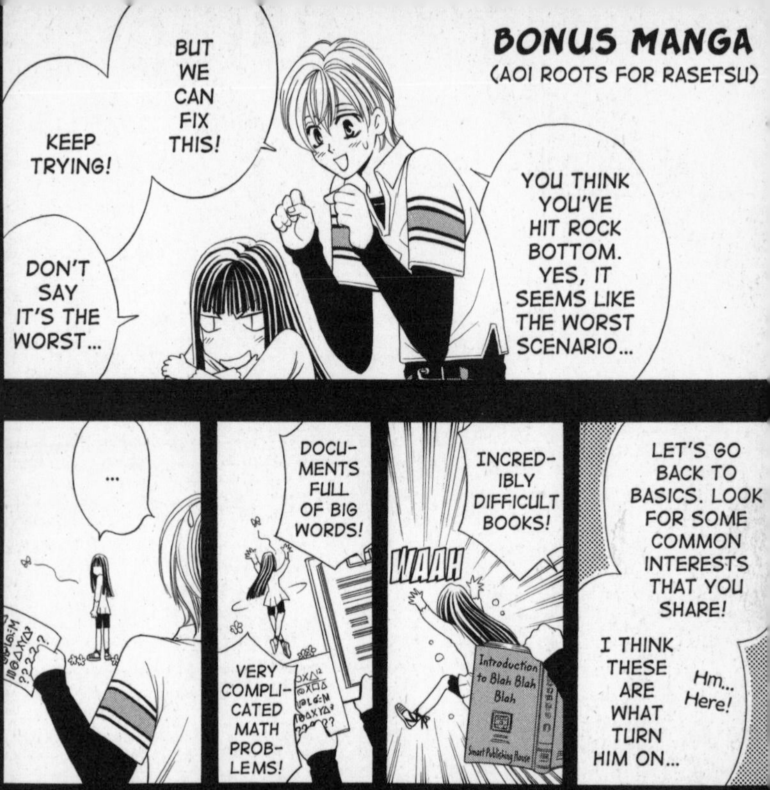
YOU THINK YOU'VE HIT ROCK BOTTOM. YES, IT SEEMS LIKE THE WORST SCENARIO...
BUT WE CAN FIX THIS!
KEEP TRYING!
DON'T SAY IT'S THE WORST...
LET'S GO BACK TO BASICS. LOOK FOR SOME COMMON INTERESTS THAT YOU SHARE!
Hm... Here!
I THINK THESE ARE WHAT TURN HIM ON...
INCREDIBLY DIFFICULT BOOKS!
WAAH
Introduction to Blah Blah Blah
Smart Publishing House
DOCUMENTS FULL OF BIG WORDS!
VERY COMPLICATED MATH PROBLEMS!
...

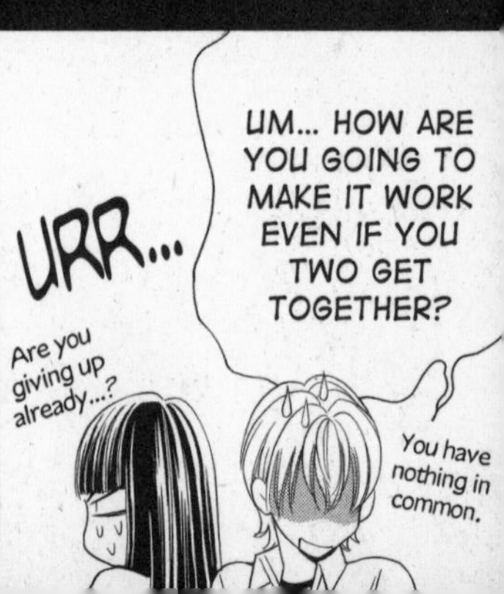
UM... HOW ARE YOU GOING TO MAKE IT WORK EVEN IF YOU TWO GET TOGETHER?
URR...
You have nothing in common.
Are you giving up already...?

EDITOR
T.YAMAKI

STAFF
K.YAMADA
N.MIYATA

CG WORKS
K.KOJIMA

SEND YOUR LETTERS TO:

CHIKA SHIOMI
C/O RASETSU EDITOR
VIZ MEDIA
P.O. BOX 77010
SAN FRANCISCO, CA 94107

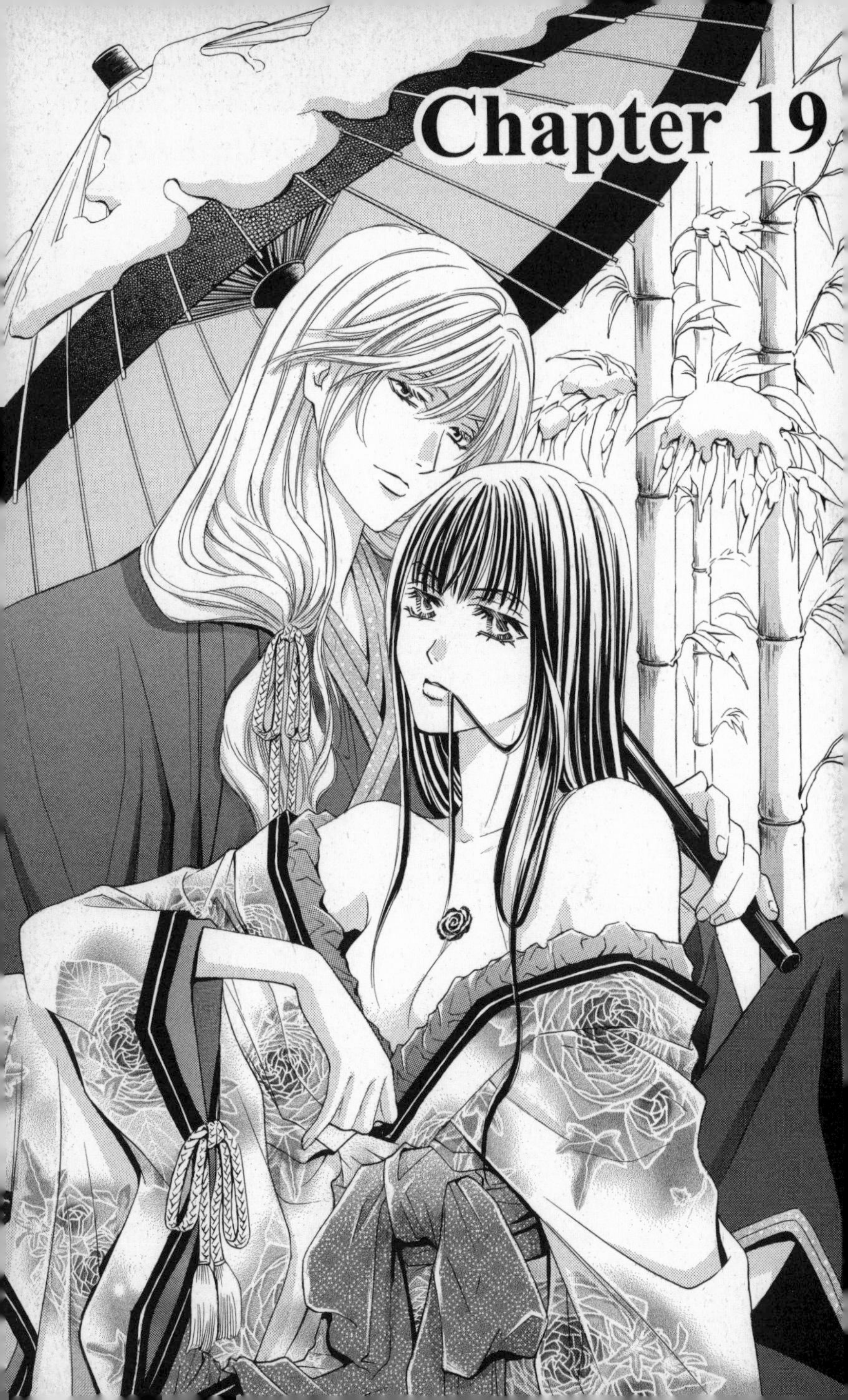
Chapter 19

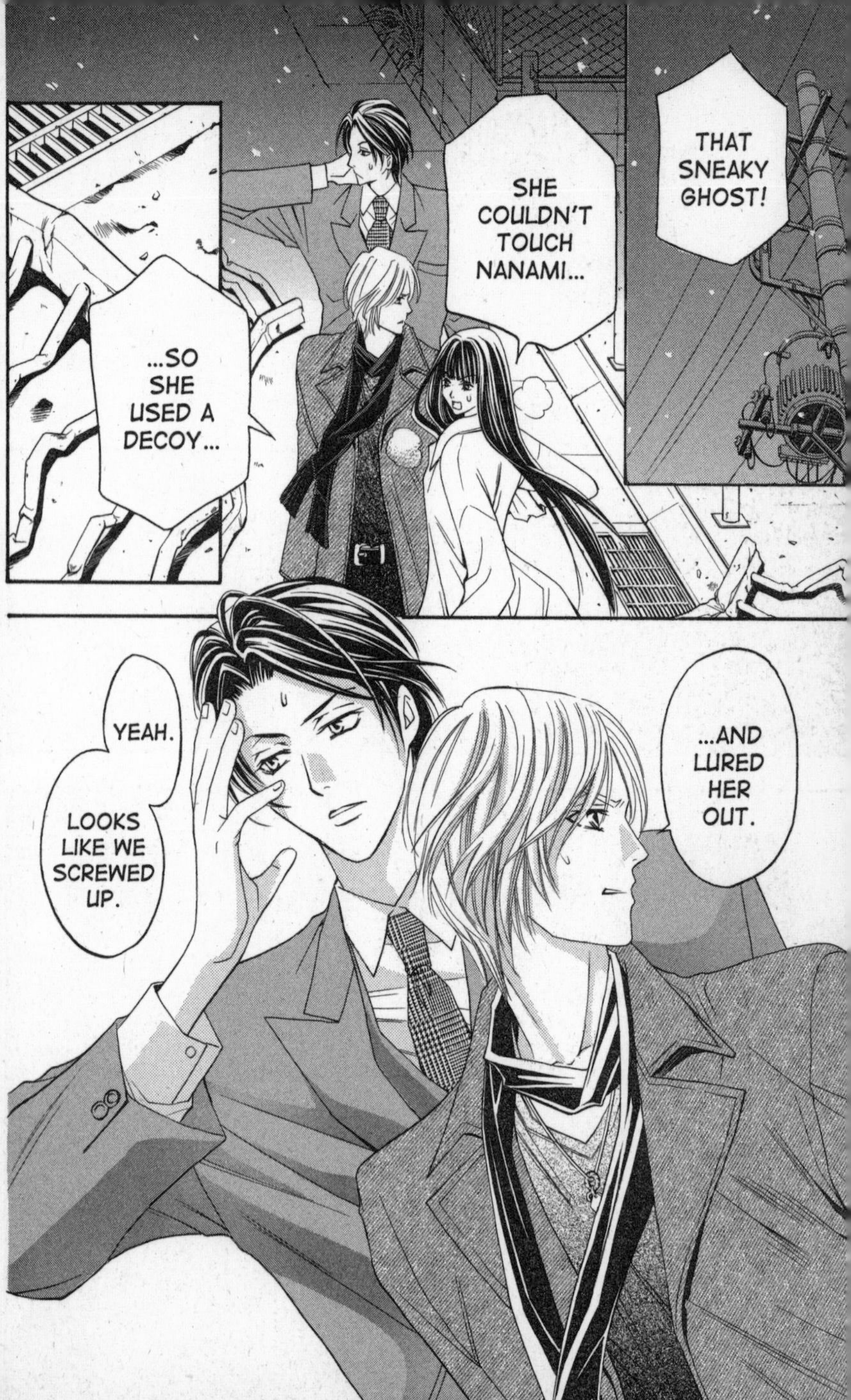
THAT SNEAKY GHOST!
SHE COULDN'T TOUCH NANAMI...
...SO SHE USED A DECOY...
...AND LURED HER OUT.
YEAH.
LOOKS LIKE WE SCREWED UP.

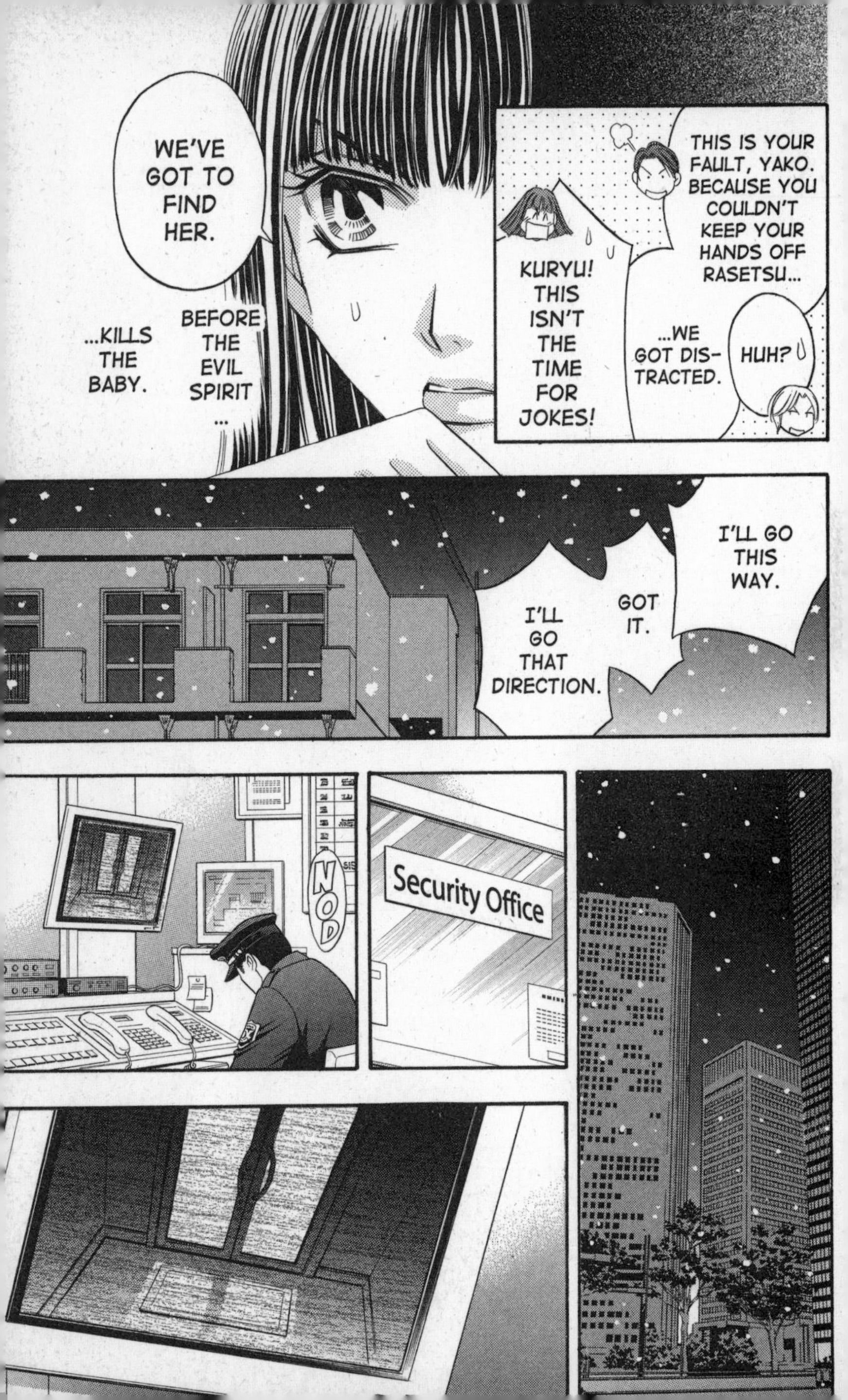
THIS IS YOUR FAULT, YAKO. BECAUSE YOU COULDN'T KEEP YOUR HANDS OFF RASETSU...
KURYU! THIS ISN'T THE TIME FOR JOKES!
HUH?
...WE GOT DIS-TRACTED.
WE'VE GOT TO FIND HER.
BEFORE THE EVIL SPIRIT ...
...KILLS THE BABY.
I'LL GO THIS WAY.
GOT IT.
I'LL GO THAT DIRECTION.
Security Office
NOD

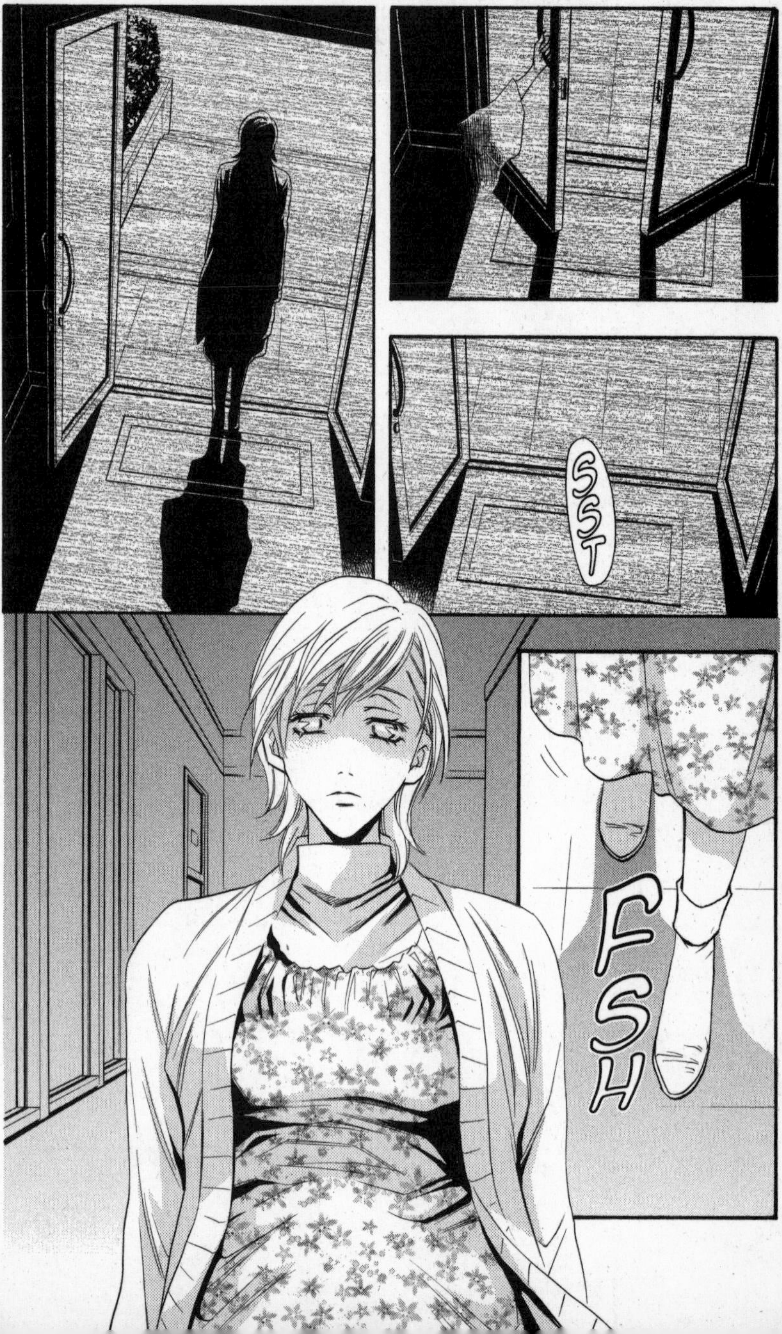
SST
FSH

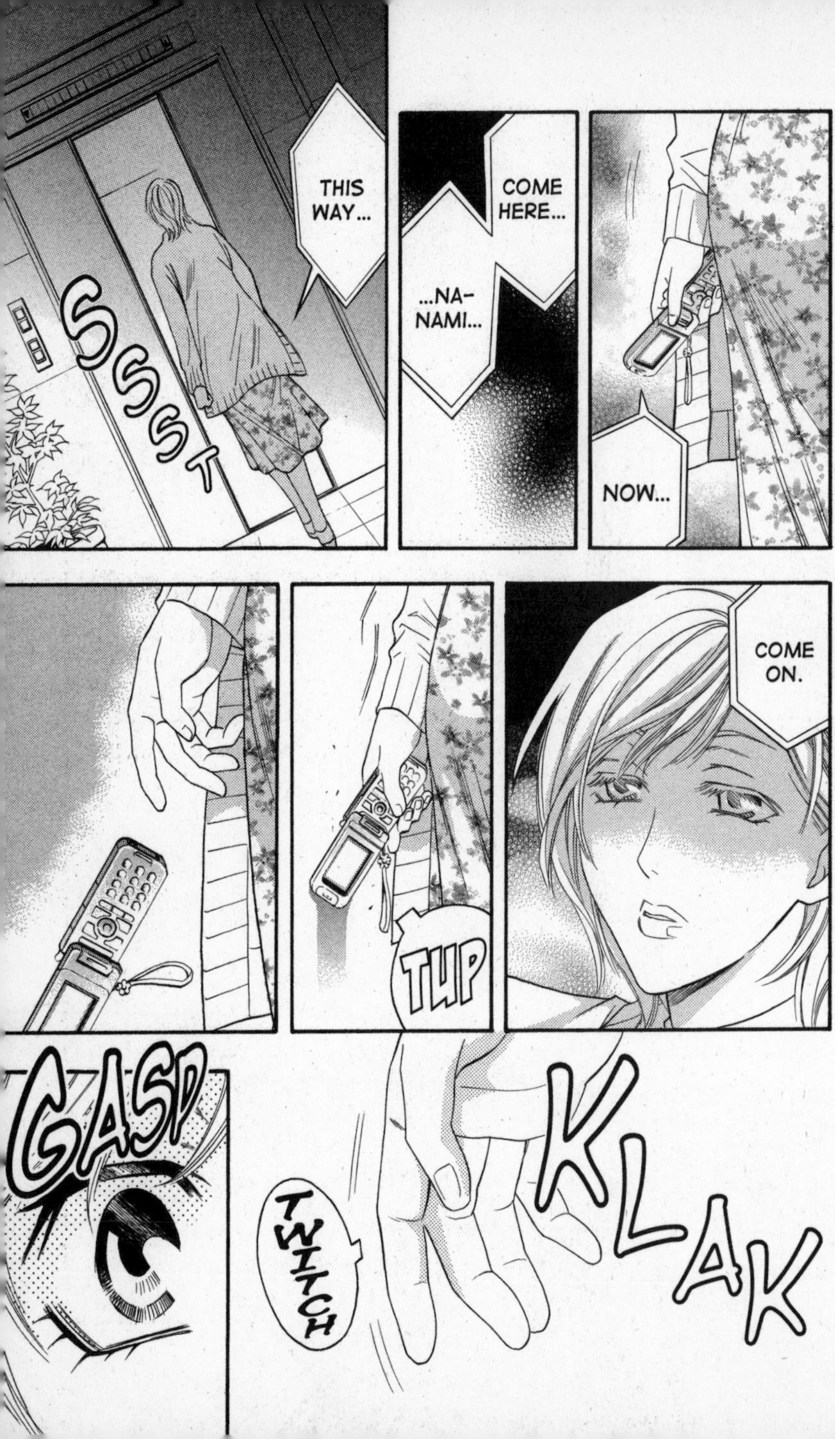
NOW...
COME HERE...
...NA-NAMI...
THIS WAY...
SSSST
COME ON.
TUP
KLAK
TWITCH
GASP

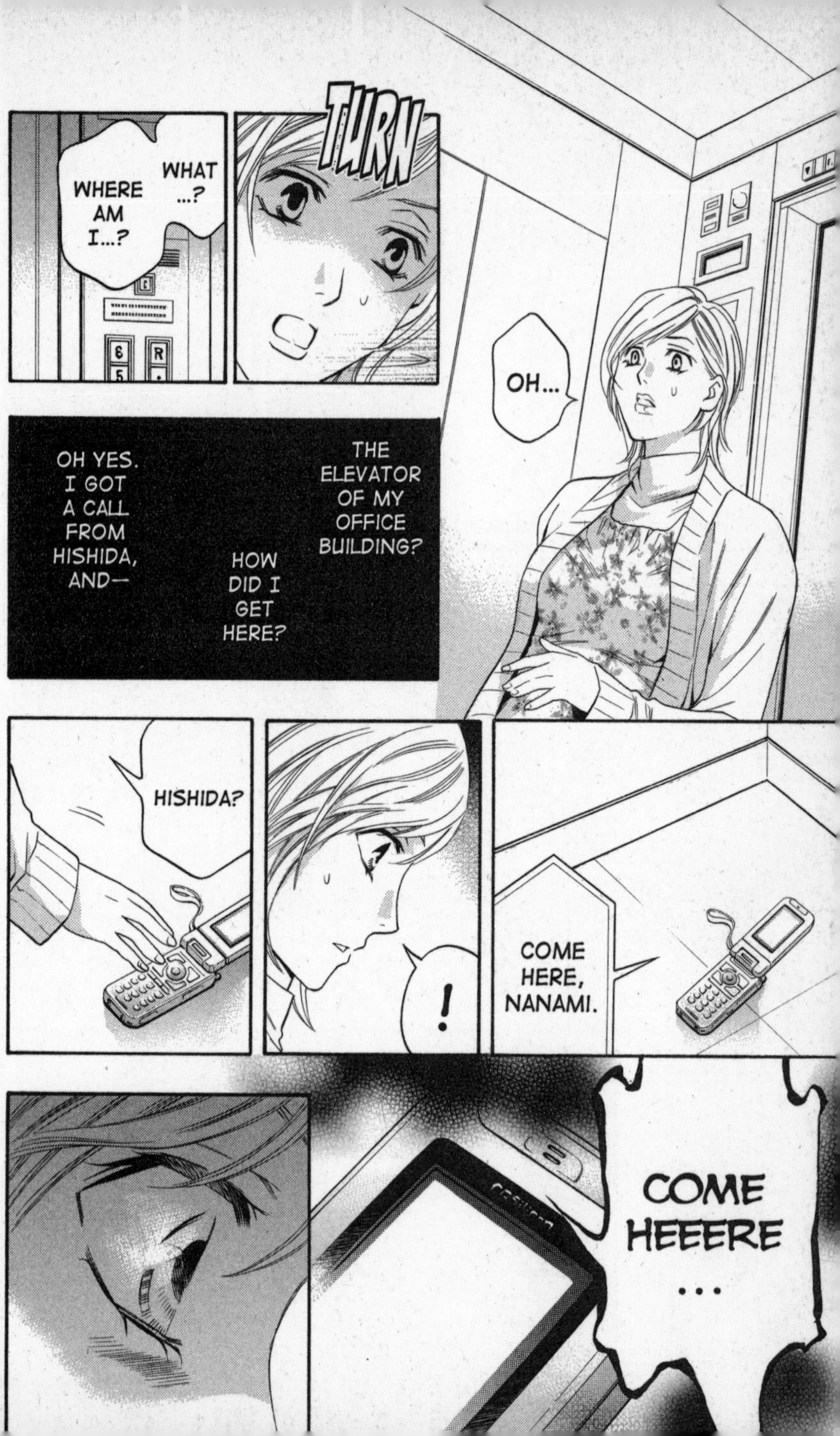
OH...
TURN
WHAT ...?
WHERE AM I...?
THE ELEVATOR OF MY OFFICE BUILDING?
HOW DID I GET HERE?
OH YES. I GOT A CALL FROM HISHIDA, AND—
COME HERE, NANAMI.
!
HISHIDA?
COME HEEERE ...

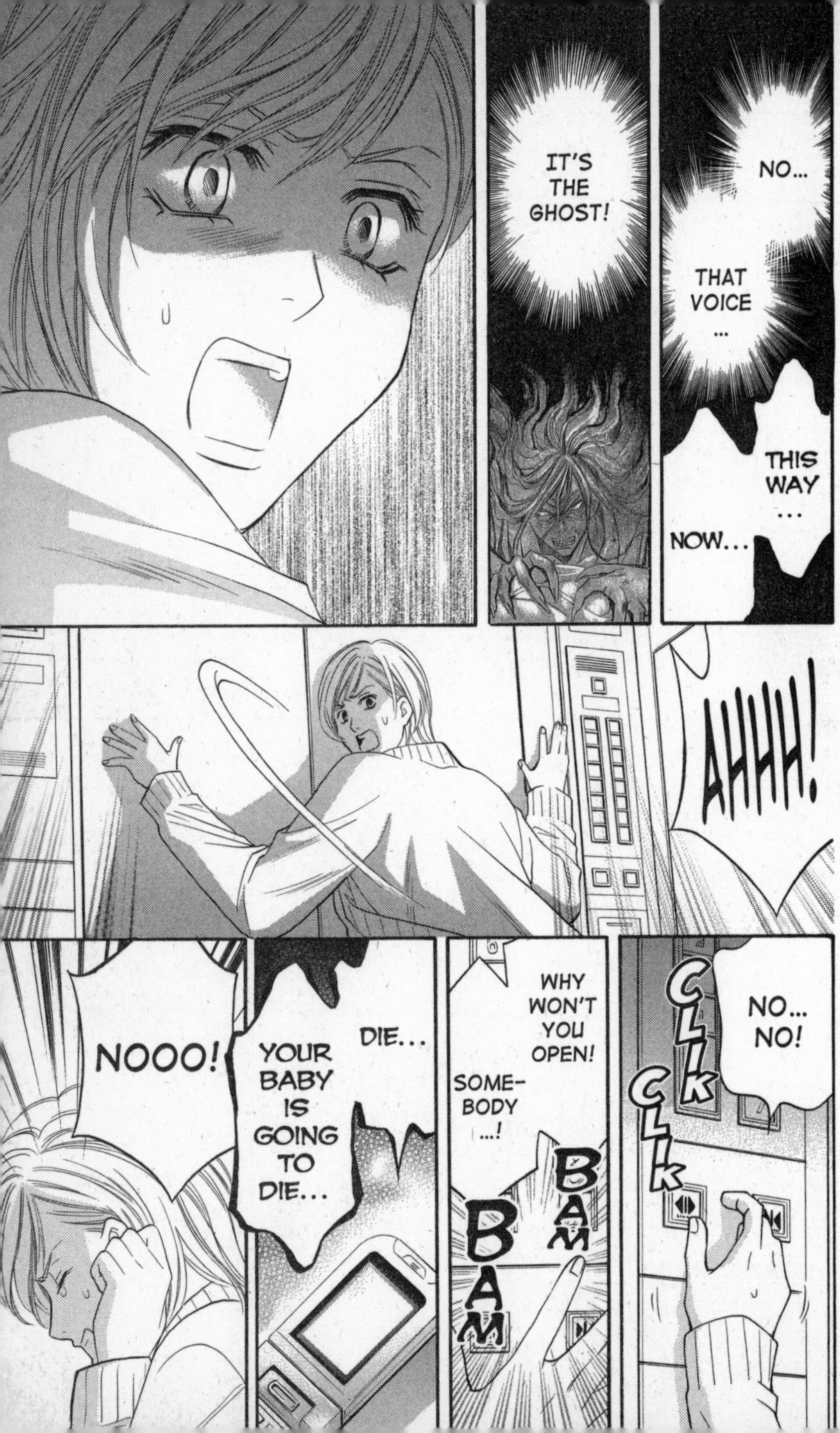
NO...
THAT VOICE ...
THIS WAY ...
NOW...
IT'S THE GHOST!
AHHH!
NO... NO!
CLIK
CLIK
WHY WON'T YOU OPEN!
SOME-BODY ...!
BAM
BAM
DIE...
YOUR BABY IS GOING TO DIE...
NOOO!

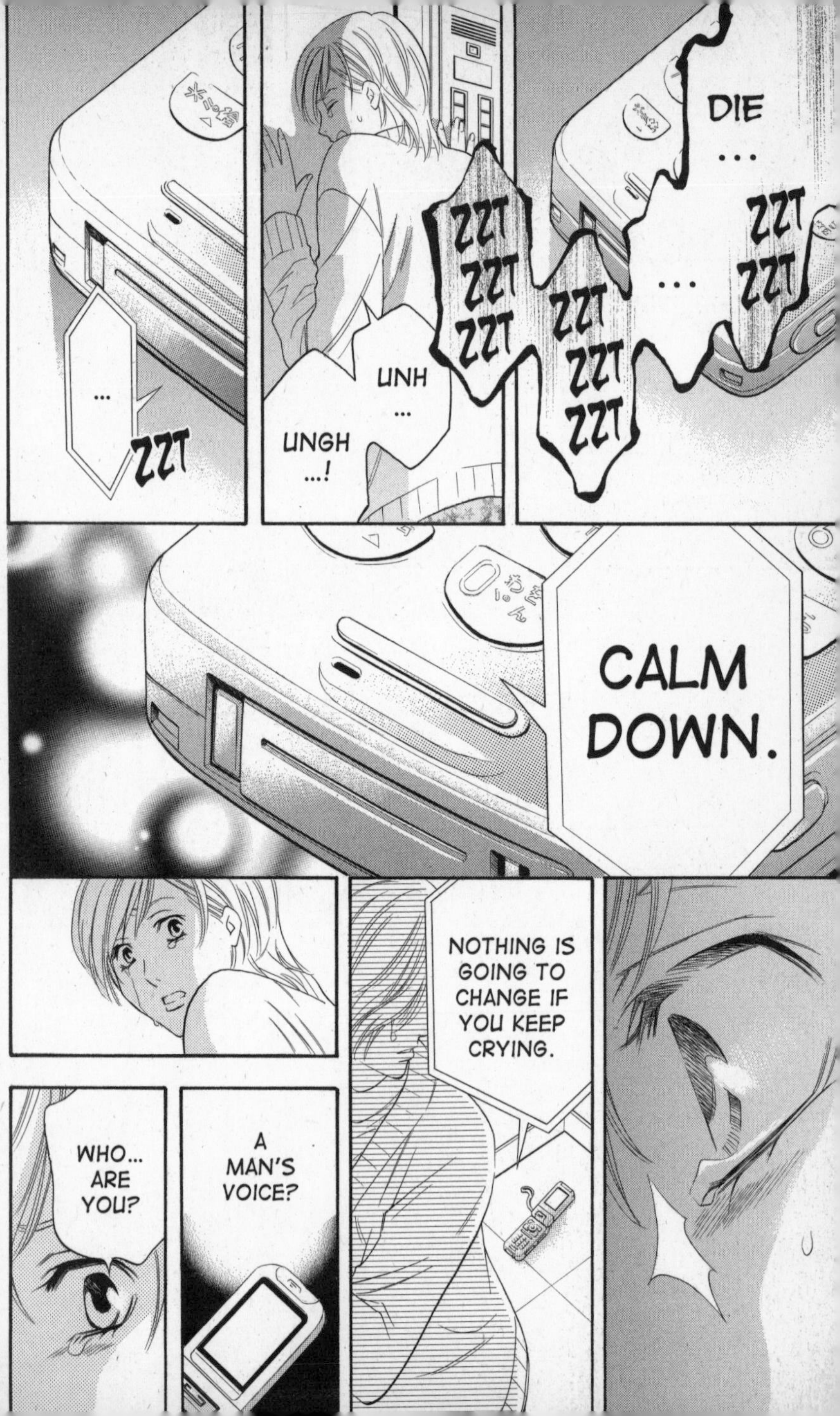
DIE ...
ZZT ZZT
...
ZZT ZZT ZZT
ZZT ZZT ZZT
ZZT ZZT ZZT
UNH ...
UNGH ...!
...
ZZT
CALM DOWN.
NOTHING IS GOING TO CHANGE IF YOU KEEP CRYING.
A MAN'S VOICE?
WHO... ARE YOU?

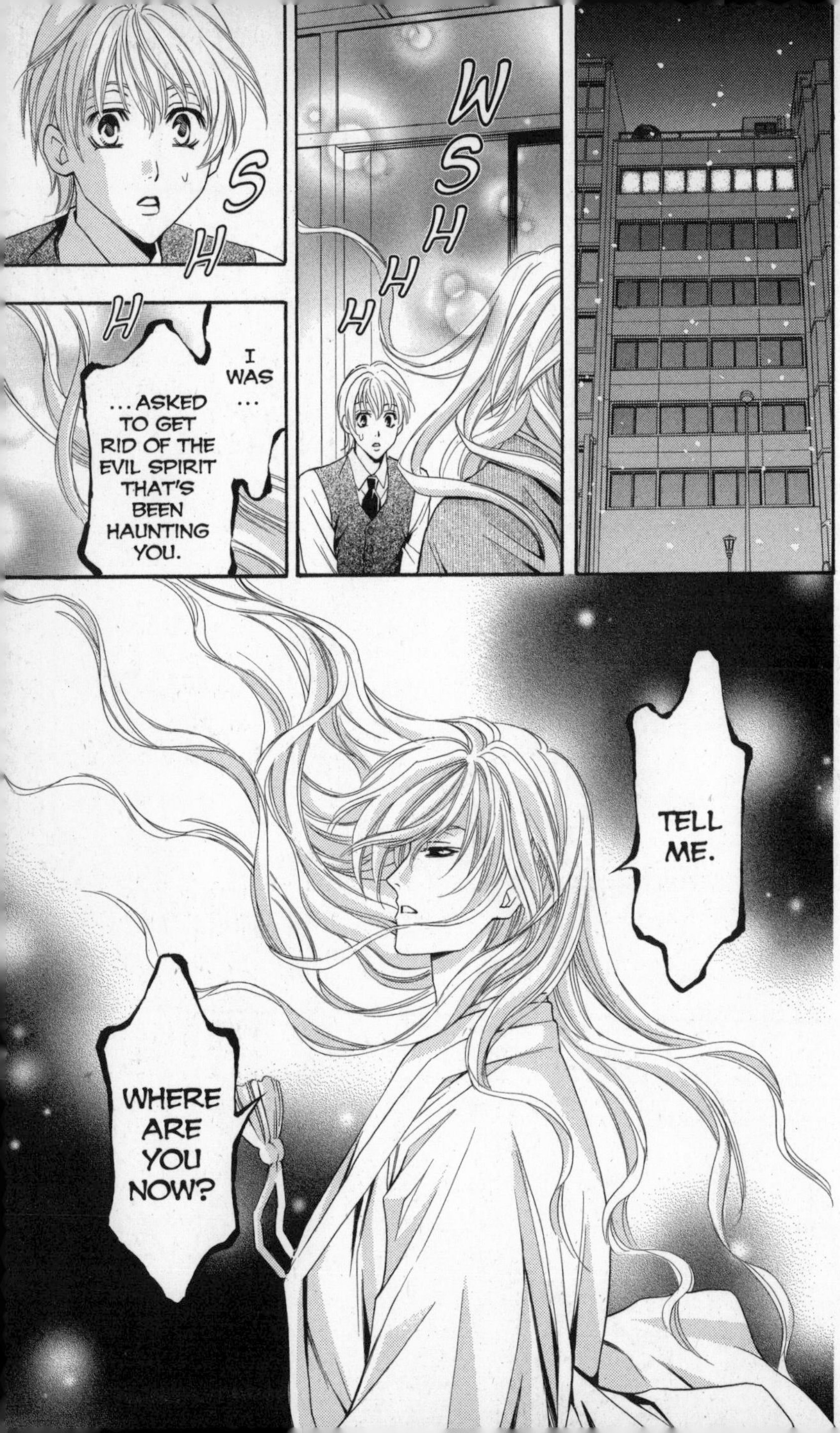
WSHHHH
SHHH
I WAS ...
...ASKED TO GET RID OF THE EVIL SPIRIT THAT'S BEEN HAUNTING YOU.
TELL ME.
WHERE ARE YOU NOW?

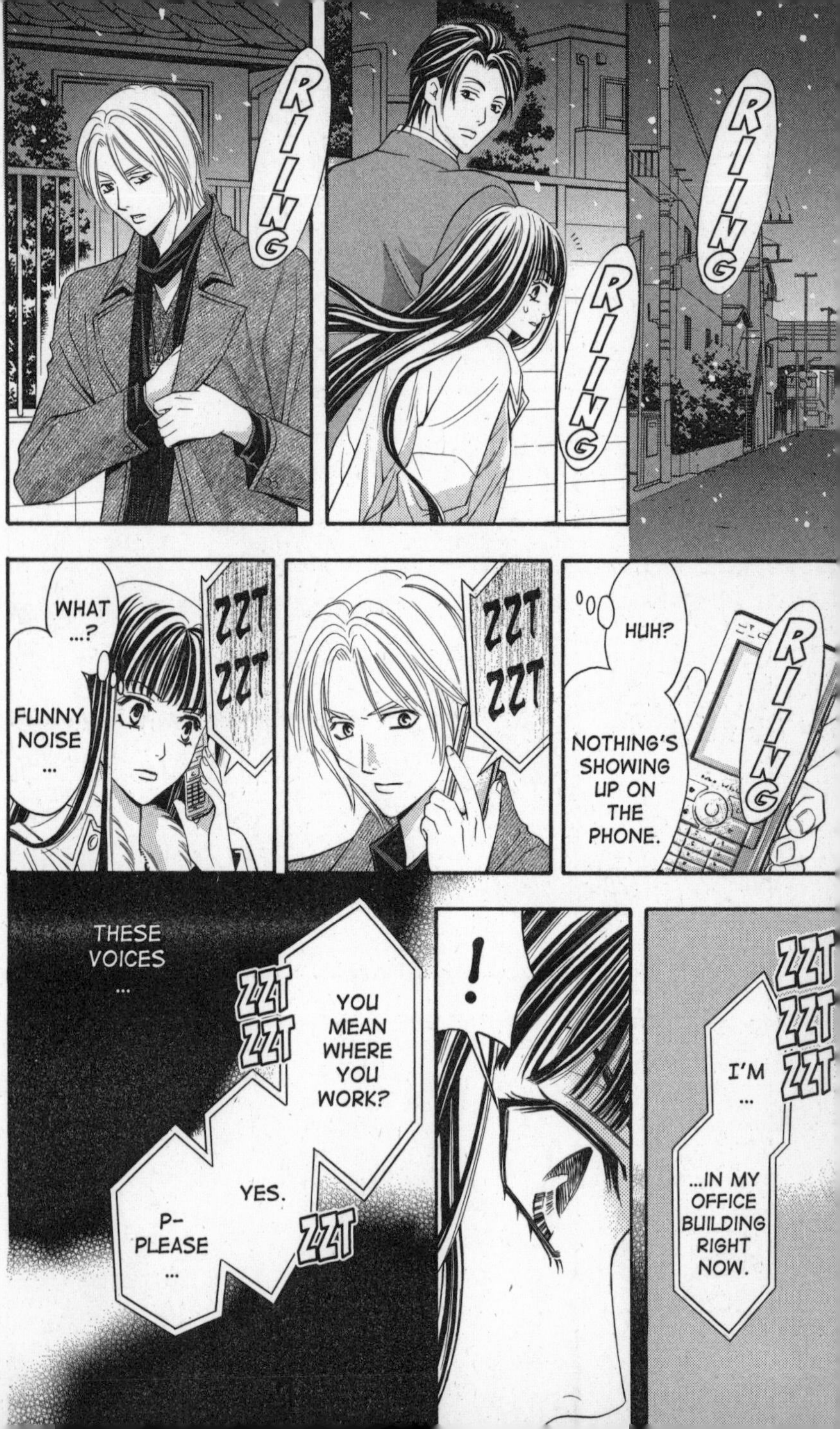
RIIING
RIIING
RIIING
HUH?
NOTHING'S SHOWING UP ON THE PHONE.
RIIING
ZZT ZZT
WHAT ...?
FUNNY NOISE ...
ZZT ZZT
ZZT ZZT ZZT
I'M ...
...IN MY OFFICE BUILDING RIGHT NOW.
!
THESE VOICES ...
ZZT ZZT
YOU MEAN WHERE YOU WORK?
YES.
P-PLEASE ...
ZZT

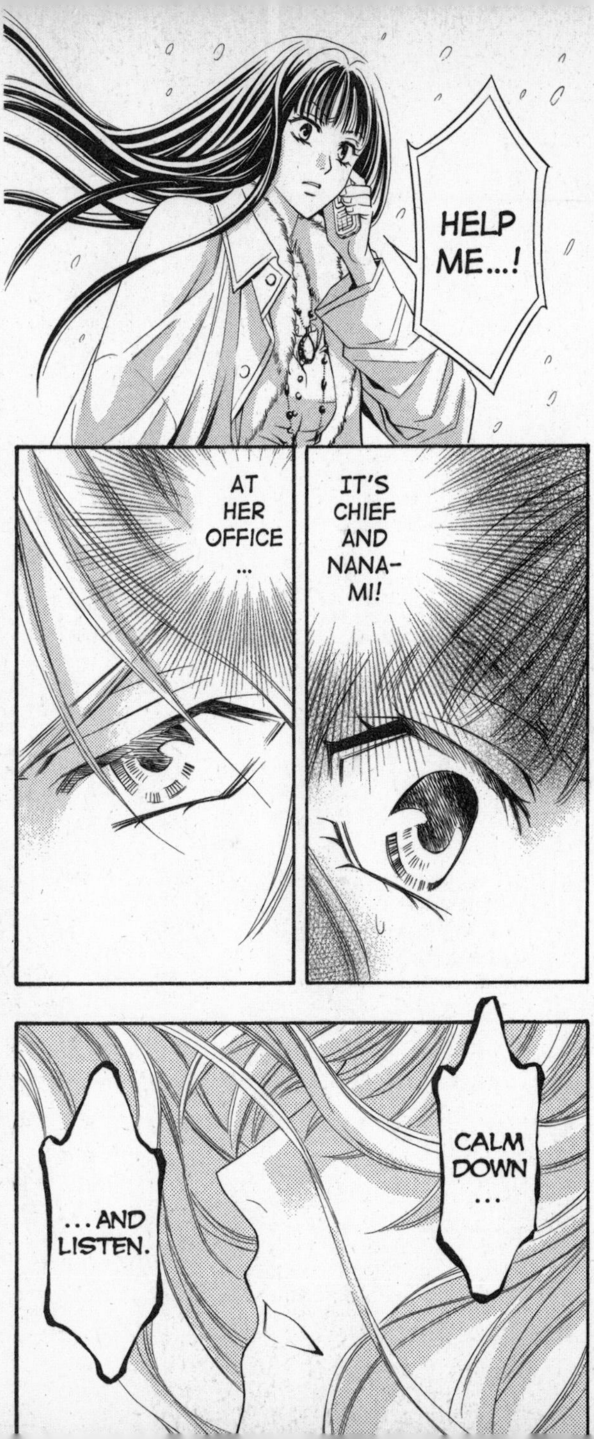
HELP ME...!
IT'S CHIEF AND NANAMI!
AT HER OFFICE...
CALM DOWN...
...AND LISTEN.

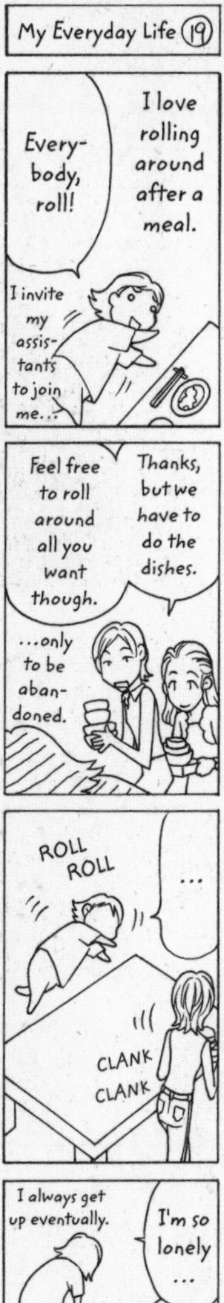
My Everyday Life 19
I love rolling around after a meal.
Everybody, roll!
I invite my assistants to join me...
Thanks, but we have to do the dishes.
Feel free to roll around all you want though.
...only to be abandoned.
...
ROLL ROLL
CLANK CLANK
I'm so lonely...
I always get up eventually.
WIPE
Really? Well, please don't mind us.
WIPE

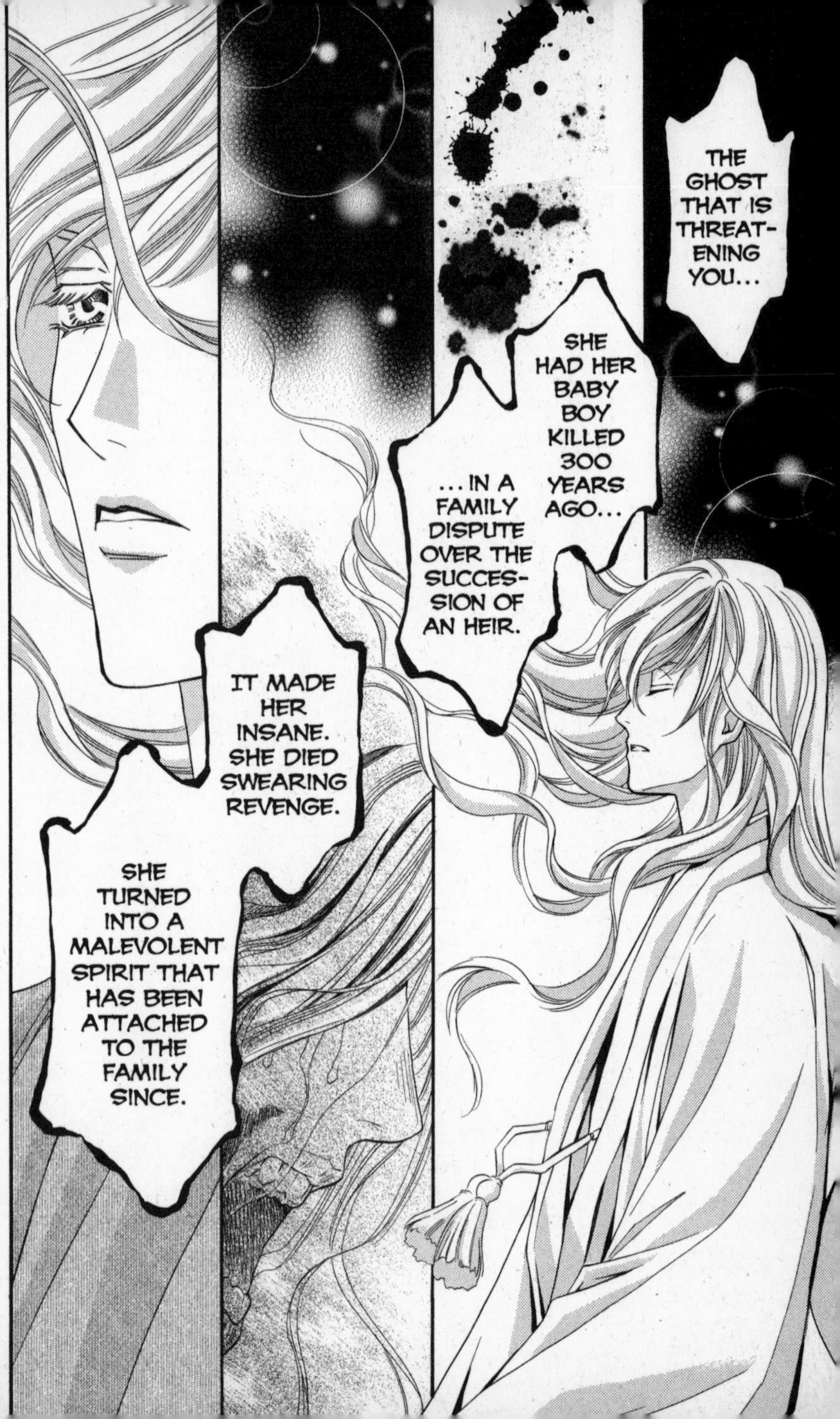
THE GHOST THAT IS THREAT-ENING YOU...
SHE HAD HER BABY BOY KILLED 300 YEARS AGO...
...IN A FAMILY DISPUTE OVER THE SUCCES-SION OF AN HEIR.
IT MADE HER INSANE. SHE DIED SWEARING REVENGE.
SHE TURNED INTO A MALEVOLENT SPIRIT THAT HAS BEEN ATTACHED TO THE FAMILY SINCE.

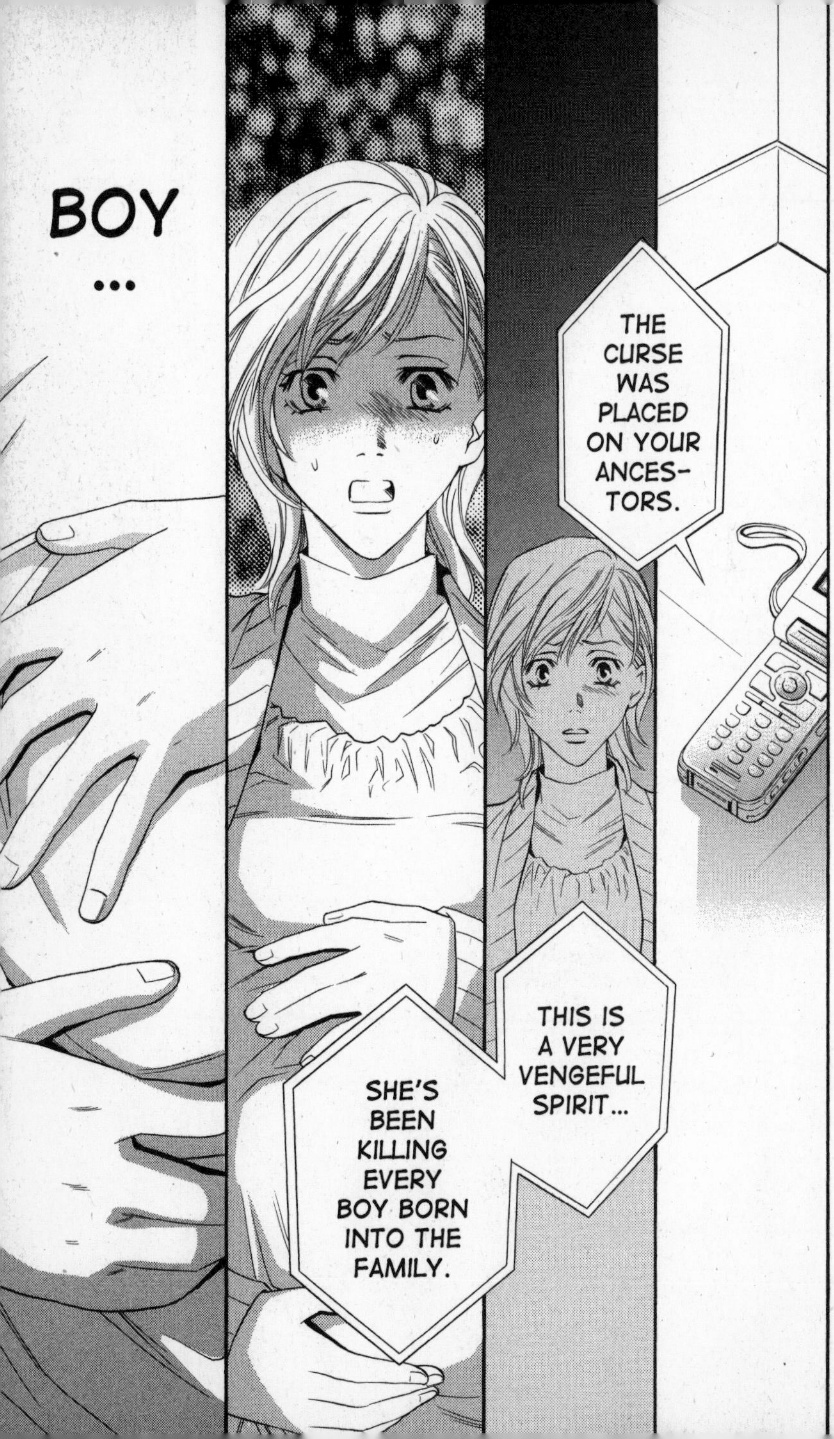
THE CURSE WAS PLACED ON YOUR ANCES-TORS.
THIS IS A VERY VENGEFUL SPIRIT...
SHE'S BEEN KILLING EVERY BOY BORN INTO THE FAMILY.
BOY ...

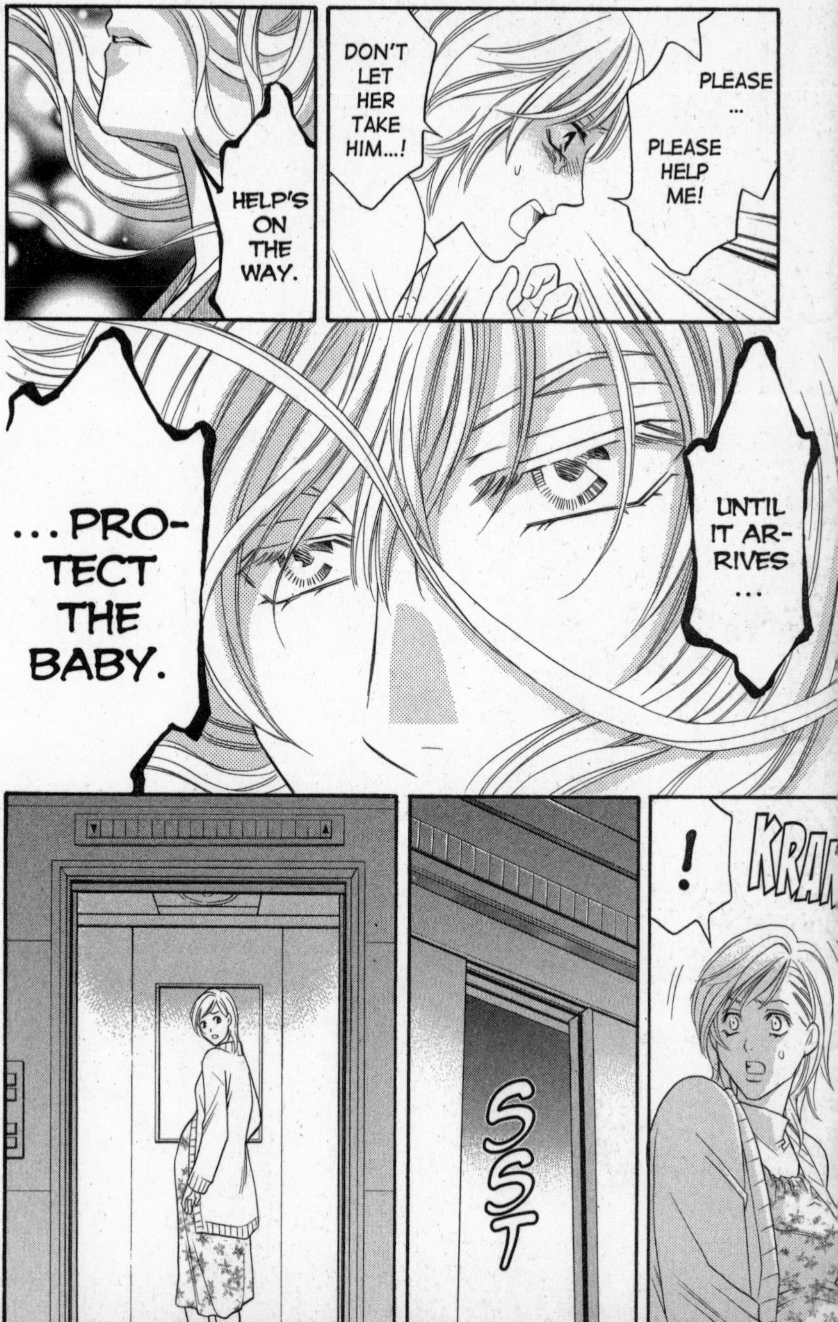
PLEASE ...
PLEASE HELP ME!
DON'T LET HER TAKE HIM...!
HELP'S ON THE WAY.
UNTIL IT ARRIVES ...
...PROTECT THE BABY.
KRAN
!
SSST

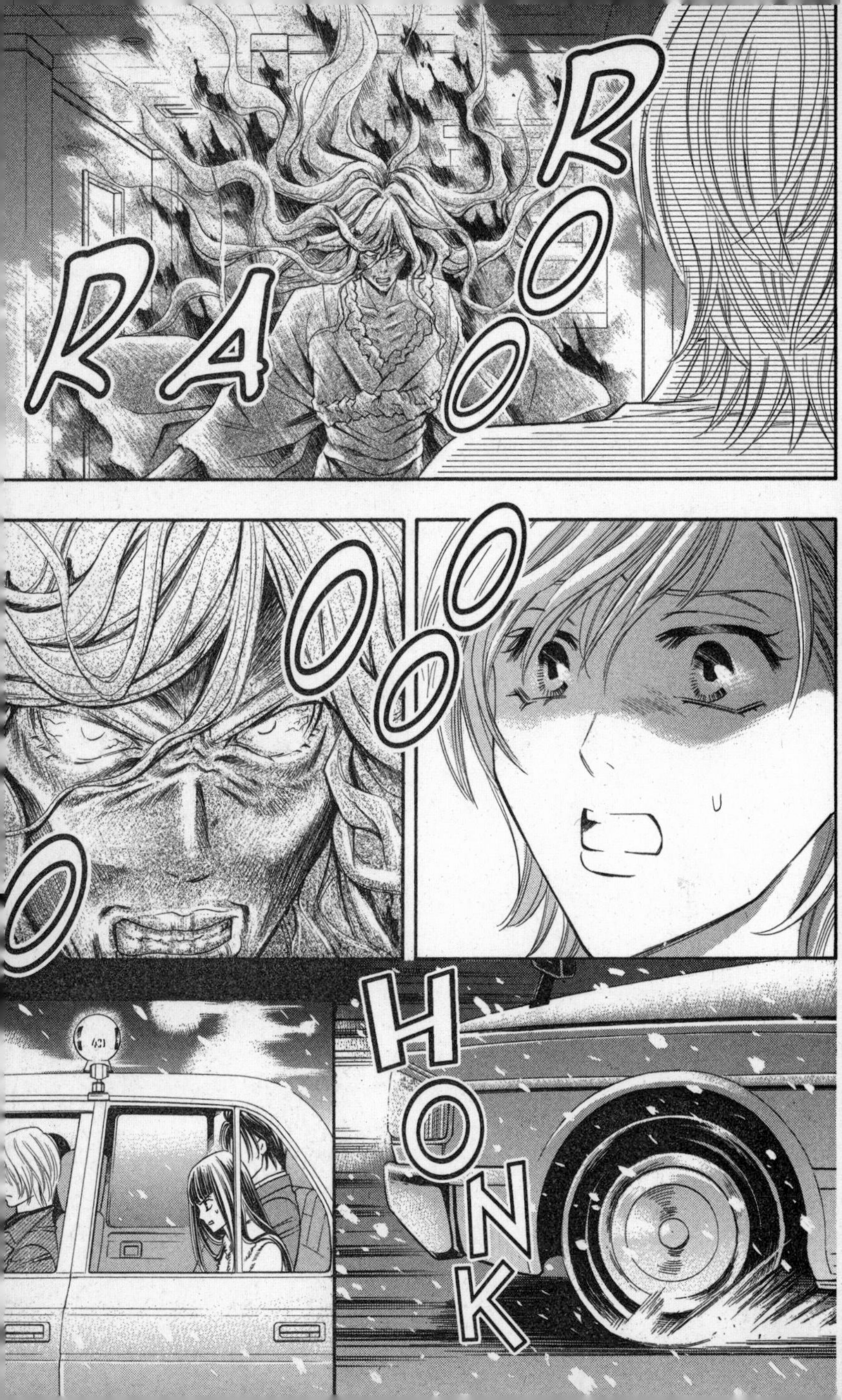
ROOOAR
OOOOOO
HONK

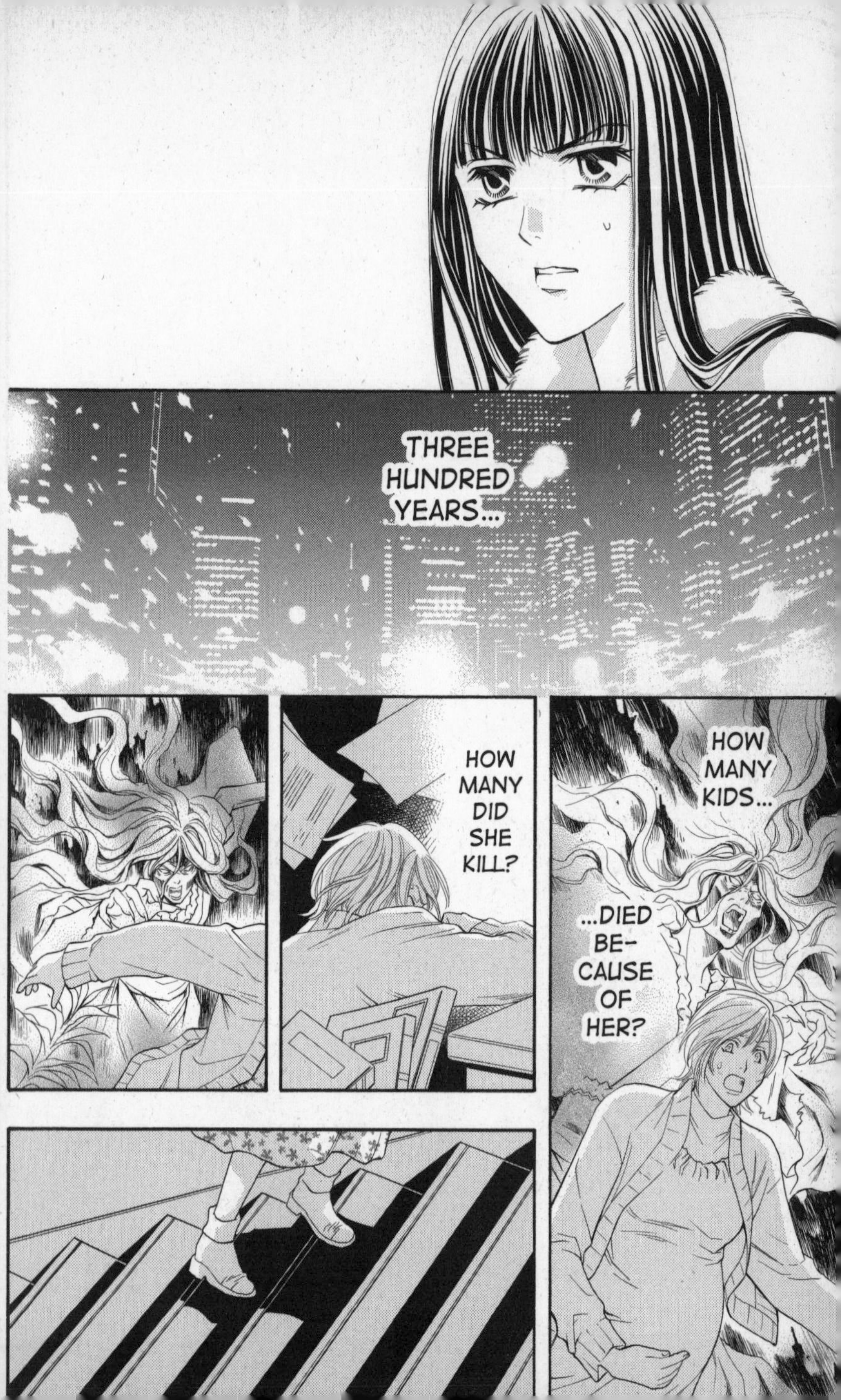
THREE HUNDRED YEARS...
HOW MANY KIDS...
...DIED BE-CAUSE OF HER?
HOW MANY DID SHE KILL?

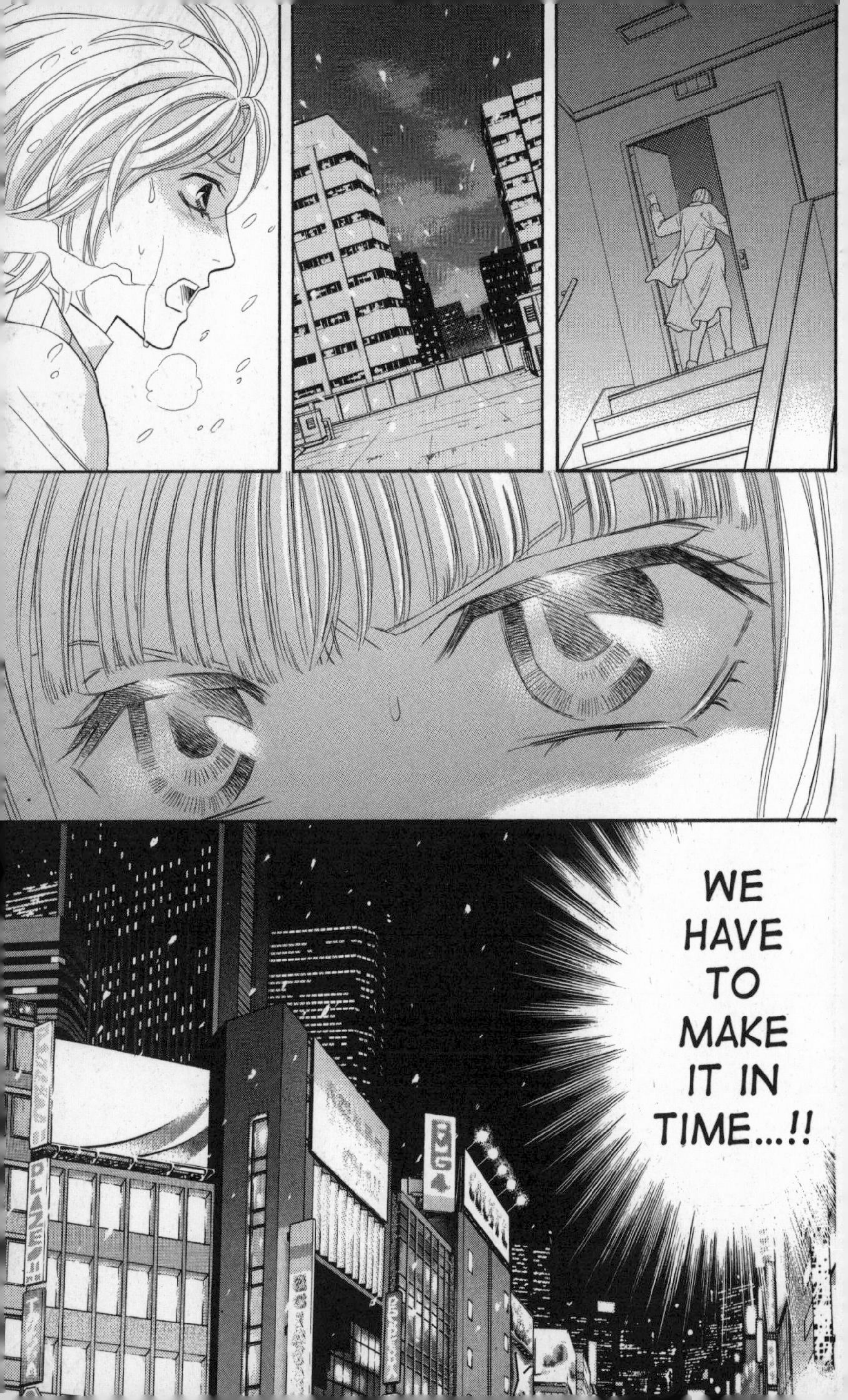
WE HAVE TO MAKE IT IN TIME...!!

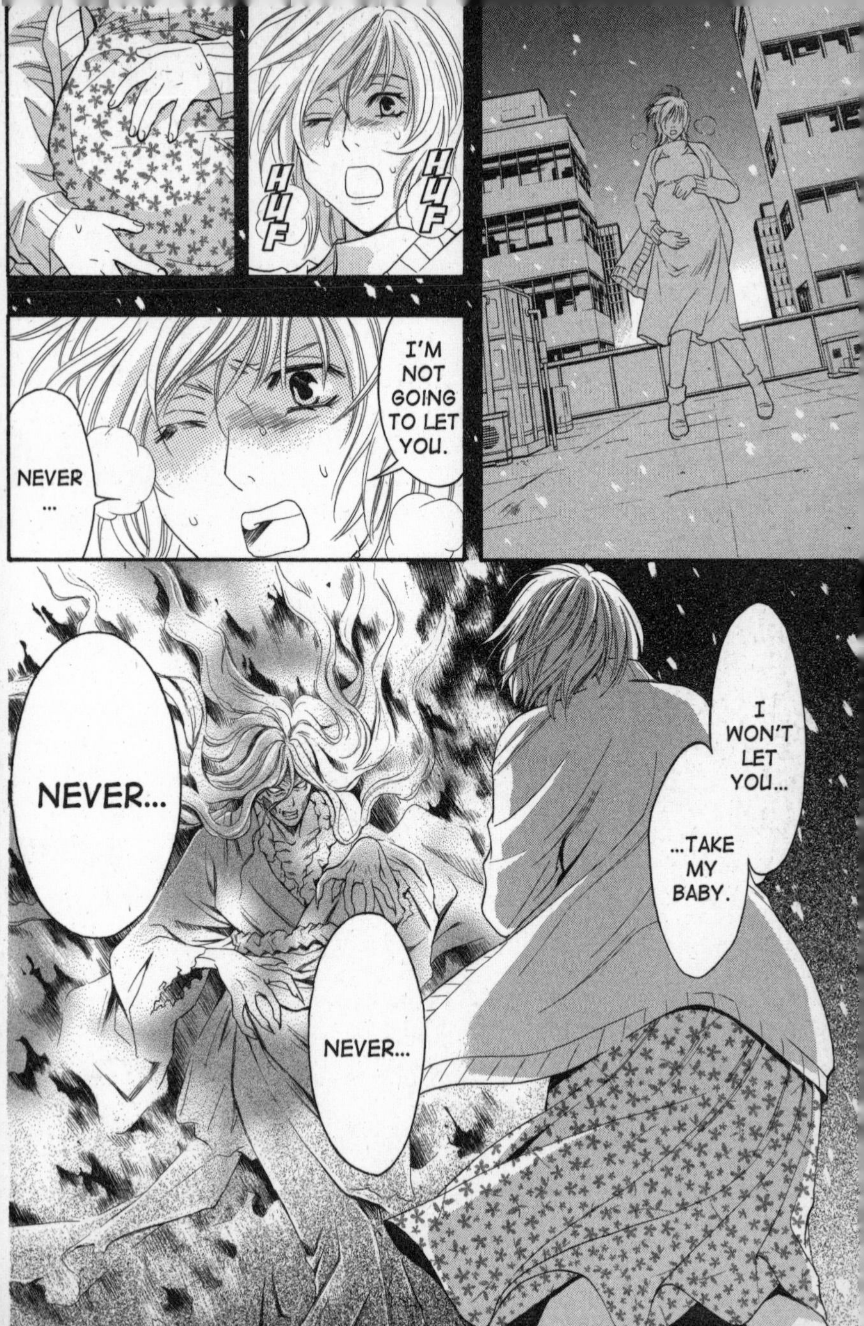
HUF
HUF
I'M NOT GOING TO LET YOU.
NEVER ...
I WON'T LET YOU...
...TAKE MY BABY.
NEVER...
NEVER...

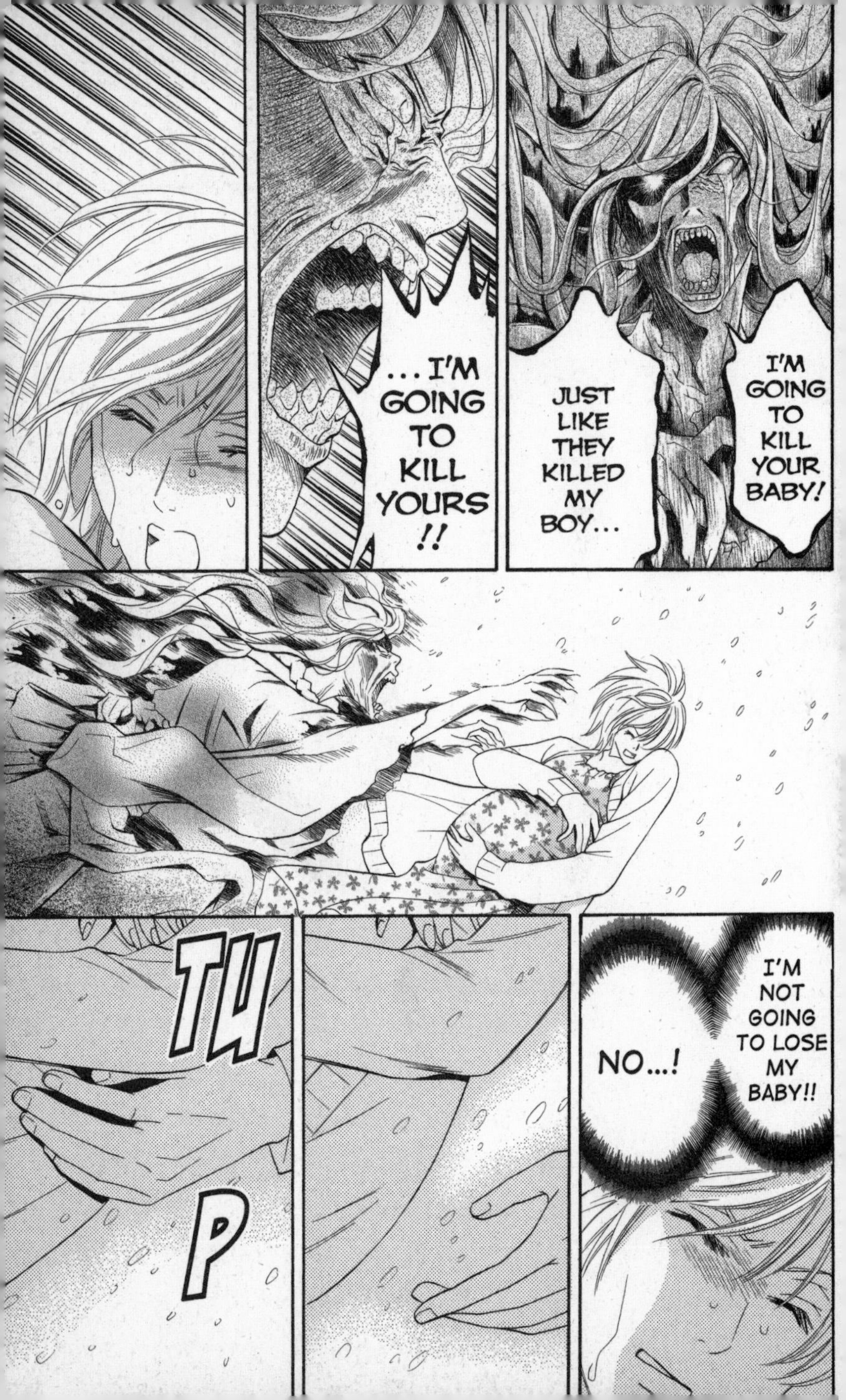
I'M GOING TO KILL YOUR BABY!
JUST LIKE THEY KILLED MY BOY…
…I'M GOING TO KILL YOURS!!
I'M NOT GOING TO LOSE MY BABY!!
NO…!
TU P

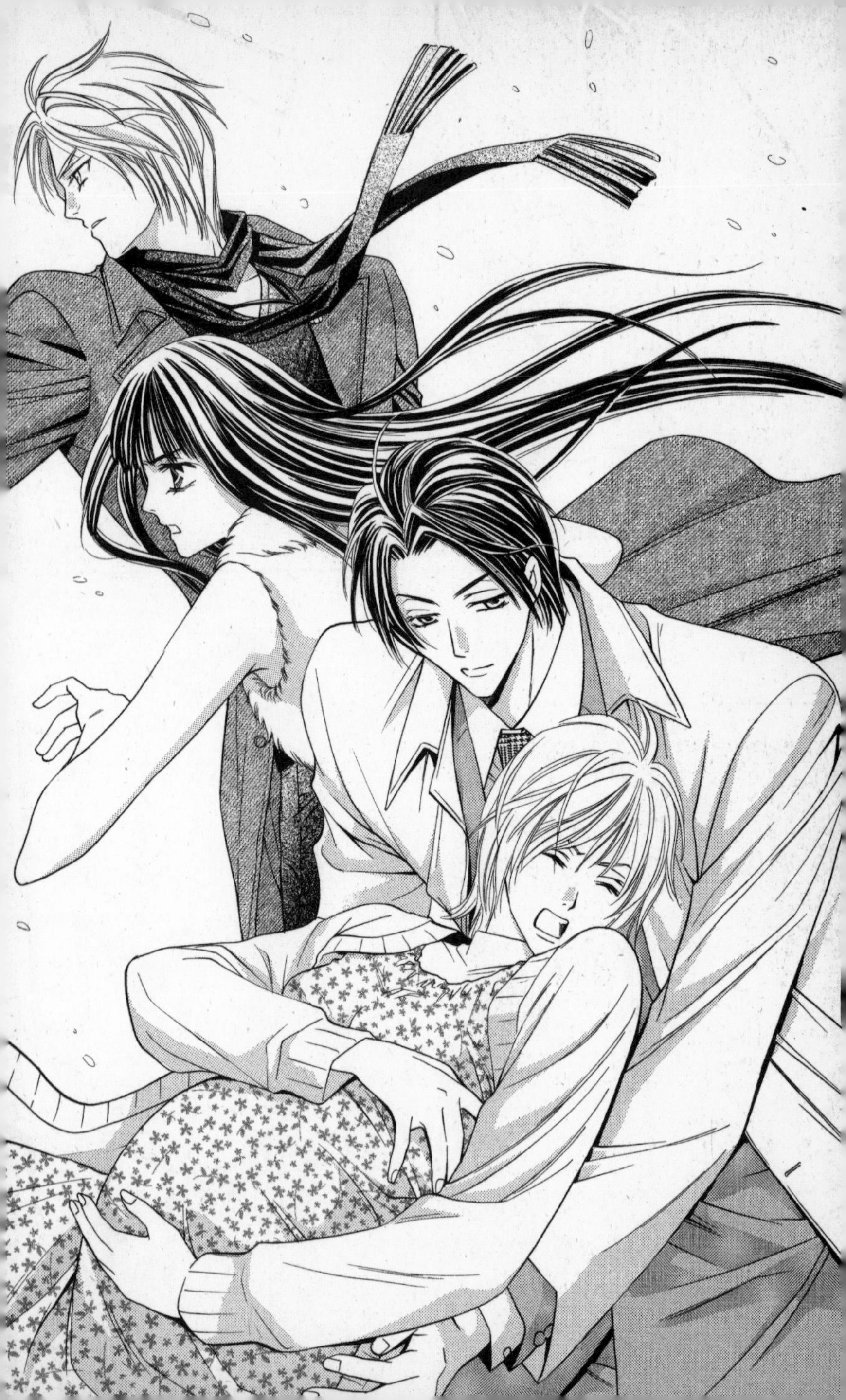

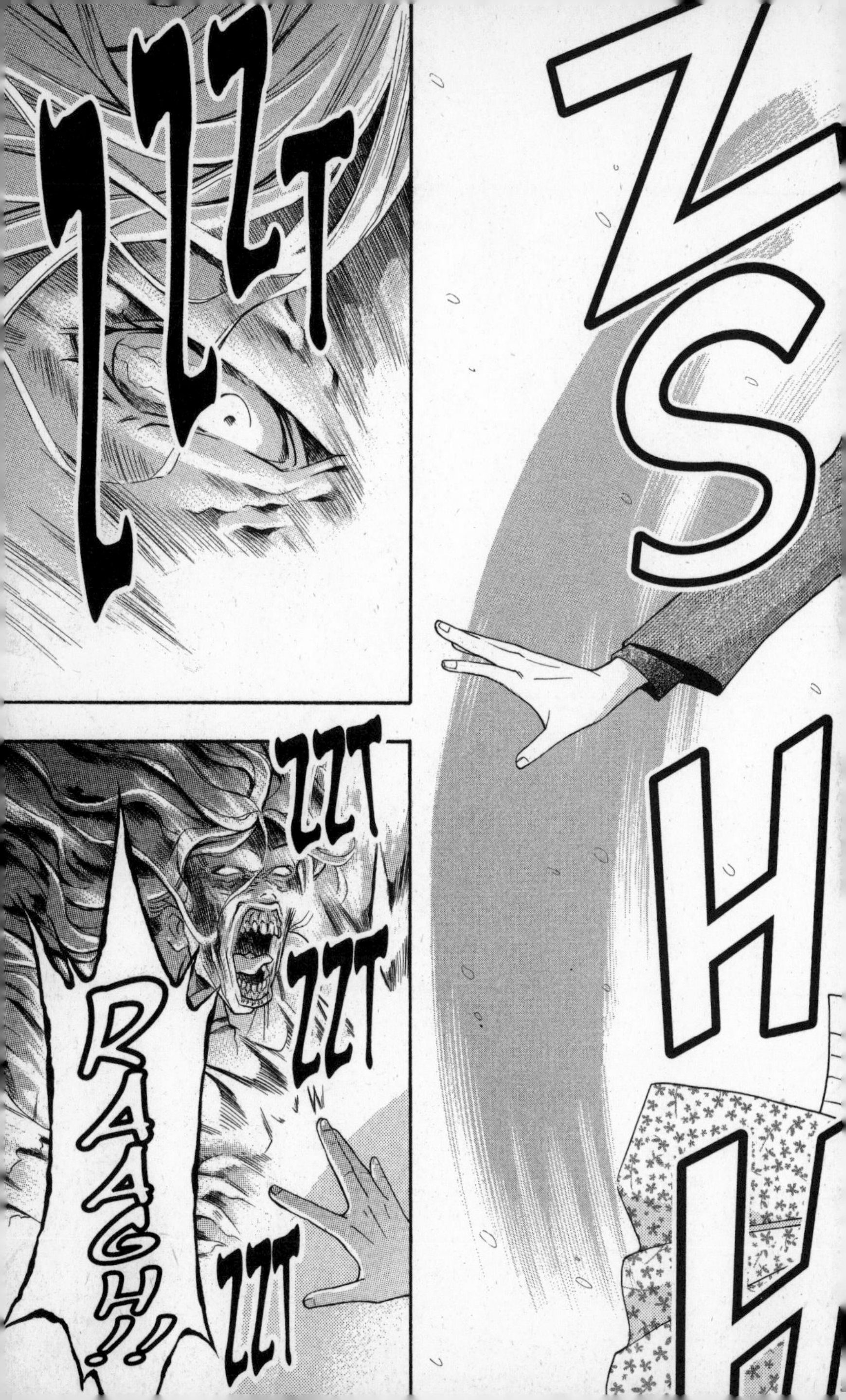
ZSHH
ZZZT
ZZT
ZZT
ZZT
RAAGH!!

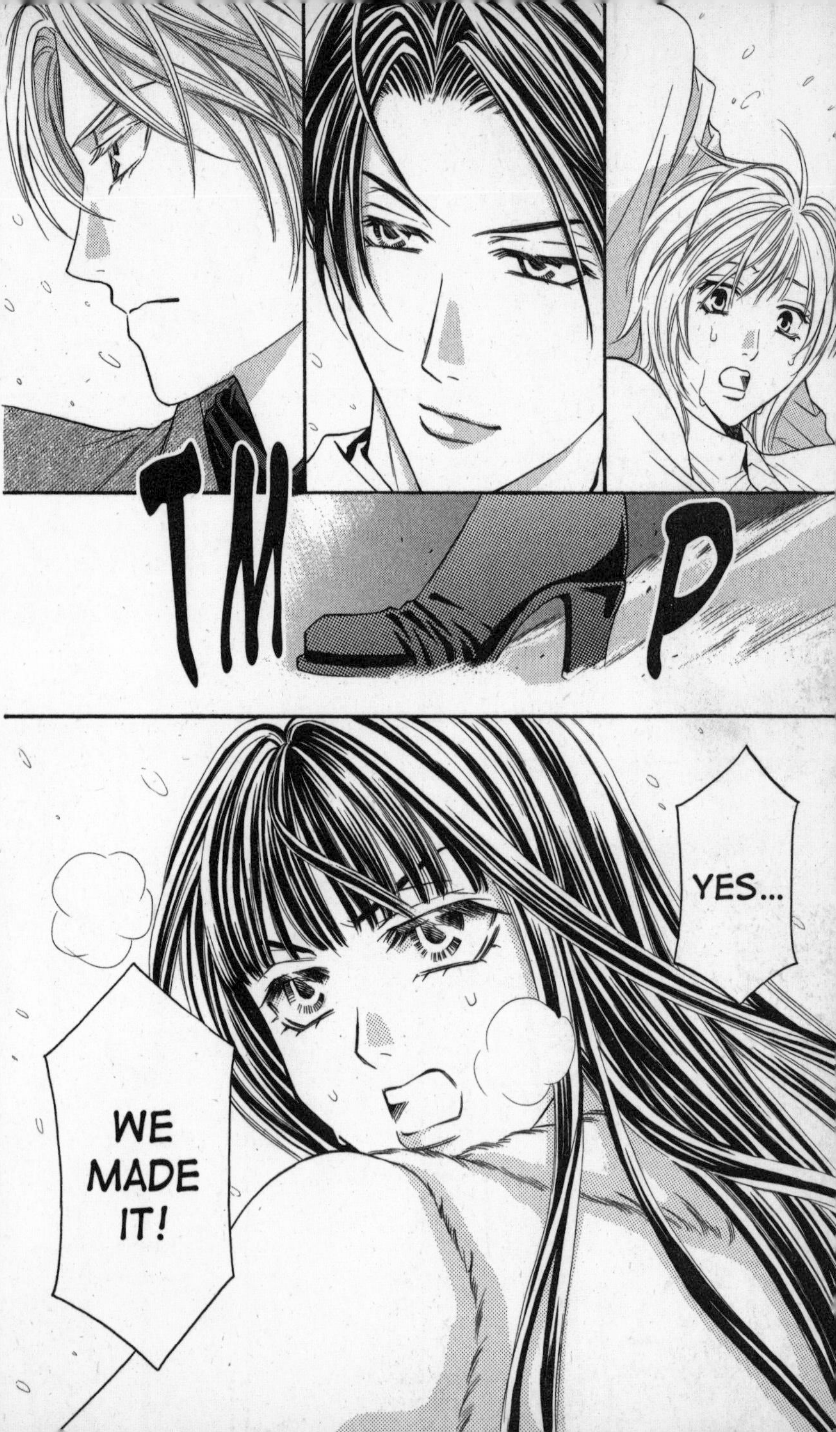
TMP
YES...
WE MADE IT!

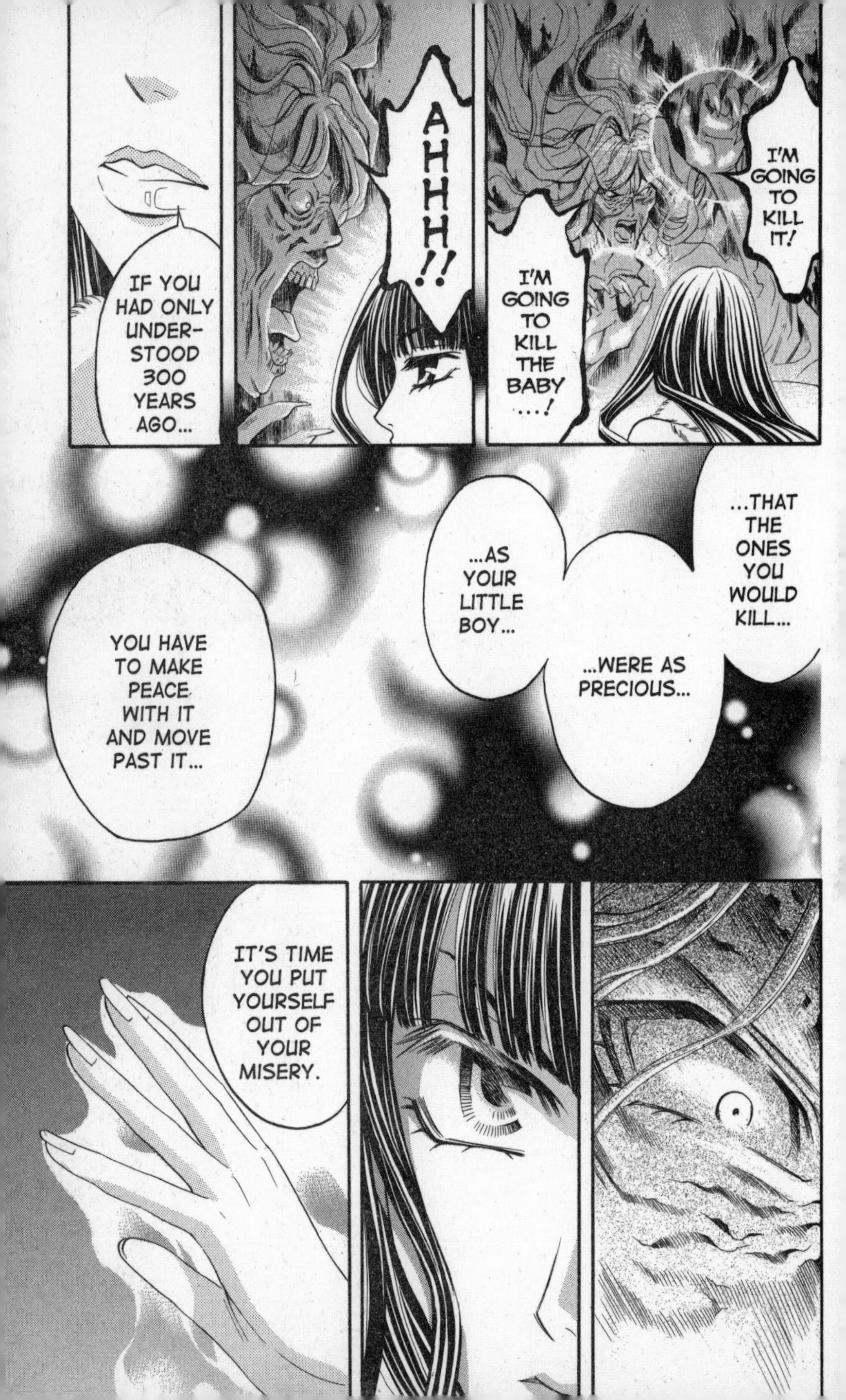
I'M GOING TO KILL IT!
I'M GOING TO KILL THE BABY...!
AHHH!!
IF YOU HAD ONLY UNDER-STOOD 300 YEARS AGO...
...THAT THE ONES YOU WOULD KILL...
...WERE AS PRECIOUS...
...AS YOUR LITTLE BOY...
YOU HAVE TO MAKE PEACE WITH IT AND MOVE PAST IT...
IT'S TIME YOU PUT YOURSELF OUT OF YOUR MISERY.

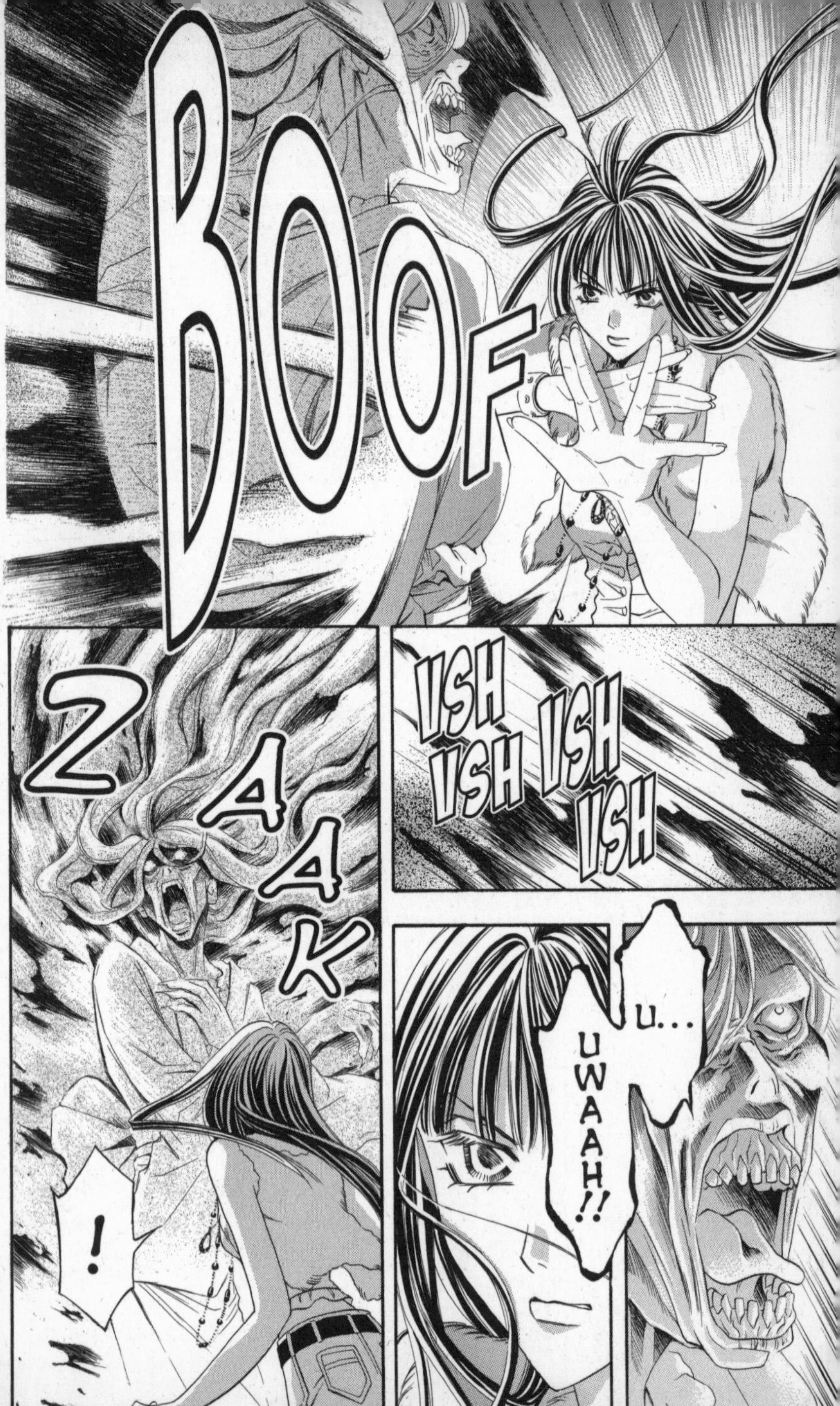
BOOF
VSH VSH VSH VSH
ZAAK
!
U...
UWAAH!!

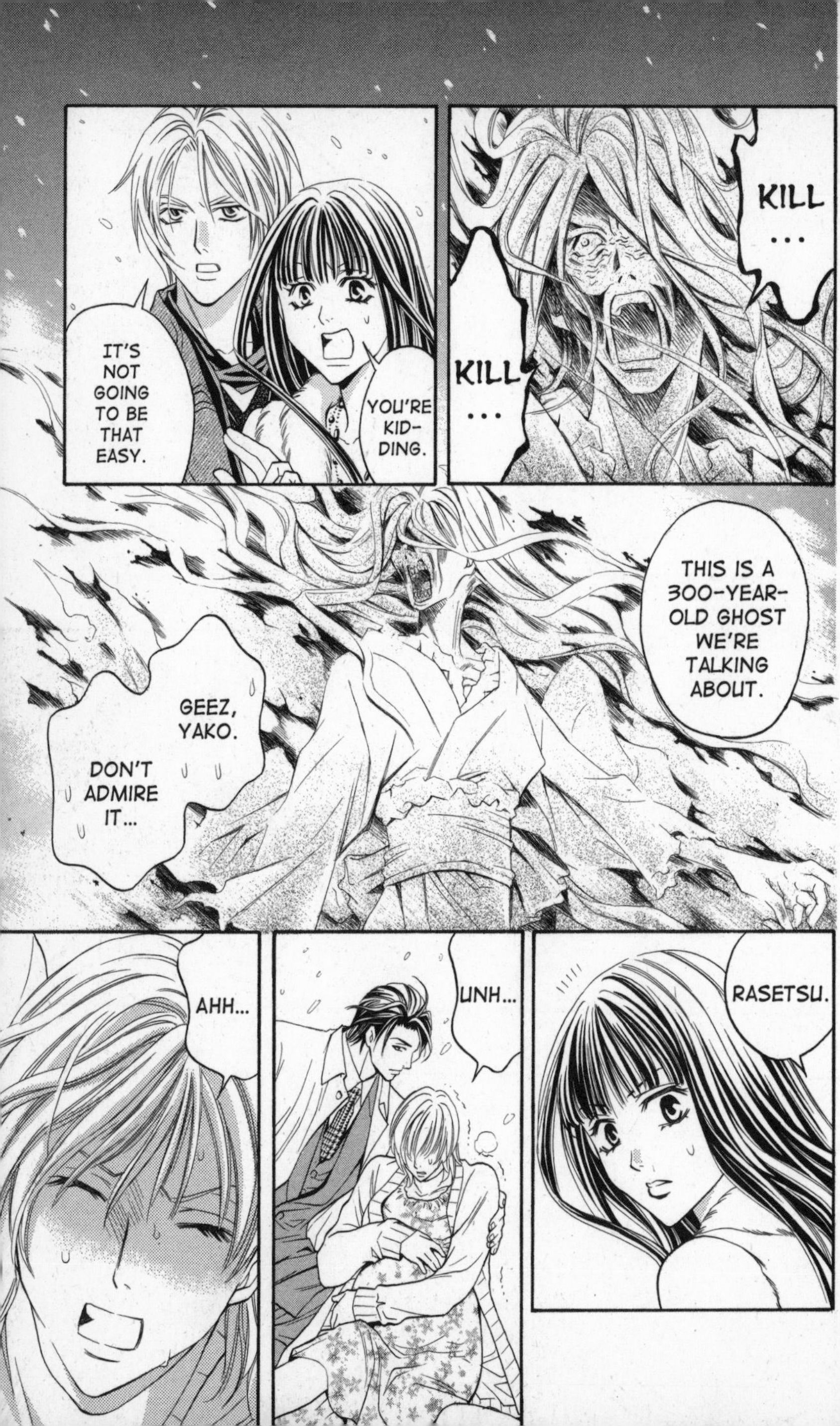
KILL …
KILL …
YOU'RE KID-DING.
IT'S NOT GOING TO BE THAT EASY.
THIS IS A 300-YEAR-OLD GHOST WE'RE TALKING ABOUT.
GEEZ, YAKO.
DON'T ADMIRE IT...
RASETSU.
UNH...
AHH...

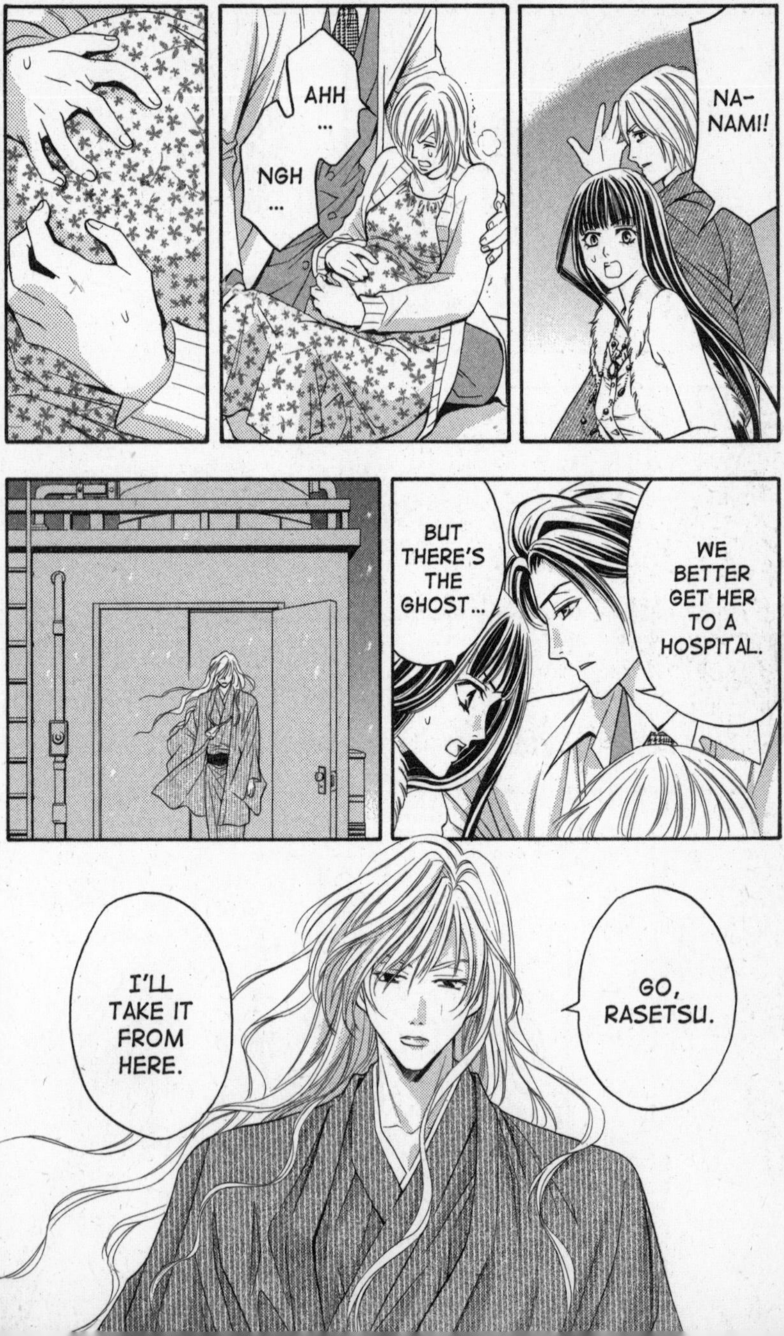
NA-NAMI!
AHH...
NGH...
WE BETTER GET HER TO A HOSPITAL.
BUT THERE'S THE GHOST...
GO, RASETSU.
I'LL TAKE IT FROM HERE.

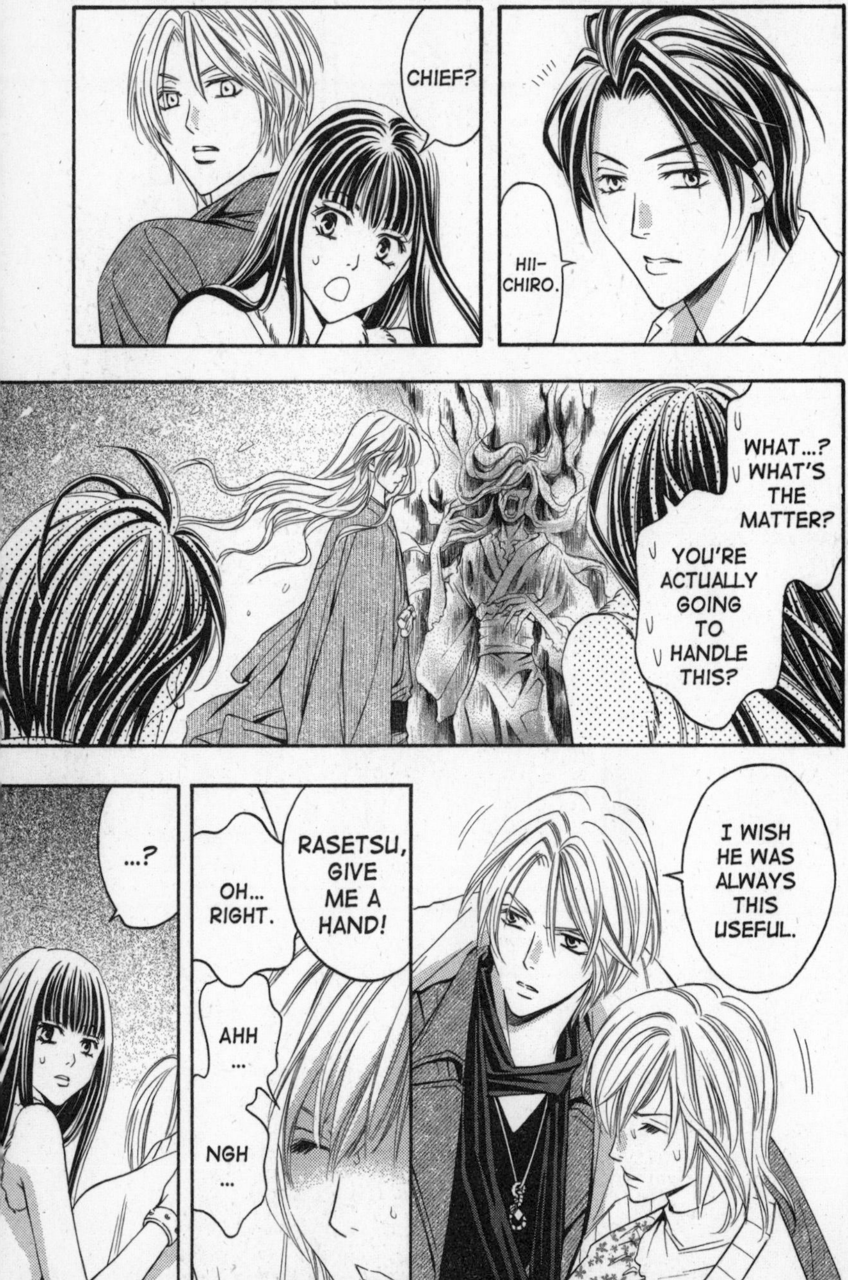
HII-CHIRO.
CHIEF?
WHAT...? WHAT'S THE MATTER?
YOU'RE ACTUALLY GOING TO HANDLE THIS?
I WISH HE WAS ALWAYS THIS USEFUL.
RASETSU, GIVE ME A HAND!
OH... RIGHT.
AHH ...
NGH ...
...?

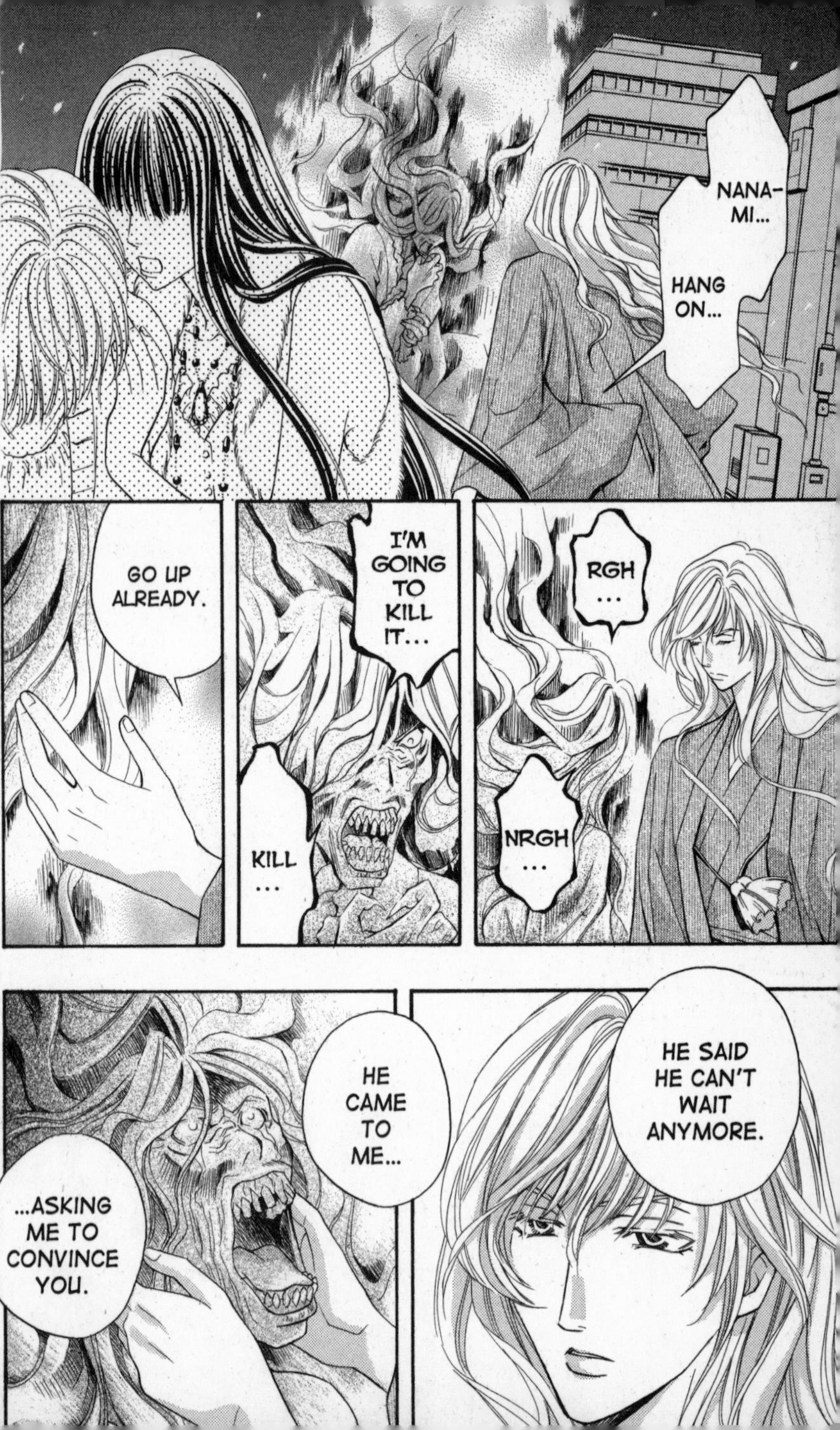
NANA-MI...
HANG ON...
RGH...
NRGH...
I'M GOING TO KILL IT...
KILL...
GO UP ALREADY.
HE SAID HE CAN'T WAIT ANYMORE.
HE CAME TO ME...
...ASKING ME TO CONVINCE YOU.

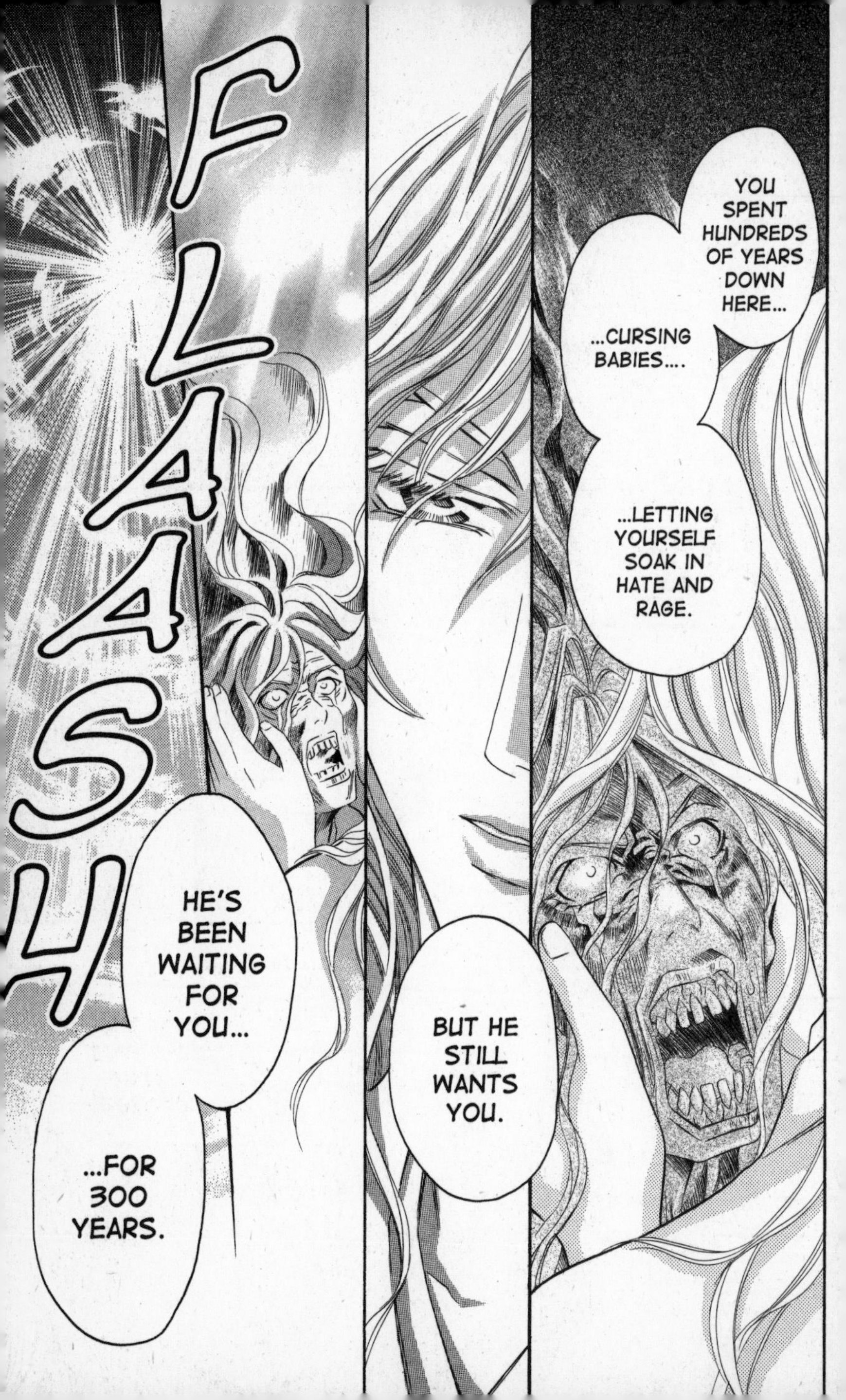
YOU SPENT HUNDREDS OF YEARS DOWN HERE...
...CURSING BABIES....
...LETTING YOURSELF SOAK IN HATE AND RAGE.
BUT HE STILL WANTS YOU.
FLAASH
HE'S BEEN WAITING FOR YOU...
...FOR 300 YEARS.

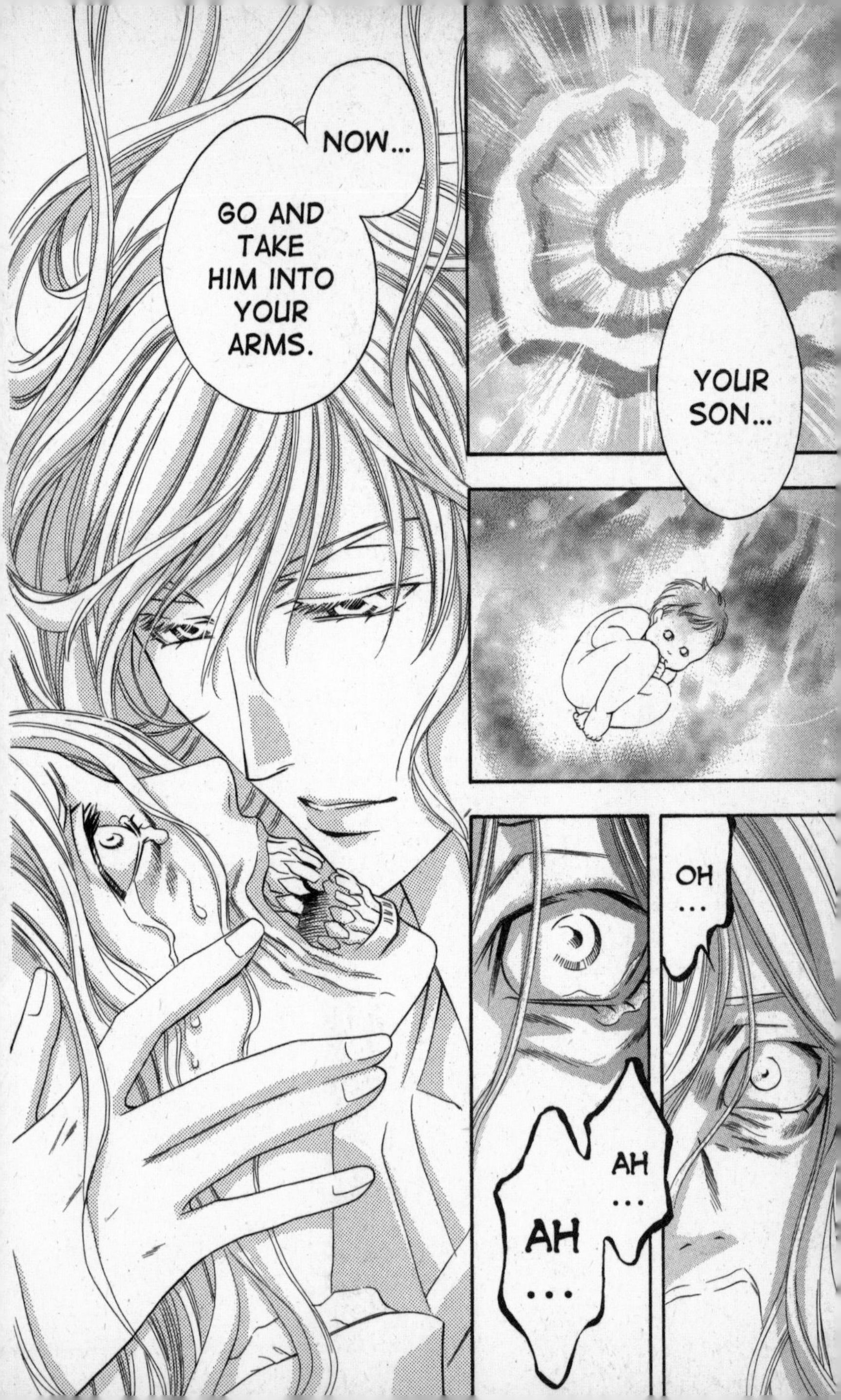
YOUR SON...
OH...
AH... AH...
NOW...
GO AND TAKE HIM INTO YOUR ARMS.

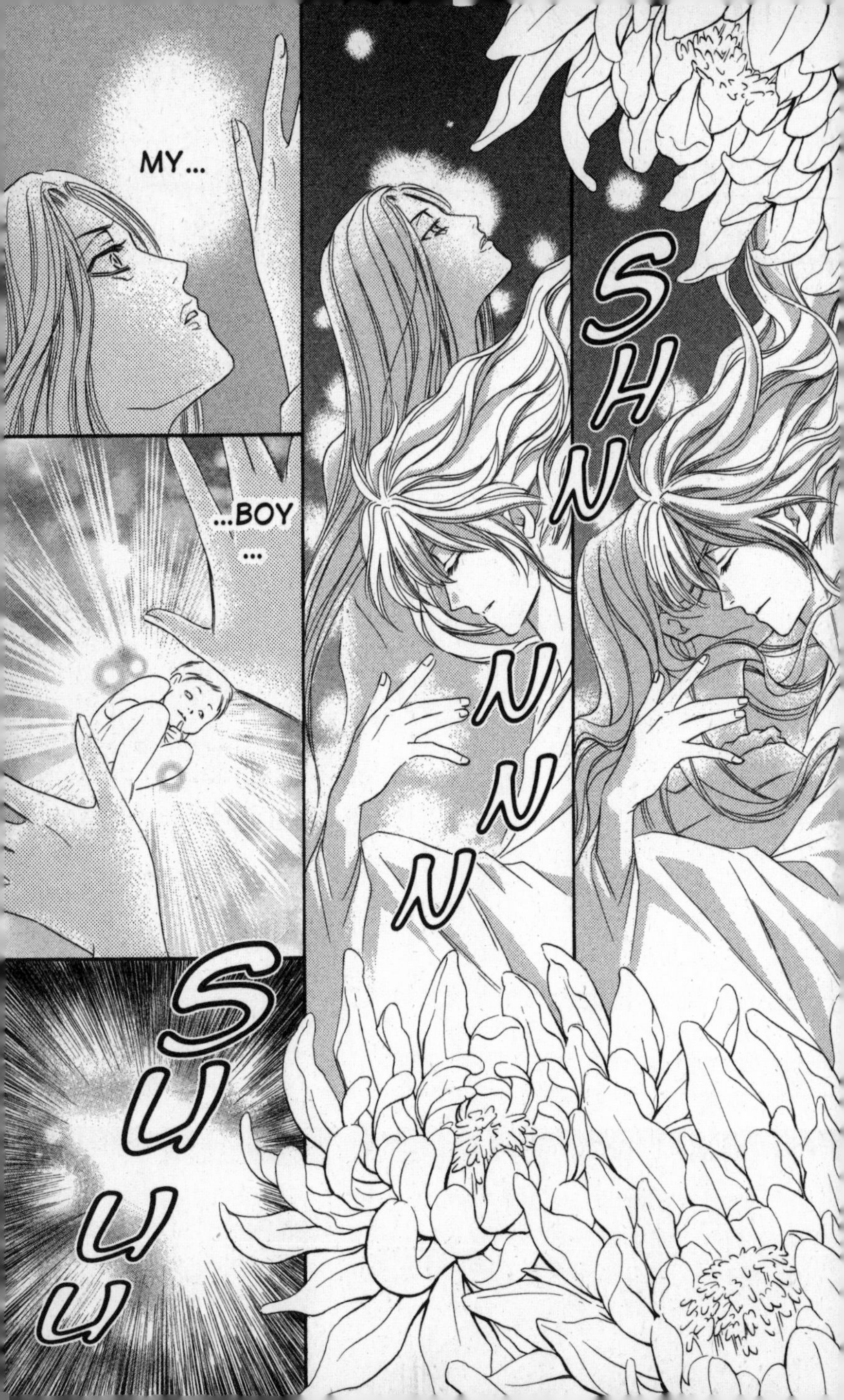
SHNNNN
MY...
...BOY
...
SUUU

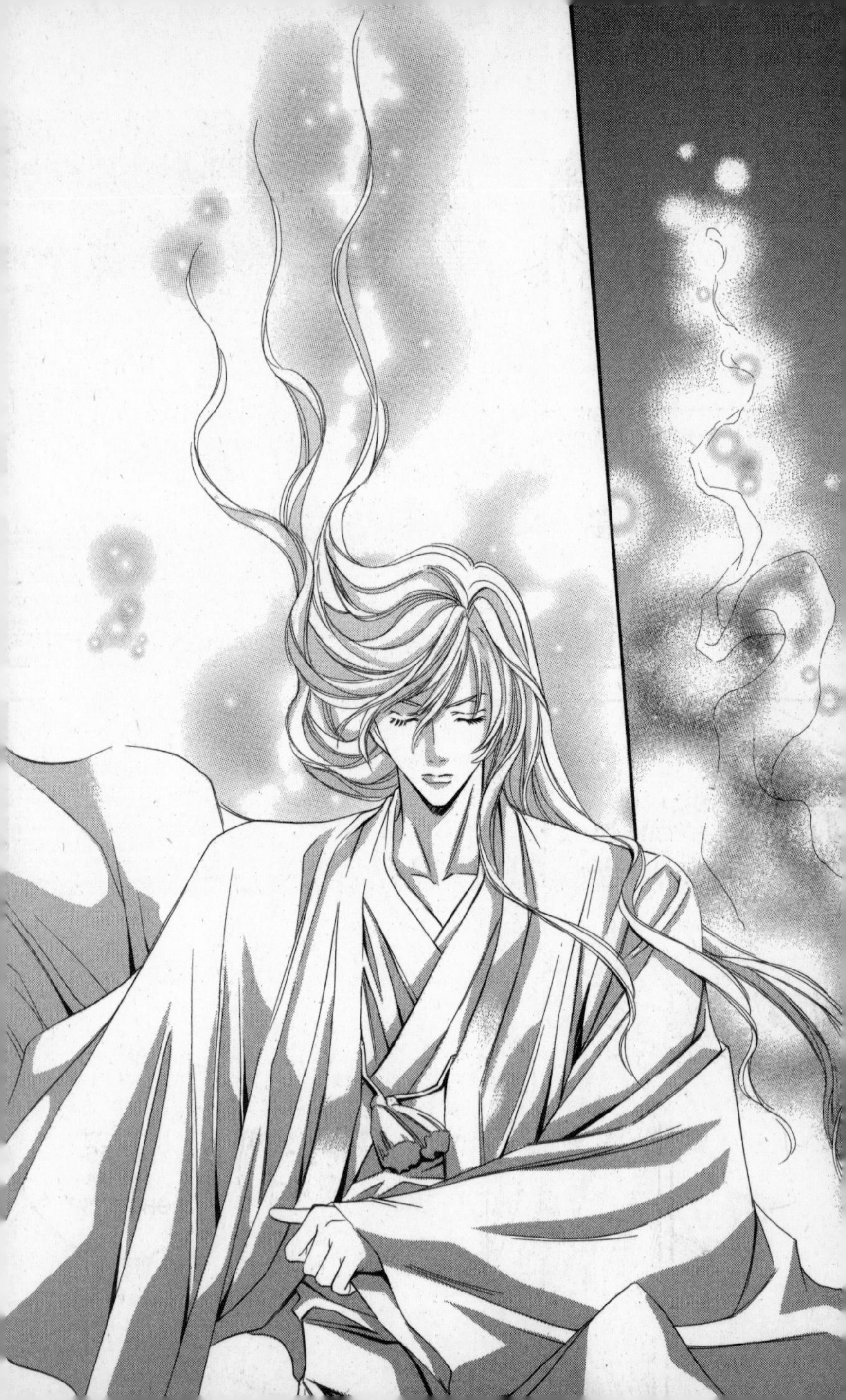

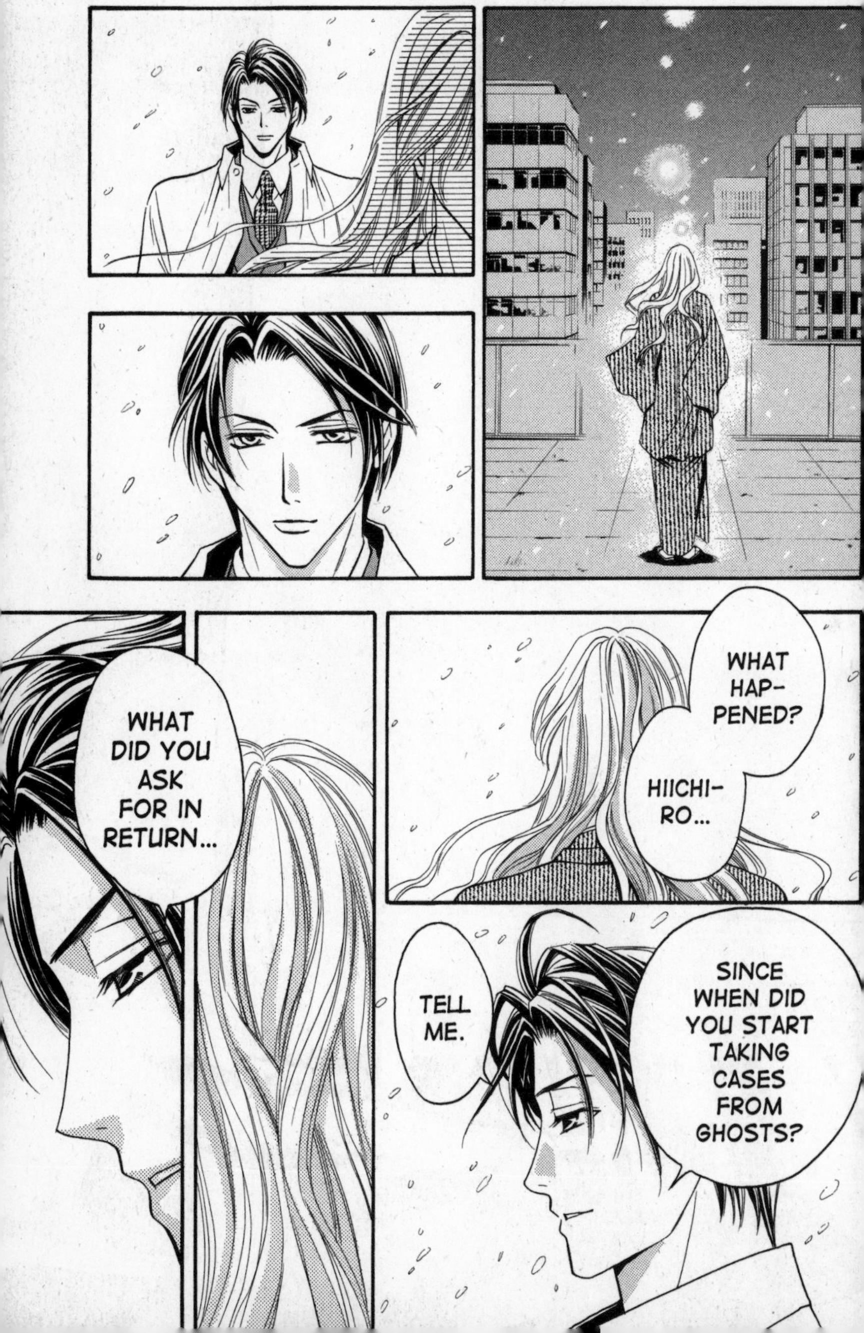
WHAT HAPPENED?
HIICHIRO...
SINCE WHEN DID YOU START TAKING CASES FROM GHOSTS?
TELL ME.
WHAT DID YOU ASK FOR IN RETURN...

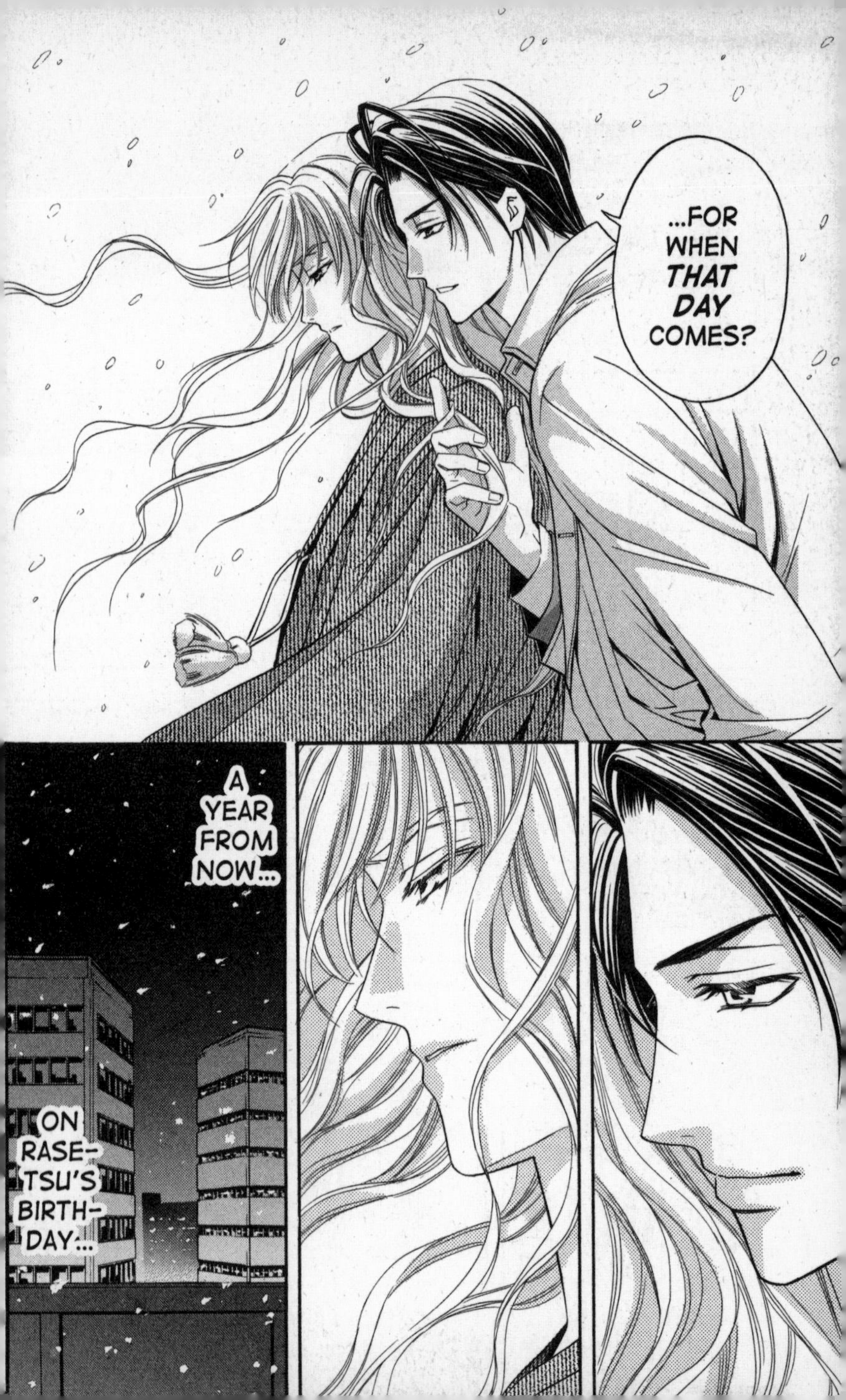
...FOR WHEN *THAT DAY* COMES?
A YEAR FROM NOW...
ON RASE-TSU'S BIRTH-DAY...

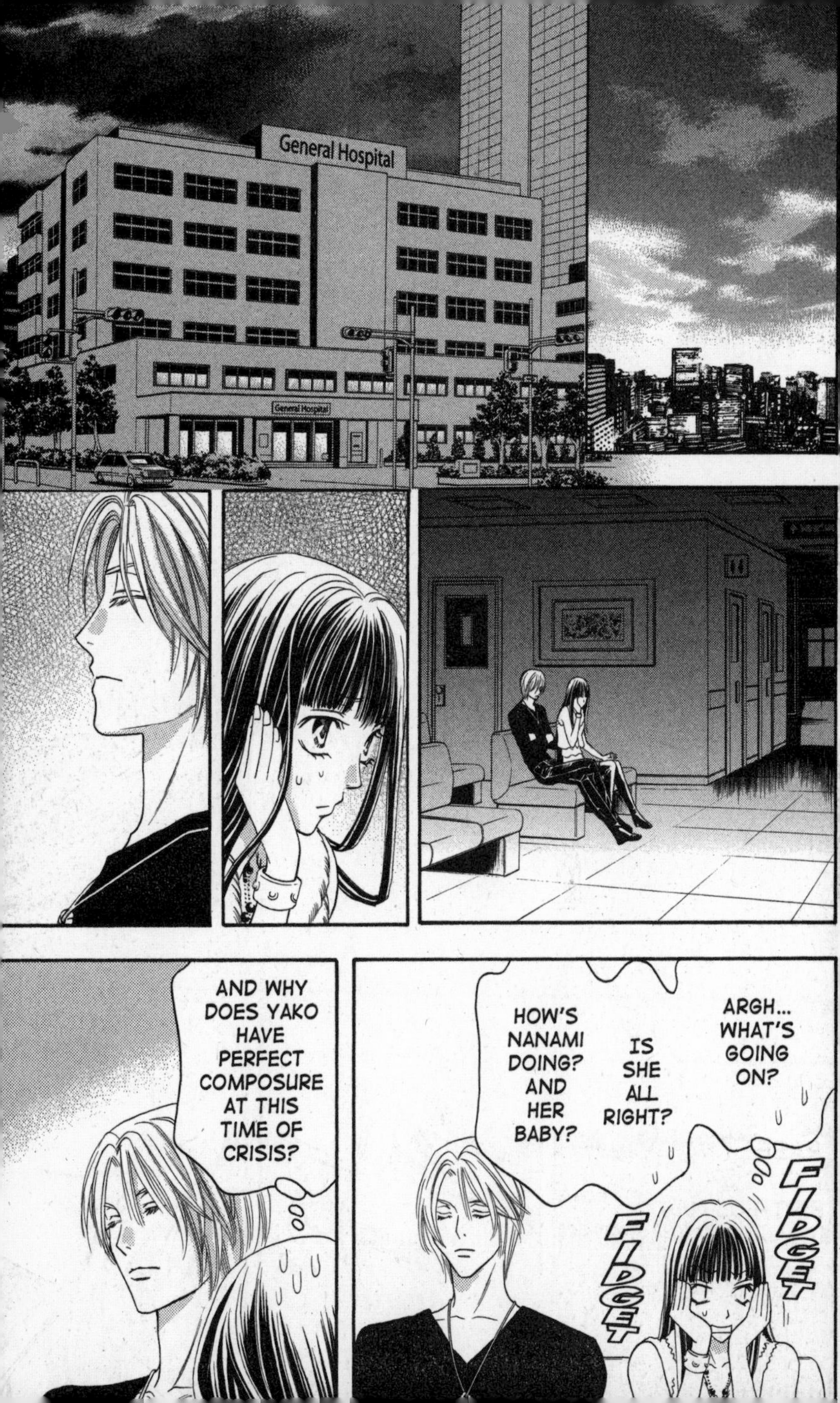
General Hospital
General Hospital
HOW'S NANAMI DOING? AND HER BABY?
IS SHE ALL RIGHT?
ARGH... WHAT'S GOING ON?
FIDGET
FIDGET
AND WHY DOES YAKO HAVE PERFECT COMPOSURE AT THIS TIME OF CRISIS?

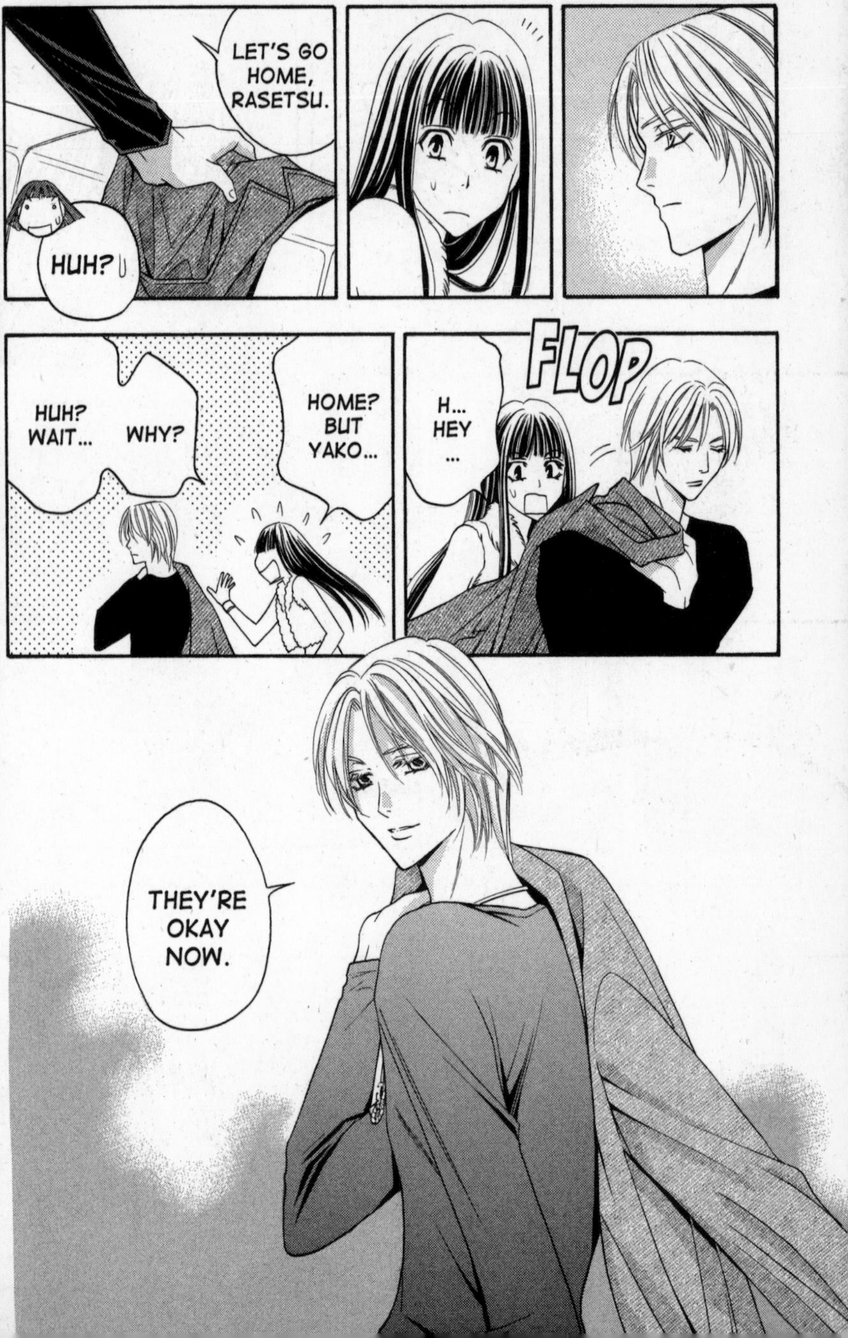
LET'S GO HOME, RASETSU.
HUH?
FLOP
H... HEY ...
HOME? BUT YAKO...
HUH? WAIT... WHY?
THEY'RE OKAY NOW.

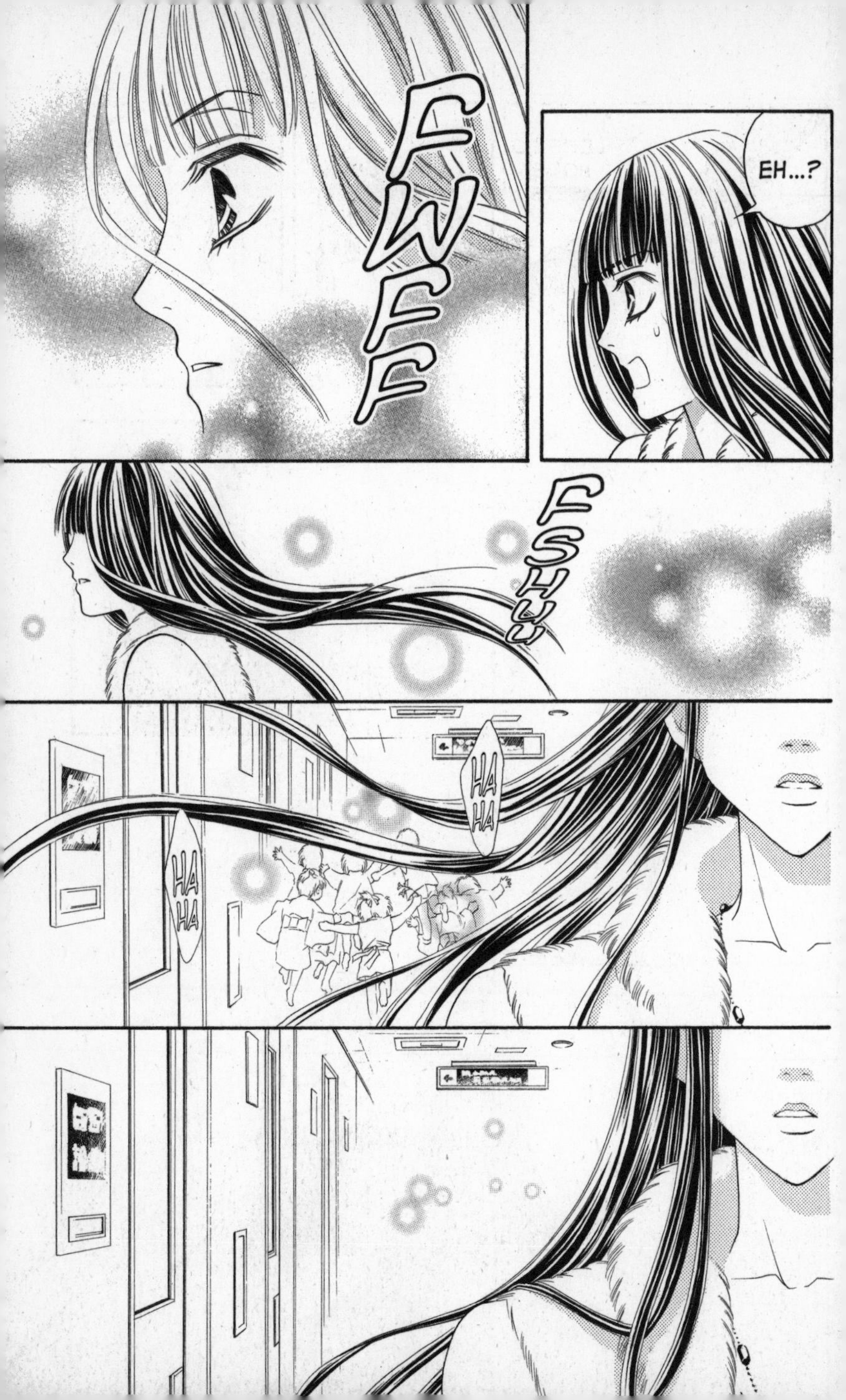
EH...?
FWFFF
FSHUU
HA HA
HA HA

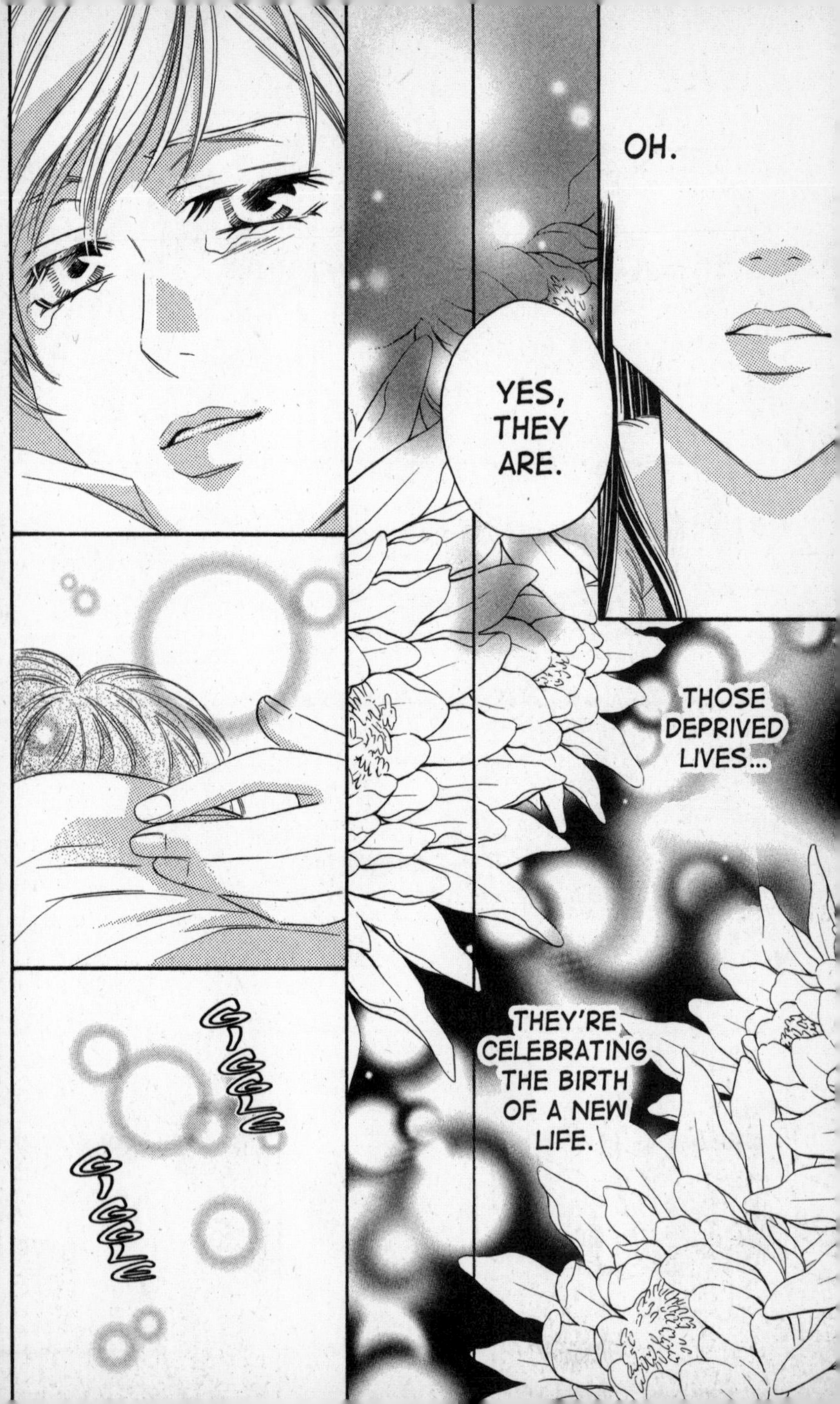
OH.
YES, THEY ARE.
THOSE DEPRIVED LIVES...
THEY'RE CELEBRATING THE BIRTH OF A NEW LIFE.
GIGGLE
GIGGLE

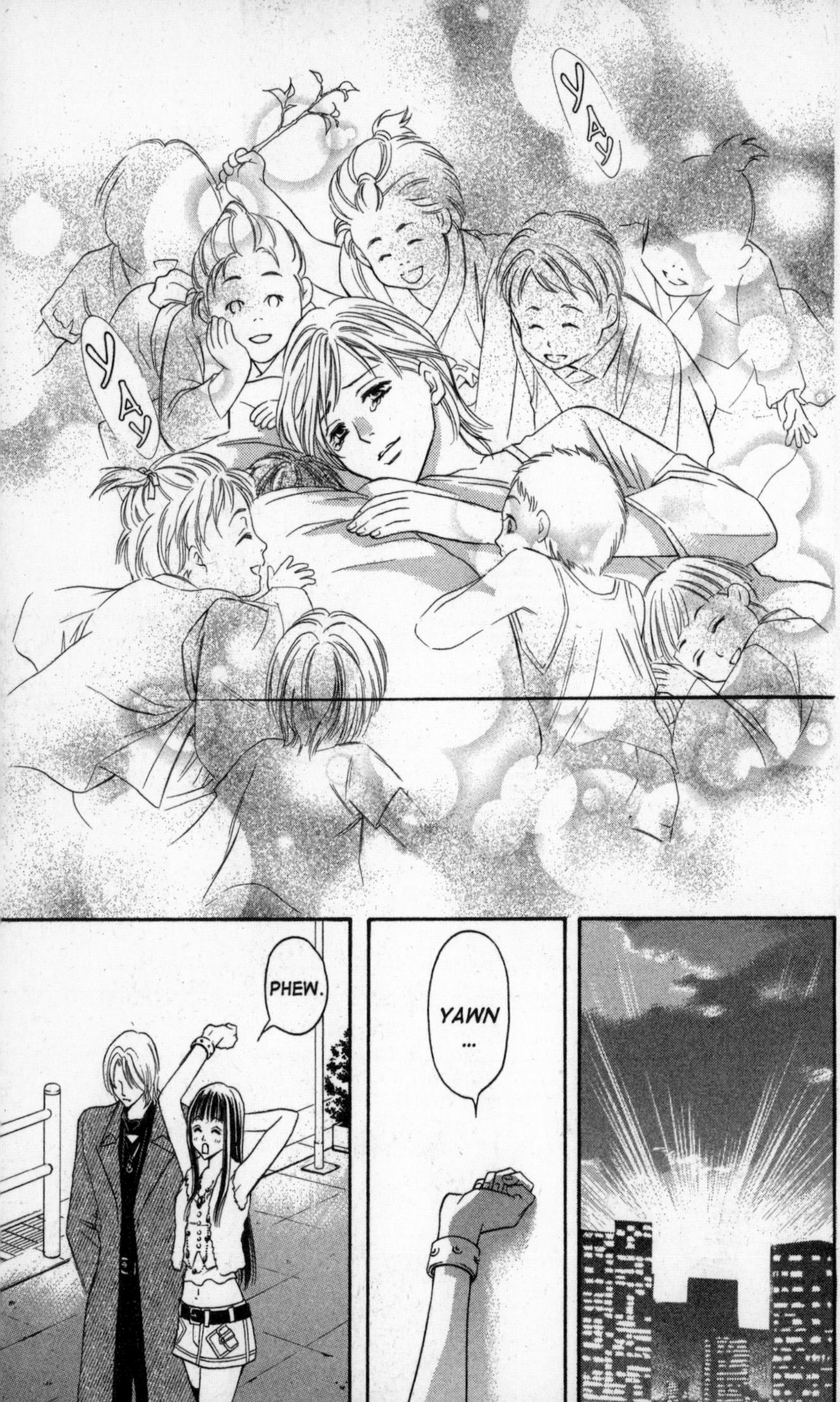

YAY
YAY
YAWN ...
PHEW.

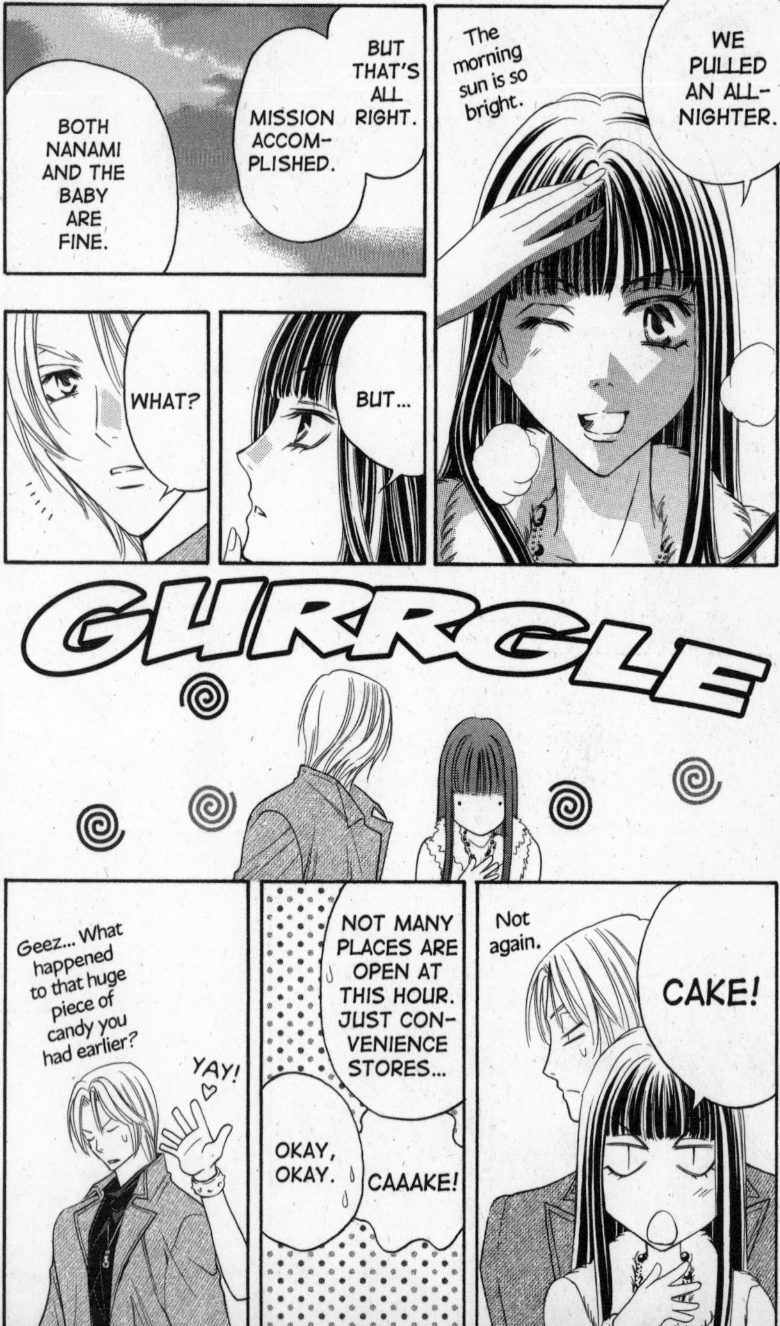
WE PULLED AN ALL-NIGHTER.
The morning sun is so bright.
BUT THAT'S ALL RIGHT.
MISSION ACCOMPLISHED.
BOTH NANAMI AND THE BABY ARE FINE.
BUT...
WHAT?
GURRGLE
CAKE!
Not again.
NOT MANY PLACES ARE OPEN AT THIS HOUR. JUST CONVENIENCE STORES...
CAAAKE!
OKAY, OKAY.
Geez... What happened to that huge piece of candy you had earlier?
YAY!

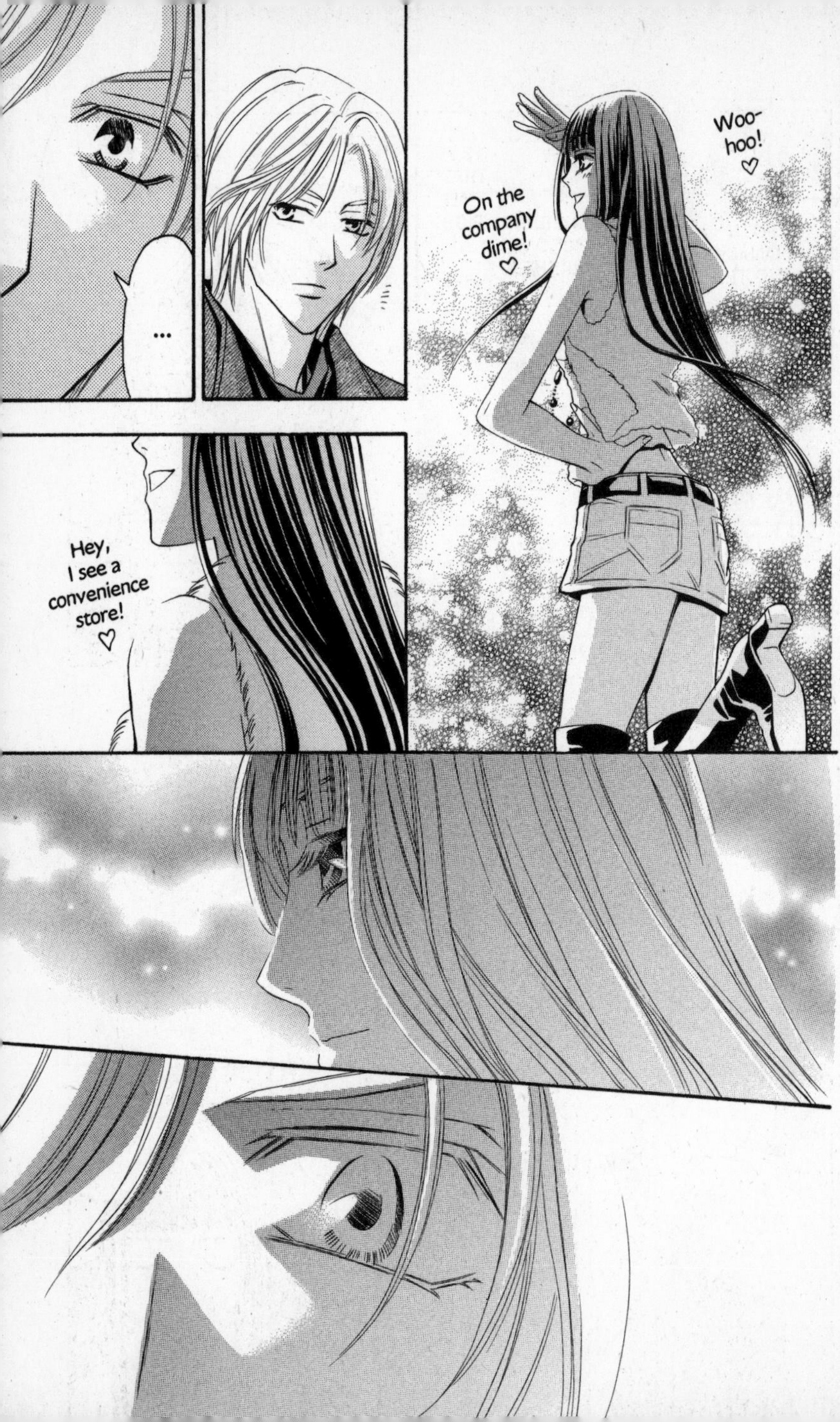
Woo-hoo! ♡
On the company dime! ♡
...
Hey, I see a convenience store! ♡

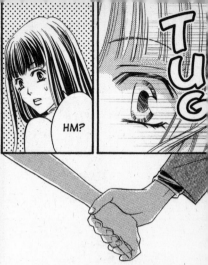

TUG

HM?

FOR A
SECOND
THERE...

YAKO
...?

DON'T
GO...

HUH?

What?

HEY
...

WHAT
IS IT?

...I
THOUGHT
SHE WAS
GOING TO
DISAPPEAR
INTO THE
LIGHT...

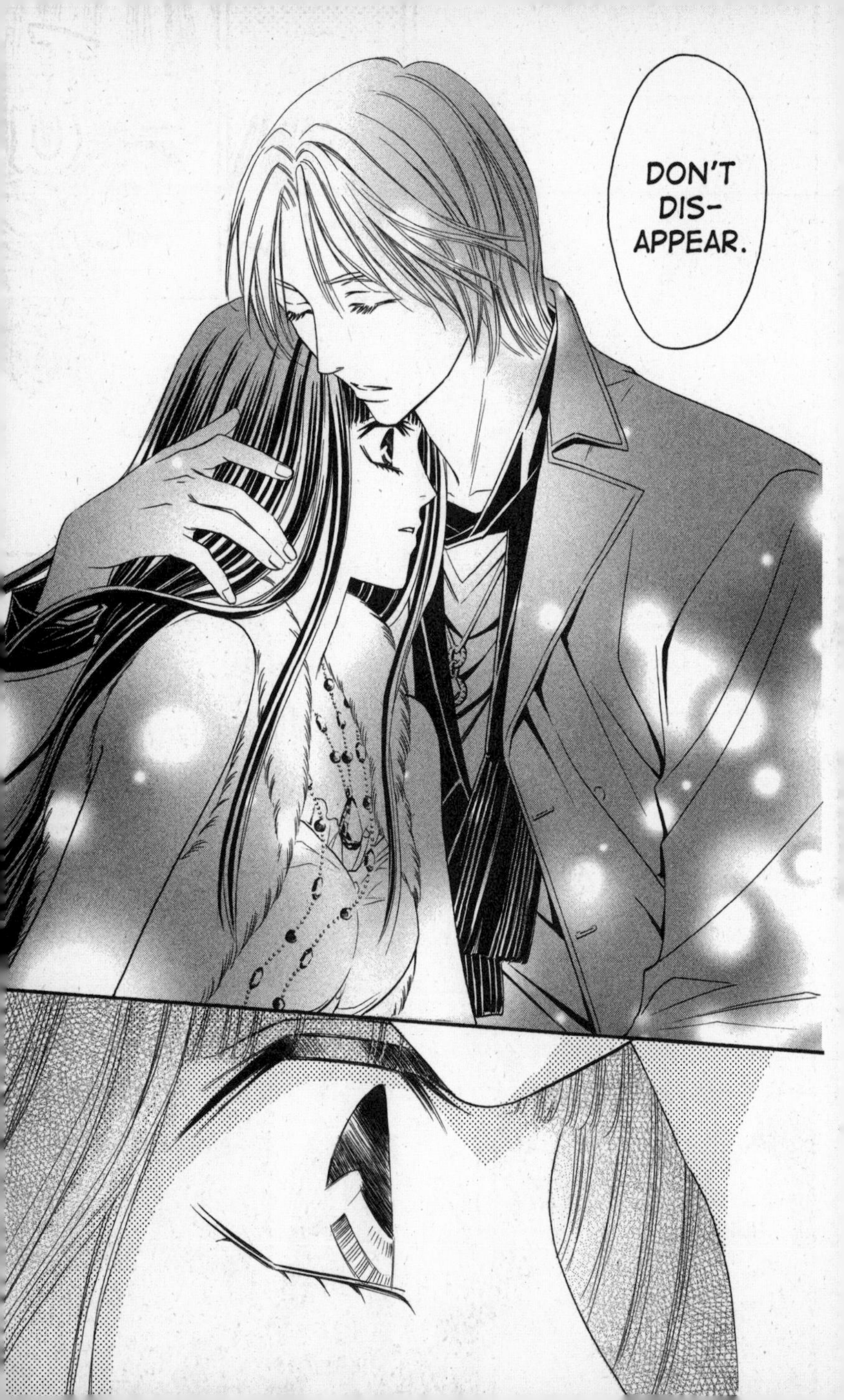
DON'T DIS- APPEAR.

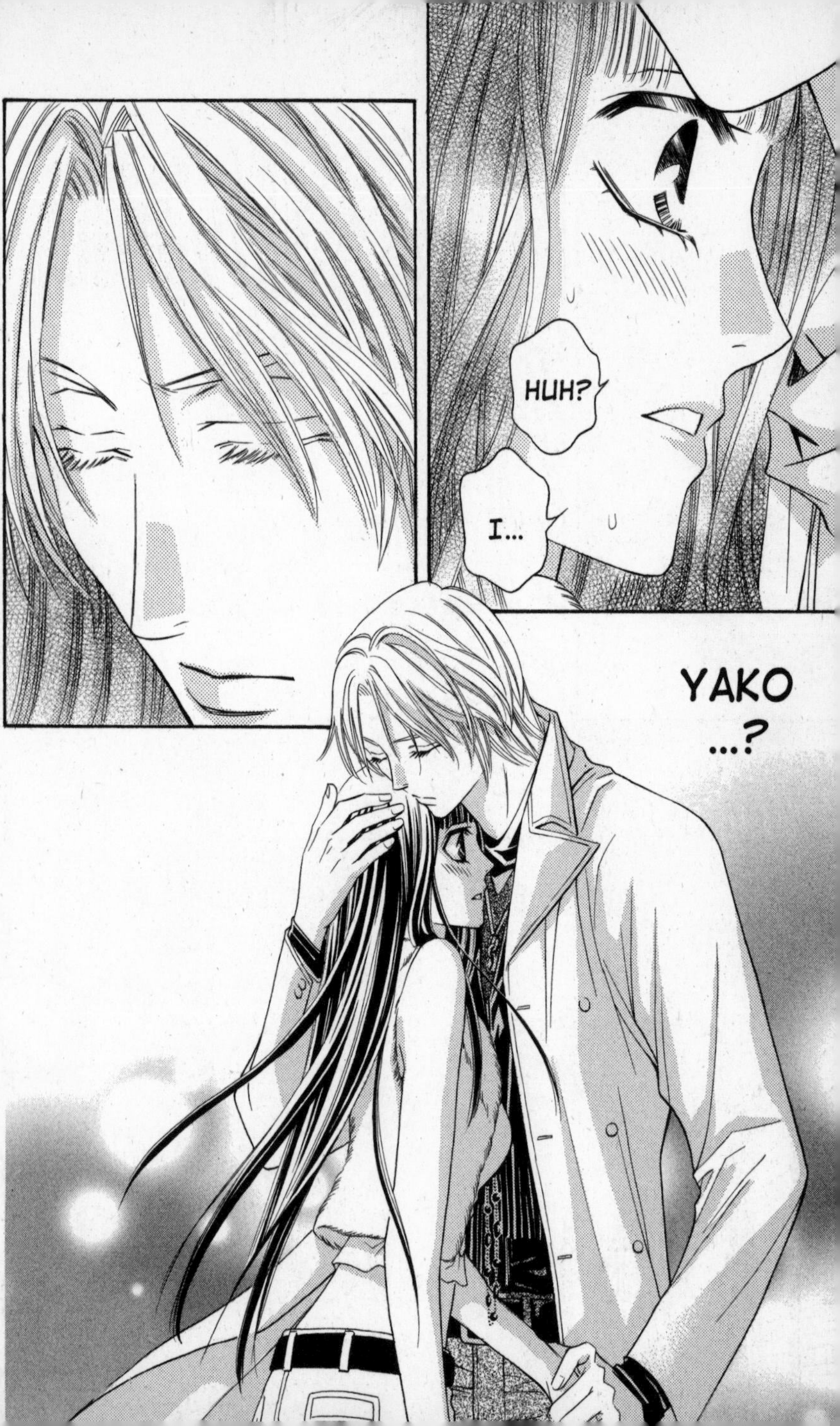
HUH?
I...
YAKO ...?

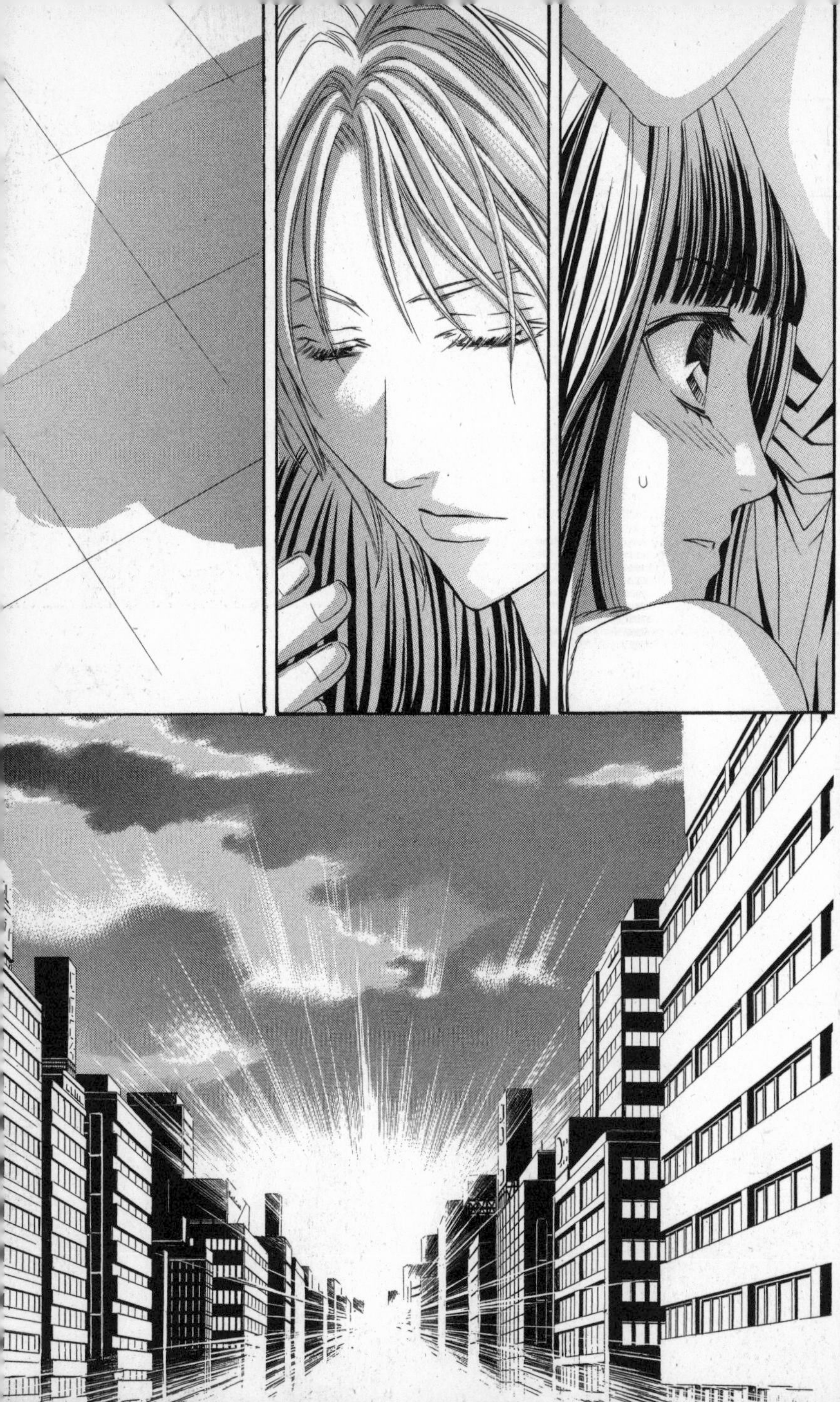

Chapter 20

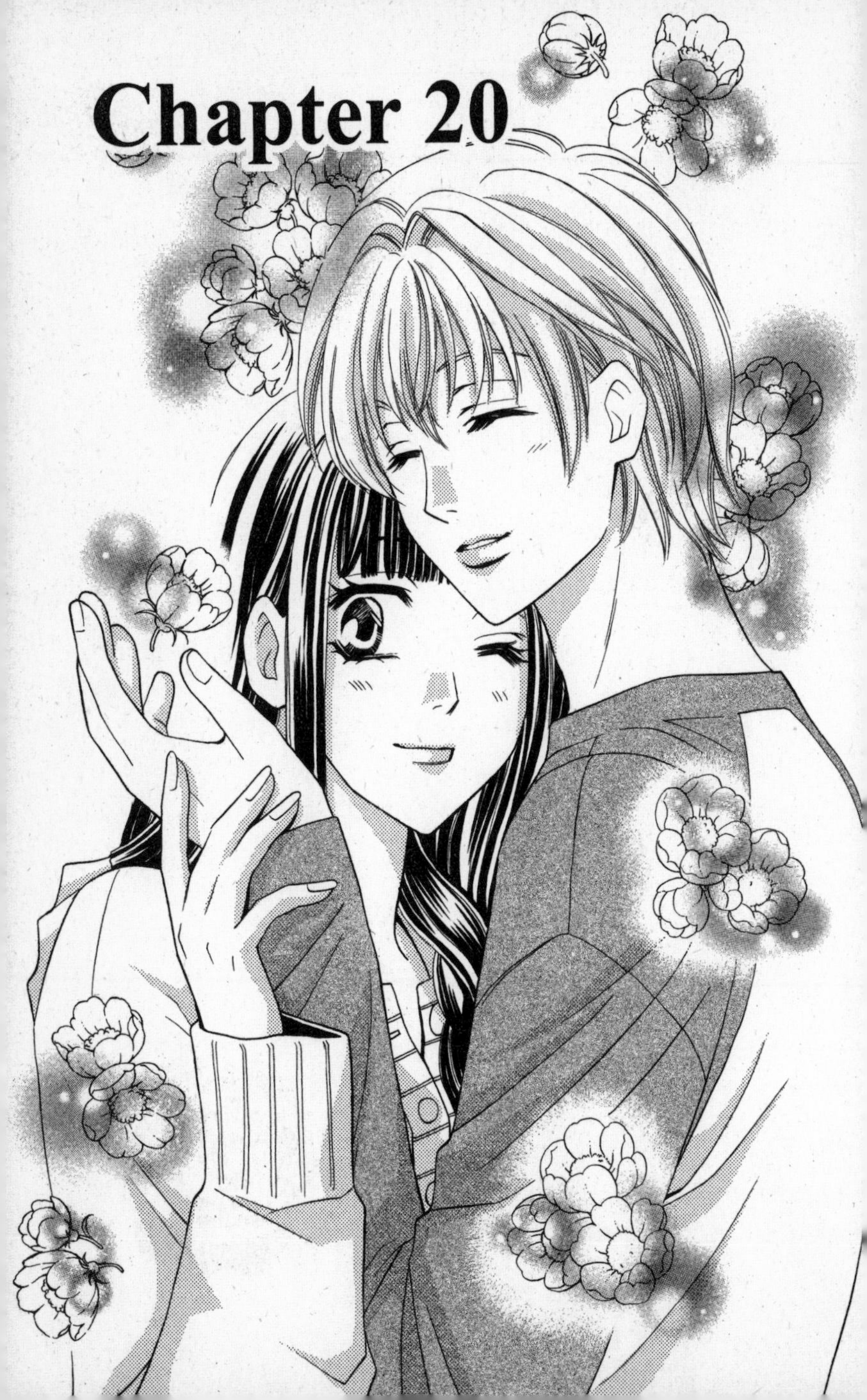

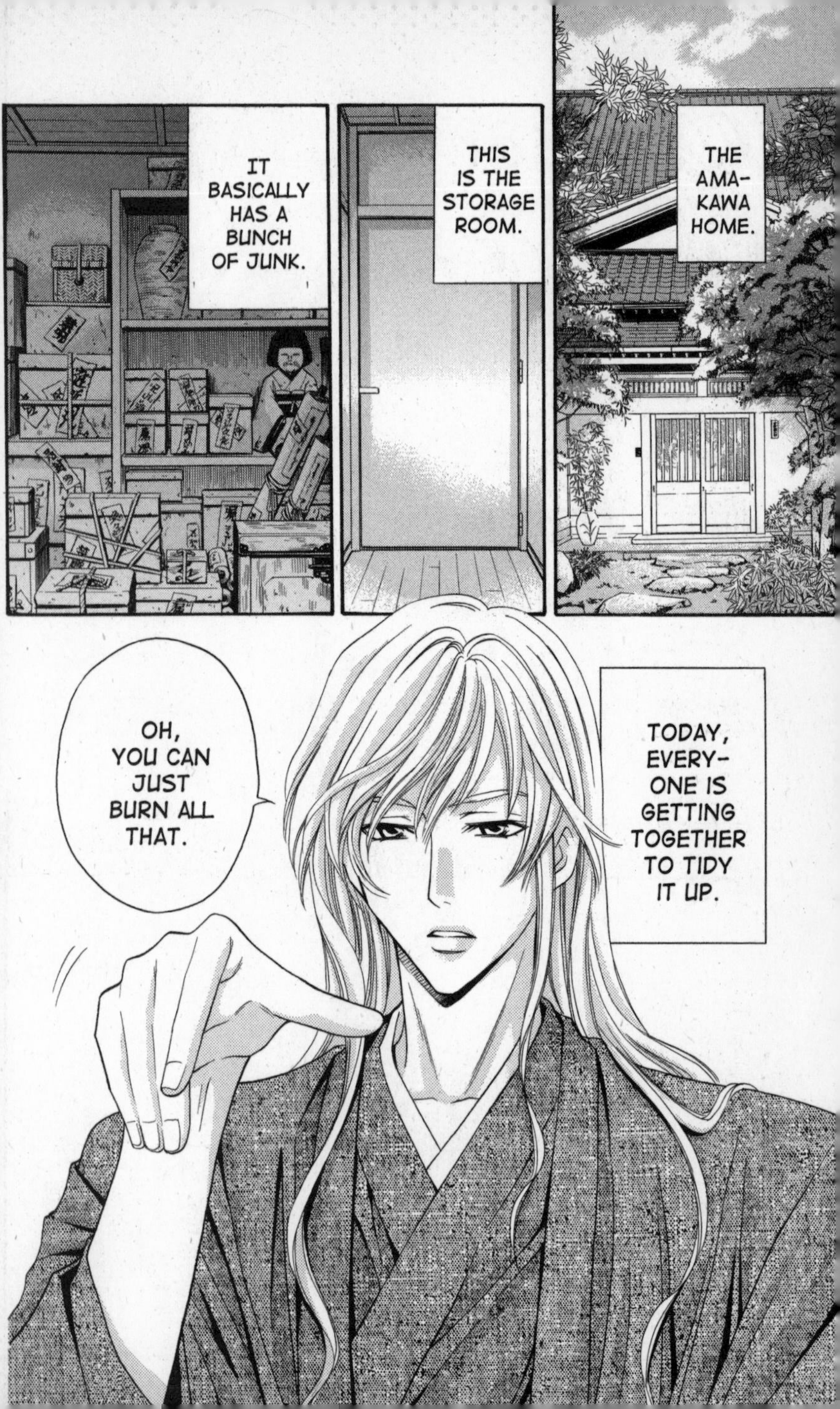
THE AMA-KAWA HOME.
THIS IS THE STORAGE ROOM.
IT BASICALLY HAS A BUNCH OF JUNK.
TODAY, EVERY-ONE IS GETTING TOGETHER TO TIDY IT UP.
OH, YOU CAN JUST BURN ALL THAT.

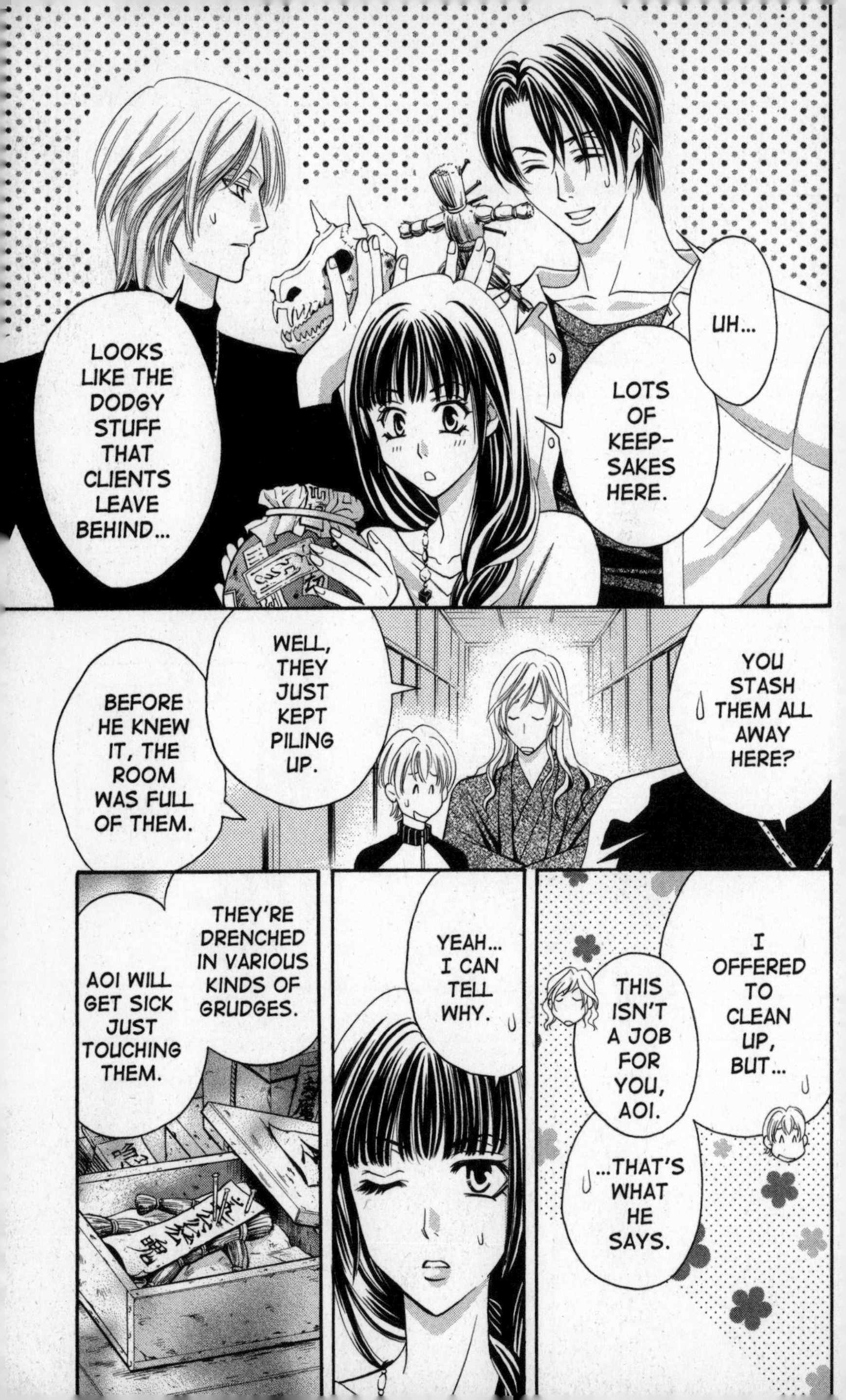
UH...
LOTS OF KEEP-SAKES HERE.
LOOKS LIKE THE DODGY STUFF THAT CLIENTS LEAVE BEHIND...
YOU STASH THEM ALL AWAY HERE?
WELL, THEY JUST KEPT PILING UP.
BEFORE HE KNEW IT, THE ROOM WAS FULL OF THEM.
I OFFERED TO CLEAN UP, BUT...
THIS ISN'T A JOB FOR YOU, AOI.
...THAT'S WHAT HE SAYS.
YEAH... I CAN TELL WHY.
THEY'RE DRENCHED IN VARIOUS KINDS OF GRUDGES.
AOI WILL GET SICK JUST TOUCHING THEM.

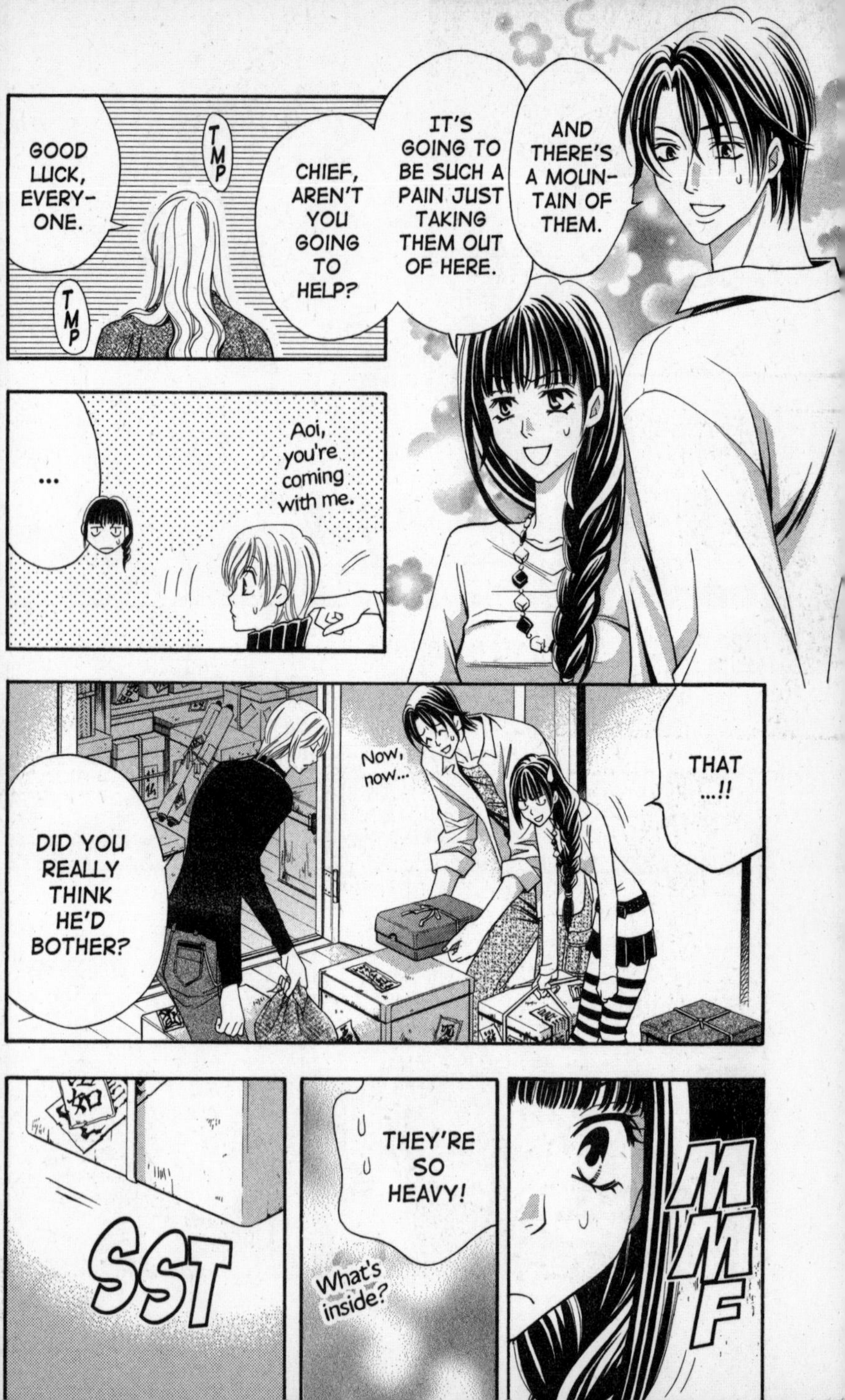
AND THERE'S A MOUN-TAIN OF THEM.
IT'S GOING TO BE SUCH A PAIN JUST TAKING THEM OUT OF HERE.
CHIEF, AREN'T YOU GOING TO HELP?
TMP
GOOD LUCK, EVERY-ONE.
TMP
Aoi, you're coming with me.
...
THAT ...!!
Now, now...
DID YOU REALLY THINK HE'D BOTHER?
MMF
THEY'RE SO HEAVY!
What's inside?
SST

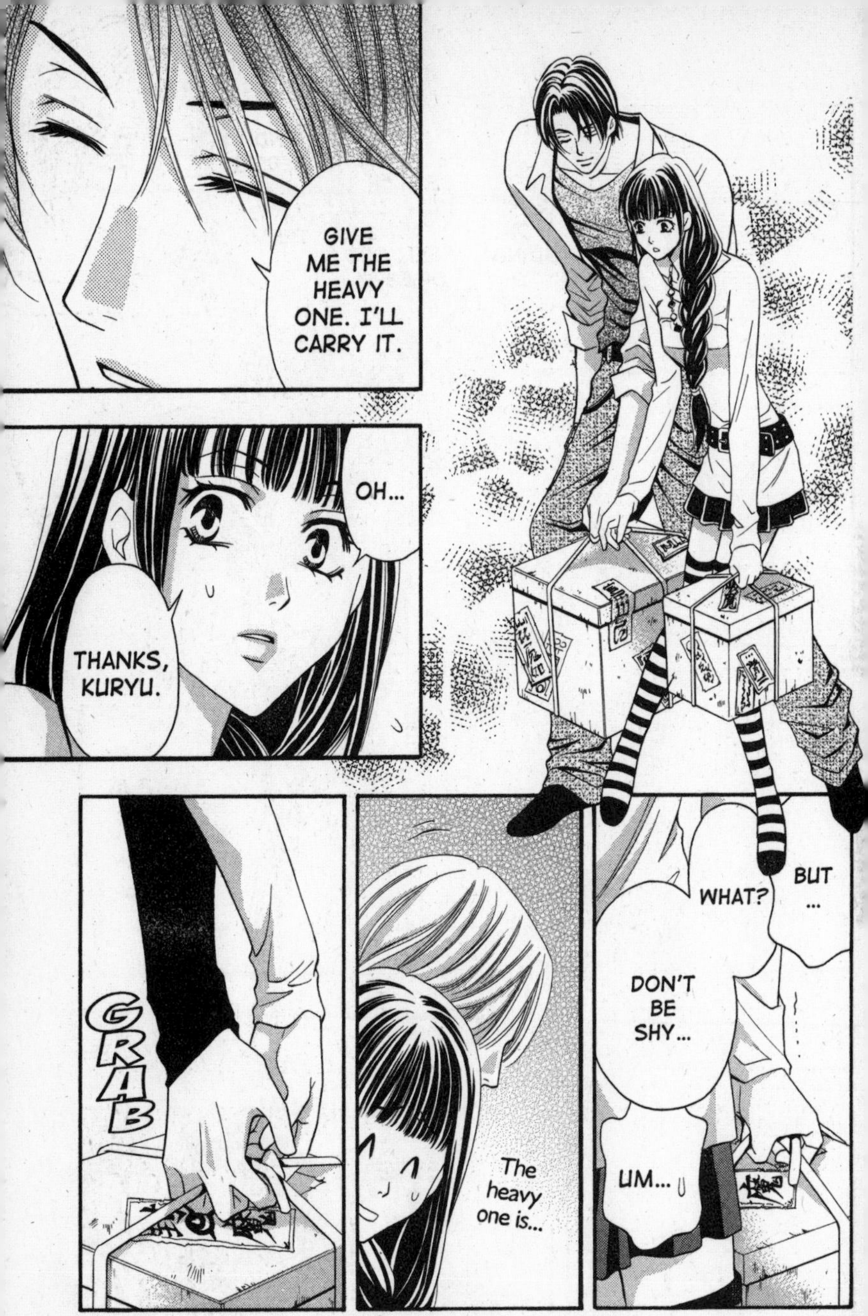
GIVE ME THE HEAVY ONE. I'LL CARRY IT.
OH...
THANKS, KURYU.
BUT ...
WHAT?
DON'T BE SHY...
UM...
The heavy one is...
GRAB

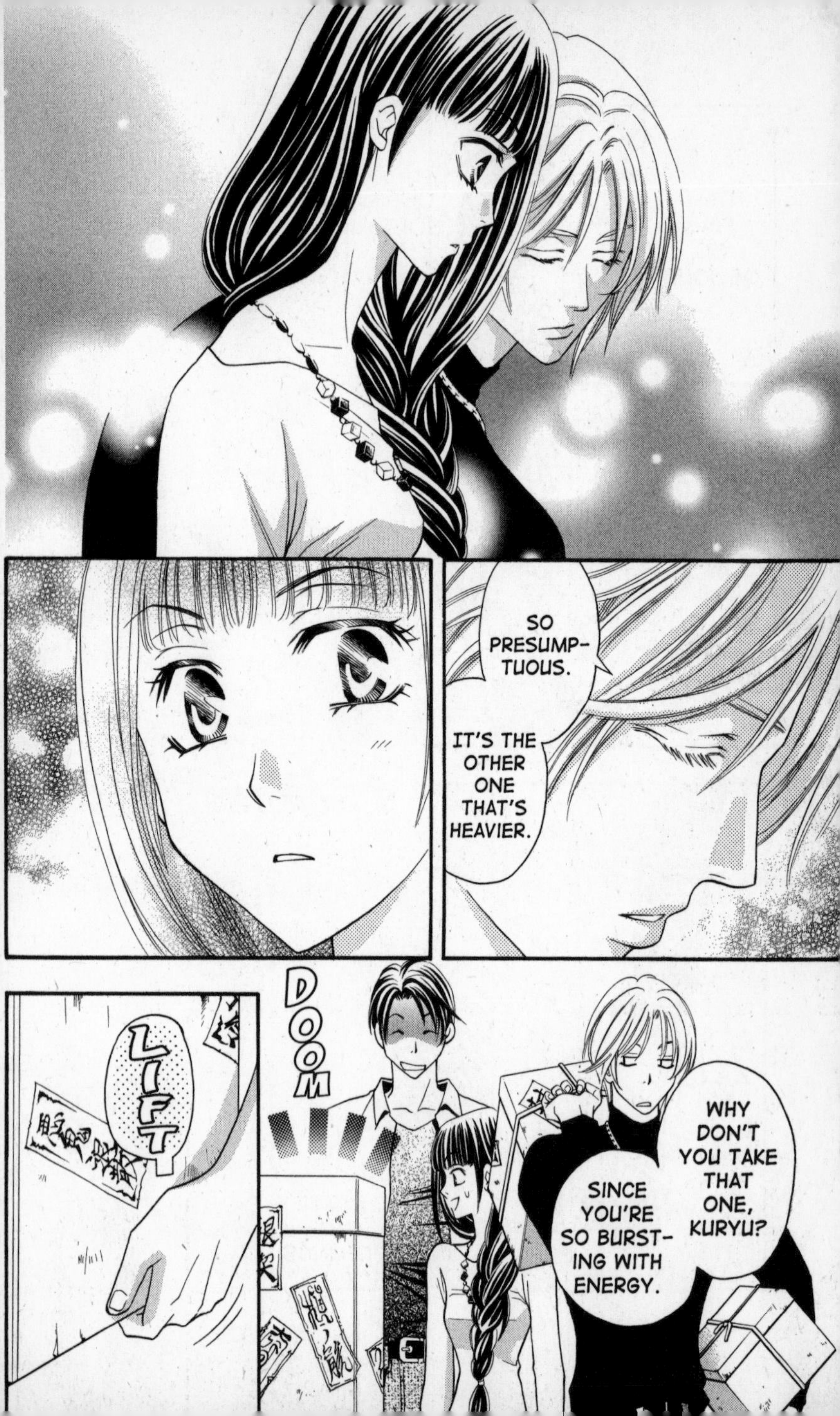
SO PRESUMP-TUOUS.
IT'S THE OTHER ONE THAT'S HEAVIER.
WHY DON'T YOU TAKE THAT ONE, KURYU?
SINCE YOU'RE SO BURST-ING WITH ENERGY.
DOOM
LIFT

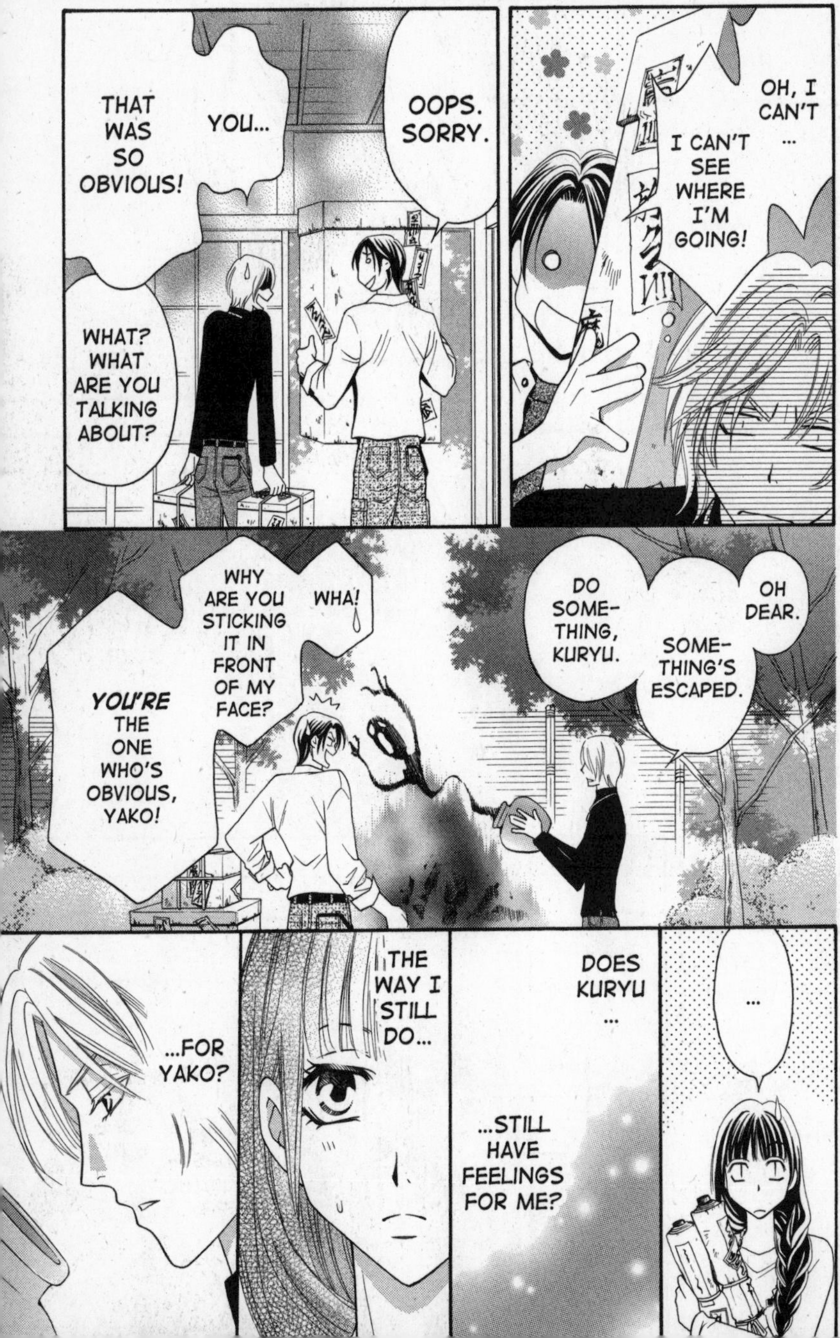

OH, I CAN'T ...
I CAN'T SEE WHERE I'M GOING!
OOPS. SORRY.
YOU...
THAT WAS SO OBVIOUS!
WHAT? WHAT ARE YOU TALKING ABOUT?
OH DEAR.
SOME-THING'S ESCAPED.
DO SOME-THING, KURYU.
WHA!
WHY ARE YOU STICKING IT IN FRONT OF MY FACE?
YOU'RE THE ONE WHO'S OBVIOUS, YAKO!
...
DOES KURYU ...
...STILL HAVE FEELINGS FOR ME?
THE WAY I STILL DO...
...FOR YAKO?

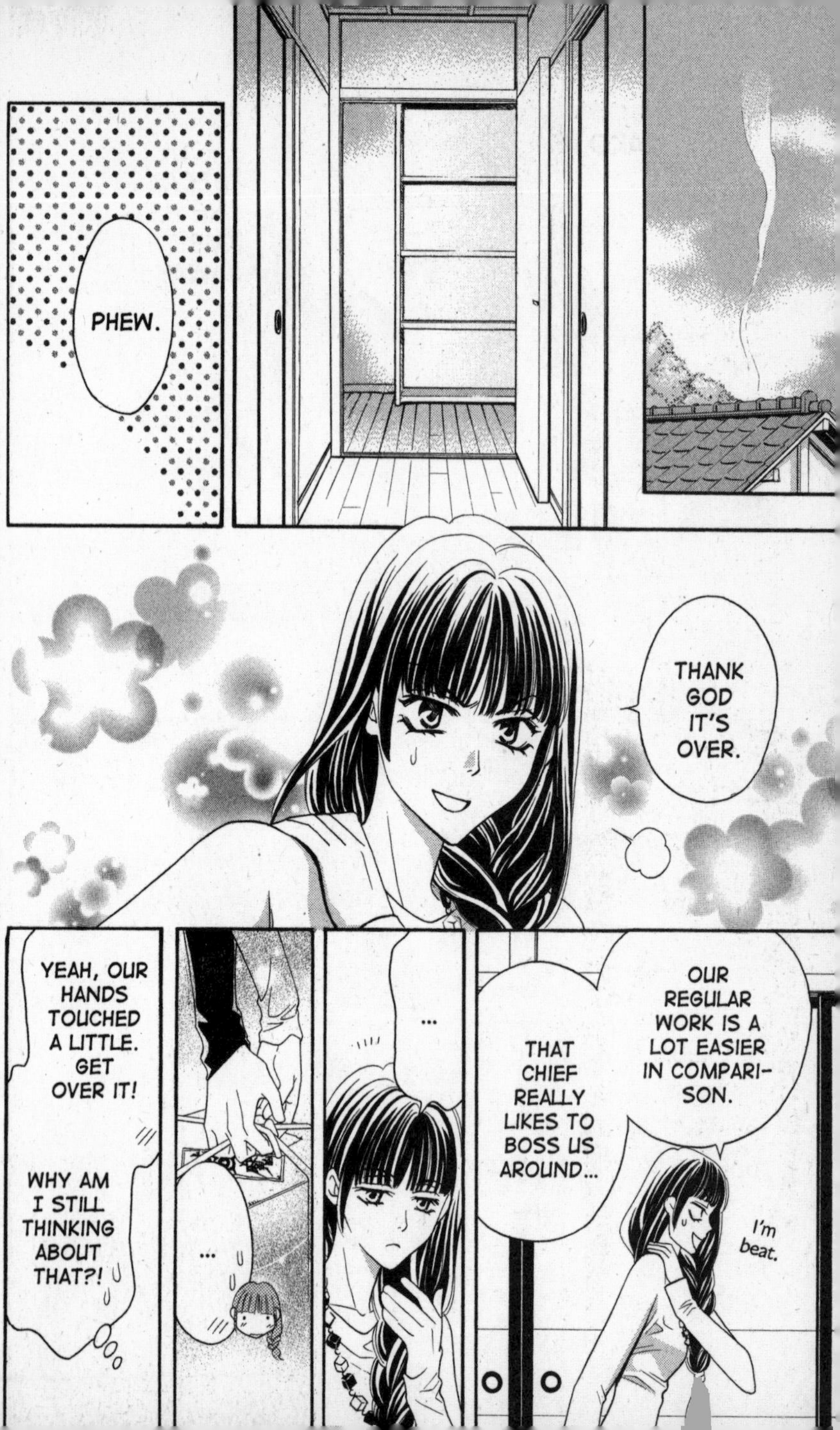
PHEW.
THANK GOD IT'S OVER.
OUR REGULAR WORK IS A LOT EASIER IN COMPARI-SON.
THAT CHIEF REALLY LIKES TO BOSS US AROUND...
I'm beat.
...
...
YEAH, OUR HANDS TOUCHED A LITTLE. GET OVER IT!
WHY AM I STILL THINKING ABOUT THAT?!

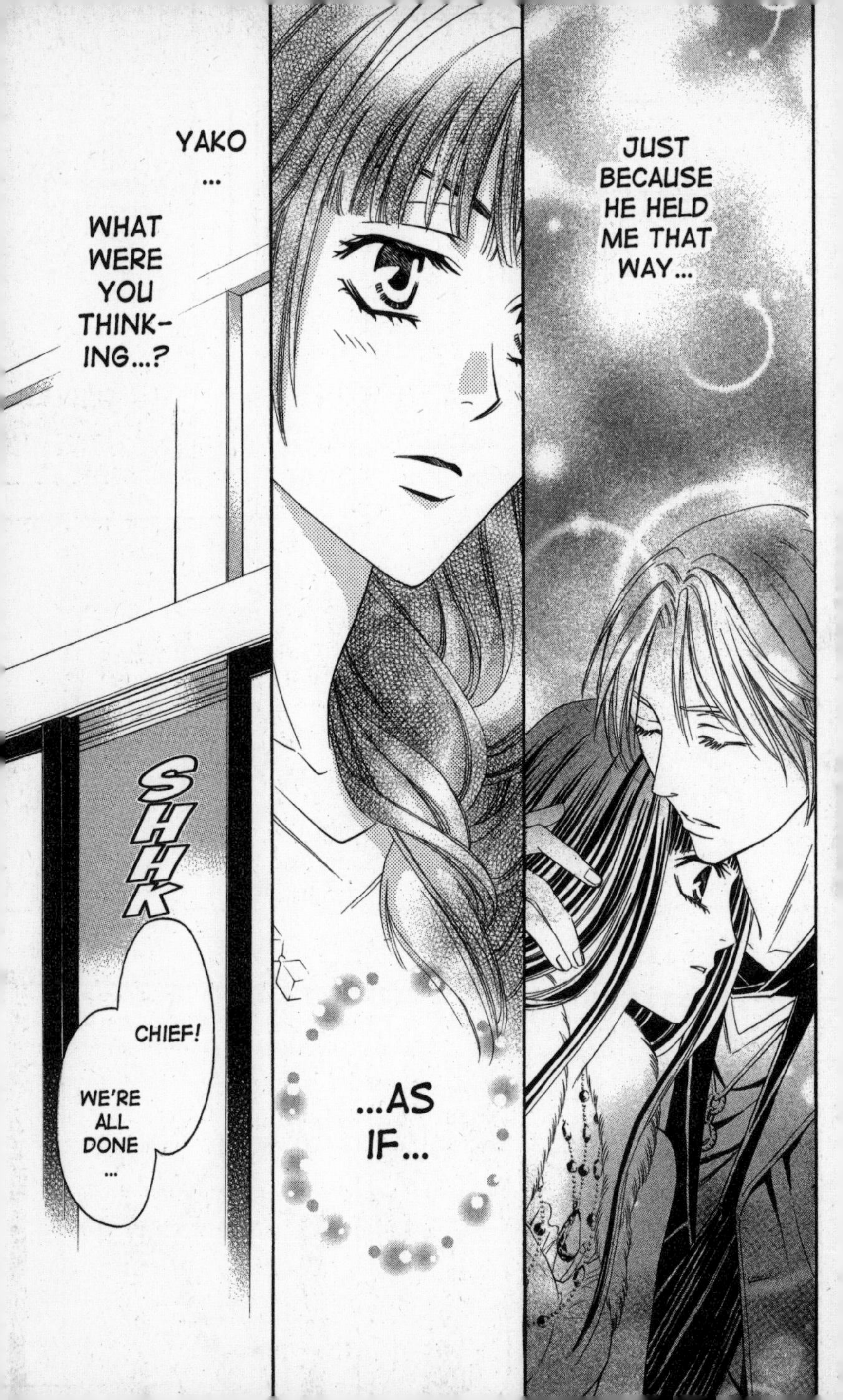
JUST BECAUSE HE HELD ME THAT WAY...
...AS IF...
YAKO ...
WHAT WERE YOU THINKING...?
SHHK
CHIEF!
WE'RE ALL DONE ...

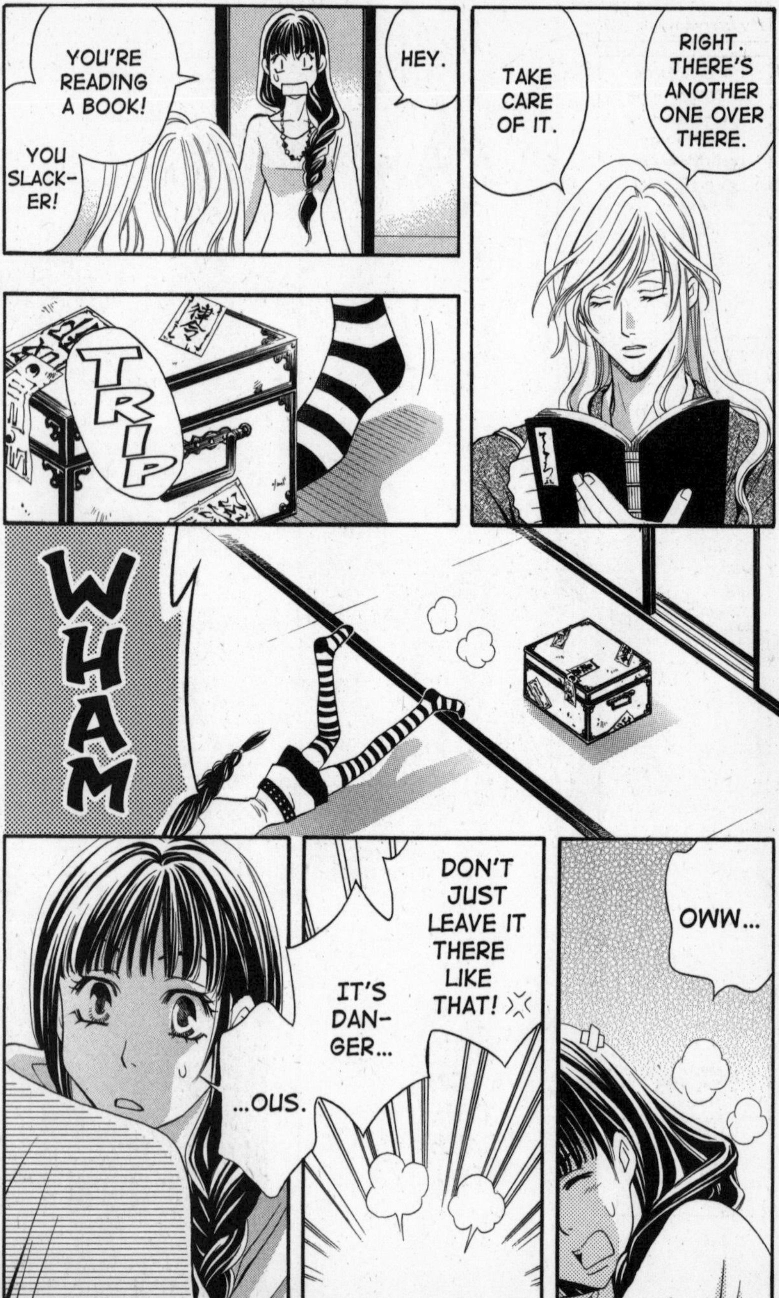
HEY.
YOU'RE READING A BOOK!
YOU SLACKER!
RIGHT. THERE'S ANOTHER ONE OVER THERE.
TAKE CARE OF IT.
TRIP
WHAM
OWW...
DON'T JUST LEAVE IT THERE LIKE THAT!
IT'S DANGER...
...OUS.

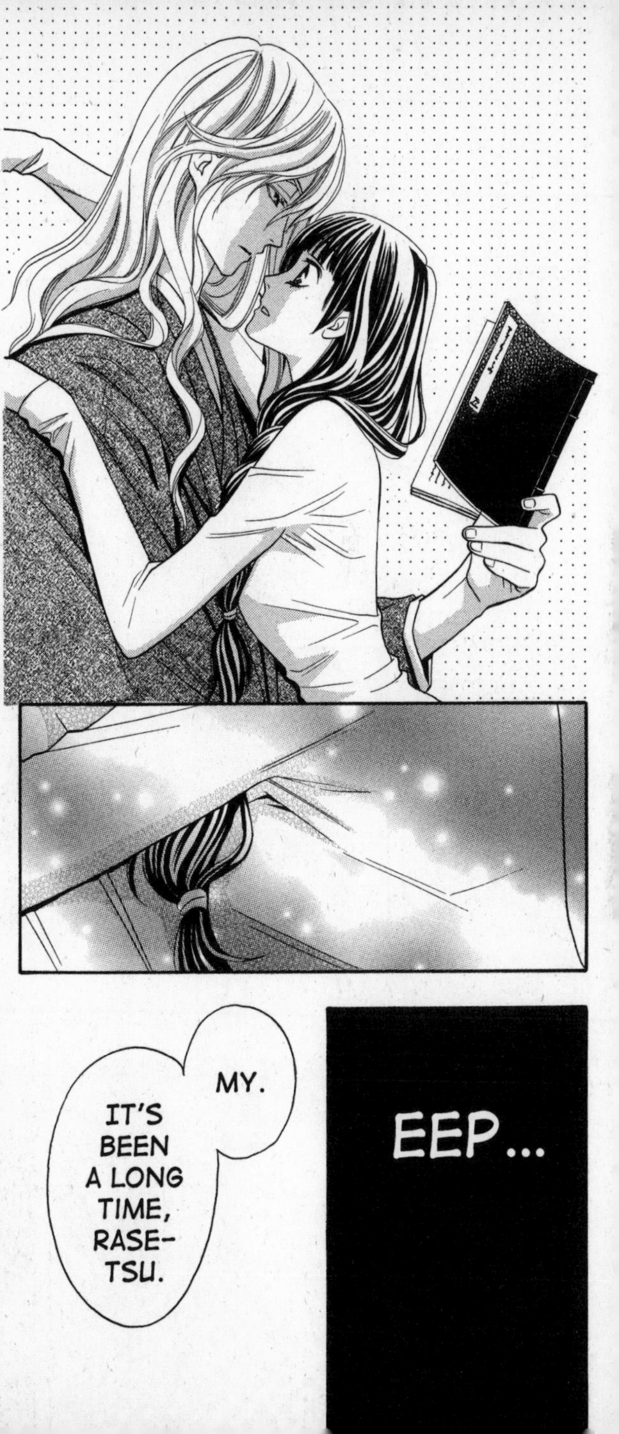
EEP...
MY.
IT'S BEEN A LONG TIME, RASE-TSU.

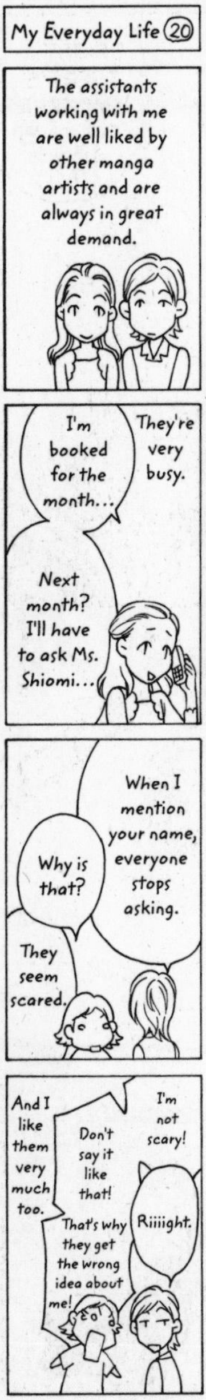
My Everyday Life 20
The assistants working with me are well liked by other manga artists and are always in great demand.
They're very busy.
I'm booked for the month...
Next month? I'll have to ask Ms. Shiomi...
When I mention your name, everyone stops asking.
Why is that?
They seem scared.
I'm not scary!
Don't say it like that!
And I like them very much too.
Riiiight.
That's why they get the wrong idea about me!

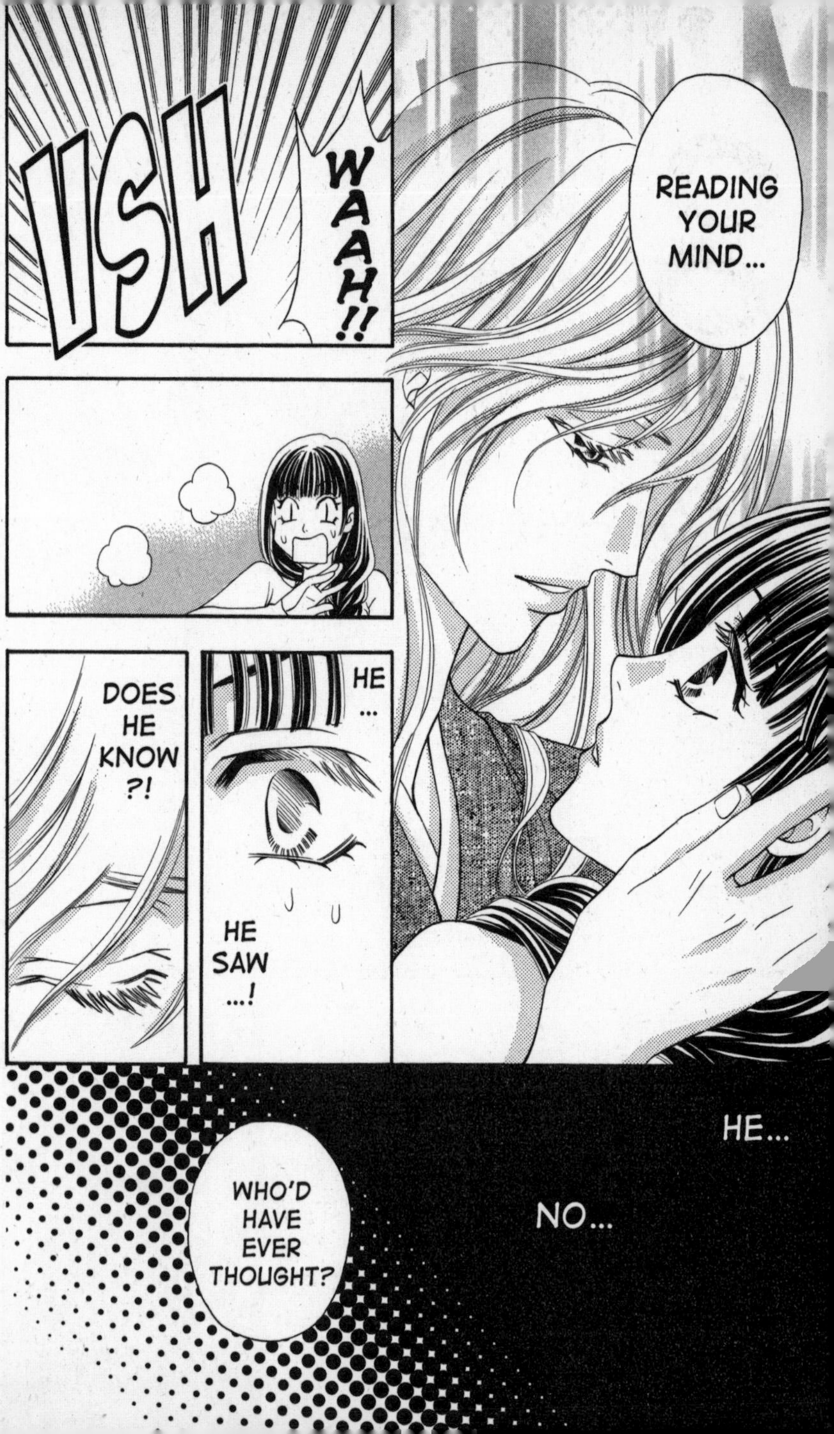

READING YOUR MIND...
WAAAH!!
VSH
HE...
HE SAW...!
DOES HE KNOW?!
HE...
NO...
WHO'D HAVE EVER THOUGHT?

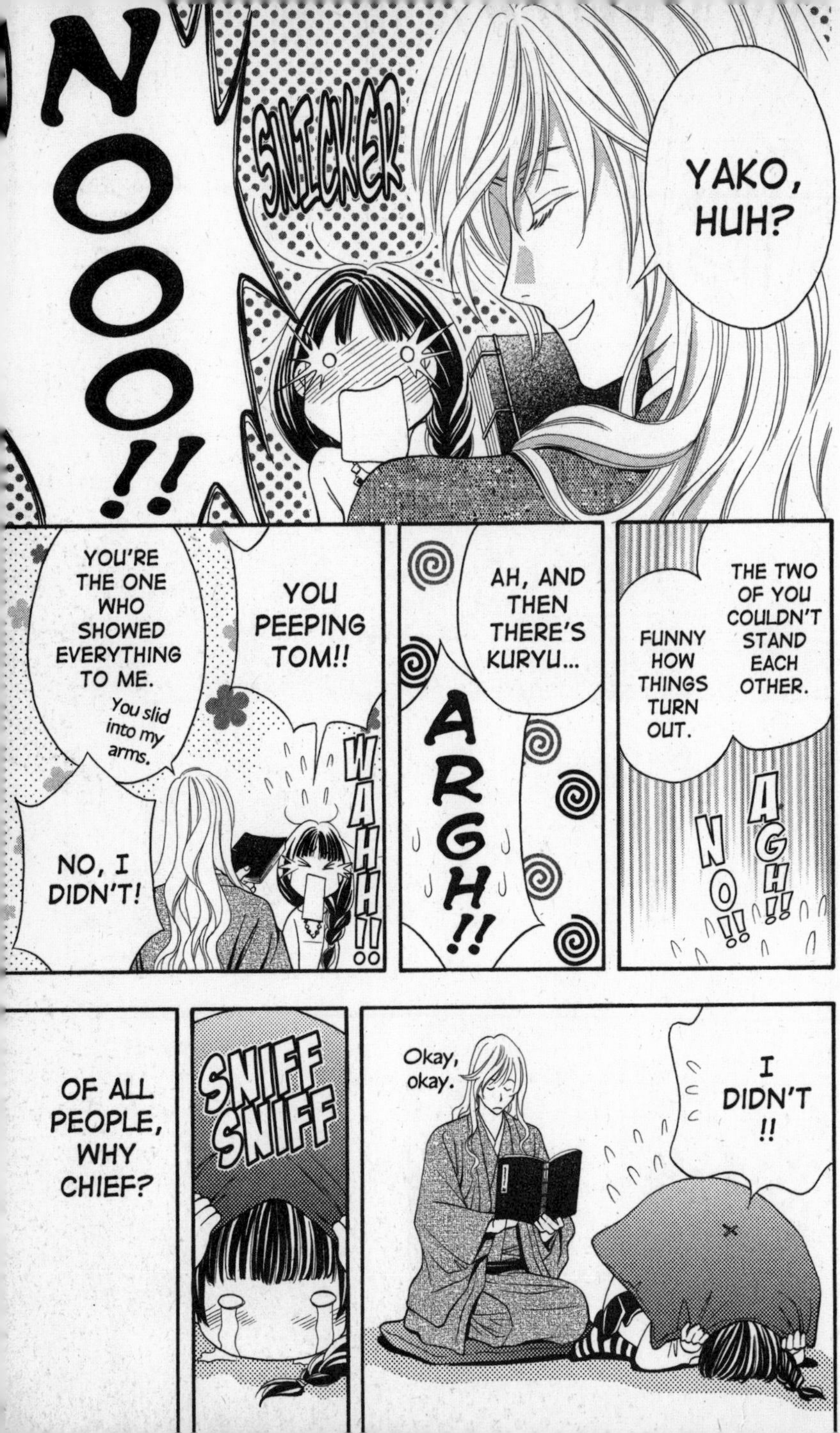
YAKO, HUH?
SNICKER
NOOOO!!
THE TWO OF YOU COULDN'T STAND EACH OTHER.
FUNNY HOW THINGS TURN OUT.
AGH!!
NO!!
AH, AND THEN THERE'S KURYU...
ARGH!!
YOU PEEPING TOM!!
WAHHH!!
YOU'RE THE ONE WHO SHOWED EVERYTHING TO ME.
You slid into my arms.
NO, I DIDN'T!
I DIDN'T!!
Okay, okay.
SNIFF SNIFF
OF ALL PEOPLE, WHY CHIEF?

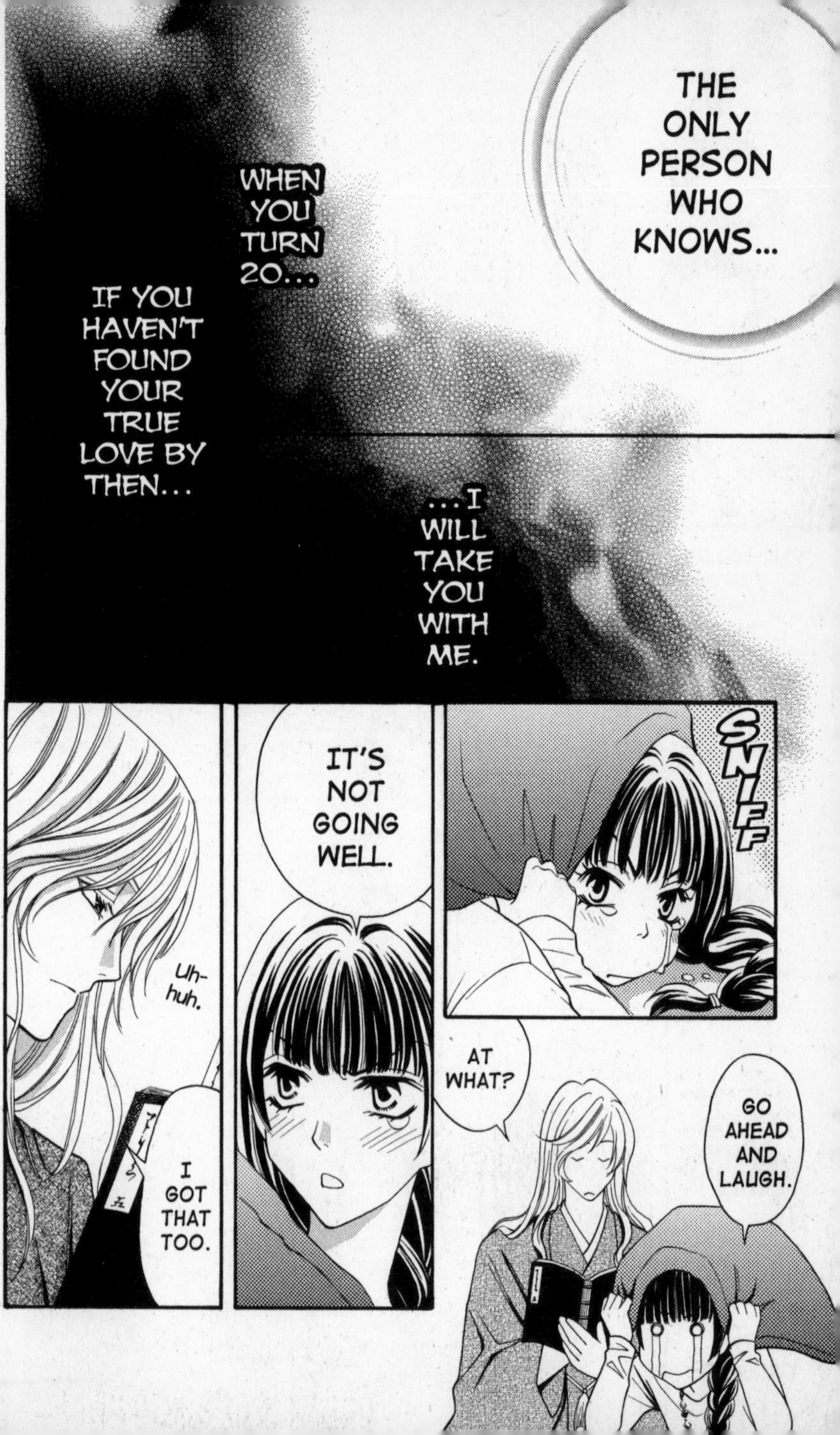
THE ONLY PERSON WHO KNOWS...
WHEN YOU TURN 20...
IF YOU HAVEN'T FOUND YOUR TRUE LOVE BY THEN...
...I WILL TAKE YOU WITH ME.
SNIFF
GO AHEAD AND LAUGH.
AT WHAT?
IT'S NOT GOING WELL.
Uh-huh.
I GOT THAT TOO.

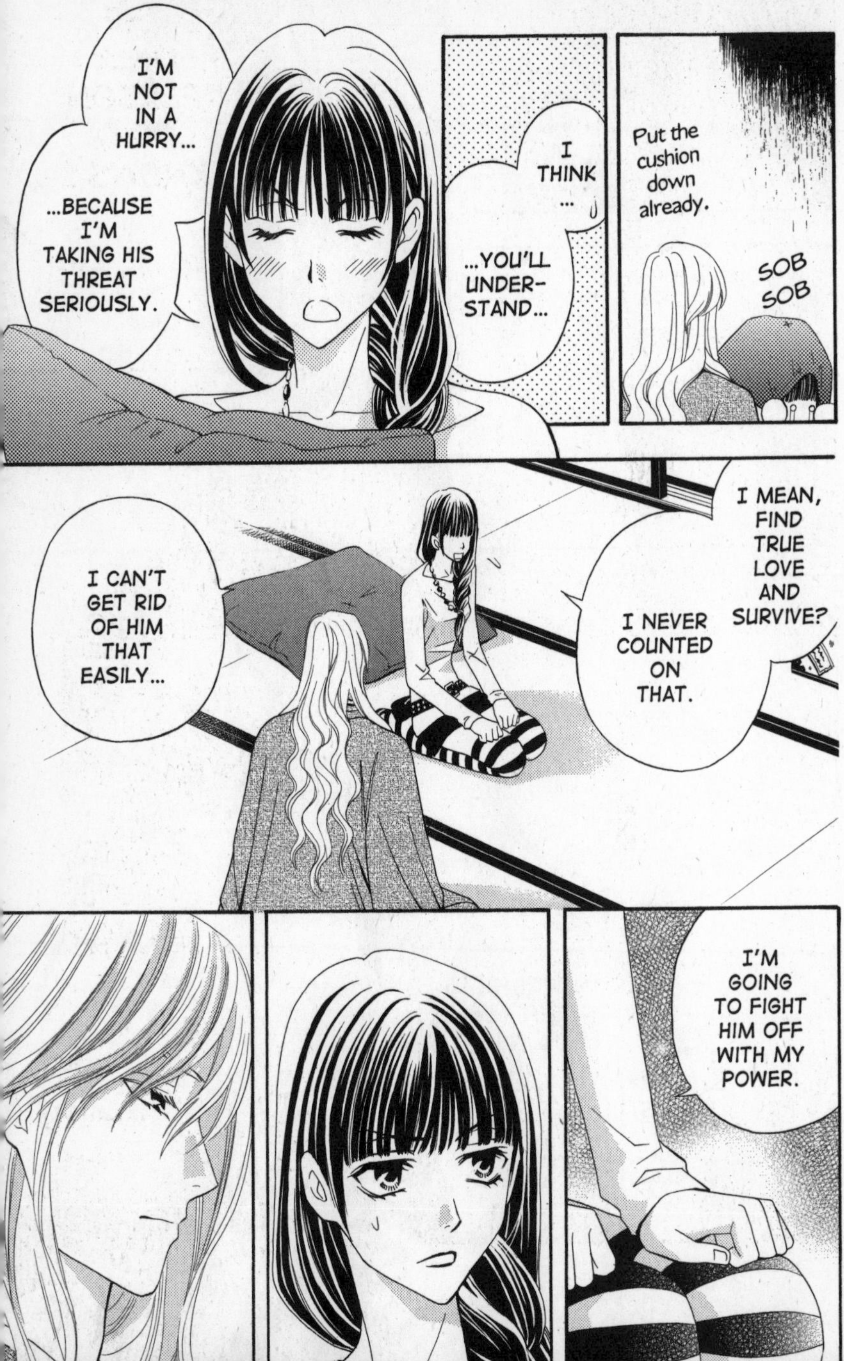
Put the cushion down already.
SOB SOB
I THINK...
...YOU'LL UNDERSTAND...
I'M NOT IN A HURRY...
...BECAUSE I'M TAKING HIS THREAT SERIOUSLY.
I MEAN, FIND TRUE LOVE AND SURVIVE?
I NEVER COUNTED ON THAT.
I CAN'T GET RID OF HIM THAT EASILY...
I'M GOING TO FIGHT HIM OFF WITH MY POWER.

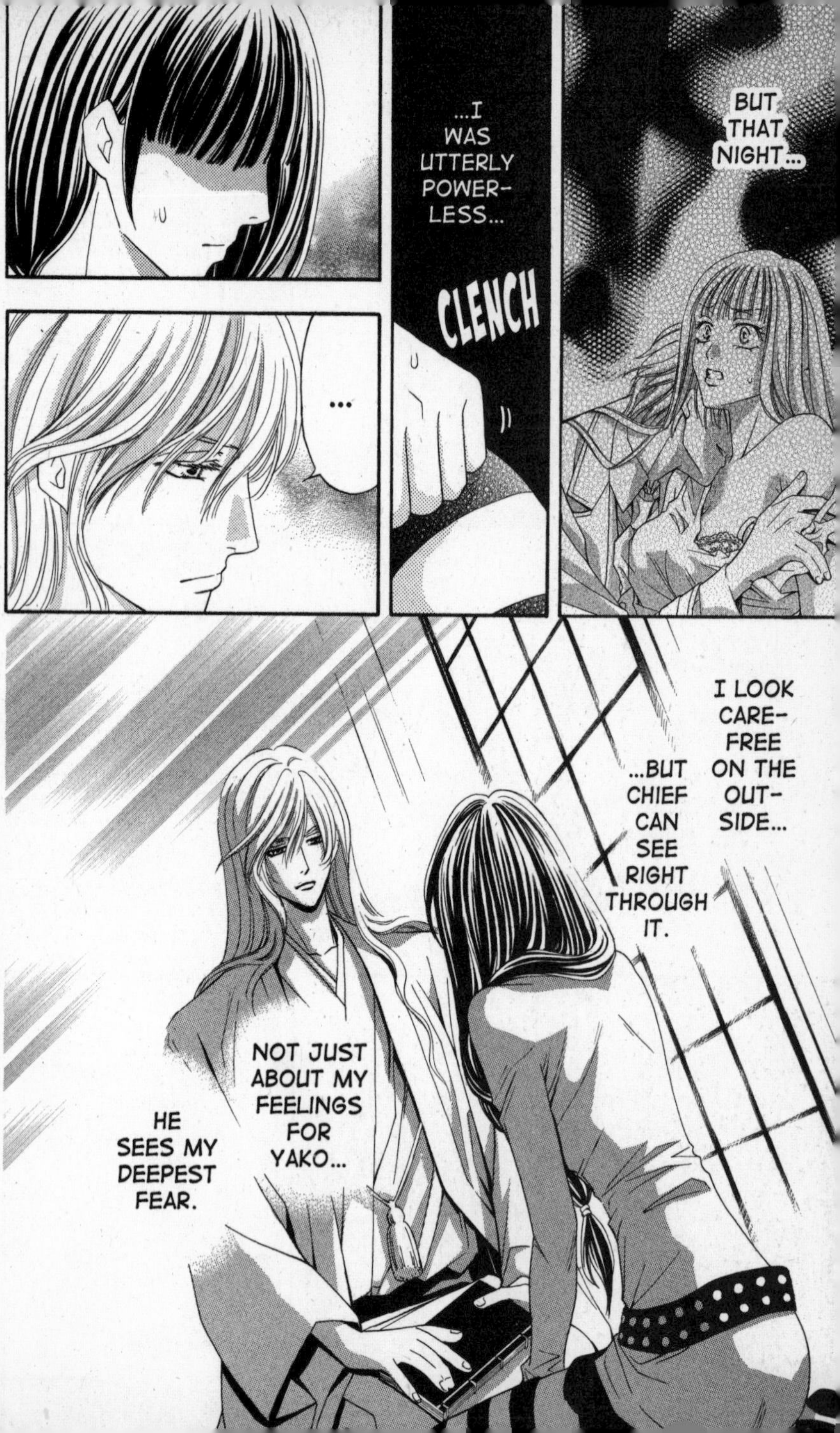
BUT THAT NIGHT...
...I WAS UTTERLY POWER-LESS...
CLENCH
...
I LOOK CARE-FREE ON THE OUT-SIDE...
...BUT CHIEF CAN SEE RIGHT THROUGH IT.
NOT JUST ABOUT MY FEELINGS FOR YAKO...
HE SEES MY DEEPEST FEAR.

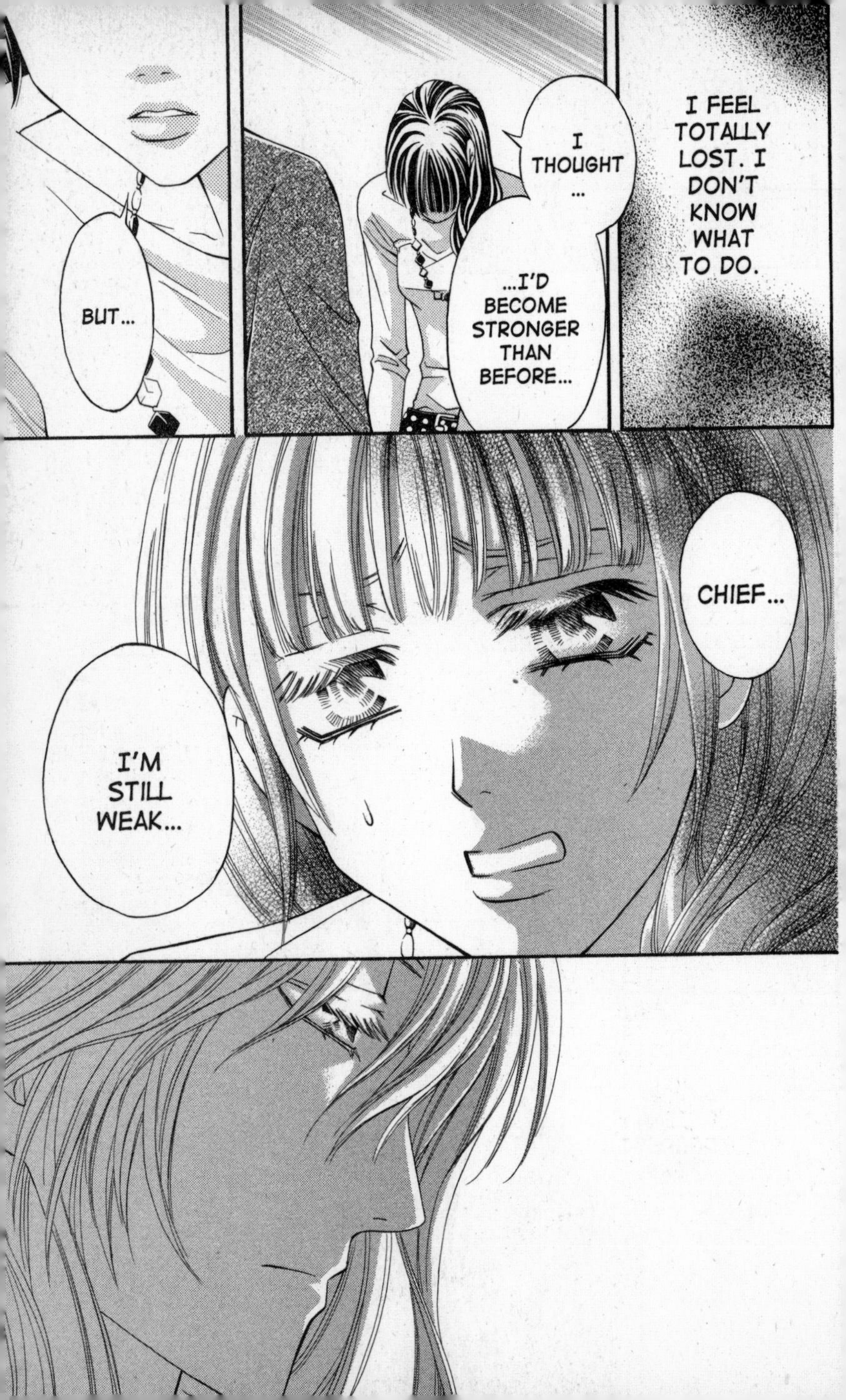
I FEEL TOTALLY LOST. I DON'T KNOW WHAT TO DO.
I THOUGHT ...
...I'D BECOME STRONGER THAN BEFORE...
BUT...
CHIEF...
I'M STILL WEAK...

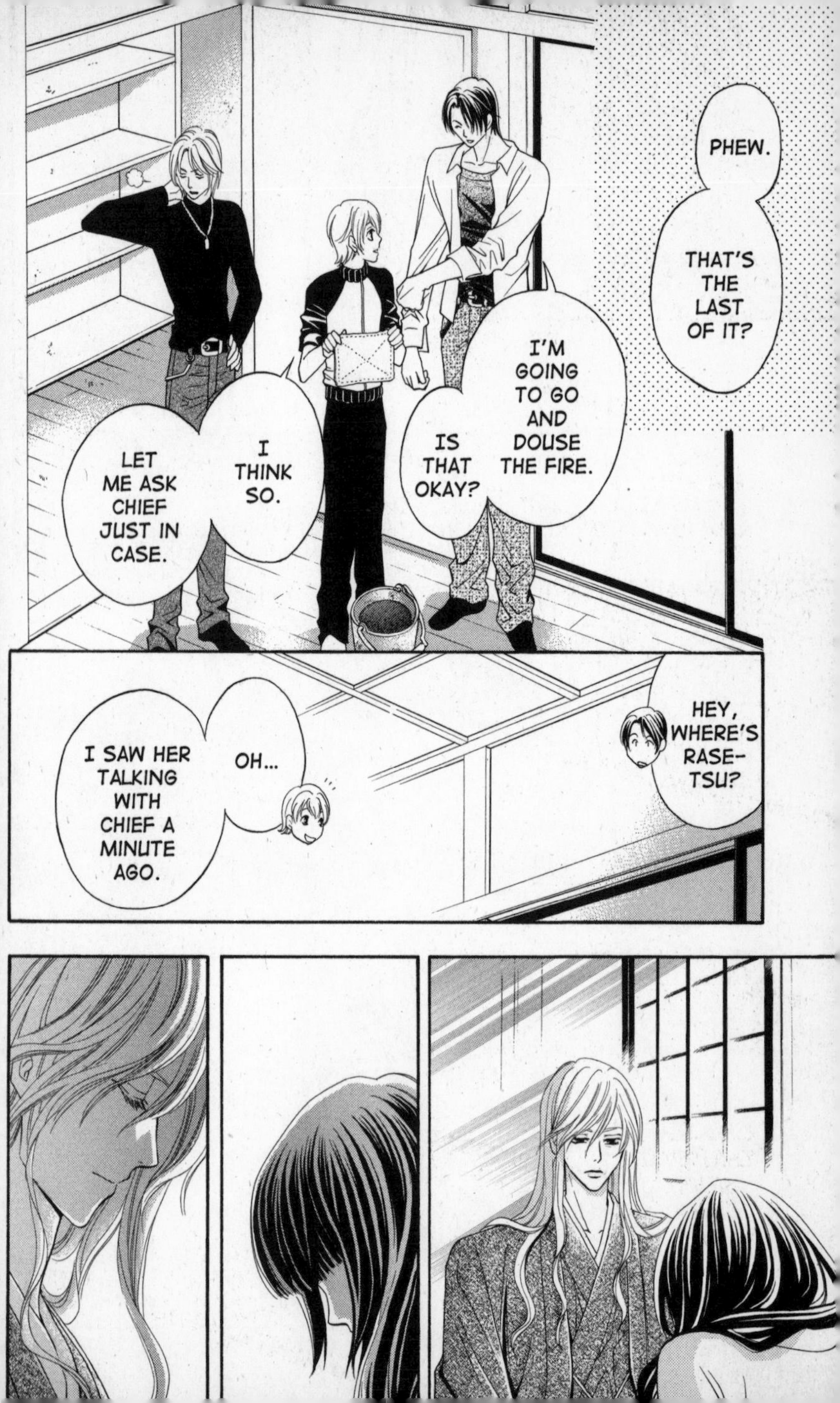
PHEW.
THAT'S THE LAST OF IT?
I'M GOING TO GO AND DOUSE THE FIRE.
IS THAT OKAY?
I THINK SO.
LET ME ASK CHIEF JUST IN CASE.
HEY, WHERE'S RASE-TSU?
OH...
I SAW HER TALKING WITH CHIEF A MINUTE AGO.

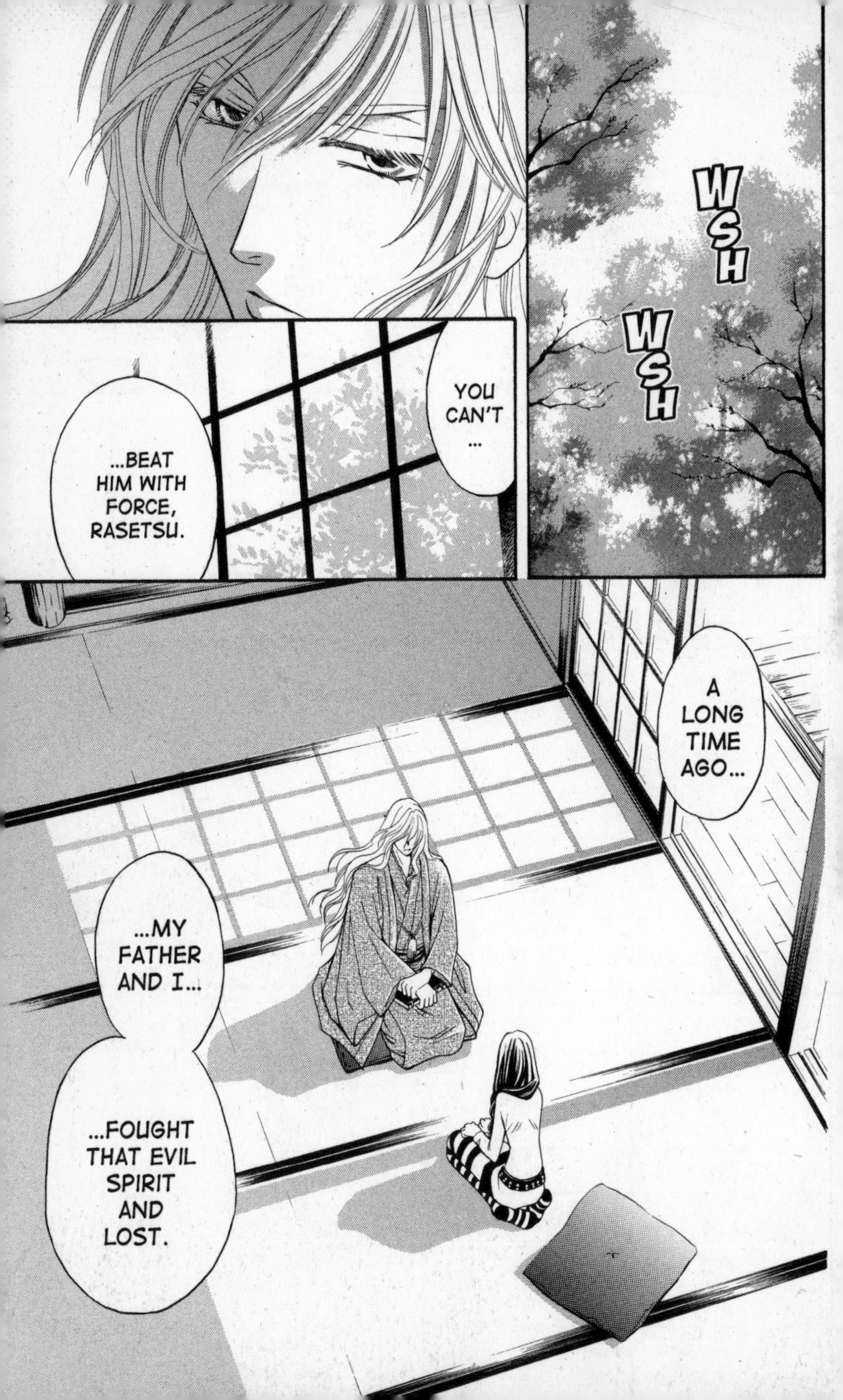
WSH
WSH
YOU CAN'T ...
...BEAT HIM WITH FORCE, RASETSU.
A LONG TIME AGO...
...MY FATHER AND I...
...FOUGHT THAT EVIL SPIRIT AND LOST.

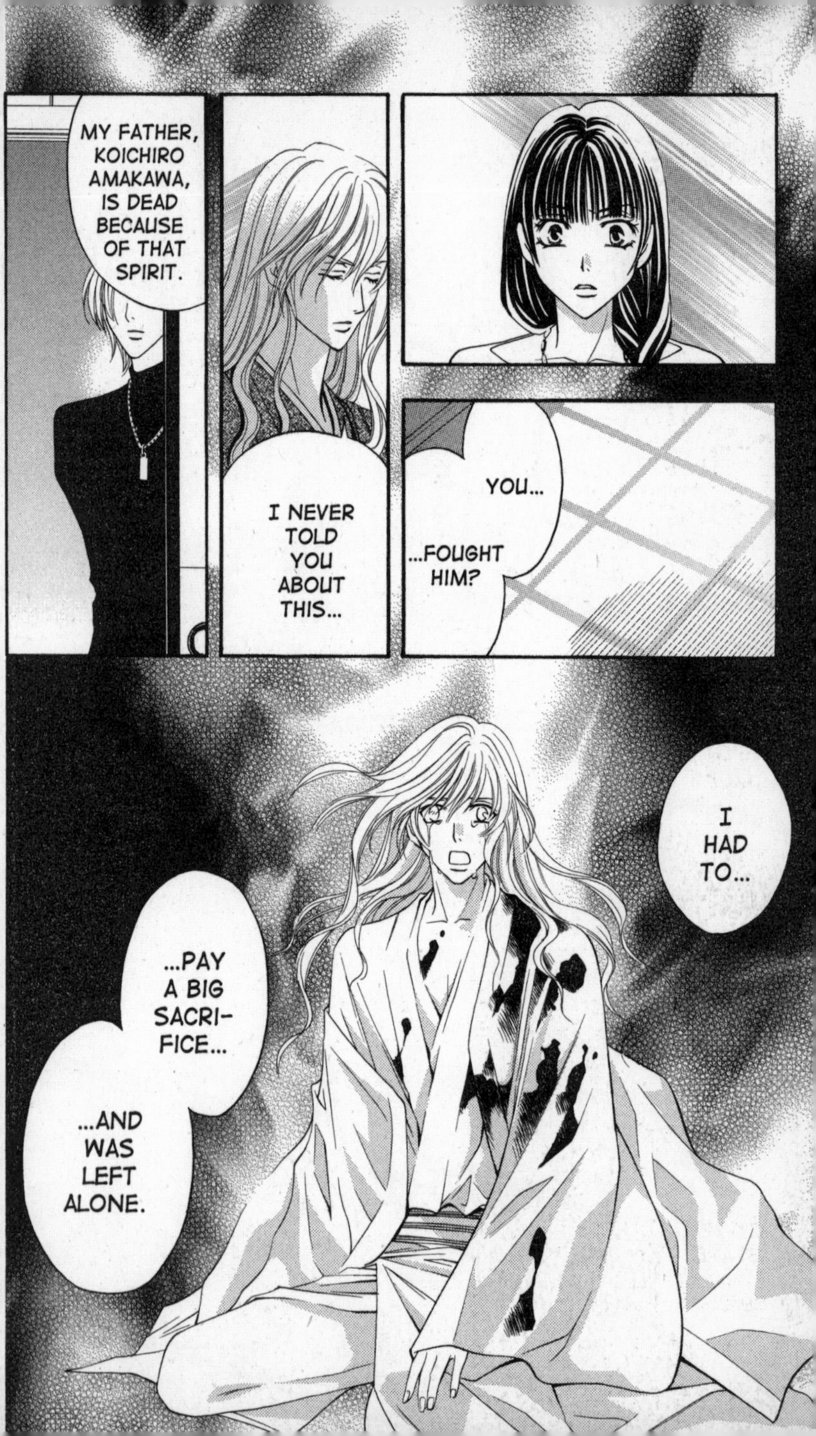
YOU...
...FOUGHT HIM?
I NEVER TOLD YOU ABOUT THIS...
MY FATHER, KOICHIRO AMAKAWA, IS DEAD BECAUSE OF THAT SPIRIT.
I HAD TO...
...PAY A BIG SACRI-FICE...
...AND WAS LEFT ALONE.

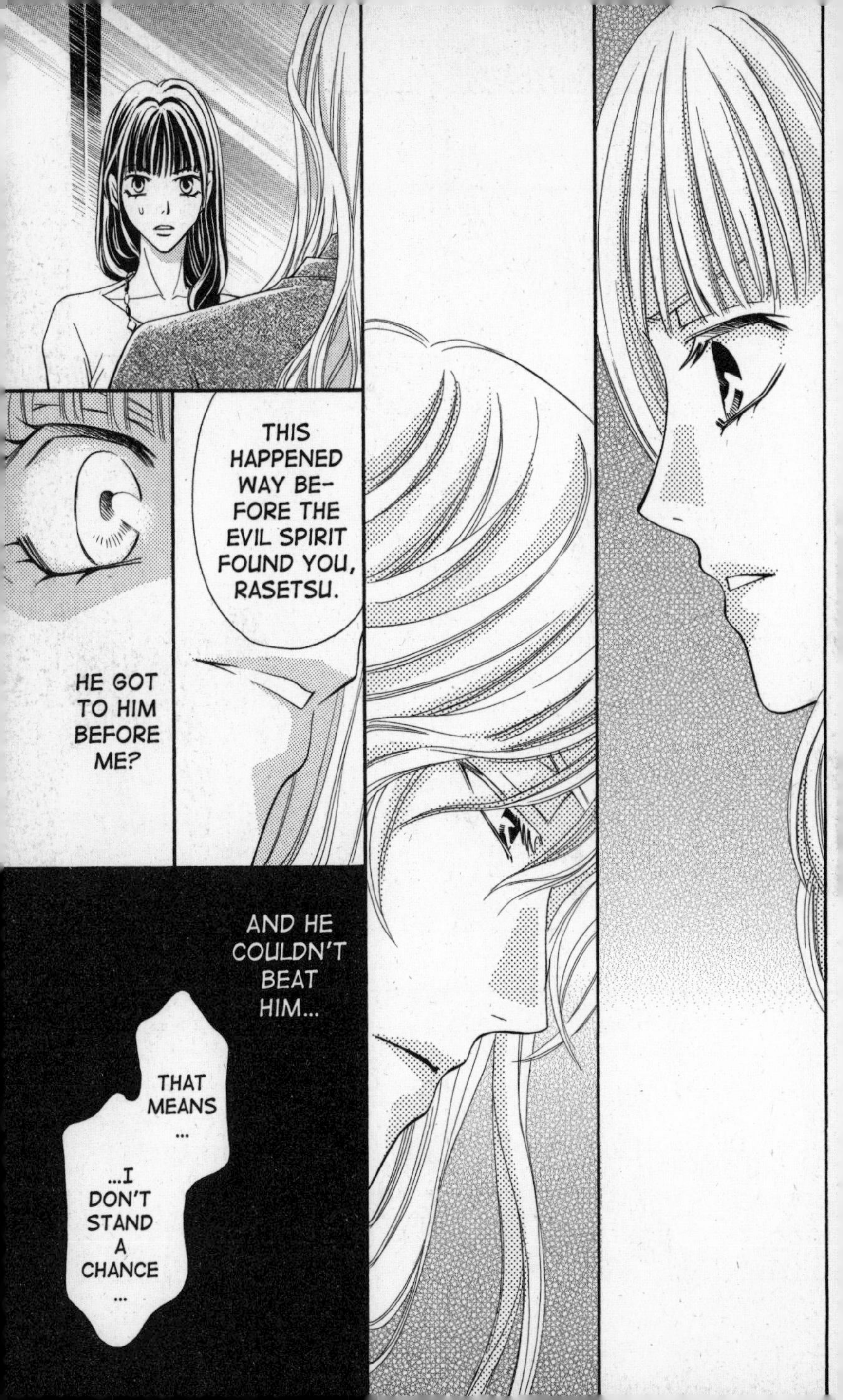
THIS HAPPENED WAY BE- FORE THE EVIL SPIRIT FOUND YOU, RASETSU.
HE GOT TO HIM BEFORE ME?
AND HE COULDN'T BEAT HIM...
THAT MEANS ...
...I DON'T STAND A CHANCE ...

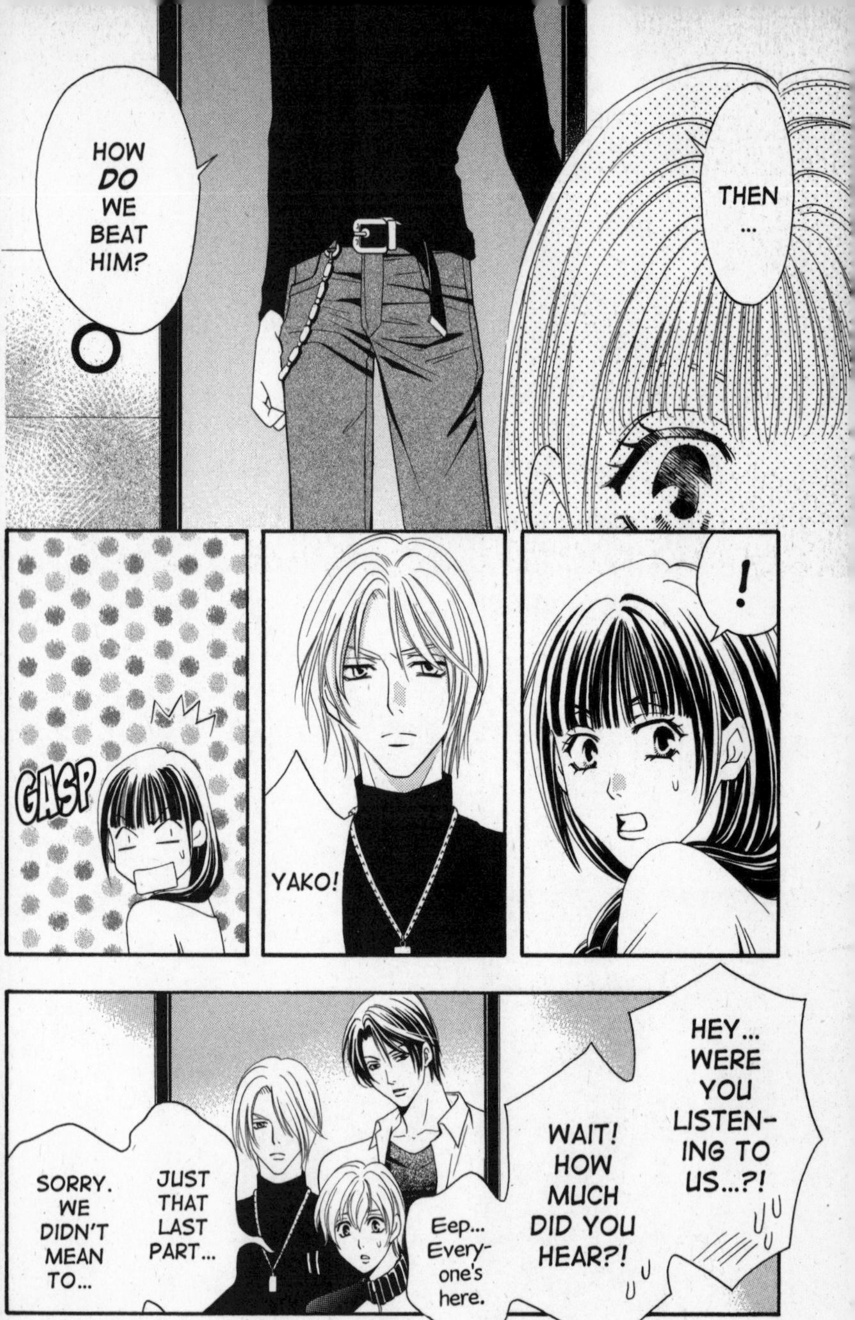
THEN...
HOW DO WE BEAT HIM?
!
YAKO!
GASP
HEY... WERE YOU LISTENING TO US...?!
WAIT! HOW MUCH DID YOU HEAR?!
Eep... Everyone's here.
JUST THAT LAST PART...
SORRY. WE DIDN'T MEAN TO...

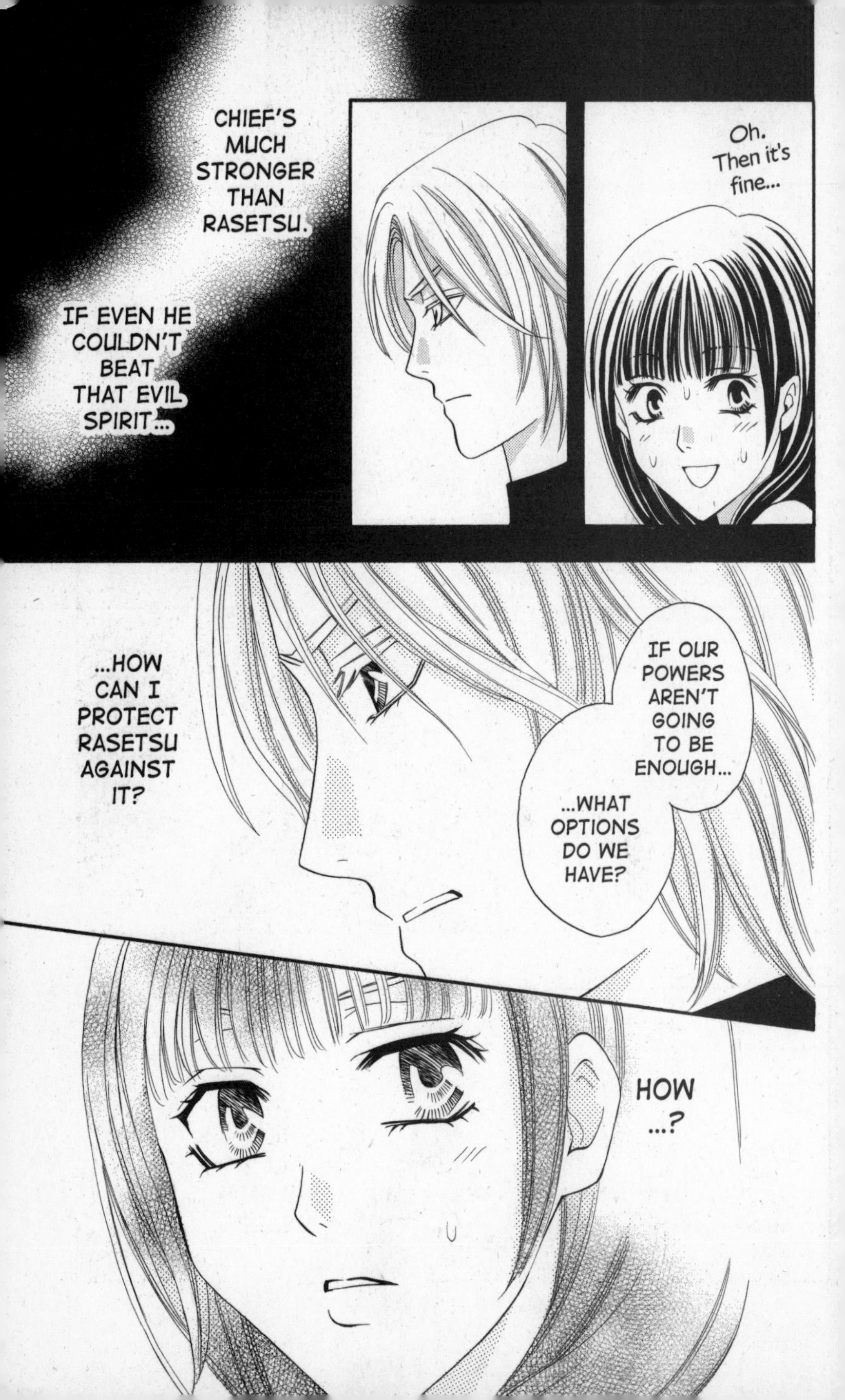
Oh. Then it's fine...
CHIEF'S MUCH STRONGER THAN RASETSU.
IF EVEN HE COULDN'T BEAT THAT EVIL SPIRIT...
IF OUR POWERS AREN'T GOING TO BE ENOUGH...
...WHAT OPTIONS DO WE HAVE?
...HOW CAN I PROTECT RASETSU AGAINST IT?
HOW ...?

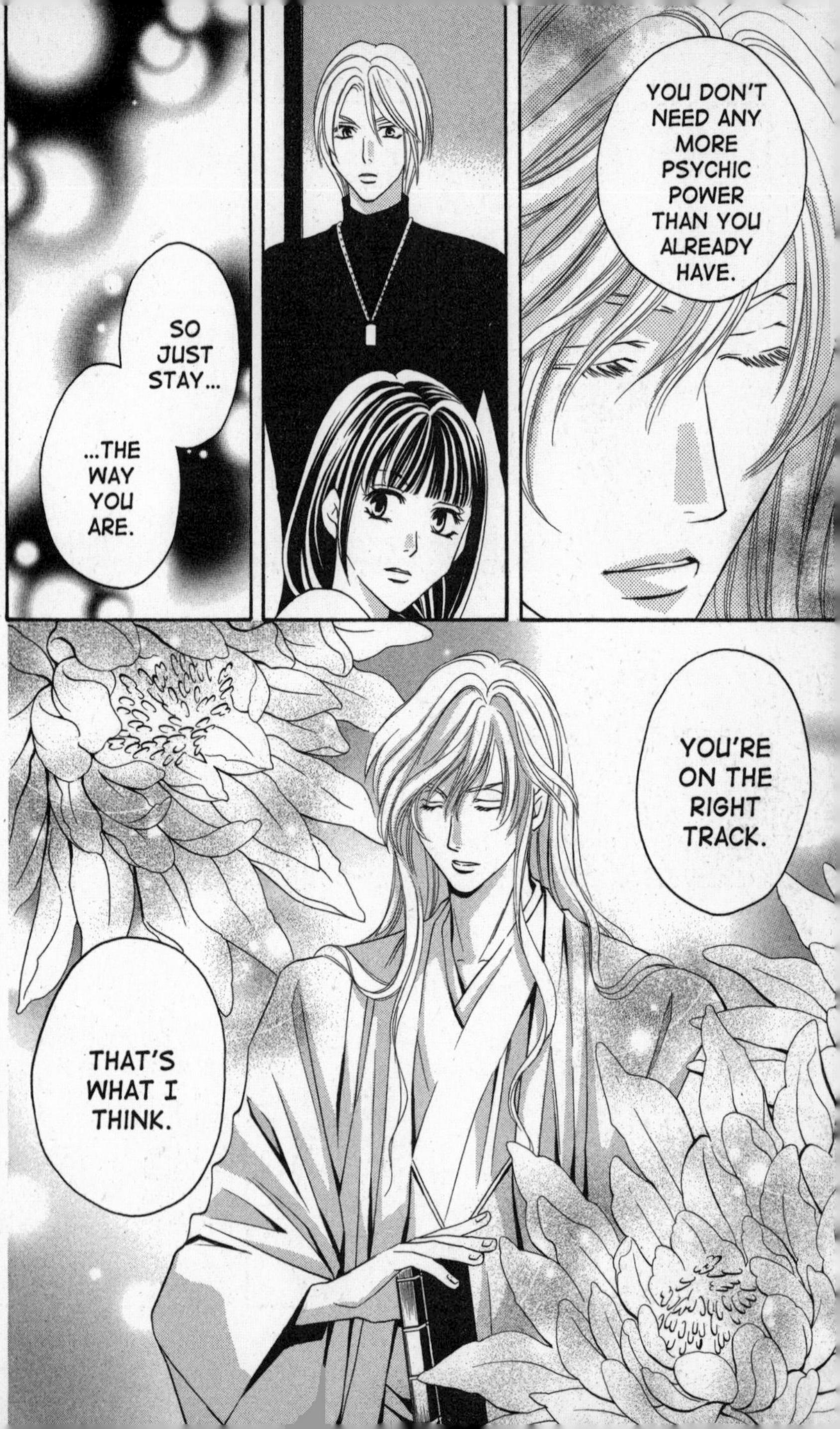
YOU DON'T NEED ANY MORE PSYCHIC POWER THAN YOU ALREADY HAVE.
SO JUST STAY...
...THE WAY YOU ARE.
YOU'RE ON THE RIGHT TRACK.
THAT'S WHAT I THINK.

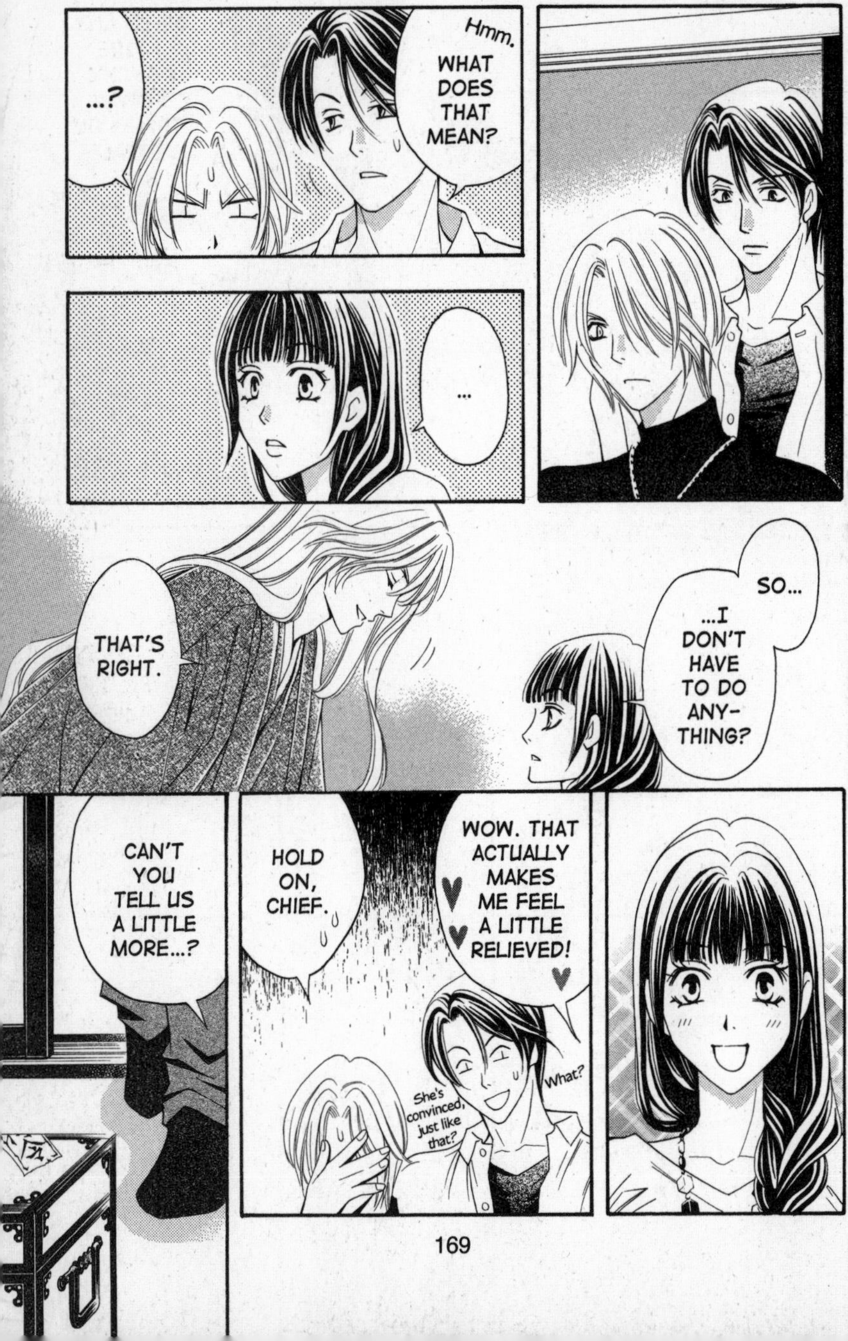
Hmm.
WHAT DOES THAT MEAN?
...?
...
SO...
...I DON'T HAVE TO DO ANY-THING?
THAT'S RIGHT.
WOW. THAT ACTUALLY MAKES ME FEEL A LITTLE RELIEVED!
What?
HOLD ON, CHIEF.
She's convinced, just like that?
CAN'T YOU TELL US A LITTLE MORE...?

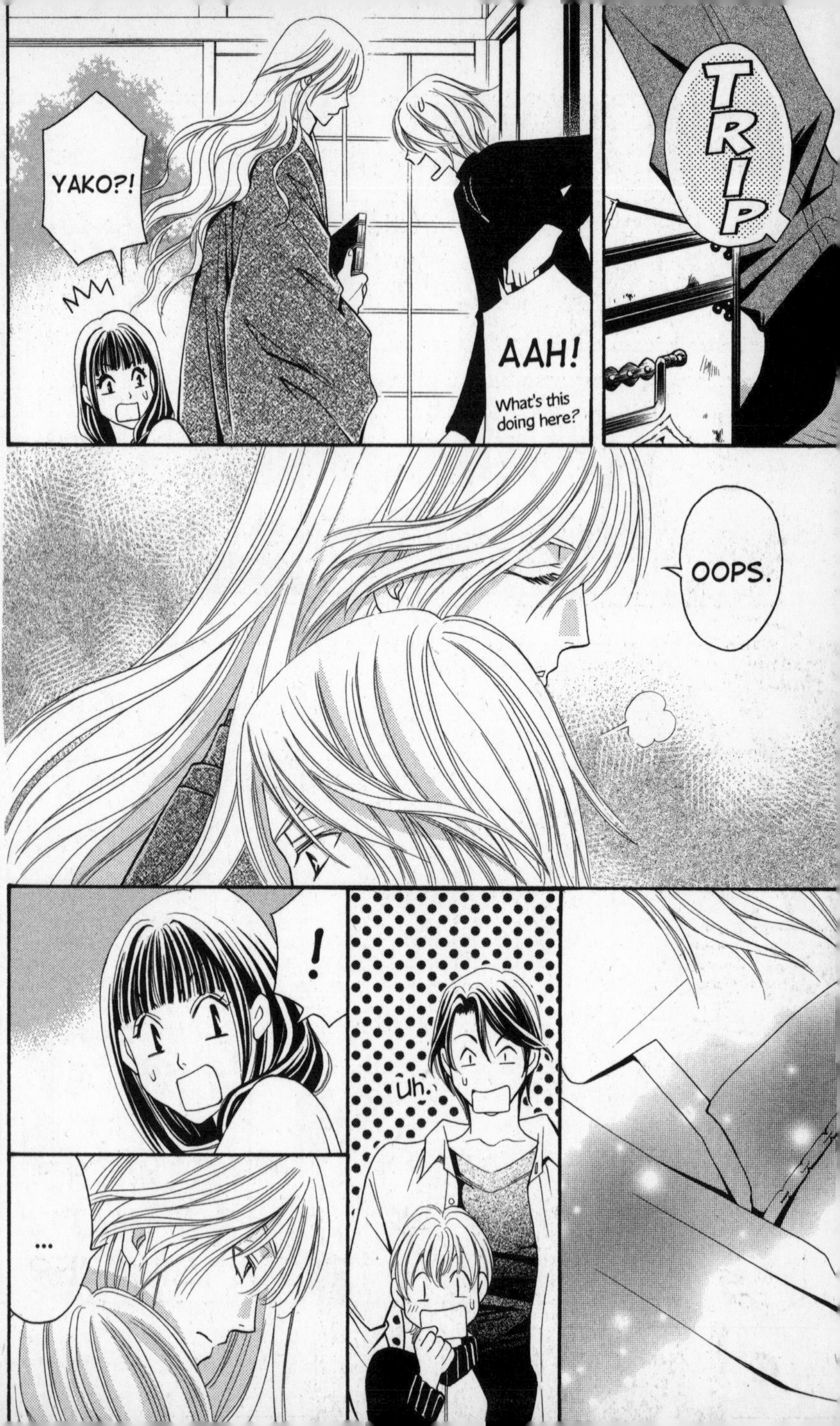
TRIP
AAH!
What's this doing here?
YAKO?!
OOPS.
Uh.
!
...

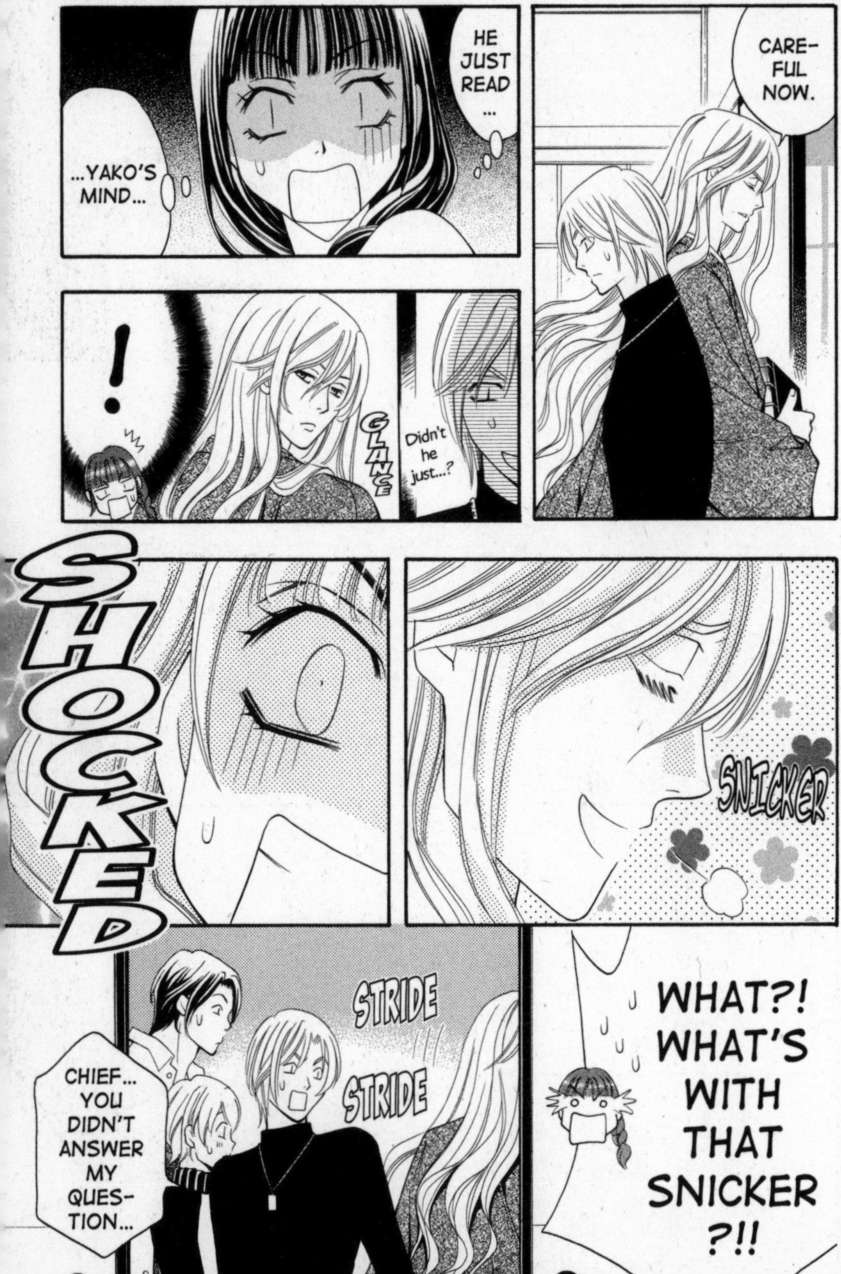
CARE-FUL NOW.
HE JUST READ ...
...YAKO'S MIND...
Didn't he just...?
GLANCE
!
SNICKER
SHOCKED
WHAT?! WHAT'S WITH THAT SNICKER ?!!
STRIDE
STRIDE
CHIEF... YOU DIDN'T ANSWER MY QUES-TION...

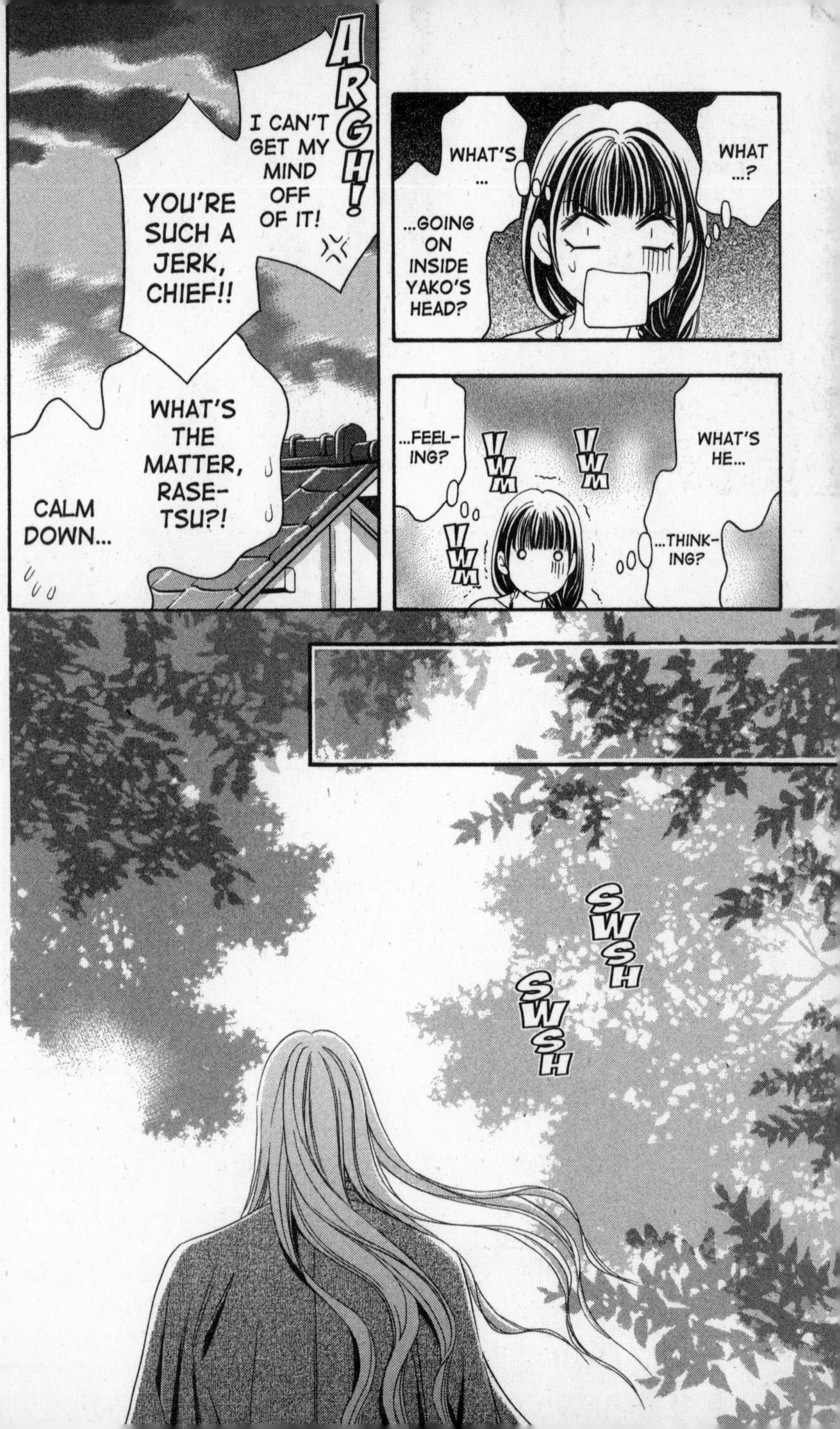
WHAT ...?
WHAT'S ...
...GOING ON INSIDE YAKO'S HEAD?
WHAT'S HE...
...THINKING?
...FEEL-ING?
VWM
VWM
VWM
ARGH!
I CAN'T GET MY MIND OFF OF IT!
YOU'RE SUCH A JERK, CHIEF!!
WHAT'S THE MATTER, RASE-TSU?!
CALM DOWN...
SWSH
SWSH

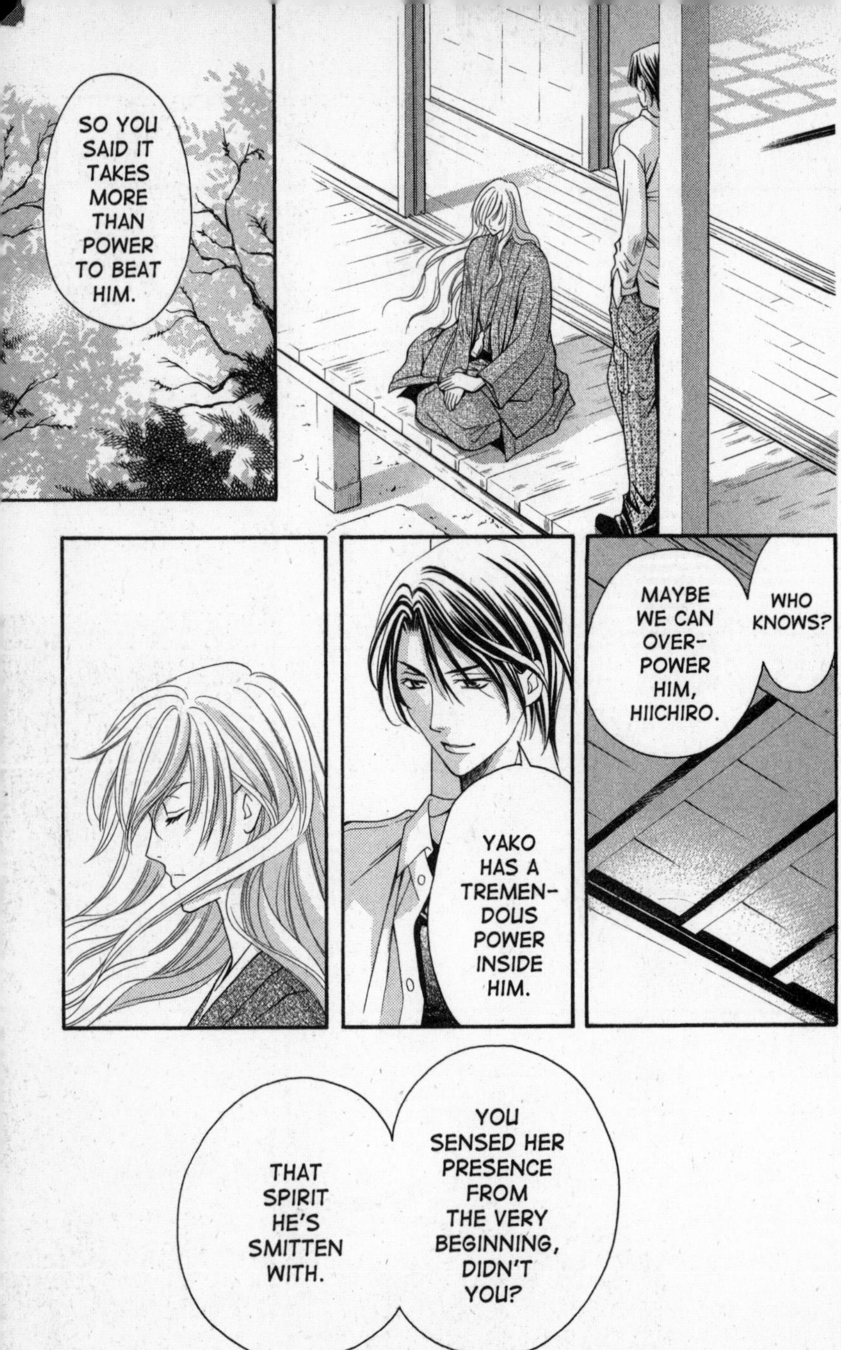
SO YOU SAID IT TAKES MORE THAN POWER TO BEAT HIM.
WHO KNOWS?
MAYBE WE CAN OVER-POWER HIM, HIICHIRO.
YAKO HAS A TREMEN-DOUS POWER INSIDE HIM.
YOU SENSED HER PRESENCE FROM THE VERY BEGINNING, DIDN'T YOU?
THAT SPIRIT HE'S SMITTEN WITH.

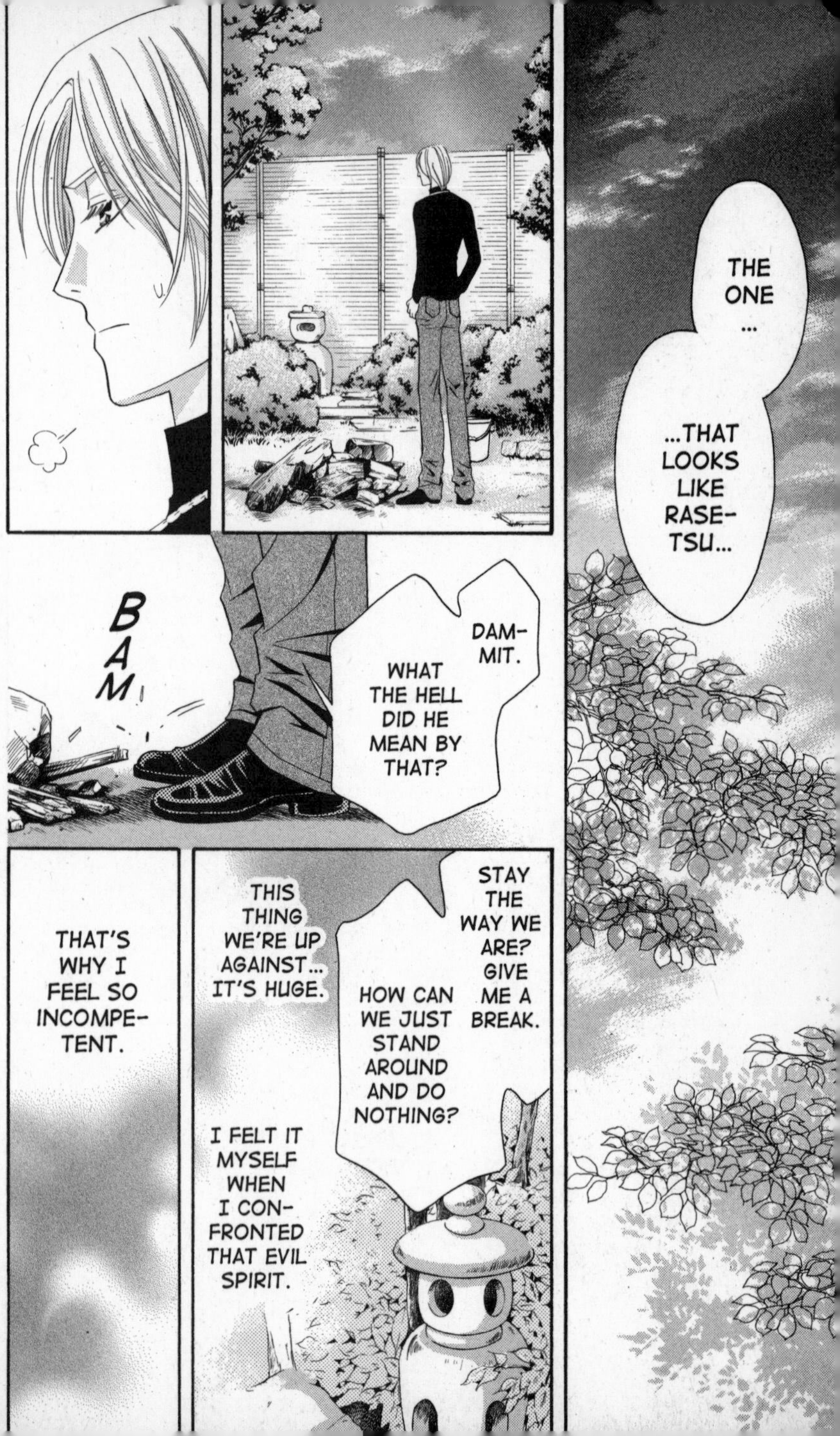
THE ONE ...
...THAT LOOKS LIKE RASE-TSU...
BAM
DAM-MIT.
WHAT THE HELL DID HE MEAN BY THAT?
STAY THE WAY WE ARE? GIVE ME A BREAK.
HOW CAN WE JUST STAND AROUND AND DO NOTHING?
THIS THING WE'RE UP AGAINST... IT'S HUGE.
I FELT IT MYSELF WHEN I CON-FRONTED THAT EVIL SPIRIT.
THAT'S WHY I FEEL SO INCOMPE-TENT.

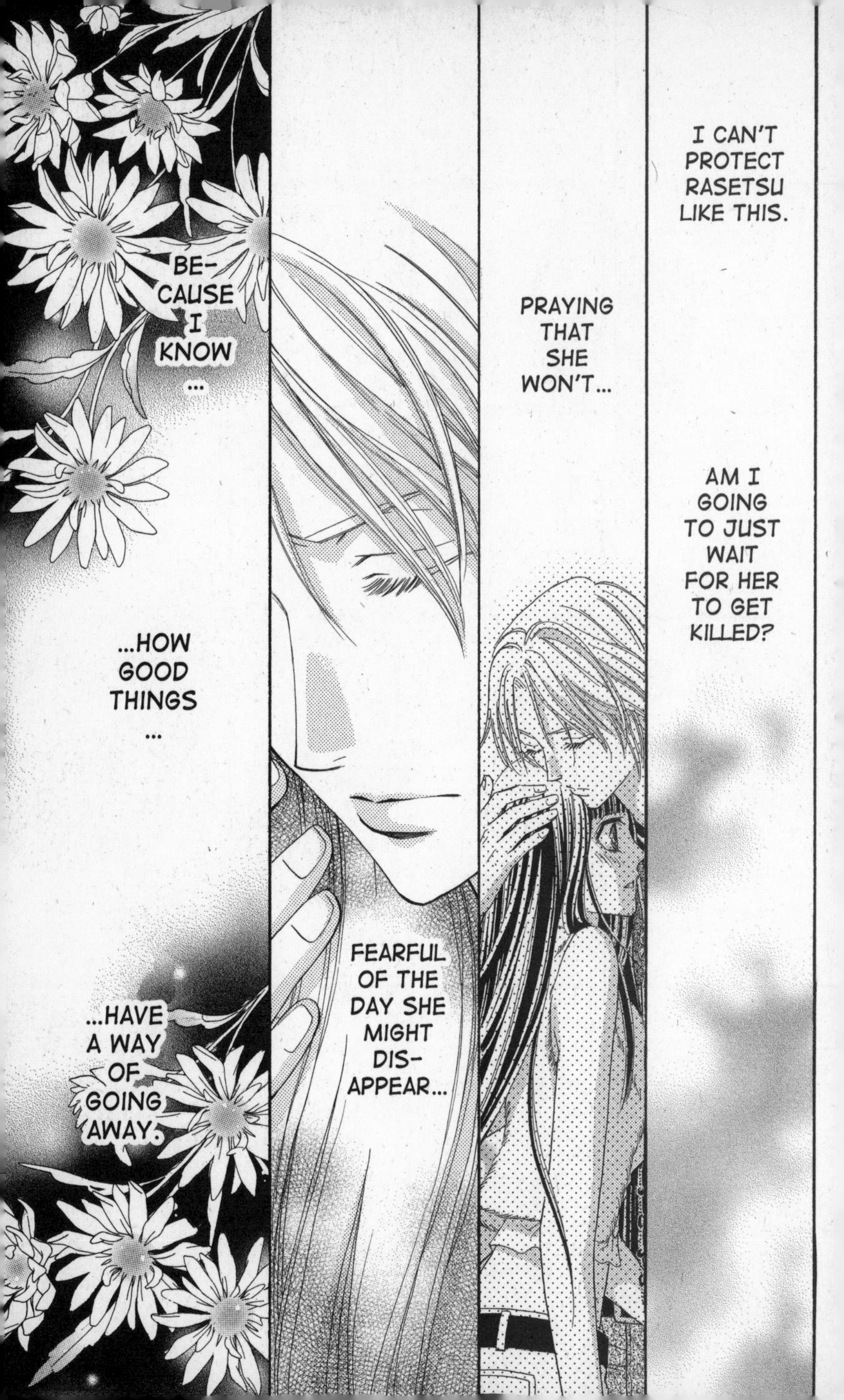
I CAN'T PROTECT RASETSU LIKE THIS.
AM I GOING TO JUST WAIT FOR HER TO GET KILLED?
PRAYING THAT SHE WON'T...
FEARFUL OF THE DAY SHE MIGHT DIS-APPEAR...
BE-CAUSE I KNOW ...
...HOW GOOD THINGS ...
...HAVE A WAY OF GOING AWAY.

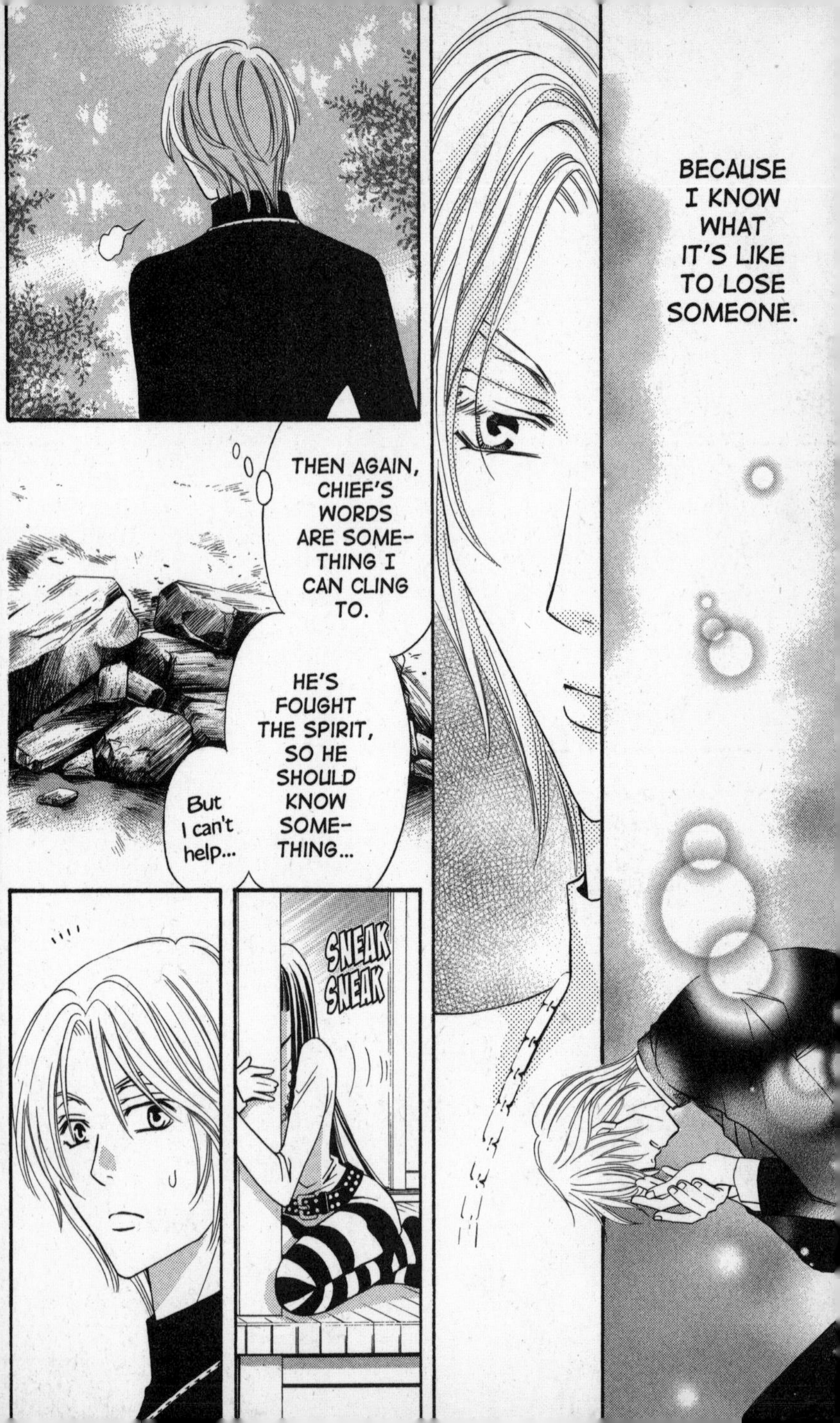
BECAUSE I KNOW WHAT IT'S LIKE TO LOSE SOMEONE.
THEN AGAIN, CHIEF'S WORDS ARE SOME-THING I CAN CLING TO.
HE'S FOUGHT THE SPIRIT, SO HE SHOULD KNOW SOME-THING...
But I can't help...
SNEAK SNEAK

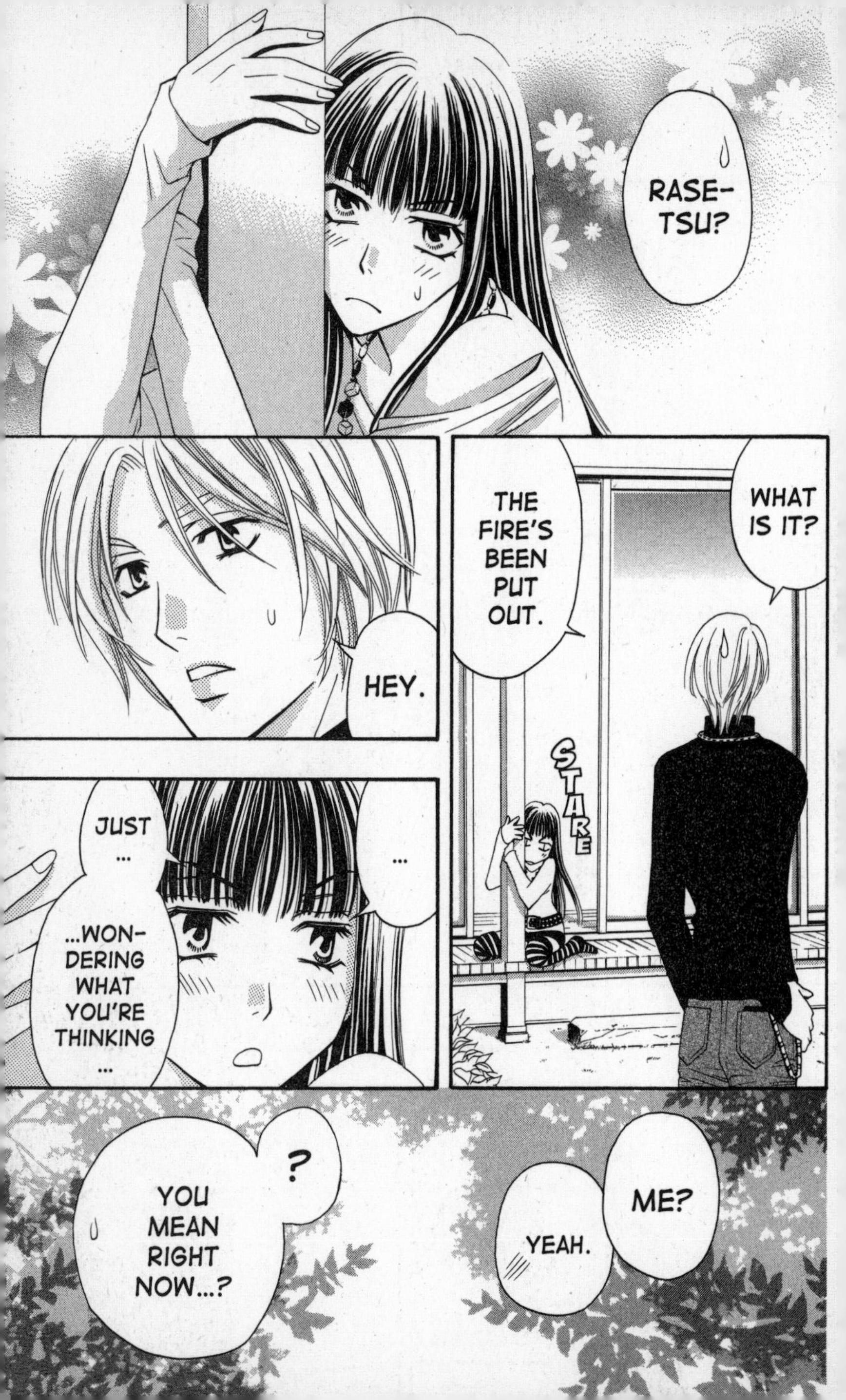
RASE-TSU?
WHAT IS IT?
THE FIRE'S BEEN PUT OUT.
STARE
HEY.
...
JUST ...
...WONDERING WHAT YOU'RE THINKING ...
ME?
YEAH.
?
YOU MEAN RIGHT NOW...?

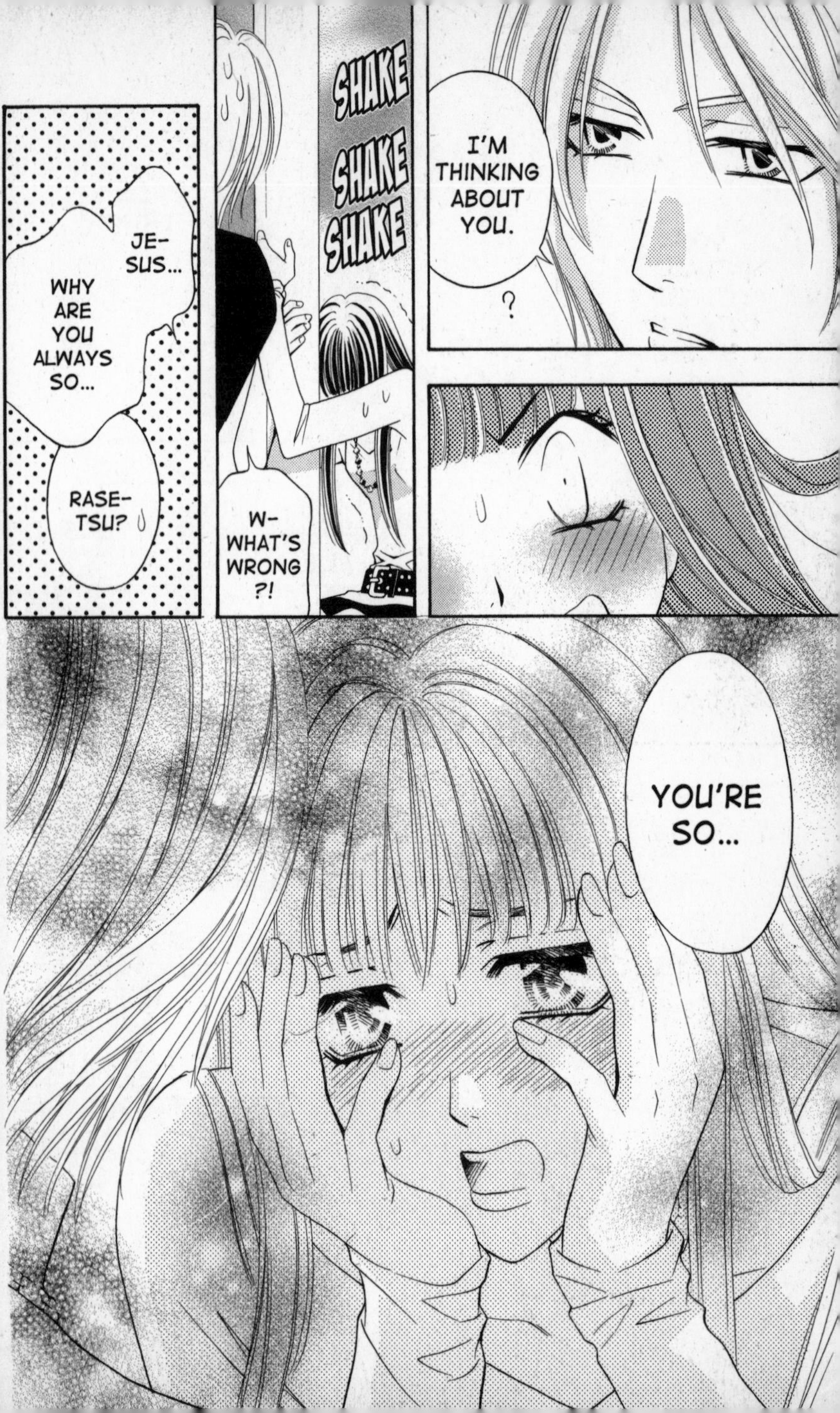
I'M THINKING ABOUT YOU.
?
SHAKE SHAKE SHAKE
W-WHAT'S WRONG?!
JE-SUS...
WHY ARE YOU ALWAYS SO...
RASE-TSU?
YOU'RE SO...

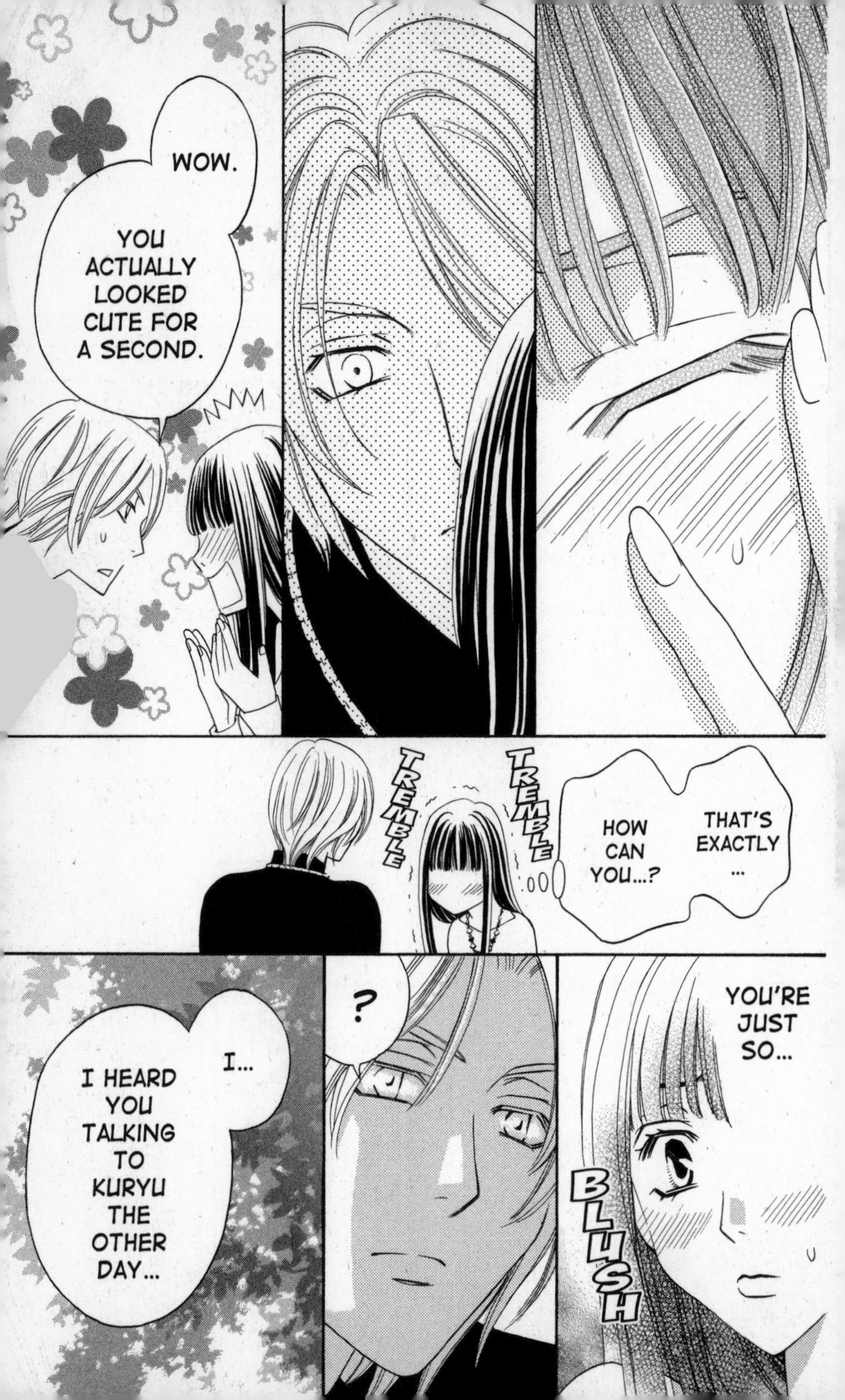
WOW.
YOU ACTUALLY LOOKED CUTE FOR A SECOND.
THAT'S EXACTLY ...
HOW CAN YOU...?
TREMBLE
TREMBLE
YOU'RE JUST SO...
BLUSH
?
I...
I HEARD YOU TALKING TO KURYU THE OTHER DAY...

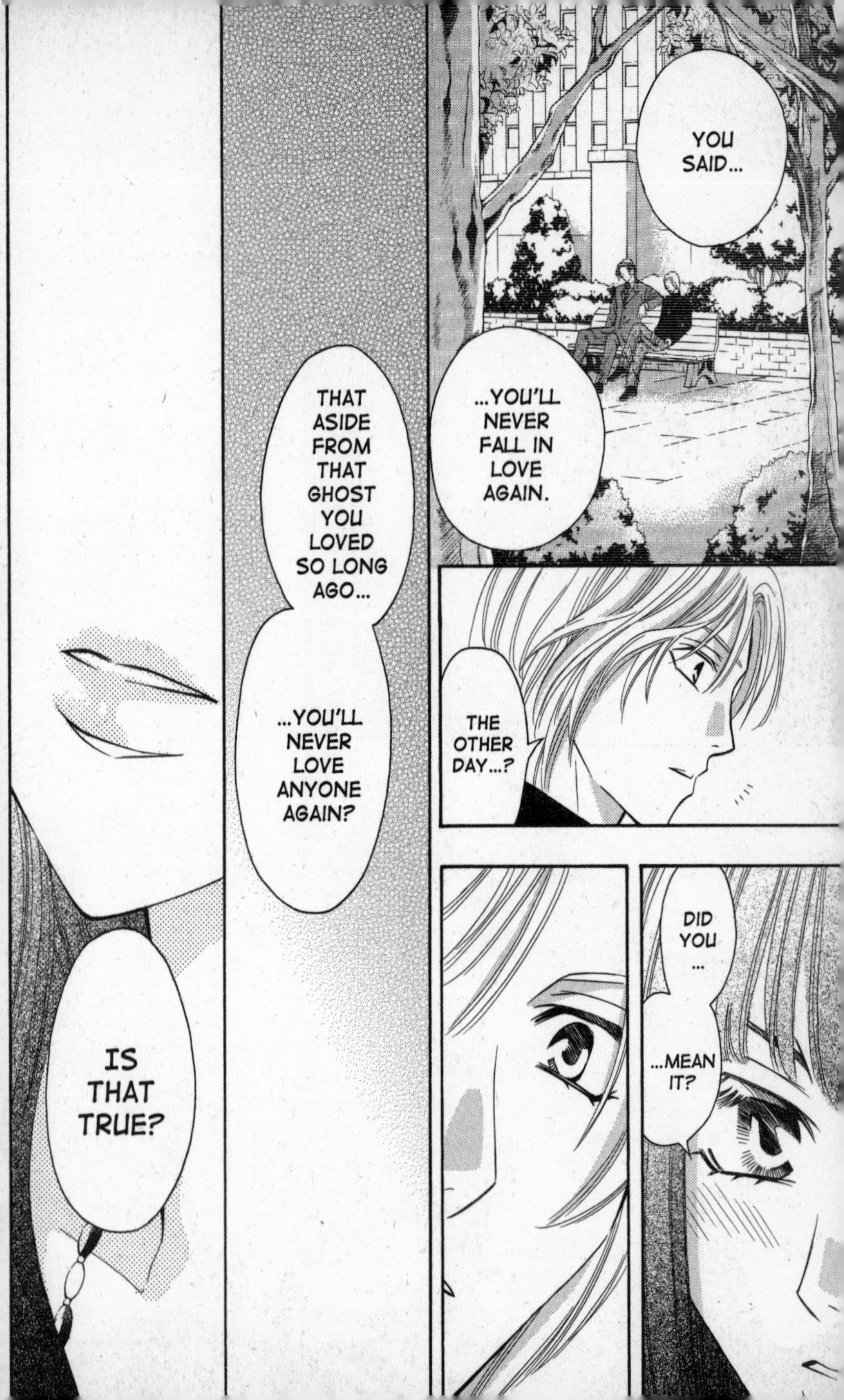
YOU SAID...
...YOU'LL NEVER FALL IN LOVE AGAIN.
THE OTHER DAY...?
DID YOU ...
...MEAN IT?
THAT ASIDE FROM THAT GHOST YOU LOVED SO LONG AGO...
...YOU'LL NEVER LOVE ANYONE AGAIN?
IS THAT TRUE?

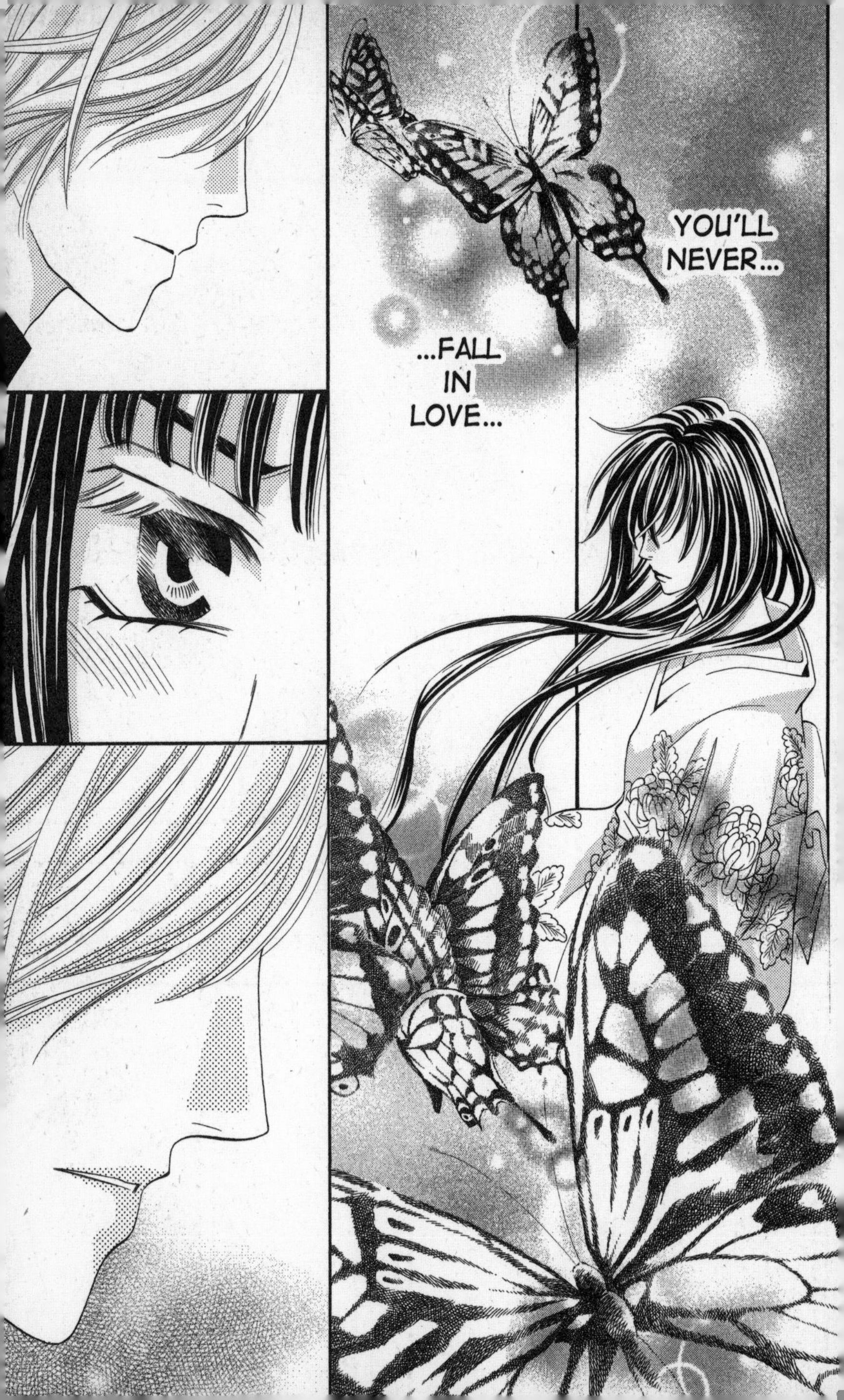
YOU'LL NEVER...
...FALL IN LOVE...

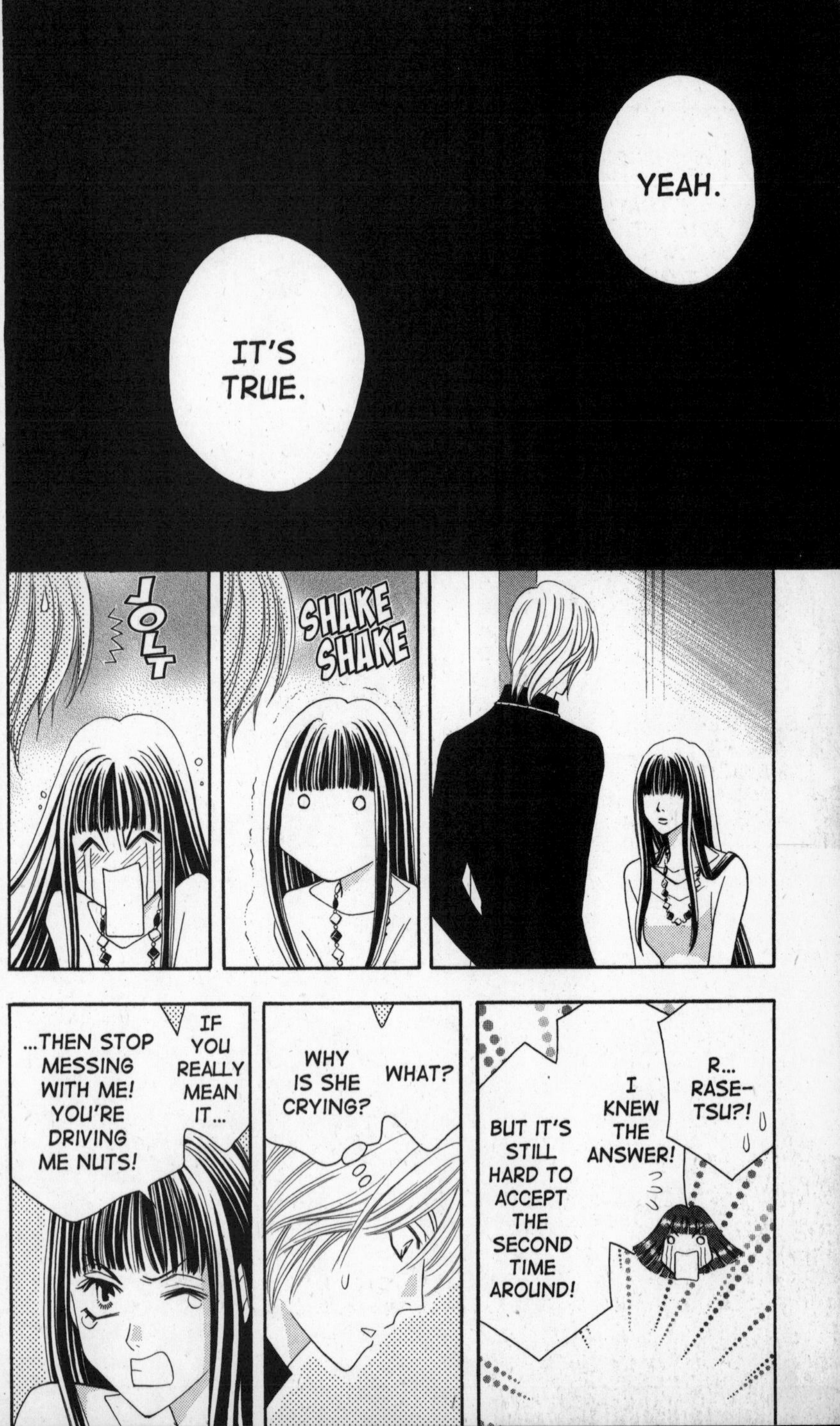
YEAH.
IT'S TRUE.
SHAKE SHAKE
JOLT
R... RASE-TSU?!
I KNEW THE ANSWER!
BUT IT'S STILL HARD TO ACCEPT THE SECOND TIME AROUND!
WHAT?
WHY IS SHE CRYING?
IF YOU REALLY MEAN IT...
...THEN STOP MESSING WITH ME! YOU'RE DRIVING ME NUTS!

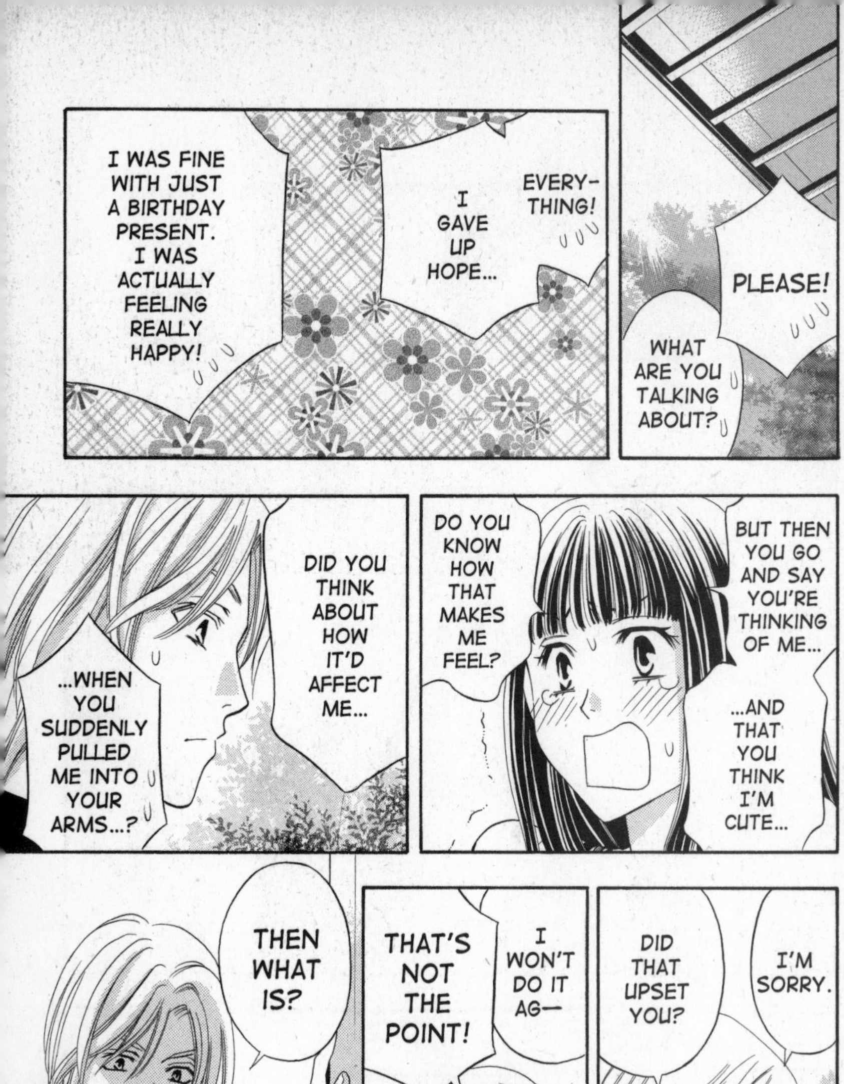
PLEASE!
WHAT ARE YOU TALKING ABOUT?
EVERYTHING!
I GAVE UP HOPE...
I WAS FINE WITH JUST A BIRTHDAY PRESENT. I WAS ACTUALLY FEELING REALLY HAPPY!
BUT THEN YOU GO AND SAY YOU'RE THINKING OF ME...
...AND THAT YOU THINK I'M CUTE...
DO YOU KNOW HOW THAT MAKES ME FEEL?
DID YOU THINK ABOUT HOW IT'D AFFECT ME...
...WHEN YOU SUDDENLY PULLED ME INTO YOUR ARMS...?
I'M SORRY.
DID THAT UPSET YOU?
I WON'T DO IT AG—
THAT'S NOT THE POINT!
THEN WHAT IS?

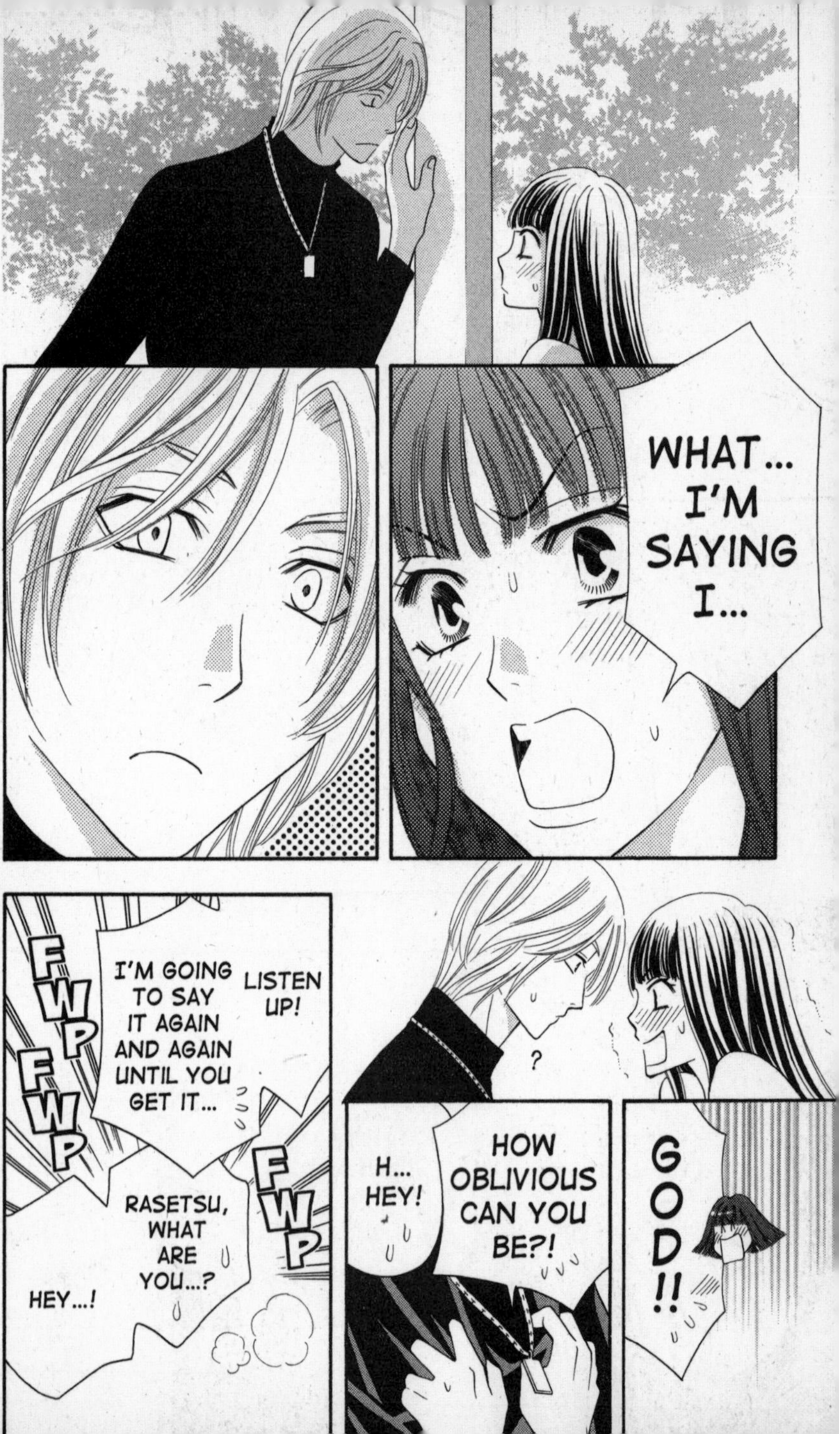
WHAT... I'M SAYING I...
?
GOD!!
HOW OBLIVIOUS CAN YOU BE?!
H... HEY!
LISTEN UP!
I'M GOING TO SAY IT AGAIN AND AGAIN UNTIL YOU GET IT...
FWP
FWP
FWP
FWP
RASETSU, WHAT ARE YOU...?
HEY...!

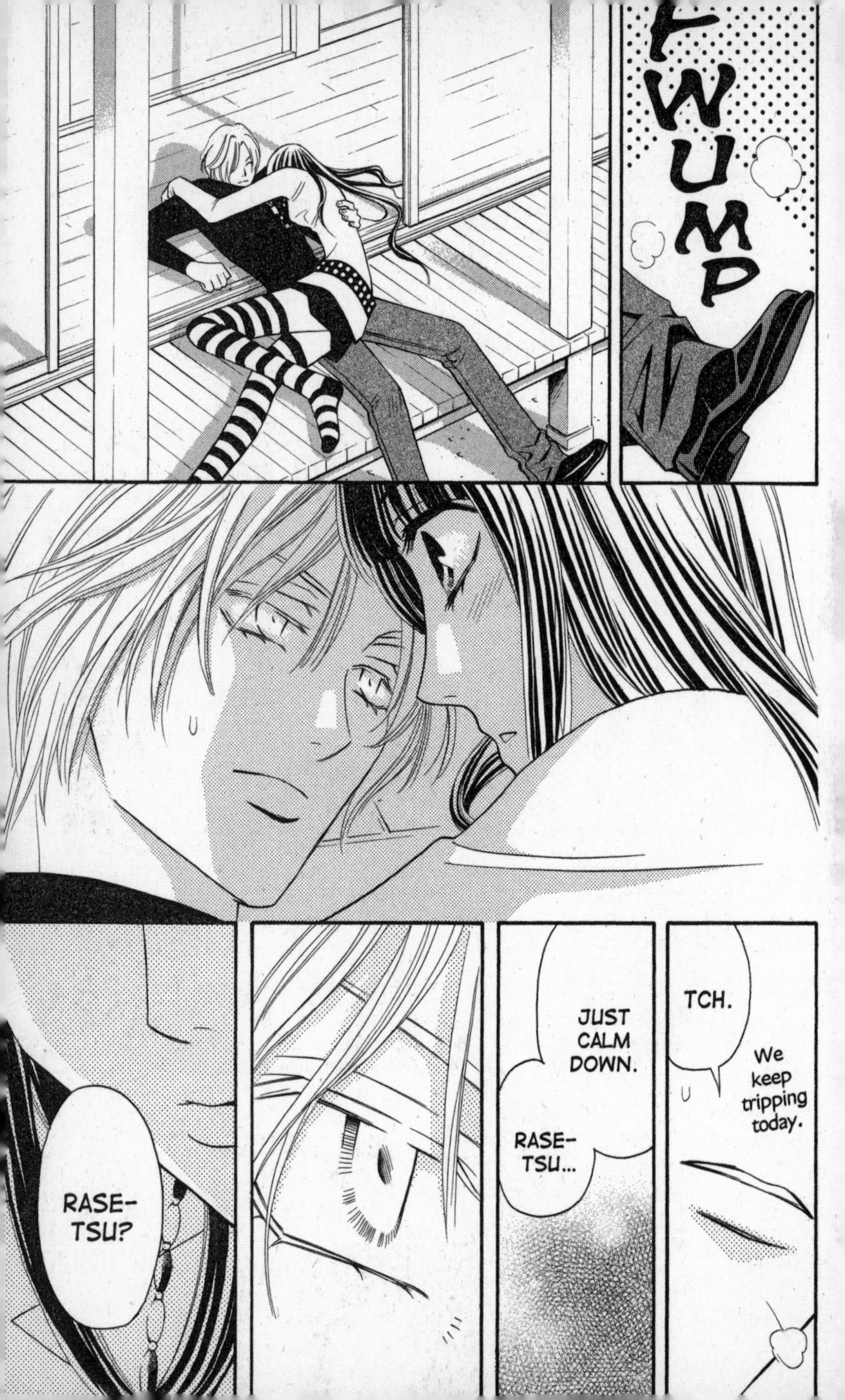
TWUMP
TCH.
We keep tripping today.
JUST CALM DOWN.
RASE-TSU...
RASE-TSU?

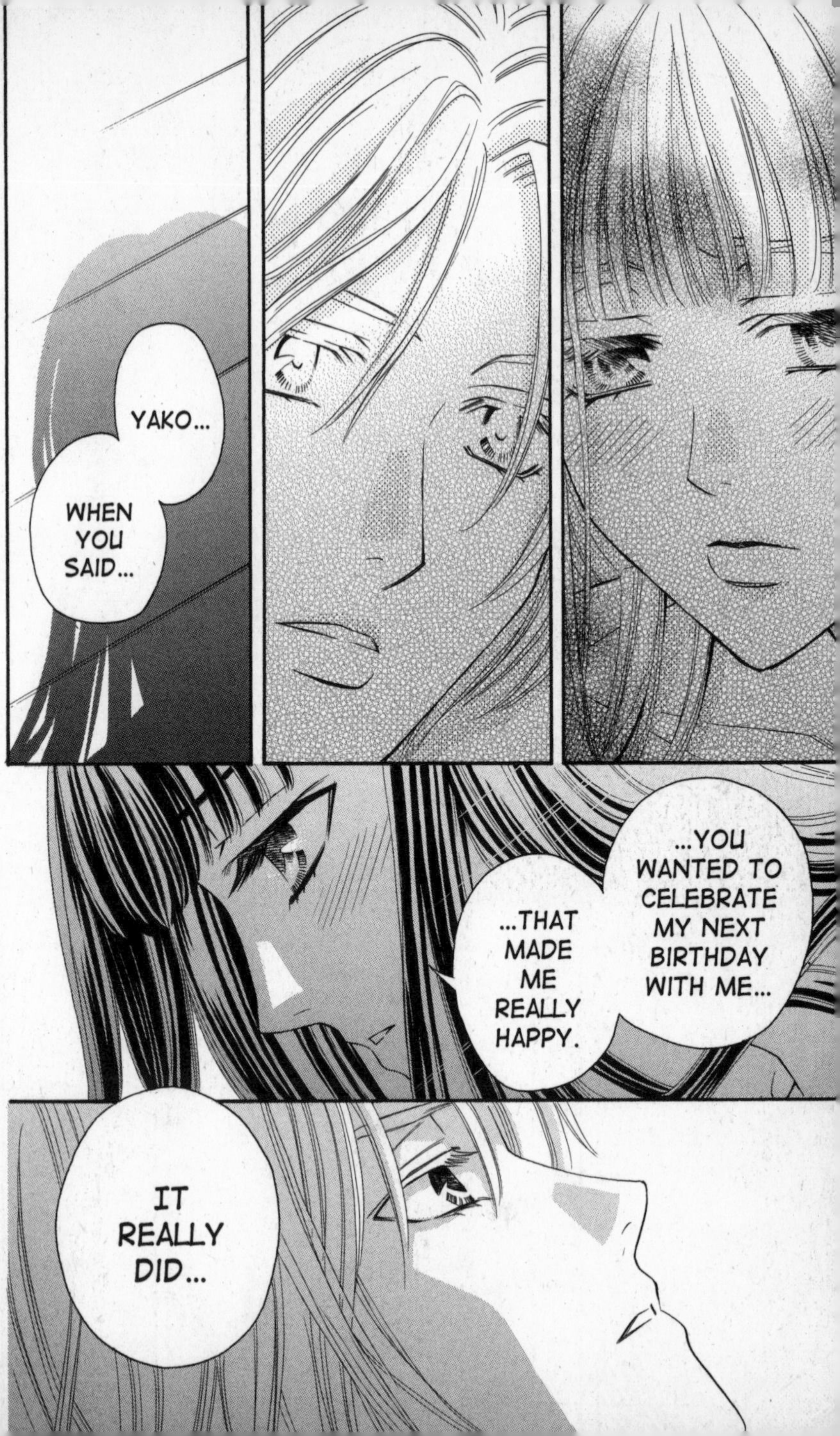
YAKO...
WHEN YOU SAID...
...YOU WANTED TO CELEBRATE MY NEXT BIRTHDAY WITH ME...
...THAT MADE ME REALLY HAPPY.
IT REALLY DID...

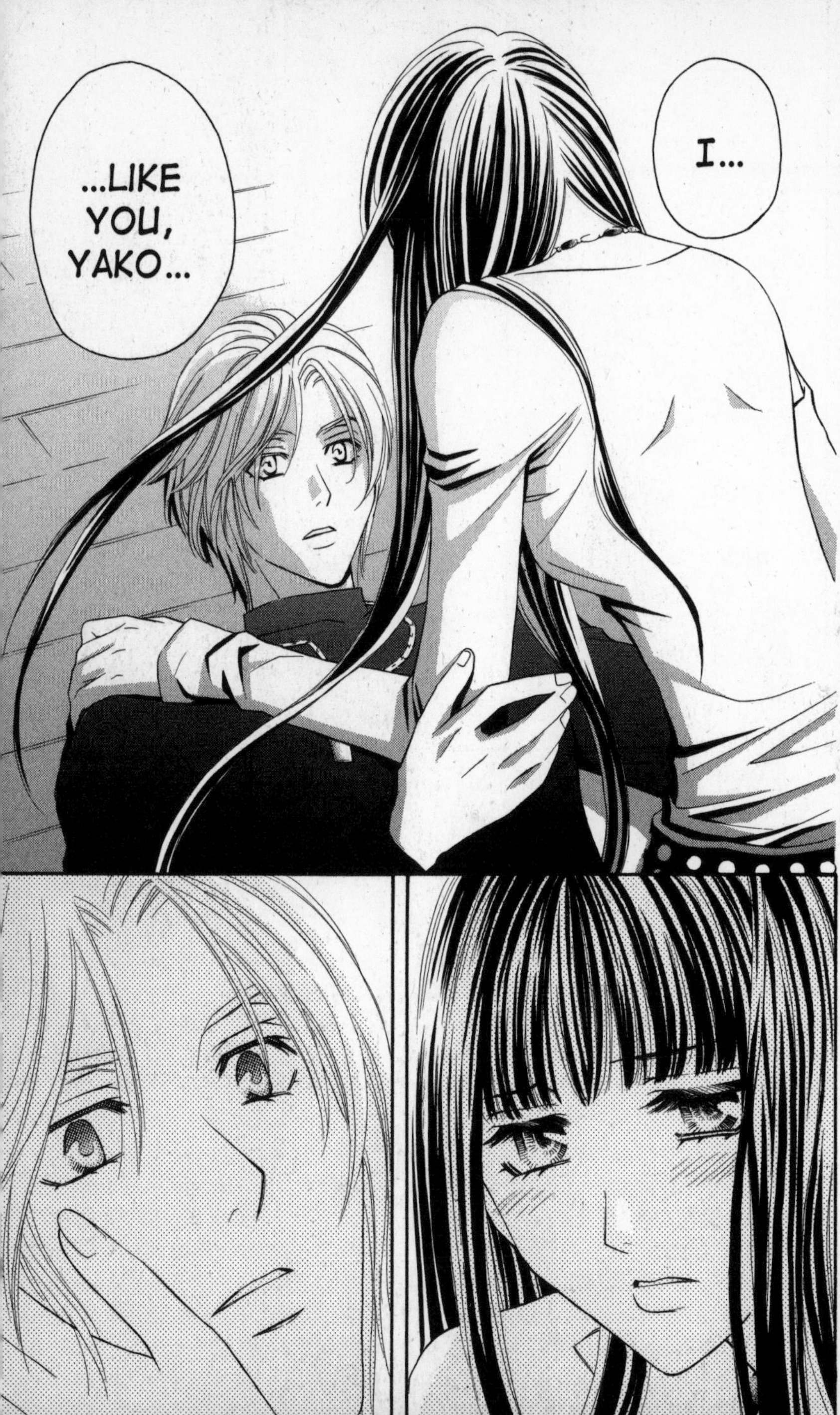
I...
...LIKE YOU, YAKO...

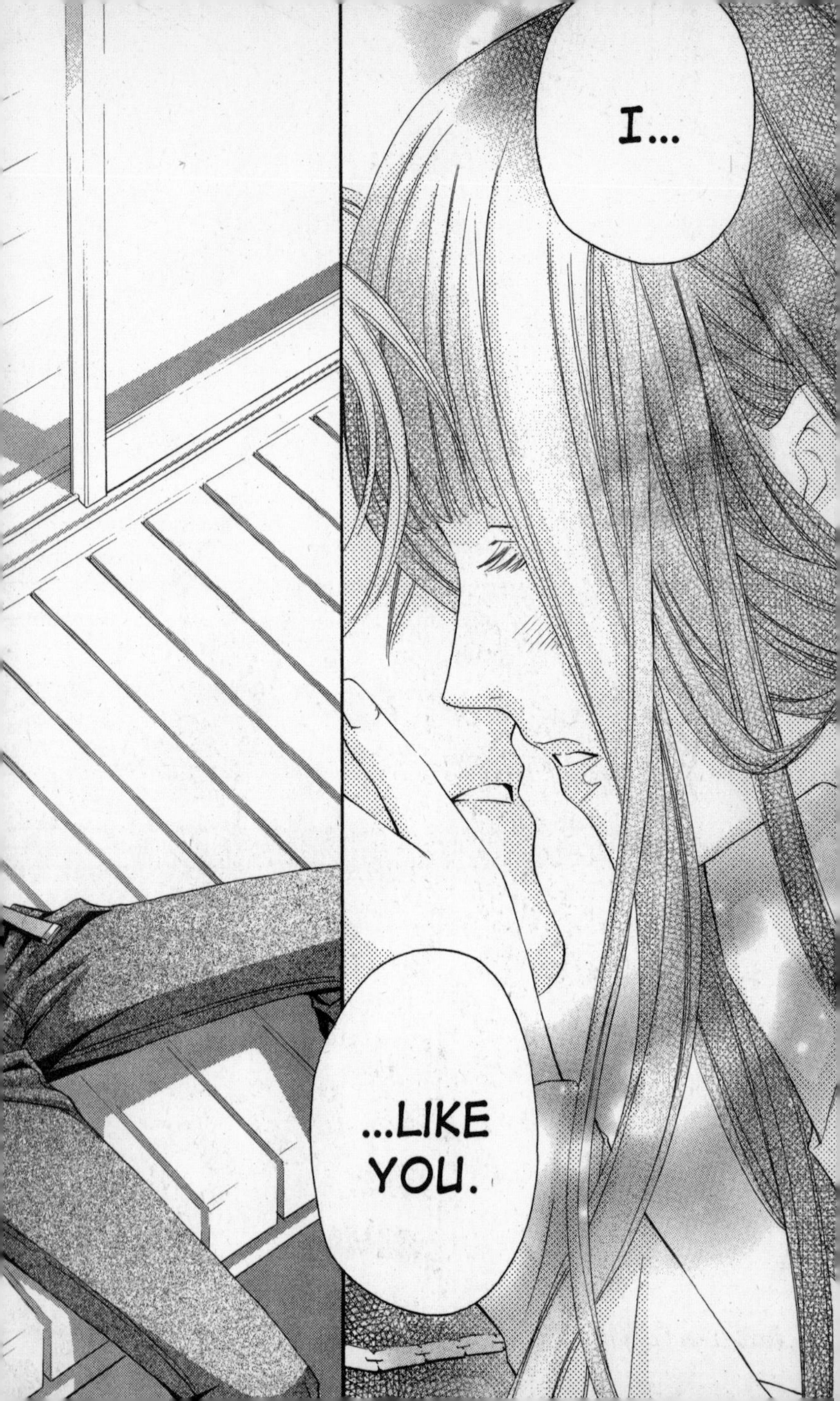
I...
...LIKE YOU.

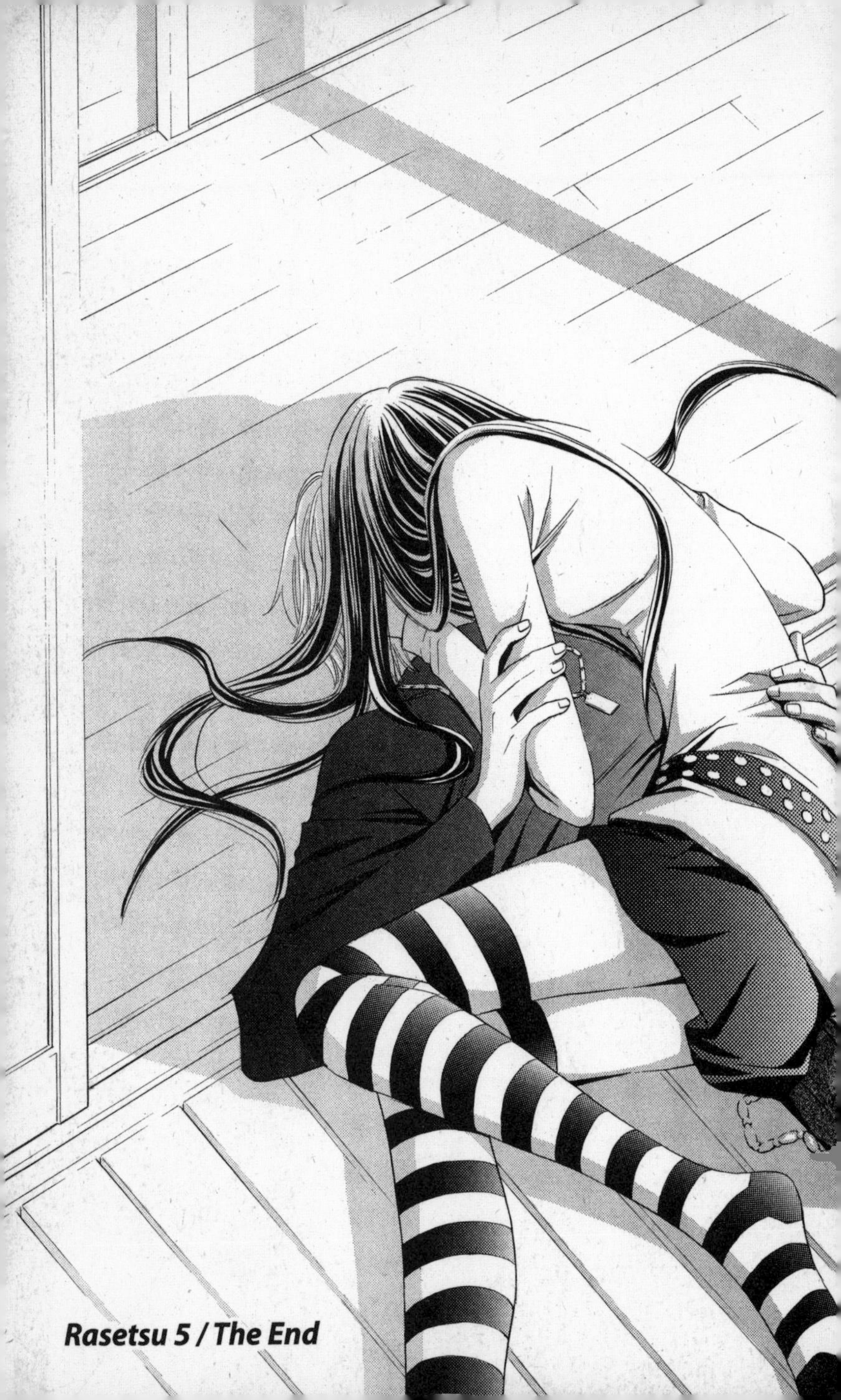

Rasetsu 5 / The End

RASETSU
VOL. 5
Shojo Beat Edition

STORY AND ART BY
CHIKA SHIOMI

Translation & Adaptation/Kinami Watabe
Touch-up Art & Lettering/Freeman Wong
Design/Hidemi Dunn
Editor/Amy Yu

VP, Production/Alvin Lu
VP, Sales & Product Marketing/Gonzalo Ferreyra
VP, Creative/Linda Espinosa
Publisher/Hyoe Narita

Rasetsu No Hana by Chika Shiomi
© Chika Shiomi 2008
All rights reserved.
First published in Japan in 2008 by HAKUSENSHA, Inc., Tokyo.
English language translation rights arranged with HAKUSENSHA, Inc., Tokyo.

Printed in the U.S.A.

Published by VIZ Media, LLC
P.O. Box 77010
San Francisco, CA 94107

10 9 8 7 6 5 4 3 2 1
First printing, June 2010

www.viz.com

www.shojobeat.com

APR 2011

Chika Shiomi lives in Aichi Prefecture, Japan. She debuted with the manga *Todokeru Toki o Sugitemo* (Even if the Time for Deliverance Passes), and her previous works include the supernatural series *Yurara*. She loves reading manga, traveling and listening to music. Her favorite artists include Michelangelo, Hokusai, Bernini and Gustav Klimt.